AMERICAN CATHOLICS

AMERICAN CATHOLICS

A History of the
Roman Catholic Community
in the United States

JAMES HENNESEY, S.J.

With a foreword
by
JOHN TRACY ELLIS

New York   Oxford
OXFORD UNIVERSITY PRESS
1981

Library of Congress Cataloging in Publication Data

Hennesey, James J.
  American Catholics.

  Bibliography: p.
  Includes index.
  1. Catholics—United States—History.
2. Catholic Church—United States—History.
I. Title.
BX1406.2.H37   282'.73   81-1074
ISBN 0-19-502946-1   AACR2

Printing (last digit): 9 8 7 6 5 4 3 2

Printed in the United States of America

for John Tracy Ellis
dean of American Catholic historians
priest—teacher—friend

Foreword

Who are we? Where do we come from? asks Father Hennesey at the outset of his absorbing story of the American Catholics. The present work furnishes abundant evidence by way of answers to these questions. That this evidence is, indeed, a genuine part of the national epic was made clear in the *Harvard Encyclopedia of American Ethnic Groups* where an alphabetical listing of over one hundred twenty groups of Americans begins with the Acadians and comes close to ending with the Ukrainians. The Acadians, who in 1755 endured a cruel expulsion by the British from their homes in Nova Scotia and the neighboring regions, were solidly Roman Catholic, and their descendants, the Cajuns of Louisiana, have remained so. If, religiously speaking, present-day Americans of Ukrainian background are of a more varied pattern, the first of their number who began immigrating from eastern Europe in the 1880s, largely from Galicia, were likewise Catholics. The fact that today they number over a half million spread through six eparchies or dioceses testifies to the variety of ethnic strains and liturgical rites within the Catholic community of the United States. And the Acadians and Ukrainians are but two of the nearly forty groups of Americans whose religious history is traced or touched upon in this volume.

At a time when ethnic history is enjoying increased popularity it is important that religious commitment and practice—or the loss thereof—should be set forth. This is especially true in an age when in the public domain religious values are either largely ignored or called in question, for no informed mind will deny that religion has been one of the prime factors in shaping humanity's cultural background from the earliest recorded history to our own day. In this respect the religious historian has to contend with the deep bias against religion that arose in the 18th century and that succeeded in coloring the efforts of many historians through the 19th and 20th centuries. Peter Gay and Gerald Cavanaugh recognized that fact, but they were not intimidated by it. "Experience shows," they remarked, "that just as skeptics and atheists can write bad history, religious men can write good history."[1]

James Hennesey is a religious man who, as the reader will find, has written "good history." His faith commitment is clear, yet it is never permitted to hamper his professional commitment, which is to tell the truth as he sees it, even when that truth reveals the unhappy side of facts relating to the Church of which he is a member. If the achievements and successes of American Catholics are recorded here, so too are their mistakes and failures. In a word, *American Catholics* is written in the spirit of Cicero's famous dictum, adopted by Pope Leo XIII when he opened the Vatican Archives to the scholarly world in August 1883, "The first law of history is to dread uttering falsehood; the next not to fear stating the truth. . . ."[2]

As has often been noted, the formal inauguration of the United States, and of the Catholic community within its borders, occurred in the same year, with George Washington taking the oath of office as president in April 1789, and John Carroll being named the first Roman Catholic bishop the following November. The strongly native cast given by the Maryland-born Carroll and his contemporary Catholics was to fade quickly thereafter, however, and within two decades following his death in 1815 there had begun the heavy Catholic immigration that completely overshadowed the original Catholic community and fastened upon it the name of the "immigrant Church."

If it was a term used in derision by many Americans in the years after 1830, it was, nonetheless, an appropriate description, for by 1920 over nine millions were added by the incoming Catholics from Europe and Latin America. In fact, it is a characteristic of this religious community that has not altogether lost its relevance for the Church of the 1980s when one recalls that only a few years ago the largest number of permanent visas were issued for Asia and Latin America to Filipinos and Mexicans respectively, natives of two predominantly Catholic countries. It is understandable, therefore, that the professor of religious history at Boston College should have devoted so large a portion of his narrative to different aspects of the "immigrant Church."

1. Peter Gay and Gerald J. Cavanaugh, eds., *Historians at Work* (New York, 1972), 1:xviii.
2. *The Tablet* (London), 62(Sept. 1, 1883):322.

One of the consequences of this immense immigration of Catholics was the arousing of the latent anti-Catholic sentiment which had been inherited from the original English colonists along the Atlantic Coast. Between the nativists of the 1830s and the Protestants and Other Americans United for Separation of Church and State of the 1940s there were five major waves of organized effort to stem the tide. Yet through the course of these unpleasant episodes the Catholics continued to multiply with a slowly increasing number and even managed to prosper. It was a painful experience for many, to be sure, but it was gradually overcome, even if pockets of anti-Catholic feeling persist in the 1980s.

The prevailing mood of this history is not, however, the negative one of anti-Catholicism. On the contrary, the story of the evolution of the tiny group of no more than thirty-five thousand—out of the new Republic's roughly four million inhabitants in 1789—to the fifty million of the 1980s who constitute between one-fourth and one-fifth of the national population, is decidedly positive. Moreover, *American Catholics* is fully abreast of the most recent developments in historiography. With admirable balance Father Hennesey provides an informed account of the Church's leadership as the bishops directed their immigrant flocks through the trying ordeals of the 19th century, affording guidance to priests, members of religious orders and congregations, and to the vast and swelling ranks of the laity. In other words, the author has not been so beguiled by the contemporary trend described as "history from the bottom up" as to neglect the essential role played by those at the top. For when one considers the raw and untutored Catholic masses that poured into the United States through most of the last century, one would be at a loss to explain their relatively orderly emergence into the body politic without guidance of this kind from above.

Yet James Hennesey has rightly sensed that the history of a people—any people—is not confined to the retelling of the plans and policies, the successes and failures, of those who rule. The overwhelming majority of Catholics in this country lived out their lives on lower levels of the ecclesiastical, social, and political ladder. For that reason he has followed the masses, for example, in the early trek of the Maryland families of the 1780s into the Kentucky wilderness where they carved out rural settlements in such places as Nelson County that remains to this day predominantly Catholic. In a similar way he has journeyed with the immigrant Germans into Indiana, Ohio, Minnesota, Missouri, and other states of the Middle West, as he has traced the influx of immigrants from Ireland into the large cities of the Atlantic Coast and into the mill towns of New England. And in the chapter "Westward the Course of Empire," the Catholic settlers will be seen as a significant group among the expanding population who dotted the great plains with their prosperous farms, and built the canals and the new railroads that by 1869 had spanned the continent, as farther west they struggled and caroused among the miners who unearthed the mineral riches of the Rocky Mountains and the fabulous gold fields of California.

All the while the Church followed with dioceses, parishes, parochial schools, and even feeble attempts at higher education. The settling of the American West was an achievement that astounded a fair portion of the world, and the Catholics, both native and foreign-born, were a discernible part of it all. In those years of the mid-century San Francisco came alive as the distant and gaudy capital of this western advance, and there in 1853 the Catholic Church erected an archdiocese with the Spanish-born Dominican friar Joseph S. Alemany as its first archbishop, while two years later an Italian Jesuit brought into existence Saint Ignatius College, which in time became a university bearing the city's name. This is to cite but a single instance, for parallel developments elsewhere are treated, such as the establishment in 1856 of the Saint John's community of Benedictines in Stearns County, Minnesota, in the midst of a solidly German Catholic settlement which again has retained that character into the late 20th century. To employ a rather tired word, Catholic Americans will find their "roots" described in these pages, a description that will likewise serve those of any or no religious persuasion whose interests are centered on ethnic history.

The dominant note of this admirable survey is, of course, ecclesiastical and religious, but the secular setting in which these events unfolded is never lost to view. Heretofore ecclesiastical history has too often been written in a vacuum, a fact deplored by the late Christopher Dawson, the distinguished historian of Western culture. That sort of approach, Dawson maintained, "destroyed the intelligible unity of culture and left the history of culture itself suspended uneasily between political and ecclesiastical history with no firm basis in either of them."[3] What, then, is necessary to understand the influence exercised by environmental factors on the Catholics of the United States is provided, and the attendant *mise-en-scène* furnishes a proper framework within which, to borrow the language of Vatican Council II, the "pilgrim Church" has charted its course in the Republic of the West.

Like all who treat the happenings of the last two decades, the author has had to confront what Geoffrey Barraclough has called "a period of explosive new dimensions" that has deposited the human family in a world "with unparalleled potentialities but also with sinister undercur-

3. Christopher Dawson, *Understanding Europe* (New York, 1952), p. 13.

rents of violence, irrationality, and inhumanity."[4] The Catholic Church, both in the United States and throughout the world, has felt the force of what has been designated in the closing chapter of this work "A Revolutionary Moment." It is an apt description, for the American Catholics have known no comparable experience to what broke over them about 1966, nor, indeed, has there been anything of a like character within universal Catholicism since the French Revolution shook the Church to its foundations. Moreover, the task of those who write on contemporary Catholicism in this country has been rendered more exacting by the fact that, with the exception of Dutch Catholicism, this revolutionary process has probably gone farther in the United States than in any other country. That impression has received fresh enforcement, incidentally, in the fascinating new book of Peter Nichols, *The Pope's Divisions: The Roman Catholic Church Today.*

It is a daunting task, to be sure. Yet *American Catholics* has brought it off with success, first due to the sober and balanced manner in which the varied and often tumultuous movements of this generation of Catholics have been treated, and, second, by the sensible attitude that Father Hennesey has adopted toward what may lie in store for his Church. The significant personalities, trends, and movements are summarized in an enlightened way, without burdening their telling with futile predictions as to the ultimate outcome. George Eliot once declared, "Prophecy is the most gratuitous form of error." When indulged in by the historian it is not only gratuitous but can be the source of confusion and ultimate distortion. If it is tempting to try, it can be said that the author of *American Catholics* overcame the temptation, a fact that redounds to his credit.

Contemporary trends have always been a strong factor in swaying the human mind, but the tendency in our time would seem to be especially powerful if not irresistible. There is need, therefore, for salutary counteraction, and history is one of the most effective of all counteractions, for as Owen Chadwick has said, "History . . . does more than any other discipline to free the mind from the tyranny of present opinion."[5] American Catholics of the 1980s—as well as others interested in their experience—will find in this work just such a liberating force. More than once the thoughtful reader, perhaps somewhat intimidated by the revolutionary character of this generation, will quietly reflect, "We have been here before." In itself that is a significant motive to justify the time spent in perusing the pages of a work that displays an impressive command of the

4. Geoffrey Barraclough, *An Introduction to Contemporary History* (New York, 1967), p. 35.
5. Owen Chadwick, *Freedom and the Historian: An Inaugural Lecture* (Cambridge, 1969), p. 39.

facts, a judicious interpretation of the data, and a literary style that shows respect for the beauty and dignity of the written word. Finally, the reader of *American Catholics* will discover here a true link between the present and the past, the kind of connection that is necessary for understanding one's own time. It was such an understanding that John Henry Newman had in mind when he stated:

> . . . the history of the past ends in the present; and the present is our scene of trial; and to behave ourselves towards its various phenomena duly and religiously, we must understand them; and to understand them, we must have recourse to those past events which led to them. Thus the present is a text, and the past its interpretation.[6]

John Tracy Ellis

Professorial Lecturer in Church History
The Catholic University of America

6. John Henry Newman, *Essays Critical and Historical* (New York, 1897), 2:250.

Acknowledgments

This book began nine summers ago, while I was teaching a course at Memorial University in St. John's, Newfoundland. It has been written in Berkeley, Rome, Chicago, and London, but mostly in St. Mary's Hall on the campus of Boston College. I am grateful to my Jesuit brothers in all those places who have been family to me—"friends in the Lord," in the old Jesuit phrase—while the work was under way. Critical readings by Professors Gerald P. Fogarty of the University of Virginia, Vincent A. Lapomarda of the College of the Holy Cross, and John Randolph Willis of Boston College prevented many a blunder and provided positive suggestions which I have tried to incorporate in the text. My personal and professional debt to Monsignor John Tracy Ellis of the Catholic University of America dates back more than two decades. He has graciously agreed to write a foreword. His meticulous and extraordinarily insightful reading of the manuscript was but another instance of the scholarly support I have known from him through the years. Edna Reed typed the manuscript and was unfailingly patient, gracious, and painstaking in doing it. At Oxford University Press, E. Allen Kelley first urged me to finish a project which had languished for several years when I was preoccupied with the responsibilities of academic administration. The Reverend Charles W. Scott and Curtis Church have been helpful, encouraging, and understanding editors. Research has been assisted by a Faculty Summer Research Grant from Boston College and by a grant from the Center for the Study of American Catholicism at the University of Notre Dame.

Chestnut Hill, Massachusetts   James Hennesey, S.J.
March 25, 1981

Contents

AMERICAN CATHOLICS

Introduction

How does one write the history of the millions of people who have been the Roman Catholic church in the United States? It has been said that, for John Gilmary Shea (1824–92), the father of American Catholic history, the church meant "the duly consecrated hierarchy and the activities sanctioned" by it.[1] That would be one approach. But the Second Vatican Council described the church as "the people of God," a community of bishops, priests, deacons, religious brothers and sisters, and laity, each with their own functions and importance.[2] The Vatican II approach coincides with the outlook expressed by many current historians who talk of writing "people history." Government, politics, and political leaders have their place, but today's historians are more interested in the people who made up a given community at a particular stage of human history. In the case of American Catholicism, this means that, while not neglecting the story of bishops and clergy, of structures and institutions, we must be more concerned with the people who *were* the community we study. Where did they come from? Why did they come to America? What of their Catholicism did they bring with them? How did the world into which they came affect that Catholicism? Finally, what does all this mean for the phenomenon we know as the Roman Catholic Church in the United States today, the largest single religious body in the nation, claiming in 1980 just under fifty million members?

American Catholic history can be approached from several different points of view. It describes a part of the worldwide spread of a religion that was, until a century ago, almost exclusively European. At the time of the First Vatican Council (1869–70), the Catholic Church had no African, no Japanese, no Chinese, no Indian bishops. Only the Near Eastern rites, and

3

North and South America, had national hierarchies with some native-born bishops. The vast majority of the council fathers represented European countries and their colonies, and the development of Catholic theological thought and church structure was shaped by European needs and conflicts. In the United States, the European cast of Catholicism was reinforced by nine and one-half million Catholic immigrants in the 19th century. Nevertheless, American Catholics were constrained to find words and structures to express their beliefs in a cultural setting that rapidly took on a distinctive non-European character.

The nation was predominantly Protestant, and its national culture had Protestant origins. Sydney Ahlstrom has spoken of the "Puritan epoch" in American history, stretching from 17th-century colonial New England to the social, cultural, and religious upheaval of the 1960s.[3] Once free of colonial domination, the United States adopted an offical stance of toleration for all religions and support for none. American separation of church and state, unlike the hostile separation stemming from the French Revolution in Europe, was characterized by mutual respect. It was, however, still colored by the deeply Protestant ethos of the nation. European models—the only models—were inadequate to cope with the new American situation. John Carroll (1735–1815), the future first Catholic bishop in the United States, saw this as early as 1783: " . . . in these United States our religious system has undergone a revolution, if possible, more extraordinary than our political one."[4]

 American Catholicism has European origins. But it also has a peculiarly American history, continuously in contact with the ideas of democracy, due process of law, representative government, religious pluralism, activism, pragmatism, and all the characteristics of this land which for so many years knew limitless frontiers, rapidly growing industry, and an aggressive, adventurous population.

American Catholics were also faced with American religious and secular self-images. The Puritans thought themselves the new chosen people, "God's New Israel." In its secularized version, this idea would later mingle with the "Manifest Destiny" of America to rule a continent from sea to sea and to export its ideas to other lands. And there was the dream of the "melting pot," an American homogeneity in which differences of race, religion, and class would disappear. No less than other Americans, Roman Catholics faced pressures to conform to contemporary norms, whether those of evangelical Protestantism is the early 19th century or liberalism at that century's end, or those of 20th-century secularism. For Catholics, the situation was complicated by the great diversity of their own ethnic origins. Too often this meant that a particular national style—the Irish, for example—came to exercise a disproportionate influence in determining church life and structure. Intramural ethnic conflicts resulted.

Each of these elements—the Catholic community's origins in and continuing ties with Europe, its specifically American experience, the conflict between dreams of homogeneity and the reality of difference—throws light on a story which began nearly six hundred years ago, when colonial adventurers first braved the western ocean and discovered a new world.

We can discover five principal groups, of unequal size, within the historic Roman Catholic community in the United States: (1) colonists, dominated by the Maryland Anglo-Americans; (2) 19th-century European immigrants; (3) migrants from Canada and Latin America; (4) the incorporated, including Native Americans (Indians), Mexicans incorporated after the 1846–48 war, Puerto Ricans after the war of 1898; and (5) converts. Special attention is owed to black Catholics, some of whom have Catholic roots deep in the slavery of Maryland, Louisiana, and Kentucky, while others come from the convert group.

These are not simply ethnic groupings. "English" America was home to Germans, Irish, French, and other nationalities. Descendants of the colonial French who were made American citizens by the Louisiana Purchase in 1803 constitute one of the heaviest proportional concentrations of Catholics in the United States today. Most present-day Mexican-Americans may be traced to a northward migration which began toward the end of the 19th century, but there are Californians and New Mexicans whose ancestry goes far back into Spanish colonial times. Nor is it simply a matter of genealogy. A cultural inheritance may be passed on to people not descended from its founders. For example, certain things characteristic of colonial English Catholicism have been perpetuated by men and women of more recent American stock. One of the continuing joys of studying history is the discovery that no set schemes or divisions can ever force millions of people into neatly separated categories.

The history of Catholicism in the United States breaks into three distinct periods—three different sets of circumstances that influenced Catholic attitudes—although there are no watertight compartments for the periods. The basic "American" period was roughly 1634–1829. The 1830s saw the start of the major immigrant period, as 245,000 Catholics descended on a church that had at the beginning of the decade numbered 318,000. Meanwhile some Catholics drifted away at the same time as gains were being made through conversion, incorporation of Indians and Mexicans, and migration from Canada.[5]

Catholicism in the immigrant period was increasingly influenced by the needs of the newcomers, who were in fact so numerous that in a real sense they *became* the American Catholic Church. The older Anglo-

American tradition, despite the efforts of some bishops and others to preserve it, faded and eventually died out as the 20th century arrived. The 19th century was a time of centralization and uniformity in world Catholicism. In the United States this tendency had its effects, not only in modifying the older independent American style, but also in fostering ethnic conflicts among various immigrant groups and in creating problems in the search for an authentic expression of Catholic life and belief among blacks, Spanish-speaking people, and Indians.

The third period in American Catholic history dates from the 1960s, when fissures opened wide in the church which the immigrants had built. For most Americans at this time, the sense of national purpose had become clouded. Face to face with a rapidly changing and vastly expanded and complex world, they began to lose confidence in the vision that had until then sustained the nation. This kind of change hardly proceeds at a uniform rate for all alike, and this fact is at the root of much contemporary confusion and disarray. Men and women understand and adjust to change at their own individual speeds; the distinction between essential Catholic belief and practice on the one hand, and what has previously been, for whatever period of time, the accepted expression of that belief and practice on the other, is not seen as clearly by all alike. One positive result of historical investigation should be an increased appreciation of the fact that forms, practices, and attitudes which have characterized either nation or church in one's own personal experience, or in the experience of the community, may not be as essential as they have seemed.

Since 1945 the face of religious America has undergone a series of rapid changes, leading two prominent sociologists of religion to conclude that "perhaps at no prior time since the conversion of Paul has the future of Christianity seemed so uncertain," a judgment which they support with empirical findings that "demythologized modernism is overwhelming the traditional Christ-centered mystical faith" and leading to doubt and disbelief on a wide scale.[6] This is scarcely surprising; in contemporary society, change has become the normal state of existence. Stable ways of life have yielded to mobility and the development of mass culture.[7] On the religious scene there was the post-World War II revival, bringing frequent confusion of religion and the American way of life. Many saw Protestantism, Catholicism, and Judaism as slightly varying approaches to that way of life.[8] The erosion of historic denominational and theological differences, already far advanced in late 19th-century Protestant circles, continued and spread beyond Protestant confines. There was the vogue for secularism and the odd contradiction of "theologians" who proclaimed the death of God.[9] For many, fascination for Eastern religions replaced commitment to inherited, if scarcely understood, Christian traditions which seemed empty of inspiration.[10]

Churches, along with other institutions of society, felt the impact of the growing emphasis on personalism and the rights of the individual. The dogmas of humanism competed with those of theology. War, civil rights, students' rights, women's rights, racial problems, ecology, and consumerism replaced concerns popularly associated with organized religion and seemed to many to render the churches irrelevant. At the same time, many church members retreated into a defensive reactionary stance; religious fundamentalism flourished and compounded the difficulty of an adequate religious response to the problems of the time. Others struggled to harmonize tradition with realistic commitment to contemporary problems and found themselves alternately condemned as too conservative and too liberal. Finally, a new form of an ancient Christian phenomenon, enthusiastic piety, found recruits among youth disillusioned with the culture they had helped to create. While it is still too early to have an accurate historical perspective on the age in which we live, it seems at this juncture reasonably sure that future generations will see this period as a major turning-point in the story of human affairs. It is no wonder that churches, like other institutions, must struggle to find proper responses to the challenges of the day.

Analyzing the phenomenon which is American Protestantism, sociologist of religion Elizabeth Nottingham has isolated among its characteristics: activism, which gave great emphasis to science and technology; stress on the sacred value of each individual human being, at times coupled with indifference to the exploitation and waste of natural resources; and a class system based on competition, rather than birth, so that success became identified with moral righteousness and failure suggested moral deficiency.[11] The contrast between rugged individualism thus theologized—and preached—and the authentic Christian doctrine of human solidarity is obvious. What Nottingham noted has not been restricted to Protestant America; the same tendencies have profoundly affected the American Catholic community as well. Henri de Lubac wrote that Catholicism "is social in a sense which should have made the expression 'social Catholicism' pleonastic,"[12] but American Catholics have enjoyed no special immunity to the pressures toward individualism endemic in the United States. The identification of authentic Catholic ideals is at issue here. The question must be raised: how deeply Catholic has the immense Catholic body in the United States, with its panoply of schools and other institutions, really been? Was it held together through the immigrant age primarily by the sociological need for collective self-defense? Are its internal resources consequently now too thin to enable it to enunciate from deeply interiorized belief a response to the changed times in which it lives?

Divisions among Catholics, previously suppressed in the overriding interest of maintaining the defensive posture of a minority, became more obvious as Catholic psychological solidarity, traceable to the immigrant status that had created the initial need for that defensive stance, began to fade in the 1960s. The tangible evidence is there: religious practice fell off sharply. Weekly mass attendance dropped in the decade 1963–72 from 71 percent to 55 percent.[13] Studies reported that on college campuses "Catholicism is the most rapidly changing tradition and the one most in danger of losing support," and that "alienation among young Catholics in the working force seems, at times, to be even greater."[14] Continuing controversies between liberal and conservative Catholics and varying degrees of inability to assimilate change produced reactions ranging from boredom with religious discussion to weariness to outright anger and rejection, both on the right and on the left. Secular humanism, which discounts all religion, and fundamentalist, highly subjective, and undogmatic enthusiasm are filling the vacuum.

However we interpret events of the past decade and a half, it is a reasonable historical judgment that the Catholic Church in the United States in 1980 was passing out of the immigrant stage which began with the 1830s. The church's responses cannot be geared to the needs of that age; they must look to the present and future. The future is not the area of the historian's competence. The past is, and it is time to tell its story.

I

Spanish America

The pre-Columbian age of discovery plays no part in the history of American Catholicism except perhaps for the strangely apposite description of their goal by St. Brendan and his legendary 6th-century sailor-monks: they sought the "promised land of the saints." Whether in a strictly religious sense, or in a secular one, the transit from Europe very early developed about it a mystic sense of destiny. Migrants thought of themselves as a specially chosen people. For Puritan New England this was put by Governor John Winthrop aboard the *Arbella* sailing to Massachusetts Bay in 1630. In *A Modell of Christian Charity* he wrote: "We shall be as a Citty upon a Hill, the Eies of all people are uppon us." The Puritans saw themselves as a new Israel, a new chosen people ordered by God to make a new world. The American national mystique combined a sense of newness and of difference from old Europe with belief in a manifest destiny to remake others in the American image, whether those others were American Indians or French and Spanish opponents in the struggle for control of a continent, or, in later days, the rest of the world. The theme of "the promised land of the saints" is vital to understanding what America has been.

North American discovery begins in the late 15th century, colonization over a century later. It is fascinating to speculate what might have developed had the explorations of Giovanni Caboto (John Cabot), sailing for Henry VII, led to permanent colonization in America before the English reformation. But it did not happen. Caboto did sail through the narrows to the site of St. John's, Newfoundland, in 1498. It was in 1583 and in the reign of Queen Elizabeth, however, that England's Humphrey Gilbert laid effective claim to the island, and the importance of St. John's for the religious history of the United States derives from its use as a way station for thousands of Irish immigrants who eventually made their way to Boston and live in New England Irish lore as "two-boaters," in contrast to their supposedly more affluent compatriots who were able to pay passage directly to the United States. Similarly, contemplating the gigantic bridge which spans the narrows between Brooklyn and Staten Island, we may speculate what the result would have been if the discovery of that estuary in 1524 by Florentine navigator Giovanni da Verrazano, acting for the king of France, had directed French explorations there instead of toward the St. Lawrence. But that is not what happened, and France's permanent entry on the North American continent was as late as England's. When it did come, French colonies stretched in a great arc from the St. Lawrence west to the Great Lakes, then down through the Illinois country along the Mississippi River until they intersected with the arc of Spanish colonies which curved for over three thousand miles from Florida to distant California.

The oldest colonial power in what is now United States territory was Spain, whose ventures spanned three centuries, from the discovery of Puerto Rico by Columbus in 1493 to the last California mission, San Francisco Solano (1824) at Sonoma, north of the Golden Gate, founded two years after Mexican independence. San Juan, Puerto Rico (1511), is the oldest diocese in present-day United States territory and its first bishop, Alonso Manso, who arrived in 1513, was the first of his rank to come to America. Before the first permanent continental settlement at St. Augustine, Florida (1565), Ponce de León had attempted a colony on the west coast of the Florida peninsula in 1521, and a half-dozen other similarly unsuccessful efforts had been made to plant a colony.[1] In 1526–27 a party headed by Lucas Vasquez de Ayllón and accompanied by three Dominican priests ranged north along the Atlantic coastline to Cape Fear in present-day North Carolina. In 1528 Panfilo de Narváez led an expedition including secular priests and Franciscans to Tampa Bay on Florida's west coast and then north to the neighborhood of modern Tallahassee before they headed west across the Gulf of Mexico to adventures which included shipwreck, slavery in Indian hands, and a trek through the American southwest before four survivors of the original 400-man expedition finally reached Mexico City in 1536. The search for gold motivated this expedition, as it did that of Hernando de Soto in 1539–42 through parts of Alabama, North Carolina, Mississippi, and Arkansas. But none of these expeditions led to permanent settlements until in 1564 a colony of French Huguenots established Fort Caroline near the mouth of the St. John's River in the area of modern Jacksonville. The colony threatened transit of Spanish treasure ships through the Bahamas Channel, and Spain sent Captain-General Pedro Menéndez de Avilés to eliminate the danger. Menéndez's ships sighted land at Cape Canaveral on August 28, 1565, the feast of St. Augustine. They continued north and engaged the French in an indecisive battle, then returned to the Indian village of Seloy, on a harbor they named St. Augustine. On September 8, Menéndez took formal possession in the name of God and the king of Spain. Several weeks later he led 500 soldiers north to Fort Caroline where they massacred its French defenders. The history of Florida had begun.

The Spaniards founded at St. Augustine the parish of Nombre de Diós, first in continental United States territory, with a secular priest, Francisco López de Mendoza Grajales, as pastor. This was the beginning of a string of such firsts for Florida: first Indian mission, launched by another secular priest, Sebastian Montero, among the Guataris of back-country South Carolina from 1566–72; first foreign-born Irish priest, Richard Arthur (1597); first hospital, La Soledad at St. Augustine (1598); first school, a Franciscan seminary (1605). Bishop Juan de la Cabezas de Altamirano of Santiago de Cuba, who visited the colony in 1606, was the first bishop recorded as having set foot on present-day American soil. He administered the sacrament of confirmation and ordained some twenty candidates, although there is no certainty that the order of priesthood was conferred. But in 1674 his successor, Gabriel Díaz Vara Calderón, did ordain seven priests at St. Augustine. In later years, three auxiliary bishops of Santiago de Cuba were assigned to live in Florida and remained there for periods varying from three weeks to ten years. A third bishop of Santiago lived in Florida in 1762–63.

Early records speak of "the enduring destitution of Florida." Over 100 Spaniards died in their first winter there. Provisions, including the most ordinary food, had to be shipped from Cuba and Mexico. For months mass could not be celebrated because bread and wine were not available. The story of the colony was one of unrelieved poverty. Maize—Indian corn—was the only crop. Florida was a mosquito-ridden military outpost of marginal value to a declining Spanish empire. The European population—soldiers, farmers, traders, civil officials, and their dependents— was never large. During the English siege of 1702, fifteen hundred soldiers and civilians took refuge in St. Augustine's Castillo de San Marcos. There were thirty-one hundred Spaniards in the peninsula sixty-one years later when Spain's flag was hauled down and Florida became a British colony.

Religious needs of Spanish soldiers and civilians were cared for by secular priests at St. Augustine and in the outlying forts. But the colony's governors wanted a religious order for the Indian missions and their first choice was the recently founded Society of Jesus. Florida was the first Jesuit mission field in North America. The missionaries' ship lost its way and, when the superior, Pedro Martínez, and a party of eight Flemish and Spanish soldiers and seamen went ashore to reconnoiter, five of them including the Jesuit, were killed by Indians on San Juan Island in 1566. Subsequent missionary efforts were unsuccessful and in 1570 eight Jesuits led by Juan Segura headed for the far north where they settled at Ajacán, between the York and James rivers in modern Virginia. There, thirty-six years before Jamestown was founded on the same peninsula, all eight were murdered by Indians.[2] Two years later the Jesuit mission in Florida was abandoned and its members transferred to Mexico.

Governor Menéndez, however, was not ready to give up the Indians and within a year of the Jesuits' departure secured Franciscan friars to replace them. Until 1587 the friars numbered only a handful, but in 1587 Alonso Reinoso brought substantial reinforcements. Initially the Franciscans found the mission as discouraging as the Jesuits had, and by 1592 all but five had left Florida. But in 1595 a major effort was begun under the direction of Francisco Marrón. Central missions and stations were opened along the Florida coast and north to Georgia, among the Guale. Mission buildings were simple: palmetto-thatched clay huts. Life was primitive, as the Franciscan provincial superior reported in 1635 to the king of Spain:

> The friars suffer greatly in this mission field. They must walk barefoot in this cold land when going about from mission to mission. The Indians are widely scattered about in forty-four missions. For this great number there are only thirty-five religious. Many times it is necessary for a missionary to walk eight or ten leagues [twenty-four to thirty miles] to hear a confession. All of these sufferings are augmented by the fact that the missionaries get very little aid in the form of assistants who might lighten some of their burdens. Some of the priests, being so overburdened with work and seeing so many Indians without hope of converting them, become discouraged and return to Spain.[3]

But if some Franciscans returned to Spain, others stayed and established a chain of forty mission stations that reached west from the coast across the peninsula and northwest to Apalache Bay. There was a heavy concentration west of the Aucilla River and as far west as the Appalachicola. When Spaniards settled permanently at Pensacola in 1698, Franciscans and Augustinians served them. Marrón was the first great Franciscan leader in Florida, the westward push was guided by Fray Martín Prieto.

Florida Indians were not easy converts. Their habits were migratory, and Bishop Calderón found them "weak and phlegmatic as regards work, though clever and quick." They lived simply, dressed, if at all, in skins and cloth made of Spanish moss. Their food was hominy, pumpkins, beans, fish, and game, their drink water.[4] But the Franciscans made considerable progress. Outstanding was Francisco Pareja, a 1595 arrival, who worked among the coastal Timucuans. He wrote a grammar and dictionary, prepared catechisms and devotional books in Timucuan, and could within a short time report that literacy was increasing and that many Indians knew their religion better than some Spaniards.

Even in its golden age, the Franciscan mission suffered two major handicaps. One was conflict with such Indian customs as polygamy, which provoked the Guale revolt of 1597 in eight Georgia villages. Fray Pedro de Corpo took it upon himself to deprive Juanillo, son of a local chief, of his hereditary rights because Juanillo refused to put away his extra wives. The Indians rebelled, five Franciscans including Corpo were killed and another, Francisco de Avila, was made a slave for some months. Fray Francisco later refused to testify against the Indians because he would not participate in a trial that could result in the death penalty. The second Franciscan handicap arose from the fact that the missions were financially dependent on the Spanish government. Mixture of sacred and secular led to increasing conflicts, as missionaries protested the virtual enslavement of many Indians by civil authorities. The problem became acute under Governors Pedro Benedit Horruytiner and Diego de Rebolledo. In 1656 Timucuans and Apalaches revolted. Rebolledo put down the uprising with particular cruelty: eleven chiefs were publicly strangled. Franciscan protests effected the governor's removal from office, and a chill fell over relations with the civil government, although the missionaries' stature with the Indians rose and for a quarter-century the missions prospered.

By 1708 the widespread Franciscan mission system was all but destroyed. The relative isolation of Florida from world affairs came to an end with founding of an English colony at Charleston, South Carolina, in 1670. For twenty years Englishmen from Virginia had been drifting south to the Spanish borderlands, but the new English presence brought Spain's outpost colony directly into the War of the Spanish Succession (1702–13, in American history "Queen Anne's War"), which pitted England and most of Europe against Louis XIV of France and his grandson, the new Spanish king Philip V. Off the Florida coast, France took the Bahamas as a base to harrass England's Atlantic colonies. Carolinians attacked Spanish Florida and Spaniards attacked Charleston. Then came the War of Jenkins' Ear (1739–42), a trade conflict between Spain and England fought in the Caribbean and along the Florida-Georgia border, the War of the Austrian Succession (1740–48, "King George's War"), and the Seven Years' War (1754–63, "French and Indian War").

The 1763 Treaty of Paris ended for twenty years the Spanish colony of Florida. The English had captured Havana and Charles III of Spain preferred to sacrifice Florida rather than Puerto Rico to obtain its return, in an agreement that also saw New Orleans and Louisiana west of the Mississippi pass from France to Spain. Not much of Florida was left. Carolinians and Georgians had made considerable inroads among the Guale, Appalachicola, Timucuan, and Apalache, while the Spaniards gradually retreated on St. Augustine. In 1702 James Moore's Carolina troops sacked the capital city while the Spaniards watched helplessly from their refuge in Castillo de San Marcos. In 1703 Moore returned to the attack, this time in the western Apalache country. Priests and Indians were brutally murdered and missions laid waste. Between ten and twelve thousand Indians were carried off into slavery. The last half-century of the first period of Spanish rule in Florida boasted no great accomplishments, and it was with considerable relief that the last of thirty-one hundred soldiers, priests, and civilians sailed for Havana in 1763. The Catholicism brought two hundred years earlier by Pedro Menéndez was effectively dead.

British rule in Florida lasted from 1763 to 1783. Despite promises of religious freedom, all Spaniards left the country. The only substantial Catholic presence in the British period was that of twelve hundred indentured servants brought out by a Scots physician, Andrew Turnbull, in 1768. Most of them were natives of the Balearic island of Minorca in the Mediterranean, a British possession from 1708 to 1783, but there was also a smattering of Italians, Corsicans, and Greeks among workers on Dr. Turnbull's plantation at New Smyrna. A Minorcan secular priest, Pedro Camps, ministered to the religious needs of the colonists and emerged as their leader in the struggle to cope with disease and harsh treatment by Turnbull's overseers. New Smyrna collapsed in 1777 and Camps led 600 survivors to St. Augustine. The Paris treaty of 1783, ending the American Revolution, returned Florida to Spain and it remained Spanish until ceded it to the United States in 1821. Despite efforts of priests like Irish-born Thomas Hassett, religious life was weak except at St. Augustine and Pensacola. Spanish remnants were overwhelmed by immigrating Americans, and Roman Catholicism became a minority religion practiced by people considered "foreigners" in the land they had helped to build.

The Spanish arc from Florida to California was broken only in the lower Mississippi country where it intersected territory held by by France from 1699 to 1769. The history of Louisiana will be considered separately. To the west was Texas, across the Sabine River.[5] Spanish reconnaissance missions from Mexico had explored that vast expanse as early as 1629, and in 1675 Franciscan Juan Larios opened a mission on the Nueces

River in southeast Texas. East Texas, land of the Asinai Indians, was eight hundred miles northeast of the Rio Grande, however, and no serious Spanish effort was made in that direction until word reached Mexico of the presence at Matagorda Bay of French adventurer René Robert Cavalier, Sieur de La Salle, whose company included three priests of the Sulpician community and some Franciscans. It was 1685. Two years later La Salle was murdered by one of his own soldiers and the remaining Frenchmen were wiped out by Indians in 1689. In that same year a Spanish expedition moved northeast to the Neches River, accompanied by Franciscans led by Damian Massanet. Fray Damian established two missions among the Asinai, but results were discouraging. When the French threat failed to materialize, soldiers and friars were withdrawn in 1693.

Fray Francisco Hidalgo caused the next Spanish move. Disappointed by his failure to interest Mexican officialdom in the east Texas Indians, he wrote to the governor of Louisiana, Antoine de la Mothe Cadillac. Cadillac had plans of his own, primary among them opening trade with New Spain, and he took the occasion of Hidalgo's letter to send a representative to the Spanish base at San Juan Bautista in Mexico to negotiate matters. In 1716 seventy-six Spaniards, nine of them Franciscans, opened four mission stations and a presidio between the Neches and Angelina Rivers. They then pushed on into the territory of the Adaés Indians in the northwestern part of modern Louisiana, where Fray Antonio Margil de Jésus established the mission of San Miguel de Linares near present-day Robeline, and some twenty miles from the French outpost at Natchitoches. Margil served as chaplain to both Spanish and French soldiers. But then Europe's wars overflowed again into America. Spain was dissatisfied with terms of the 1713 Treaty of Utrecht and in 1717 resumed war against Hapsburg Emperor Charles VI. Britain and France supported the emperor and echoes were felt in the Adaés country when in 1719 French troops fell on the nearby Spanish garrison and destroyed the presidio and mission. Spanish forces in east Texas beat a general retreat to San Antonio, but they were back by 1721 and the mission continued for another fifty years until it was abandoned in 1773, ten years after the Spanish takeover of Louisiana.

A French traveler, Pierre de Pagés, has left a description of the Adaés Settlement as he found it in 1767: "a collection of forty miserable houses constructed with stakes driven into the ground . . . situated on the declivity of a hill, the top of which, formed into a square and inclosed with Palisadoes . . . served as a kind of fortress to the village." Across a small valley on another hill stood the church and house of the Franciscans. He found the site unappetizing: "A few straggling trees, and a heath overgrown with briars and thickets, and bounded everywhere by woods, compose the cheerless prospect of the inhabitants." The soil was poor, rations were primitive. Pagès thought the Spanish cavalrymen "half-savage," but admitted they were fine horsemen. The Indians were for him "noble savages," whose only vices were those learned from Europeans.[6] Despite the efforts of Margil and others, the mission among the Adaés was not one of the more successful Franciscan ventures.

The second major focus in eastern Texas was at San Antonio, where a military post and the mission of San Antonio de Valero (The Alamo) were begun in 1718, largely at the urging of Fray Antonio de San Buenaventura Olivares. It served as a link in the chain that stretched from the Rio Grande to east Texas, and was the site of the first civilian settlement in Texas when a colony of Canary Islanders arrived in 1731. Pagès also visited San Antonio in 1761. He found a palisaded fort too large for the number of soldiers stationed there, partially in ruins and surrounded "by several miserable villages." The Canary Islanders lived in "a multitude of huts."

Spanish Texas was always thinly populated. Apart from San Antonio there were only soldiers and Indians. Franciscans found the tribes frustrating. The Indians were reluctant to gather in villages, and Spanish authorities refused requests from the friars that they be coerced to do so. A few Indians lived around the presidios and missions, where they were used as cattlemen and herders. But religious results were meager. This was even more so in the case of the Apaches. San Sabá mission (near Menard) was established among them in 1757, but a Comanche attack in the following year cost the lives of two friars and the mission never prospered. Toward the end of the 18th century the Franciscans asked that the Texas missions be secularized, because their accomplishment was so small. As Spanish rule faded in 1810 there were only 4,155 Europeans in the territory, 1,033 of them soldiers. Americans had begun to immigrate illegally after the sale of Louisiana to the United States in 1803, and the future was theirs.

Spanish activity in the Southwest was more impressive than it was in Texas.[7] Dreams of reaching the legendary Seven Golden Cities of Cibolá had drawn Francisco Vásquez de Coronado to the Zuñi pueblos and the uncharted northern plains of the Gran Quivira in 1540. His expedition travelled the Texas Panhandle and reached Kansas. Smaller parties discovered the Colorado River, the Rio Grande, the Grand Canyon.[8] Fray Juan de Padilla remained among the Wichita in Kansas and at their hands became the first American martyr sometime in 1542–43.[9] More Franciscans died in 1580–81 among the Pueblos. Then in 1598 Juan de Oñate led a full-scale expedition to what was already called New Mexico.[10] Santa Fé was founded in 1609.

In New Mexico Spanish and Indian races and cultures merged, creating a native American and American Catholic tradition second in seniority only to that of the Indians, that of "La Raza."

By 1630 Fray Alonso de Benavides reported fifty thousand Indian baptisms in New Mexico.[11] There were ninety friars in two dozen missions. The Pueblos were a peaceful agricultural people who lived in villages of adobe or stone houses.Spaniards introduced cattle-raising and improved farming methods. Makeshift chapels grew into vividly decorated adobe churches, surrounded by Indian homes, small craft-shops and blacksmith's forges. The Pueblos joined in the friars' liturgical prayers and choir schools were founded for them. It all seemed very different from the failures of Florida and Texas.

The idyll did not last.[12] Pueblo tribal organization had been deeply religious, with rites centering on rain-making and fertility and medicine men forming a ruling caste. Ceremonies were held in underground rooms set aside for religious purposes, called *kivas*. This ancestral religion ran strong under the surface of Pueblo life. External forces created problems. Raiding parties of nomadic Apache, Ute, Navajo, and Comanche reminded mission Indians that they were not as free as they had been. Quarrels between friars and civil officials confused them. In 1631 Benavides protested imposition of forced labor and tributes on the natives. Many refused baptism for fear that it meant slavery. Some Indians had already been sent as slaves to Mexico. Proud chiefs resented being treated as vassals. Extensive land grants to Spaniards deprived Indians of ownership. Finally, five years of secret planning by medicine men under El Popé resulted in the great Pueblo uprising of 1680, which swept Spain from New Mexico and forced missionaries and soldiers back on El Paso. The region had counted 2,800 Spaniards, 32 Franciscans, and 35,000 Christian Indians in 1680; 400 Spaniards, 21 friars among them, died. The missions were wiped out and never fully recovered. The Spaniards returned in 1692, but by 1776 there were only 18,344 Christian Indians. By then Spanish zeal had devolved into bitter exchanges between government and church, and within the church successive bishops of Durango criticized Franciscan management of the missions, charging among other things that the friars had failed to learn the Indian languages and that at best Christianity had only superficially taken root.[13] Near-total collapse occurred after Mexican independence in 1821 and the departure of most of the priests, so that when the United States took New Mexico after the war of 1846–48 the Catholic community had to be completely rebuilt.

New Mexico developed slowly.[14] An arid, sun-bleached land of deserts and mesas sweeping up from the flatlands of the Rio Grande to the Sangre de Cristo mountains in the north, it achieved only a subsistence agriculture, although ranches prospered. There were three major towns: Santa Fé, Albuquerque and Santa Cruz de la Cañada. By 1810 there were perhaps 35,000 Spaniards and people of Spanish-Indian ancestry and 10,000 Pueblos. Society was feudal, controlled by important families, with the poor reduced to peonage and captive Apaches and Comanches held as slaves. The church was cut off from the world outside and decayed in the twilight of the Spanish era and under Mexican rule. Virtually abandoned by the church, New Mexico Catholics struggled as best they might. Sometimes they went strange directions, as in the case of "Los Hermanos de los Penitentes," the flagellant brotherhoods of the Sangre de Cristo which developed out of the third order of St. Francis and have continued a shadowy existence into the 20th century. Nevertheless, the Spanish legacy is strong in the continued Catholicity of the Pueblos, oldest native American members of the church, and of the descendants of the most successful mingling on United States soil of European and Indian, La Raza.

Moving westward we come to the only major non-Franciscan Spanish mission, that of the Pimería Alta in northern Sonora and Arizona south of the Gila River. Even here a friar was first to arrive, Marcos de Niza, who explored the Zuñi pueblos in 1539–42. Later Franciscan attempts among the Hopi and Moqui were discouraging and ended in 1680. Next to come were Jesuits from missions which had pushed north from the Mexican Sierra Madre to Sonora and then to the area of modern Tucson, where San Xavier del Bac mission was founded in 1700. The Arizona-Sonora missions cannot be separated from the name of Eusebio Kino, Tyrolese Jesuit, defender of the Indians, missionary (he personally baptized over four thousand and claimed a total of thirty thousand converted by Jesuits), cattle rancher, explorer, and geographer. Riding thousands of miles, he established conclusively that California was not an island, as had been believed by mapmakers who thought that the Gulf of California extended as far north as the Columbia River. Jesuit missions were established among the Pima, Papago, and Maricopa, but the arid land of mountain, desert, and cactus resisted the Spanish advance fiercely. Nomadic Yuma and Apache remained hostile and with Kino's death in 1711 the missions declined. A revival set in after 1722 and more German Jesuits worked in the area, but a Pima uprising in 1751 cost the lives of two missionaries, and in 1768 Spain's expulsion of the Jesuits effectively ended everything. Three dilapidated missions were handed over to Franciscans. In 1776 the first Spanish presidio was founded at Tucson. There were only 180 Europeans in the province. Most prominent of the Franciscans was Francisco Garcés, who rivaled Kino as traveller and chronicler, and who made a vain effort to convert the Yuma until he and three companions were killed in a 1781 uprising. The Papago built the new church at San Xavier del Bac in 1797, but with Mexican independence the missions were abandoned, the last Franciscan leaving in 1828. From that time until establishment of the vicariate apostolic of Arizona in 1868 church life was virtually non-existent, except for the occasional itinerant missionary. On Arizona's southern border with the Mexican state of Sonora live two fascinating survivals of the Jesuit mission period: the Yaqui, since 1918 largely resident in Arizona, who for centuries refused the ministry of other priests and whose religious practice is reminiscent of 18th-century Catholicism; and the Sonora Catholics, who have fused dim memories from the Jesuit period with Indian religion.[15]

First explorer of the six-hundred-mile California coastline was Juan Rodriguez Cabrillo (1542–43), who reached Drake's Bay in modern Marin County. Bartolomé Ferrelo sailed to the California-Oregon line (1543). Sir Francis Drake anchored in San Francisco Bay (1579). Sebastiáno Vizcaíno accompanied by Carmelite friars landed in Monterey Bay (1602). But not until czarist Russia thrust south from Alaska in 1741 did authorities in New Spain become concerned about the distant lands of Alta California.[16]

Cabrillo vividly described distant mountain ranges, plains, groves, and savannahs sweeping down to the sea. He was impressed by large Indian pueblos along the Santa Barbara Channel.[17] But the Indians were in fact scarcely removed from the Stone Age. Men went about naked; women wore skirts of antelope, deer, and beaver skin. The California Indians were nomads who hunted with bow and arrow, fished from pinewood canoes, and supplemented their catch by gathering seeds and acorns. Agriculture was unknown and there were no domestic animals. Tools were made of flint. There were six major languages and hundreds of dialects. In the south the Indians lived in semi-circular brush huts. They were a generally passive people, disdainful of work, usually friendly and hospitable, although town occasionally fought town and mountain Indians regularly raided the coastal settlements. Their religion was shamanistic.[18]

While Spain hesitated, Russian seamen and traders hunted sea-otter down the coast. In 1811 they established Fort Ross in present Sonoma County. Not until 1825 were the activities of the Russian-American Fur Company restricted to the czar's Alaska colony. The Spanish decision to move north was made as far back as 1768. Inspector-General José de Gálvez and Fray Junípero Serra, president of the Franciscan missions in Lower California, planned the expedition as a joint missionary-military enterprise with a triple target.[19] Settlements were made on San Diego

Bay, at Monterey, and at Santa Barbara. By 1772 there were five missions: San Diego, San Carlos (Carmel), San Gabriel (near Los Angeles), San Antonio, and San Luis Obispo. During the next fifty years under friars like Serra, Francisco Palou, and Fermín Lasuén, sixteen more foundations were spaced out a day's journey apart, extending as far north as the neighborhood of the Russian fort in Sonoma.[20] Serra himself founded nine missions before his death in 1784. They were the economic center of California life. Hundreds of thousands of cattle, sheep, and other farm animals roamed their acres, fields yielded wheat, corn, and barley, orchards blossomed with oranges, apples, pears, figs, and peaches. Olive trees were introduced. Vineyards produced grapes from which wine and brandy were made. A flourishing export trade developed.

In 1773 the friars were given total authority over baptized Indians. A majority of California's Indians never came within the system, but those who did, once they were baptized, were not free to leave the mission. Punishment for infractions was severe. Flogging was used and misdemeanors could result in chains or the stocks. Runaways were hunted down by soldiers. Some 98,000 Indians were baptized over the mission period. The greatest number in the missions at any one time was 38,000. They lived and worked in tile-roofed adobe houses laid out in town patterns. Indians were trained as cattlemen, shepherds, carpenters, blacksmiths, masons, and weavers. Village bands and choirs were organized. Mission property was held in trust by the Franciscans, who clothed, fed, and housed the Indians. In return the Indians worked the fields and herds and learned Christian doctrine and prayers. They also felt painfully their loss of freedom.

More can be said about this darker side of the otherwise impressive accomplishments of the California missions. Nomadic and generally indolent Indians did not take easily to the confinement of mission life. Even in its moderate Spanish form, the work ethic was not for them. Immorality among Spanish soldiers hardly recommended Christianity. Within a year of settlement at Monterey, Serra moved San Carlos mission five miles south to present-day Carmel to avoid interference from military officers and the bad example of the garrison. The soldiers treated the Indians badly—a favorite "sport" was to lasso Indian women—and they also introduced venereal and other diseases which soon reached epidemic proportions. The psychological and physical hardship of being wrenched from the Stone Age into the 18th century told heavily. In 1814 it was reported that three-quarters of the children born at prosperous San Gabriel mission died before they reached their first birthday, and that most Indians did not live to see twenty-five years. By 1832, the end of the mission era, the native population had dropped to 98,000. Life was even harder after the American takeover: by 1880 there were only 20,500 Indians in all California.

Outside the missions Spanish presence was sparse. Presidios of wood and mud construction were built at Monterey, San Diego, San Francisco, and Santa Barbara, each manned by a few hundred soldiers. Towns grew at Los Angeles and San José. In 1839 only fifty people huddled in the village of Yerba Buena, soon to become San Francisco. There were 1,200 Europeans in California in 1800 and by 1846 the number had risen to only 4,000. It was an isolated land, its contact with the world outside mainly by ship. During the Mexican period (1821–46) California became a sort of Siberia, a place of exiles for *cholos*—scoundrels—shipped from Mexican prisons.

Mexican independence ended the California mission era.[21] Even before the Mexican Revolution there was considerable feeling—shared by many Franciscans—that the missions should be placed under secular control, with the friars freed for explicitly spiritual work. Disintegration of government under the Mexican regime hastened matters. A dozen rebellions broke out after 1828. Supplies were short and pay was in arrears. The presidios increased their demands on the missions and the Indians were overworked. Spanish friars who would not swear allegiance to the new republic left the country. In 1834 the long-expected secularization of the missions was carried out. It was to have been a carefully phased operation, with land and livestock turned over to the Indians. Instead greedy local politicians partitioned millions of acres of land among themselves. Some families gained control of as many as three hundred thousand acres. The Indians were simply turned loose. Massive looting occurred, cattle, sheep, and horses were slaughtered, fields laid waste. Mission paternalism yielded to anarchy and the brief rule of the "dons," the *gente de razón* who called themselves Californios.

For fifteen years California was like a western version of the Old South.[22] Indians and *cholo* peons herded cattle on vast ranches in return for their keep. The Indian death rate was twice that of black slaves on America's other coast. The Californios lived a free and lazy life, riding madly about the countryside, enjoying brutal blood sports. They were an illiterate lot, innocent of cultural influence. There were no schools, no newspapers. There was almost no government. Religion declined. If older people still said their prayers and went to mass, their sons were either indifferent or influenced by the wave of 19th-century enlightenment liberalism which swept Spanish America. The church struggled as best it might. A diocese of the Two Californias was established in 1840, but its first bishop, Francisco Garcia Diego, faced hopeless odds. He died in 1846. In all California there were only thirteen priests. An American Catholic naval officer wrote that some were "very old, others very ignorant and others again I am sorry to say, but it is true, very bad; none of them, I expect, suitable for the present population emigrating to Upper California."[23]

California Catholicism was in complete disarray when the last Mexican forces surrendered to the United States in 1847. A year later James W. Marshall discovered gold at Johann Sutter's sawmill on the American River in the Sacramento valley. Another year and California's population had swelled to 100,000 as hopeful prospectors and hangers-on from the four corners of the world swarmed in. Spanish California was overwhelmed. Its Catholic history was about to take a dramatic new turn.

II

New France

The first French settlement in what is now the United States was on Ste. Croix (De Monts) Island in Maine's Scoodic river, where Father Nicholas Aubry was chaplain in 1604–5. The main French garrison was across the Bay of Fundy at Port Royal in modern Nova Scotia. Jesuits arrived in 1611, but disputes in the colony and France led to their removal in 1613 to Mount Desert Island off the Maine coast. In September of that year a Virginia captain, Samuel Argall, plundered the French outposts and scattered the missionaries. Jesuit Brother Gilbert du Thet was killed in the attack at Mount Desert. It was another twenty years before missions were begun among the Abenaki Indians of Maine.[1]

Among Port Royal's colonizers was Samuel de Champlain, who until his death in 1635 dominated the Canadian scene. In 1608 he founded Québec. He also began a century of Iroquois hostility by making alliances with the Ontario Hurons and the Montagnais and Algonquins of the Ottawa valley. French thinking was dominated by concern for lines of communication to the west and its lucrative fur trade. For security reasons the Iroquois had to be pushed south into present-day New York State. They became France's enemies while the Hurons, Montagnais, and Algonquins were French allies. Consequences for the French empire and for French missionaries were momentous.

Recollect Franciscans came to New France in 1615 and Jesuits returned ten years later. Missions were established as far west as Georgian Bay. But in the Anglo-French War of 1627–29 Québec was captured, and France's American colony was not restored until the treaty of St. Germain-en-Laye in 1632. King Louis XIII's chief minister, Cardinal de Richelieu, sent the

23

Jesuits to the Huron, Algonquin, and Montagnais and the Capuchins to Acadia (Nova Scotia). Maine remained a wilderness frontier area, divided at the Kennebec River between New England and New France. Sporadic visits from Franciscans, Québec seminary priests and Jesuits kept contact with the Abenaki, who lived between the Ste. Croix and Kennebec rivers. Gabriel Druillettes, S.J., was an important missionary among them. Capuchins ranged south from Acadia as far as Penobscot Bay. But from 1654 to 1670 Acadia was controlled by the English, and King William's War (1689–97) kept the frontier in constant turmoil. Competing European powers enlisted Indian support and paid bounties for scalps. Villages were destroyed on both sides, their inhabitants brutally killed.

Greatest of the Maine missionaries was Sébastien Râle, S.J., who came there from the Illinois country in 1694 and spent thirty years with the Abenaki, a tribe that became completely Catholic. The 1697 Treaty of Ryswick brought temporary peace, but France and England were at war again from 1702 to 1713 (Queen Anne's War), and in 1704 the Abenaki sacked Deerfield, Massachusetts, and massacred its population. The Treaty of Utrecht in 1713 increased the confusion, since it involved cession of Acadia to Britain but left boundaries in Maine unclear. If Acadia extended to the Kennebec, the Abenaki now became British subjects; if the boundary was at the Ste. Croix, they were French. Québec's governor wrote Râle in 1720, urging him to mobilize Indian resistance. Meanwhile Râle was embroiled in controversy with a Protestant minister who had been sent from Boston in the hope of winning over the Indians; Massachusetts offered a £200 reward for the Jesuit's capture. Two years later war was declared, and in 1724 a band of Mohawk Indians and New England militia attacked the village of Norridgewock, where Râle had his headquarters. Lieutenant Stephen Jacques shot and killed Râle, and his scalp and those of some of the Indians were paraded in Boston.

Peace returned to Maine in 1726. Efforts were made to rebuild the mission, but the Treaty of Paris of 1763, ending the Seven Years' War, followed in 1764 by government suppression of the Jesuit order in France and its empire, effectively ended organized church life in Maine.

The chief French mission effort was that of the Jesuits among the Hurons. Their story, which belongs to the history of Canada, is told vividly in the pages of the *Relations,* annual reports covering the years 1632–73.[2] A recent historian has summed up the tale:

> From these pages, written in a simple and direct style, rise up vivid pictures of the cultivated and refined Black Robe, squatting in a circle of filthy savages, or paddling his canoe across a wide wind-swept lake, or sleeping in a smoke-filled hut, or standing as an object of jeering Indian derision.[3]

The difficult Huronia mission continued for fifteen years and then ended in an orgy of fire and death as the Iroquois unleashed a genocidal war on the Hurons in 1648–49. At stake was the western fur trade, for which the Hurons were the principal channel. Torture, mutilation, and running the gauntlet were only some features of these fiery days which saw ten thousand Hurons die and the remnant scattered. Among the victims of Iroquois fury were five Canadian Jesuit martyrs, canonized in 1930. Another Jesuit mission had ended in apparent failure.[4]

Who were the Iroquois?[5] Before the arrival of the French they had been driven south, out of the St. Lawrence lowlands. Somewhere between 1559 and 1570 they formed a confederacy, the Five Nations, to which in 1715 were added the Tuscarora moving north from the Carolinas. When European colonizers reached the area, the Five Nations were spread across northern New York: the Mohawks on the east flank, then, in order, the Oneida, Onondaga, Cayuga, and Seneca, whose lands on the west touched Lake Erie. The Mohawk Valley and the Finger Lakes region were Iroquois territory. The Five Nations looked south to Dutch New Netherland for support, and Dutch guns helped them destroy the Hurons. After New Netherland became New York in 1664, the Iroquois transferred their alliance to the English. Their continuing hostility to the French was a factor in the eventual destruction of France's American empire.

Despite the obstacles, Jesuits attempted missionary work among the Iroquois. The first venture was less intended than accidental.[6] In 1642 Jesuit Isaac Jogues and several lay helpers, accompanied by a party of Hurons, were travelling from Québec to the mission among the Chippewa at Sault-Ste.-Marie in present-day Michigan. They were captured by Mohawks and taken to the village of Ossernenon in the Mohawk River valley, west of Albany. Jogues's companion, René Goupil, was tomahawked, but the priest, after enduring incredible tortures which left him with mutilated hands, escaped in 1643 and made his way back to France by way of the Dutch colonies at Fort Orange (Albany) and New Amsterdam. He returned to Iroquois territory in 1645 as a peace ambassador, but in 1646 was again taken captive. The Indians blamed the missionaries for crop failures and sicknesses which had reached epidemic proportions, and in 1646 Jogues, Jean de LaLande, and a Huron Christian suffered martyrdom somewhere near the present site of Auriesville. Goupil, Jogues, and LaLande were canonized along with the Canadian martyrs by Pope Pius XI.[7]

The next Jesuit effort among the Iroquois was among the Onondaga. In 1654 Father Simon LeMoyne accepted an invitation to visit their principal towns on the Oswego River. It seemed an important breakthrough. The

Onondaga, in the center of the Five Nations' confederacy, were hosts to the regular meetings of the league. They were the "keepers of the council" and the "keepers of the wampum." For three years a French fort on Lake Onondaga was the center of missions that reached out also to the Seneca, Cayuga, and Oneida. but the Mohawks remained hostile, and in 1657 secret warnings of impending disaster put the French to flight. The Iroquois mission was resumed again from 1668 to 1686, but results were relatively meager, and many of the Christian Indians moved to Canada. Among them was the Mohawk girl Kateri Tekakwitha, who died in 1680 and was declared "Blessed," the final stage before canonization, by Pope John Paul II in 1980.

Political considerations bulked large after 1683 when the aggressive Irish Catholic Thomas Dongan became the Duke of York's governor in New York. Dongan sought English priests for the Iroquois, but was unsuccessful. The French mission withered under the strain of constant warfare and Iroquois resistance to Christianity. From 1748 to 1760 a Sulpician priest, François Piquet, directed La Présentation mission near modern Ogdensburg, but by the time France abandoned her continental possessions in North America in 1763 the Iroquois missions were more memory than reality. The small French presence—in 1754 there were seventy thousand French in America, and two million in Britain's colonies—the hostility created by the Huron alliance, the subordination of other purposes to the all-important fur trade, the bad example of French soldiers and trappers, the introduction of guns and liquor among the Indians, all played their part.[8] Ultimately, the missions were pawns in the struggle of France and England for a continent. They depended on the French crown for their financial survival and on the French army for protection. Examples of religious heroism abound among Indian converts and missionaries alike, but the fact remains that the Iroquois were not in any large number won for Christianity.

George Bancroft's line about French Jesuit missionaries in North America is famous: "Not a cape was turned, nor a river entered, but a Jesuit led the way." It is however, inaccurate in omitting mention of Franciscans and Québec seminary priests and, as Jesuit historian William Bangert has pointed out, it is "overgenerous because frequently the actual pioneers were the fur traders." "But," he adds, "the priests were not far behind."[9] The rape of Huronia had severed communications with the west.[10] First to reestablish them were the *coureurs de bois,* roughhewn trappers and traders. They reached Michilimackinac and the Sault, then pushed on to modern Wisconsin and into the lands of the Ottawa who lived above Georgian Bay and Lake Huron. It was not until ten years after the end of the Huron mission that an Algonquin Chippewa tribe, the Ojibwa, brought Jesuit René Ménard to the shores of Lake Superior. He doubted he would return and wrote to another Jesuit in words that tell the motivation of the missionaries:

> This is probably the last word that I shall write to you, and I wish it to be the seal of our friendship until eternity. . . . In three or four months you may include me in the Memento for the dead, in view of the kind of life lived by these peoples, of my age, and of my delicate constitution. In spite of that, I have felt such powerful promptings, and have seen in this affair so little of the purely natural, that I could not doubt, if I failed to respond to this opportunity, that I would experience an endless remorse.[11]

Ménard died somewhere in Wisconsin looking for a band of wandering Catholic Hurons, but four years later the Jesuit Ottawa mission was founded with the arrival in Wisconsin of Father Claude Jean Allouez.[12] He served Hurons, Potawatomi, and Illinois around Lake Superior and traveled as far as what are now the states of Michigan, Illinois, and Indiana before his death among the Miami near Niles, Michigan, in 1689. Mission headquarters was located after 1670 at St. Ignace on the Straits of Mackinac, where the priest was Jacques Marquette.[13] In 1673 Marquette extended the mission's horizons when he accompanied Louis Jolliet on the voyage of discovery down the Mississippi River, a 2,700-mile round trip which reached the confluence of the Mississippi and Arkansas rivers. Marquette then worked among the Kaskaskia and spent a winter at what is now Chicago. He died in 1675 near present-day Ludington, on Lake Michigan's eastern shore.[14]

Priests from the Québec seminary, which was modeled on the Foreign Missions Seminary of Paris, went to the Mississippi valley in 1689 and settled in the region of Vicksburg and Natchez, among the Taenses, Tonica, and Tamaroa. After some unpleasant jurisdictional quarrels with the Jesuits had been resolved, they established their headquarters at Cahokia.[15] Franciscans accompanied René Robert de LaSalle on his explorations of the Great Lakes in 1679–80, and we owe our first description of Niagara Falls to a friar, Louis Hennepin. In 1680 Hennepin and other Franciscans explored Minnesota and were held captive by the Sioux for a half-year. LaSalle had Franciscans with him on his expedition to the mouth of the Mississippi in 1682, and Franciscans and Sulpicians went to their deaths on his ill-fated voyage to the Gulf of Mexico which ended in tragedy at Matagorda Bay, Texas, in 1689. A Franciscan, Constantin Delhalle, was with Antoine de la Mothe Cadillac at the founding of Detroit in 1701 and gave his life in 1706 while trying to negotiate peace with the tribes.[16] Cadillac dreamed of a "Québec of the West," with the Ottawa, Huron, Miami, and Potawatomi gathered around the fort. This mingling of French and Indians ran counter to the Jesuit policy of segregating Indians from the bad example of French settlements, and, rather than acquiesce in it, they abandoned all their stations in Ottawa country except the one at Green Bay. The Jesuits also made forays farther west, into Minnesota, the Dakotas, and perhaps as far as Montana, but the Sioux proved resistant to conversion and nothing came of these efforts. At Detroit Franciscans continued to serve the parish until 1782, twenty years after the British takeover.

The principal Jesuit mission among the Illinois was founded at Kaskaskia in 1703. From it developed a series of riverfront stations which after 1717 were attached to the colony of Louisiana. Frequently the site of the missions changed as priests followed migratory Indians from place to place. Gradually stability was achieved in such towns as Kaskaskia, Prairie du Rocher, Fort de Chartres, St.-Philippe, Cahokia, and on the west bank Ste.-Geneviève. Outlying posts were at Fort Arkansas on the river of that name, Fort Orléans on the Missouri and, 240 miles to the east, in modern Indiana, Post Vincennes on the Wabash. Each boasted some settlers, but they were mainly garrison towns to protect the fur trade. The history of the Illinois missions is spotted with conflicts between priests and local authorities over the liquor trade, gambling, and prostitution of Indian women. The trafficking in brandy was particularly vicious. Nowhere in the United States had Indians distilled liquor before the coming of Europeans, and its spread helped break down the structures of Indian society. Still, the missions survived and French churches grew up. Local government had something of the town meeting about it with the village church serving as a meeting place for both civil and religious business. The government, when it remembered to do so, supported the clergy, who supplemented this income with revenues from farms worked by hired help and black slaves. The slaves, in some villages half the population, had originally been brought upriver to work in the lead mines which were another source of colonial income.

There was no fighting in the west during the Anglo-French wars of 1689–97 and 1702–13, and France's soldiers continued to push into the Mississippi valley. Forts were built at Mackinac, Detroit, and at the mouths of the Kaskaskia and the Illinois. Settlers from Canada trickled down the great river. But disaster came with the outbreak of the French and Indian War in 1754. France's fortunes turned for the worse after 1758 and a year later Québec fell to General Wolfe. Canada surrendered on September 8, 1760. France ceded New Orleans and the west bank of the Mississippi to Spain in 1762. The rest of New France, except the fishing islands of St.-Pierre and Miquelon off Newfoundland, went to Britain in the 1763 Treaty of Paris.

Suppression of the Society of Jesus in France ended organized Jesuit mission work in the Illinois and Ottawa country in 1763. Only Sébastien Meurin stayed on until his death at Prairie du Rocher in 1777, four years after Pope Clement XIV decreed the worldwide end of his order. With the forced departure of the Jesuits, religious ministry in the vast Illinois territory dwindled almost to the vanishing point. Only with the coming of priests like Pierre Gibault, a missionary from the Québec Seminary, who arrived in 1768, did matters improve. From his base at Kaskaskia on the Mississippi he sent to Bishop Briand of Québec a description of his reception by the people of Vincennes when he came there as the first priest they had seen in seven years:

> Some threw themselves on their knees and were quite unable to speak; others spoke only by their sobs; some cried out: Father, save us, we are nearly in hell; others said: God has not then utterly abandoned us, for it is He who has sent you to make us do penance for our sins; and others again exclaimed: Ah! Sir, why did you not come a month ago, then my poor wife, my dear father, my loved mother, my poor child would not have died without the sacraments![17]

Meurin was dead, but Gibault was still travelling through the Illinois country when the Americans, in the person of George Rogers Clark and his rangers, arrived in 1778.

The Treaty of Paris did not put an end to resistance in the west. France's Indian allies, who had not been defeated by the British, tried to continue the battle against advancing frontiersmen. The Ottawa chief Pontiac rallied Ottawa-speaking tribes and laid siege to Pittsburgh and Detroit. Involved were the Delaware, Miami, Shawnee, Ottawa, Pottawatomi, and Ojibwa. But his support melted away, and Pontiac was murdered by an Indian at Kahokia in 1769.

During the American Revolution, the Indians supported the British, and their opposition to American encroachment lasted well into the 19th century. In 1794 General Anthony Wayne defeated them in the battle of Fallen Timbers near Maumee, Ohio, and in 1811 William Henry Harrison started on his way to the White House with the victory of Tippecanoe in western Indiana. The great Indian leader Tecumseh died fighting for the British in 1813, and intermittent struggles continued until the defeat of the Sauk and Fox under chief Black Hawk in 1832. Within a dozen years the greater part of the Indian population had been removed to the Trans-Mississippi West. The era of the French missions was over. They were themselves long gone from the scene. A new Catholic population was coming. Representative of it was Colonel John Francis Hamtramck, of Luxemburg descent and a veteran of the Revolution. He served under

Wayne, commanded the First Regiment of the new American army and died commandant at Detroit in 1802.[18]

There is one other footnote to the colonial story. Despite provisions of the 1783 Treaty of Paris, Great Britain retained control of military posts at Detroit and elsewhere in the old Northwest until 1796. There was talk of an Indian barrier state to block United States expansion to the west. The fur trade remained largely in British hands, and Revolutionary War veterans and other frontiersmen swarming over the mountains to take up new lands felt hemmed in. All this ended with the final defeat of the Indians. In the meantime, while French villages in Indiana and Illinois were being integrated into the new nation, the French at Detroit, who had been loyal to the crown during the Revolution, continued for thirteen years under British rule. French secular priests replaced the Franciscans in 1782. But on June 1, 1796, in the final year of George Washington's presidency, the British withdrew and the last French mission came under the diocese of Baltimore. In 1798 the Bishop of Baltimore assigned a young Sulpician priest, Gabriel Richard, as assistant pastor.[19] Before his death in 1832, Richard had introduced the first printing press and edited the first Catholic newspaper in the United States. No other minister was available, so he gave regular lectures to the Governor and territorial officials of Michigan. He was one of the founders of the University of Michigania, in which he was vice-president and professor (at $12.50 per subject) of six of the thirteen subjects taught. When the University of Michigan began in 1821, Richard was a trustee. From 1823 to 1825 he was the first Catholic priest to serve in the United States Congress, as Michigan's delegate. By then the French period was a memory. Apart from place names, it left no lasting heritage comparable to that of the Spaniards in the southwest. The Indians among whom Jesuits, Québec Seminary priests, and Franciscans had worked were driven across the Mississippi. French colonists, few enough at the best of times, disappeared into the general American population. The substantial Franco-American population later to be found along the nation's Canadian border was the product of 19th-century migration from the north.

III

Louisiana

Louisiana was the most cosmopolitan and heterogeneous region of either Spanish or French America.[1] It was made up of the towns along the Mississippi and the Gulf Coast, plus a vast hinterland. The United States would double in size with the Louisiana Purchase in 1803. Control by France (1699–1766) and Spain (1766–1803) left its mark, but Creole society was spiced also by infusions of Rhinelanders and German Swiss brought out by John Law in the heyday of mercantilism and after 1755 by deportees from faroff Acadia, the ancestors of today's Cajuns. Black slaves were imported in great numbers for the plantations and for lead mines upriver. Americans from Kentucky and Tennessee multiplied after the end of the Revolution. New Orleans, founded in 1718, became an international port, the gateway to the Gulf of Mexico, the Caribbean, Latin America, and Europe for trade flowing down the Mississippi and its tributaries.

The Gulf Coast's first French settlement was at Biloxi, Mississippi, where Pierre LeMoyne, Sieur d'Iberville, built a chapel and fort in 1699. A Franciscan naval chaplain accompanied the expedition, but did not remain in the colony. The Jesuit Paul du Ru was at Biloxi in 1700, but then Québec seminary priests replaced him. Until 1720 they were Louisiana's only priests.

The seminary priests began missions among the Choctaw and Chickasaw, but neither they nor others who followed were very successful. The same was true of efforts to convert the Arkansas Indians on the west bank of the Mississippi. Missions among the Yazoo and Natchez had hardly begun when the Indian revolt of 1729 wreaked havoc. The brandy trade, arbitrary and often brutal treatment of Indians by civil officials and soldiers, the use of Indian women for prostitution, laws which forbade Indian widows to inherit their husbands' property, all diluted the impact of the gospel preached by the priests. The example of white Christians was one of the greatest obstacles for the missionaries to overcome. Indians were also sometimes enslaved, although most slaves, including those who after 1727 worked plantations owned by the Jesuits, were blacks brought in from the Caribbean. The *Code Noir* or Black Code of 1724 attempted to regulate conditions of slave labor. Religious instruction was required, a prescription often ignored. Slaves might not marry without permission. Miscegenation, in or out of marriage, was forbidden. The *Code Noir* also forbade public religious services other than Roman Catholic and ordered expulsion of Jews.

Exploitation of Louisiana was turned over to commercial companies, the most famous of which was the Company of the West, headed by Scots entrepreneur John Law, which controlled colonial trade until 1732. In 1722 the Bishop of Québec, in whose jurisdiction the territory lay, allowed the Company to divide religious responsibilities among four groups: Jesuits and Québec seminary priests were to work above the confluence of the Mississippi and Ohio; Capuchins in the lower Mississippi, including New Orleans; and Carmelites around Mobile. The Carmelites soon withdrew, and the Jesuit territory was extended to just above Natchez in 1723. In 1726 all Indian missions came under Jesuit control. Jesuit-Capuchin conflicts flared regularly after this time until the French government expelled the Jesuits in 1763.[2] More productive than these quarrels was the arrival in 1727 of Ursuline nuns who established a school for girls. Their agreement with the Company of the Indies called for them to supply six nuns. Their tasks included hospital nursing, teaching both white and black girls, hospitality for young women who came from France in search of husbands, and care also for "correction girls" sent to the colony. For these services the Company gave the Ursulines a house, eight *arpents* of land and eight black slaves.

Spanish Louisiana lasted for thirty-seven years, from the coming of acting Governor Antonio de Ulloa in 1766 until a two-month interim French regime before the American takeover in 1803. Church jurisdiction passed from Québec to Santiago in Cuba. Priests were in short supply, a situation aggravated by the departure of many French clergy. In 1785 New Orleans received its first bishop, the Capuchin Cirillo Sieni, a native of Barcelona who was appointed auxiliary to the bishop of Santiago and, after 1787, to the bishop of Havana. His eight years in office were equally divided between Cuba and Louisiana, with trips also to Florida. In 1793 Pope Pius VI established the diocese of Louisiana and the Floridas, centered in New Orleans, which therefore ranks third in American seniority, after San Juan

(1511) and Baltimore (1789). A Cuban bishop, Luis de Peñalver y Cardenas, arrived in 1795 and stayed until 1802. His impressions of Louisiana's forty-five thousand Catholics and twenty-two priests were very negative. Practical toleration of the presence of Americans, he thought, encouraged poor Catholics to neglect their religion. "The emigration from the western part of the United States," he complained, "and the toleration of our government have introduced into this colony a gang of adventurers who have no religion and no knowledge of God." The influence of the Enlightenment and of French revolutionary ideas was strong. Religious practice was at a low ebb. In 1795 the bishop reported to Spain:

> The inhabitants do not listen to, or, if they do, disregard all exhortations to maintain in its orthodoxy the Catholic faith, and to preserve innocence of life.

Peñalver estimated Sunday mass attendance in the cathedral parish at 25 percent, and claimed that only three or four hundred of the eleven thousand parishioners received communion at least once a year. Most men, married or not, kept mistresses. The one bright spot was the Ursuline convent. Its graduates were "less vicious than the other sex." The royal Spanish school for boys was ineffective. Its students left it too early and at home they heard "neither the name of God nor of King, but daily witness[ed] the corrupt morals of their parents." The bishop was likewise unhappy about the lot of slaves in the colony, noting that, with rare exceptions, they were not permitted to marry legally. Peñalver reserved some of his strongest hostility for Anglo-American interlopers, and for French and Irish priests who did not speak Spanish and refused to conform to Spanish ways. Even the Ursulines came in for criticism because of their attachment to French language and customs. Reaction to their new bishop among the French Creoles may be left to the imagination.[3]

There were other complicating factors. Pinckney's Treaty of 1795 had finally secured for Americans the right to use the Mississippi as a trade route and to transship goods at New Orleans, but in 1797 a new Spanish governor withdrew most religious toleration. Bishop Peñalver was delighted. Freedom of conscience was restricted to the first generation. Children of non-Catholic parents had to be baptized as Catholics or the parents would be expelled. No Protestant ministers were allowed in Louisiana. The picture was spoiled for the bishop only by the problem of Fray Antonio de Sedella, known to French Louisianians as Père Antoine.

Antonio de Sedella, a Capuchin friar, first arrived in New Orleans in 1781. In short order he became superior of the Capuchins, vicar-general and pastor of St. Louis cathedral. An able, aggressive, and ambitious man, he used the period of Bishop Cirillo's absence in Cuba from 1785 to

1789 to consolidate his position as real leader of the Catholic community. He knew how to use power. In 1787 he was made Commissary for the Inquisition.[4] From this position of strength he resisted for three years the efforts of bishop and governor to expel him from the colony, threatening on one occasion to use his position as inquisitor to stamp out the "American heresy" tolerated by the government. He was forcibly deported in 1790, only to return five years later with a royal warrant ordering his restoration as pastor in the same ship that brought Bishop Peñalver. Of Sedella's popularity there is no doubt. His reputation for indulging moral weaknesses among his flock had endeared him to many of them; to still more he was a familiar figure. The stern new bishop was a stranger. Conflict between the two was inevitable, and controversy did not end with the bishop's departure in 1802. Sedella's supporters tried to enlist Emperor Napoléon's support for his appointment as bishop. What followed was one of the most vigorous efforts in American history by lay people—the *marguilliers,* or church wardens—to assert their right to a share in church administration.

Peñalver's departure coincided with the final shift in political control of Louisiana. By the secret Treaty of San Ildefonso (1800), Napoleon regained Louisiana for France, but no French commissioner arrived until 1803, and then only to pass the territory on to the Americans, who had bought it for $15 million. Meanwhile, church administration was a shambles. Peñalver had named an Irish priest, Thomas Hassett, as administrator of the vacant diocese, a position he held until his death in 1804 when a second Irishman, Patrick Walsh, succeeded him. When Père Antoine defied his authority, Walsh withdrew his official authorization to preach and to hear confessions. The church wardens then elected the Capuchin as their pastor. Walsh's position was effectively undercut. He died in 1806.

The United States had taken over a territory with a church-state tradition substantially different from that which developed under the Articles of Confederation and was continuing to develop under the new Federal Constitution. The superior of the Ursuline convent at New Orleans, Sister Thérèse Farjon, inquired of both President Thomas Jefferson and Bishop John Carroll of Baltimore what impact the American system would have on the sisters and the property they had received from the previous government. On May 15, 1804, Jefferson explained:

> . . . The principles of the constitution and government of the United States are a sure guarantee to you that [the property] will be preserved to you sacred and inviolate, and that your institution will be permitted to govern itself according to its own voluntary rules, without interference from civil authority. . . .

"Whatever diversity of shade," Jefferson continued, "may appear in the religious opinions of our fellow citizens," none would be indifferent to the "charitable objects" and "wholesome purposes" of the nuns and their school, and this would "ensure it the patronage of the government it is under." He closed by assuring Sister Thérèse that the nuns and their school would "meet with all the protection" his office could give.[5]

Catholic problems in Louisiana were internal rather than external. In September 1805, Bishop John Carroll of Baltimore was named by Rome as administrator of the diocese of Louisiana and the Two Floridas. He consulted Secretary of State James Madison on the situation, particularly about appointment of a bishop. Madison talked with President Jefferson, then sent two replies. In an official letter, he pointed out that the United States government could not concern itself with a purely ecclesiastical affair, although he did suggest that Carroll's own patriotism would undoubtedly see to it that the candidate combined with "professional merits a due attachment to the independence, the constitution and the prosperity of the United States." A second, private, letter was more explicit. The Secretary of State told Carroll that he shared his views on Père Antoine, and that the *marguilliers'* attempt to solicit foreign support for the Capuchin's nomination was "manifestly reprenhensible."[6]

In this fluid situation no bishop was named until 1815, when a scholarly Sulpician, William DuBourg, who had managed to survive three years as administrator of New Orleans, was consecrated in Rome. The new bishop was not anxious to face Sedella and his supporters. Half the Louisiana parishes were vacant, and only ten priests were active, several of them old or sick. DuBourg made his way instead to St. Louis. Not until two years later did he venture a visit to New Orleans, and only in 1823 did he begin to live there. Three years later he resigned the see and returned to France. Père Antoine was pastor of St. Louis cathedral in New Orleans when he died in 1829 and was buried with Masonic rites. Difficulties with the church wardens continued until 1844.

IV

English America: Maryland

The civilization and culture which laid the foundations of the future United States was English and Protestant. England's continuing 16th- and 17th-century religious reformation is therefore central to an understanding of religious aspects of American colonization. Early explorers were sent out towards the end of the 15th century by a Catholic king, Henry VII, but actual settlement was delayed and only under James I were permanent roots put down at Jamestown, Virginia, in 1607. By then, separation of the church in England from Rome was an accomplished fact. The intellectual center of English America developed in Massachusetts where Pilgrims in 1620 and their fellow Puritans who founded Massachusetts Bay in 1630 represented the dissenting wing of England's reformation, strongly Calvinist in theology and sternly opposed to Roman Catholicism and to Catholicizing influences in English Protestantism. Opposition to "papists" was all-pervasive. It stemmed from complex historical, religious, and political factors.

For the Puritan, Catholicism was a corruption of the Christian message; Rome was Babylon, the pope the anti-Christ of the Apocalypse. Theological judgments were reinforced by memories of the fires of Smithfield and elsewhere, where nearly 300 Protestants were burned between 1555 and 1558 under Queen Mary I. Ancestral memory was kept fresh by widespread circulation in England and the colonies of works like John Foxe's *Book of Martyrs* (1563) illustrating Protestant martyrdoms at Cath-

36

olic hands. The tradition was intensified by tales of the 1605 Gunpowder Plot, when Guy Fawkes and a group of madcap Catholics planned to blow up King James and the houses of Parliament, and by Titus Oates's false charges of Catholic complicity (the so-called "Popish Plot") in a 1678 scheme to assassinate Charles II. International politics were involved too. France and Spain were England's enemies and they were Catholic. Pope Pius V in 1570 excommunicated Elizabeth I and declared her subjects released from their allegiance. The alliance of his successor, Gregory XIII, with Spain gave weight to charges that adherence to Catholicism meant treason.

On the American side of the Atlantic, French soldiers and their Indian allies threatened New England on the north and west, while in the south Spaniards from Florida warred with Englishmen from Georgia. Religious and political hostility poisoned the colonial atmosphere. Laws were passed banning Catholics. A Massachusetts statute of 1647 threatened priests with death:

> all and every Jesuit, seminary priest, missionary or other spiritual or ecclesiastical person made or ordained by any authority, power or jurisdiction, derived, challenged or pretended, from the pope or see of Rome . . . shall be deemed and accounted an incendiary and disturber of the publick peace and safety, and an enemy to the true Christian religion, and shall be adjudged to suffer perpetual imprisonment, and if any person, being so sentenced and actually imprisoned, shall break prison and make his escape, and be afterwards re-taken, he shall be punished with death.[1]

Similar, if less sanguinary, laws were enacted elsewhere. In actual fact, prosecutions of Catholics were rare, not so much because laws were winked at as because neither priests nor lay Catholics were to be found in most of the colonies. Goodwife Ann Glover, hanged as a witch on Boston Common in 1688 after reciting for Cotton Mather the Lord's Prayer in Latin, Irish, and English ("But she could not end it," he noted), may be a lone example. She died forgiving her enemies and executioners and told the magistrates: "I die a Catholic." The Catholic martyrology in English America hardly compares with that of the Quakers, who suffered bitterly at Puritan hands, but Catholic settlement was effectively prevented and foundations laid for the anti-Catholicism which observers have noted as endemic to the American scene.[2]

Despite anti-papist laws and a generally hostile climate some Roman Catholics did find their way to English America, principally to Maryland and Pennsylvania, but also to Virginia, New York, and New Jersey. The most substantial Catholic settlement was in Maryland, a proprietary colony granted by King Charles I in 1632 to Caecilius Calvert, second Baron Baltimore, and named for the ill-fated monarch's French queen, Henrietta Marie. The Maryland colony was to be founded from "a laudable and pious zeal for extending the Christian religion, and also the Territories of our Empire." Baltimore's purposes were certainly political and mercantile. They were also religious. Like his father before him, he was a Roman Catholic—a proscribed papist. His business and political fortunes were bound up with that fact.

Caecilius Calvert's father, Sir George Calvert, had served King James I as one of two principal Secretaries of State.[3] He engaged at the same time in a range of profitable financial ventures: the silk trade, Irish properties, a colony in Newfoundland, investments in the East India, Virginia, and New England companies. It is not known when George Calvert became a Roman Catholic, but it was public knowledge in London by the winter of 1624–25 when he resigned his office and was raised to the Irish peerage as Baron Baltimore of Baltimore in County Longford. At Charles I's accession in the spring of 1625 he lost his rank as Privy Councillor because he could not in conscience swear the required oaths. Much of the rest of his life he devoted to his tiny colony, Ferryland, on distant Avalon peninsula in Newfoundland. The religious arrangements made there foreshadowed developments in Maryland's history.

Calvert provided his colony in Newfoundland with an Anglican clergyman. When he went out himself in 1627 he brought along two English Catholic secular priests to join the Protestant "Parson of Ferryland." Anglicans and Catholics shared Baltimore's own house for worship services, to the evident distress of Pope Urban VIII's nuncio at Brussels, as we know from a report to Rome in 1630. But George Calvert was not made for the rigors of northern life. Newfoundland was a "wofull country" where "crosses and miseryes is my portion," he wrote, and as autumn approached in 1632 he was sailing south to Virginia where he was denied admission for refusing the oath of supremacy acknowledging King Charles as "only supreme governor of this realm . . . as well in all spiritual or ecclesiastical things or causes, as temporal." He returned to England and petitioned that same king for the grant of a proprietary colony in the territory lying to the north of Virginia.

George Calvert died in 1632 before the royal charter for Maryland was issued to his son Caecilius, second Lord Baltimore, on June 20. The colony had a large measure of autonomy, its laws were to be

> consonant to Reason and be not repugnant or contrary, but (so far as conveniently may be) agreeable to the Laws, Statutes, Customs and Rights of Our Kingdom of England.[4]

Along with the charter went Baltimore's instructions to the colonists, dated November 13, 1633. They reflected a realistic pragmatism in the thorny matter of founding in England's empire a colony where Roman Catholics might practice their religion. The governor and commissioners were to

> be very careful to preserve unity and peace amongst all the passengers on Shipp-board, and . . . suffer no scandal or offense to be given to any of the Protestants, whereby any just complaint may heerafter be made by them, in Virginea or in England, and . . . for that end . . . cause all Acts of Romane Catholique Religion to be done as privately as may be, and . . . instruct all Romane Catholoques to be silent upon all occasions of discourse concerning matters of Religion; and . . . treat the Protestants with as much mildness and favor as Justice will permit.[5]

With these directives, some two hundred colonists sailed from England in the 360-ton *Ark* and 40-ton *Dove* in November 1633. Four months later they anchored in the Potomac estuary and landed on the island now called St. Clement's.

One of the "Gentlemen Adventurers," as the principal colonists were called, recorded the events of Maryland's first day:

> On the day of the Annunciation of the Most Holy Virgin Mary [March 25] in the year 1634, we celebrated mass for the first time on this island. This had never been done before in this part of the world. After we had completed the sacrifice, we took upon our shoulders a great cross, which we had hewn out of a tree, and advancing in order to the appointed place, with the assistance of the Governor and his associates and the other Catholics, we erected a trophy to Christ the Saviour, humbly reciting, on our bended knees, the litanies of the Sacred Cross with great emotion.[6]

That description is from the pen of Father Andrew White, S.J., onetime dean and philosophy professor at St. Alban's English Seminary in Valladolid, Spain. He was drafting his annual report to the Jesuit superior-general in Rome, Muzio Vitelleschi. With two Jesuit companions, Father John Altham (who sometimes used the alias Gravenor) and Brother Thomas Gervase, White accompanied the colonists who sailed in the *Ark* and the *Dove*. By April the three Jesuits were settled in an old Indian cabin at the new town of St. Mary's and Catholic life in Maryland had begun.

The Gentlemen Adventurers, their wives, families, and servants were a religiously mixed group. Protestants were in the majority, as they would be throughout Maryland's history, but there was a substantial Catholic element, including the Governor, young Leonard Calvert; the military captain, Thomas Cornwallis; and the secretary, John Lewger. Maryland was unique in the history of English-speaking Roman Catholicism in America. Catholics belonged to the political and social elite of the colony. Religious attitudes growing in that context inevitably differed from those which grew in the later 19th-century immigrant Catholic community when it intruded on a nation born of cultural and religious forces largely alien and often hostile to it.

Colonial Maryland's history was stormy. Economics played an important role in the development of a predominantly single-crop tobacco economy, leading to reliance on black slavery and domination by a relatively few wealthy families. The Baltimores' style was also a factor. Their proprietary rule was authoritarian. Struggles between assembly and governor were regular. Religion lay just under the surface. The Calverts discriminated in favor of family and friends—fellow Catholics—and that did not go unnoticed. At the same time, Reformation fervor was at its height; Puritans streamed into the colony and were welcomed. The makings of a religious donnybrook fell into place.

Catholic fortunes varied under the several types of government which Maryland experienced, the rule of the lords proprietor and their governors, Puritan interludes, and a quarter-century of direct royal rule. The Proprietors resisted Jesuit efforts to claim privileges and immunities traditional in Catholic countries of Europe. Puritans could not abide papists. Under royal governors anti-Catholic penal laws were passed and periodically enforced. In the course of dressing down the Jesuit mission superior, William Hunter, and the first American-born priest, Robert Brooke, Governor Seymour observed in 1704:

> It is the unhappy temper of you and all your tribe to grow insolent upon civility and never know how to use it and yet of all people you have the best reason for considering that if the necessary laws that are made were let loose they are sufficient to crush you.

Hunter was charged with consecrating a chapel, and Brooke with offering mass in the chapel at St. Mary's City. Seymour was tired of Catholic "gawdy shows and serpentine policy":

> In plain and few words Gentlemen if you intend to live here let me hear no more of these things for if I do and they are made good against you I'll chastize you. . . . Pray take notice that I am an English Protestant gentleman and can never equivocate . . . be civil and modest, for there is no other way for you to live quietly here.[7]

If religious harrassment was not violent, it was constant. Only in the early years when Catholics controlled the government, was there universal religious toleration. Robert Baird, never loath to criticize the Roman Catholic Church, later admitted that:

> Think what we may of their creed, and very different as was this policy from what Romanism elsewhere might have led us to expect, we can not refuse to Lord Baltimore's colony the praise of having established the first government in modern times in which entire toleration was granted to all denominations of Christians.[8]

The first statutory reference to toleration occurs in an ungrammatical 1639 declaration of the Maryland Assembly: "Holy Churches [*sic*] within this Province shall have all her rights and liberties."[9] Marylanders understood the subject and the object of the sentence. The "rights and liberties" were those guaranteed by Magna Carta. The meaning of "Churches" was made clear in a criminal prosecution before the Provincial Court in 1661. Arrested for exercising his priesthood, Jesuit Francis Fitzherbert based his successful defense on the 1639 Code combined with an interpretation of the word "Churches" taken from the 1649 Act Concerning Religion. he took the stance that he was:

> neither denying nor confessing the matter here objected since by the very first Lawe of this Country [the code of 1639] Holy Church within this Province shall have and Enjoye all her Rights, libertyes and Franchises wholy and without Blemish, amongst which that of preacheing and teacheing is not the least. . . .

"Neither imports itt," Fitzherbert argued,

> what Church is there meant, since by the true intent of the Act Concerning Religion [1649] every Church professing to believe in God, the father, Sonne and Holy Ghoste is accounted Holy Church here.[10]

The outbreak in 1642 of England's Civil War had begun a troubled twenty years in Maryland's history. Governor Leonard Calvert fled to Virginia, returned, and died in 1647. The church had a hard beginning. Of fourteen Jesuits who came out in the first twelve years, four were back in England within twelve months of arrival. Four more died of yellow fever. Their superior, Ferdinand Poulton, was mysteriously shot dead while crossing the St. Mary's River. Three young priests died exiled in Virginia. White and Thomas Copley, the last two priests in Maryland, were taken to England in chains in 1645 and there charged with violating the penal law prohibiting priests ordained abroad from entering the country. They were banished to Flanders.

By 1648 proprietary rule was reestablished and a year later the Assembly adopted the Act concerning Religion. Themes of religious toleration from the colony's earlier tradition were incorporated, but, as Matthew Page Andrews wrote, the Act "represented a compromise with the intolerant element that had entered the Province in increasing numbers since 1642."[11] Penalties were set for those who contravened the act—treble damages, fines, whipping, and imprisonment. Blasphemy or denial of the Trinity or the divinity of Christ was subject to the death penalty. These innovations were the contribution of the Puritans in the Assembly, echoing parliamentary acts in England like that of May 2, 1648, against heresies and blasphemies.

Puritans again seized the government after their victory in the 1655 battle of the Severn. With the Stuart Restoration of 1660 the Baltimores resumed control and Catholicism prospered, although its adherents were, by 1676, only one-twelfth of the 20,000 colonists. The 1688 Glorious Revolution and the activities in Maryland of John Coode and the Protestant Associators ended toleration for Catholics. From 1691 to 1715 the colony was a royal province. Only after the fourth Lord Baltimore conformed to the Church of England in 1713 was the proprietorship restored to his Protestant son in 1715. Anglicanism was established in 1702, taxes were levied for its support, attendance at its services made compulsory. A series of penal laws was enacted. Catholics could not vote or hold public office, although after 1712 they might worship privately.[12]

Despite burdens, many Catholics prospered handsomely. Diggeses and Brookes lived in some splendor on the Potomac, as did Sewalls at Mattapany on the Patuxent. When a rider attached to the Supply Bill of 1756 imposed double taxation on Catholics, Charles Carroll of Annapolis was so enraged that he considered emigration to French Louisiana, but he was still British America's richest man. His son, Charles Carroll of Carrollton, returned from sixteen years' European education to marry cousin Molly Darnall. They were the toast of Annapolis society. Mr. Carroll accepted an invitation to join the Homony Club, where he mingled with Maryland's bluest bloods.[13] Galling as it was to suffer religious discrimination where their own ancestors had introduced toleration, the fact is that most Maryland Catholics paid no substantial penalty for their faith.

Catholics lived chiefly in St. Mary's and Charles counties. They numbered in 1708 three thousand, a minuscule one-tenth of the population. Nearly half lived in St. Mary's County. By no means all were wealthy planters, and those who were also did the work of traders, businessmen, and financiers. They attended mass with small farmers who worked their own fields or lived as tenants on larger estates. Some plied the trades—such as blacksmithing and carpentry—of a rural economy. There were boatmen, oystermen, and sailors on the ships which regularly traded along the Atlantic coast. So many Irish indentured servants were imported in the wake of the Williamite sweeps of their native land that in 1699 the Assembly passed an act "to prevent too Great a number of Irish Papists being imported into this Province." But in the tobacco fields they were far outnumbered by black slaves.

Jesuits and lay Catholics bought, kept, and sold black slaves, perhaps as far back as 1634 or 1635 when the Jesuits' annual report announced arrival of "Matthias Sousa, a Molato" and "Francisco, a Molato." In 1638 the priests bought four servants—black or white they do not say— "for necessary services." The pattern was set. There is evidence that Catholics instructed their slaves in Christianity, baptized them, and shared the church's sacraments with them. They took pains to avoid separating black married couples. Never was there an indication that either priests or lay people saw slavery as morally wrong. John Carroll, named in 1784 to head the Catholic Church in the United States, reported to Rome that there were three thousand Catholic slaves in Maryland. When in 1789 an Irish priest attacked the Maryland clergy for mistreatment of their slaves, Carroll was content to say in their defense only that the priests

> treat their Negroes with great mildness and guard them from hunger and nakedness. . . . They work less and are much better fed, lodged and clothed, than labouring men in almost any part of Europe.

Corporal punishment of adults, he continued, was "rare indeed, and almost unknown. . . . A *priest's negro* is almost proverbial for one, who is allowed to act without control."[14]

Between 1634 and the Revolution, over one hundred Jesuit priests, a single Jesuit scholastic (seminarian), and about thirty Jesuit brothers served in Maryland and Pennsylvania. Most were English. Of forty-one Americans who entered the order (the first was Robert Brooke in 1684) twenty worked later in America, five decided after trial to follow other callings, two died as students, and the rest served in Europe. Three Americans were ordained as secular priests for work in England. Two English secular priests sent out by Lord Baltimore worked with the Jesuits in the 1640s, as did a half-dozen English Franciscans from 1672 to 1720. Mission staffing did not consistently reach double figures until the 18th century. The largest number of priests before the Revolution in the combined Maryland-Pennsylvania region—all of them Jesuits—was twenty-three, the figure for 1773.

Relations with the Proprietor's government were not always smooth. As the Secretary of the Council, John Lewger, suggested in twenty "Cases" he prepared in 1638, church-state relations "in such a country as this"—part of a Protestant empire—were not amenable to canonical rules shaped in and for the Catholic countries of Europe.[15] The Jesuits tacitly admitted this by coming to Maryland not as chaplains, but as gentlemen adventurers. Father Thomas Copley, who succeeded White as Jesuit superior, was not satisfied. He objected to Baltimore's omission in a draft code sent over in 1637 of traditional clerical immunities like exemption from civil court jurisdiction, taxation, and assessments for military purposes. Matters came to a head over lands given to the Jesuits by Indian chiefs. Under the royal charter all land in Maryland lay in the Proprietor's gift. He denied that the Indian donation conferred valid title. Copley warned of the excommunication incurred by usurpers of church property. The Jesuit superior-general ended the debate by ordering his men to claim no rights not theirs in England. "I should be very sorry," he wrote in 1643, "to see the first fruits which are so beautifully developing in the Lord nipped in their growth by the frost of cupidity."[16]

Under the Conditions of Plantation, Jesuit gentlemen adventurers took up land on the same terms as their lay counterparts. They began with four hundred acres of town land and three-thousand acre manor at St. Inigo's and St. George's Island in 1641. St. Thomas Manor, four thousand acres in Charles County, followed in 1649. Both estates were put in the hands of lay trustees. Other farms were acquired by purchase, came as gifts, or accrued from inheritances which individual Jesuits made over to the order.

The situation of the Jesuit "Gentlemen of Maryland" has sometimes been idealized. The mission was in fact neither easy nor attractive. Pastoral demands were routine, but strenuous and insistent. Those who lived on Jesuit manors doubled as farmers, husbandmen, and veterinarians. They managed grain mills, sawmills, and tobacco sheds. Others depended for support on a Catholic magnate, not always a happy situation, as Charles Carroll of Carrollton revealed when he wrote of his chaplain, the cantankerous Irishman John Ashton: "I wish we had never sent for a priest. They are troublesome animals in a family."[17]

Joseph Mosley had a third lifestyle—this priest lived alone for seventeen years on Maryland's Eastern shore. He saw his nearest priest-neighbor perhaps once a year. Whether from central manor houses or from a lonely outpost like Mosley's, priests rode circuit by boat and on horseback to outlying stations in parishioners' homes. It could mean from three to four hundred miles of hard riding a week. Provisions were scarce: "I've asked, when I've been fainting," Mosley wrote, "for a mouthful of bread and a glass of milk and could not get it."[18] Even when food could be had, the itinerant priests were held to rigid rules of fasting before celebrating the Eucharist. At each stop they heard confessions, said mass, and preached. For the children there was catechetical instruction. They made a special point of visiting the sick and administering the church's last rites. Some sense of how they understood their ministry comes through in a letter of Mosley:

> What part of our labours can we cut off, without neglecting our duty? Must I refuse when the sick want me? Must I neglect my Sunday church exercise to ease myself by staying at home? Must I, when at the chapel, refuse to hear half that present themselves? Must I, if call'd to the sick in the night, sleep till morning, and thus let the sick die without assistance? Must I, if call'd to a dying man in the rain, stay till it's fair weather?[19]

In 1638 several leading men in the colony were directed in the spiritual exercises of St. Ignatius Loyola, but there is no evidence that this became a regular feature of colonial Catholic life. Maryland piety resembled that of contemporary English Catholics. It was quiet and reserved. The Jesuits promoted devotion to the sacred Heart of Jesus, understood as symbol of Christ's redeeming love for humankind. The Eucharistic reservation normal in settled parish life could not be had where there was a scarcity of priests and public Catholic churches were prohibited; so men and women joined a league of prayer in honor of the Eucharistic presence of Christ. They agreed on assigned days to spend a private half hour kneeling in prayer in their homes.

There was talk of a school in Maryland in 1640, but nothing came of it until in 1653 well-to-do farmer Edward Cotton left the Jesuits his horse and mare, "the stock and all its increase to be preserved and the profit made use of for the use of a school."[20] Catholic education in the eastern seaboard colonies began at Newtown Manor. Onetime Jesuit seminarian Ralph Crouch was the schoolmaster. The program was "grammar," the initial cycle in the Jesuit educational system. Crouch's school was ecumenical: he was "ready some years to teach eyther Protestant or Catholikes."[21] After he went back to Europe in 1659 to rejoin the Jesuits, the school dropped for a time from the annual reports. But concern for education continued: in 1674 six girls and twelve boys sailed for English Catholic schools in Flanders. Regular "educational convoys" of this type became the pattern.[22]

By 1677 Newtown was again flourishing, with courses offered in the humanities, the second cycle in the Jesuit system. A few years later, two alumni were doing well in further studies at the English Jesuit college in St. Omer, French Flanders. They "yielded in ability to few Europeans for the honour of being first in their class."[23] A second Jesuit school, on Bohemia Manor at the head of Chesapeake Bay, was open for several years in the 1740s. It is remembered as *alma mater* to the first Archbishop of Baltimore, John Carroll, and to other leading Catholics of the Revolutionary generation.

V

English America: Virginia, Pennsylvania, and New York

Despite his shares in the defunct Virginia Company of London, George Calvert had in 1629 been turned away from its former colony as a popish recusant. Maryland and its neighbor to the south inevitably shared an uneasy coexistence. Puritans from Virginia were major disturbers of Maryland's colonial peace, while the Calverts' territorial designs on the Potomac's right bank hardly promoted detente. Inherited suspicions lingered. When Father John Altham made initial contact with Archihù, uncle of the *tayac* (chief) of the Piscataways, his interpreter was Henry Fleet, "one of the Virginia Protestants." Reporting the encounter, Andrew White remarked: "We do not much trust the Protestant interpreters."[1] Religious peace in Maryland was always fragile.

While Virginians made armed forays against the Proprietor's government and harrassed its Catholic supporters, the Jesuits found their colony both a field for ministry and a refuge in difficult times. A 1638 despatch to Rome reported on a pair of Catholic indentured servants bought in Virginia. Other Maryland Catholics joined in the rescue crusade. Beneficiaries were in ample supply: Catholic servants were "very numerous" in Virginia. They lacked there the spiritual support of a Catholic community and lived "among men of the worst sort." Doubly satisfying to the Jesuits was the case of another Virginian, a Catholic long careless of his religion who went through the spiritual exercises of St. Ignatius Loyola. His resolution to lead a model Christian life was a prelude to his pious death.[2]

Virginia had sweeping laws against popish recusants. Public office was denied those who would not swear the oaths of allegiance and supremacy. As for priests,

> it shall not be lawful . . . for any popish priest that shall hereafter arrive to remain above five days after warning given for his departure by the Governour or commander of the place, where he or they shall bee, if wind and weather hinder not his departure.[3]

Despite the cold hospitality, it was to Virginia that the author of the first catechism in the Piscataway tongue, Father Roger Rigby, and two companions fled in 1645 to escape the attentions of the Puritans who were challenging the proprietary government.[4] The three refugees all died within the year. Prospects were mysteriously brighter when Thomas Copley returned as superior of the American Jesuits in 1648. A "land route of two days journey" had been opened through the forest between Maryland and Virginia and it was now possible to combine work in the two provinces. He expected to visit the Governor of Virginia after Easter and had high hopes for the interview.[5]

Unfortunately more typical was an incident that occurred sometime between 1655 and 1658, during the Puritan ascendency at Annapolis. Virginia marauders raided a Maryland Jesuit manor house. The priests managed to escape and slipped across the Potomac to take refuge with friendlier Virginians. A report in 1656 described their state as like that of St. Athanasius exiled from Alexandria: "They live in a mean hut, low and depressed, not unlike a cistern or even a large tomb."[6]

The refugees returned to Maryland once order was restored. After that the sole Jesuit in Virginia was a priest who ministered there "under the pretext of being schoolmaster to the sons of a very rich businessman who is not at all hostile to the Catholic religion."[7] But even this outpost had to be abandoned in the wake of the Glorious Revolution.

Was the "very rich businessman" a friendly Protestant? or one of the Catholic Brents? Since 1651 that family had been prominent in the Aquia Creek region of Virginia's "Northern Neck," the peninsula between the Rappahannock and the Potomac.[8] First to come were Giles Brent, former acting governor of Maryland, and his sisters Mary and Margaret. A third sister, Anne, had been Leonard Calvert's wife. Mistress Margaret Brent ("the first American feminist") was among Maryland's larger landowners. During Claiborne's 1646 rebellion, when a militia unit she had raised went unpaid she used her authority as the Proprietor's agent to sell some of his cattle and meet the payroll. She also demanded voice and two votes in the assembly, one as freeholder and one as executrix of Leonard Calvert's estate. The demand was rejected and not long after she joined her brother Giles across the Potomac. Between 1651 and 1660 the Brents patented eleven thousand acres in Virginia.

Despite the Catholicism of which he made no secret, Giles Brent of Richland was a major figure in civil and military affairs on the Virginia frontier. At his death, family leadership passed to a cousin, George Brent of Woodstock. Landowner, surveyor, captain of the "Stafford Rangers," George was a leading attorney, as was his brother Robert. In 1684 the House of Burgesses voted him formal thanks for services in a campaign against the Seneca Indians. Two years later, when James II was king, he was Attorney General of Virginia and a Burgess himself.

After King Louis XIV revoked the Edict of Nantes in 1685, London was crowded with Huguenot refugees looking to England's American colonies. In 1687 George Brent was partner in a scheme to settle a group of them on thirty thousand acres in the Northern Neck. By warrant King James allowed to all living in the area "the full exercise of their Religion without being prosecuted or molested under any penall laws or other account for the same." Religious toleration which included Catholics ended with the accession of William and Mary. Virginia Whigs saw the chance to bring down the Brents, who were both Tory and Catholic. Rumors spread that with their connivance the Senecas and Catholics from Maryland planned an invasion. George Brent's stature was proof against the charge. He later served as Ranger-General and as co-agent for the principal Proprietor, the fifth Lord Fairfax. He did not neglect Catholic interests. When the Franciscan priest Richard Hobart was driven from Maryland in 1689 he stayed at Woodstock, Brent's estate. In the same year Brent raised with his business partner William Fitzhugh the possibility of a "Refuge and Sanctuary for Roman Catholicks" on the land to which they had hoped to attract Huguenots.

On Brent's death in 1699, Robert "King" Carter became the proprietor's agent and Brent family participation in Virginia politics lessened. Richland at least remained a Catholic center. It was there, at Bobby Brent's Landing, that the future Bishop John Carroll stopped first on his return home from Europe in 1774. The lady of the plantation was his oldest sister, Anne. Her husband, Robert Brent, had been John Carroll's schoolfellow at Bohemia Manor. A second sister, Eleanor, was married to William Brent, of a branch of the family that seems to have conformed to the established church.

In social and hierarchical structure colonial Maryland Catholicism followed the English Catholic pattern. In Virginia Catholic presence meant Brents and plantations. It was Pennsylvania, chartered to Quaker William Penn in 1681, that provided models for the urban and rural future of American Catholicism. Religious toleration was real in William Penn's colony, even if the required oaths of allegiance and supremacy and a test act denied membership in the assembly and public office to Roman Catholics. Colonists came in several waves. Irish Catholic servants accompanied English and Welsh Quakers in Penn's 1682 party. By mid-18th century the Proprietor's agents had recruited and settled about one hundred thousand Rhineland and Palatinate Germans in Philadelphia and on rich farmland in the eastern part of the colony. There were Mennonites, Amish and Dunkers, Lutherans and Moravians. There were German Catholics. The third immigrant wave, Scotch Irish from Ulster, generally moved on to the Alleghanies and the Indian frontier, but a steady flow of Catholic southern Irish tended to congregate in the thriving port city on the banks of the Delaware. Philadelphia soon became British North America's largest city, but still a walking town, only a few streets deep. Its prosperous citizens lived near the water, the poor on the outskirts. The population was cosmopolitan. Street signs and advertisements appeared in "Dutch and English," but few nationalities and peoples went unrepresented.[9] The religious complexion of the city was variegated. It was not long before an alarmed Anglican parson was reporting to London that "this city is very much infested with Popery."[10]

The first Jesuit move northward had come in 1706 when Father Thomas Mansell patented a tract of vacant land on Little Bohemia Creek in Maryland's northeast corner.[11] From Bohemia Manor missionaries travelled the Chesapeake's Eastern Shore and moved into Delaware and Pennsylvania. The Reverend John Talbot notified the Society for the Propagation of the Gospel in London in February 1708, that mass had been "set up and read publicly in Philadelphia."[12] Penn was taxed with this and wrote his deputy, James Logan: "Here is a complaint against your government, that you suffer publick mass in a scandalous manner."[13] Perhaps the improvised chapel was in Elizabeth McGauley's house on the Nicetown Road.[14]

By 1729 Father Joseph Greaton was Philadelphia's resident priest. Sometime in 1733–34 he opened a tiny (18 by 22 feet) permanent chapel in a house in the meadowland off Walnut Street, next to the Friends' almshouse. St. Joseph's (its Willings Alley address came later, when the alley was put through) was the first urban Catholic church in the thirteen colonies. It started with less than forty Irish, English, and German parishioners, a number that reached twelve hundred by the American Revolution. They were tradespeople, tavern keepers from locals like "The Three Jolly Irishmen" and "The Lamb," laborers, servants, and sailors. French-speaking Acadians, immortalized by Longfellow, settled along Pine Street in 1755:

> Under the humble walls of the little Catholic churchyard,
> In the heart of the city they lie, unknown and unnoticed.

Roman Catholics were normally well treated in Philadelphia, but harrassment occurred during King George's War and after Braddock's defeat on the Monongahela in the summer of 1755. Colonel George Washington was among those taken in by false rumors "of very unnatural and pernicious correspondence, held with the French by some Priests." Arrival at Philadelphia in 1755 of a boatload of Acadians sparked fears of papist revolution. In 1757 Catholics were forbidden to bear arms. The French were Catholics and so were the people who went to church in Willings Alley. That was evidence enough. As rumors spread in coastal cities Governor Sir George Hardy of New York warned his Pennsylvania colleague, Robert Morris, to beware the "ingenious Jesuit" in Philadelphia.[15]

A happy by-product of hysteria over a "popish plot" was the 1757 order from British commander-in-chief Lord Loudun for a census of Roman Catholics. In all, 692 men and 673 women over the age of twelve were counted. Germans made up 70 percent; 30 percent were English-speaking. In Philadelphia, Germans outnumbered all others by 228 to 150.[16]

The congregation came to include a prosperous element. Much of Philadelphia's trade was with Spain, Portugal, and France, nations with which English and Irish Catholics had good contacts. Pews at old St. Joseph's and later at St. Mary's were occupied by families of young shipping executives and traders like George Meade, his Irish-born brother-in-law Thomas FitzSimons, the four Moylans from Cork, and ship captain John Barry of Wexford. The urbane Robert Harding succeeded Greaton as pastor in 1753. He moved easily in polite society, was a subscriber to the drive for Benjamin Franklin's hospital, and organized relief efforts for the Acadian boat-people. His Irish parishioners formed the Catholic minority in the Friendly Sons of St. Patrick; their pastor was a founding member of the Sons of St. George.

The earliest information on rural Pennsylvania missions is from the pen of a Marylander, Father Henry Neale, who in 1741 wrote to his patron, Sir John James, Bart., of Bury St. Edmunds: "We have at present all the liberty imaginable in ye exercise of our business, and are not only esteemed, but reverenced." Prospects at Philadelphia were good. "More hands and a larger house" would soon be needed. Neale was Greaton's assistant, with charge also of the outlying stations. "The necessarys of life," he found, were "as dear, & several dearer, than at London itself. . . . Among other expenses I must of necessity keep a horse in order to assist poor people up and down ye country. Some twenty miles, some sixty, some farther off."[17] Financial help was badly needed.

Neale's plea was successful. Sir John died in September 1741, and left his fortune to Bishop Challoner in London. £40 a year was to stay in England to support two priests working among London's poor. Income from the remainder went to Pennsylvania's country missions. Bequests to Catholic charities were illegal under English law and the will was broken, but capital of £4000 was saved and invested in East India annuities and in the French East India Company. In later financial statements, the James bequest figured as "salary from London." It was one of the sources which supported the missionaries, along with farm income, ground rents on town properties and, in Philadelphia but not in the country districts, "regular gratuities," contributions from the parishioners.

Settlement in southeastern Pennsylvania came from two directions. In 1717, armed with a patent from the Baltimores, John Digges of Maryland laid claim to 10,000 acres of rolling hills in southeastern Pennsylvania's Conewago valley. When the Mason and Dixon Line was drawn forty years later, part of the agreement between Penns and Calverts was that these patents be honored. The Maryland settlers were soon joined by Catholics from the Rhineland and Palatinate. Greaton asked his superiors in England to arrange with the German Jesuit provinces for priests to minister to the new immigrants. He thought that a £20 annual stipend would provide them "a tolerable sufficiency," since they "would spend the greatest part of their time among their countrymen and meet with assistance from them." Henry Neale was less sanguine: "Little or nothing can be expected from the country Catholiks, who, tho' very numerous, are most of them servants or poor tradesmen, and more in need oftentimes of charity themselves, than capable of assisting others."

The first German priests to arrive were Theodor Schneider from Speyer and Wilhelm Wappeler, a Westphalian. They sailed up the Susquehanna in July 1741, and lodged, as Wappeler recorded, "with a certain Catholic Hibernian, Thomas Doyle," at Lancaster, which the Germans called Neustatt.[18]

"Their presence is very much wanted," Neale had written to James. "My heart has yearned when I've met with some poor Germans desirous of performing their duties, but whom I have not been able to assist for want of language." The German priests soon remedied this. They divided the missions between them. From Lancaster Wappeler served the Susquehanna area, with stations at Conewago which had a Jesuit farm, and

York. Schneider was based at Goshenhoppen, site of a second Jesuit farm. He worked the Schuylkill and Delaware valleys and visited German glass workers at Salem in the Province of West Jersey. Their personalities differed. Wappeler, whose poor health forced his return to Europe in 1748, was at home in Pennsylvania Dutch country. Forty years later John Carroll wrote of his "candour and artless disposition of heart," and wondered, "What does he think of the great *overgetumbeling* of this American continent?"[19] Schneider, a "great strong man" who had been a philosophy professor and in the academic year 1738–39 presided over the University of Heidelberg as its *Rector Magnificus,* was remembered in Pennsylvania for good business sense and for his "consummate prudence and intrepid courage."[20]

A series of German missionaries followed, most famous of them the Swabian Ferdinand Steinmeyer, known in America as Ferdinand Farmer. He went first to Lancaster, vacant since Wappeler's departure. Then for thirty years, 1756–86, he was Philadelphia's first permanent German pastor. Dressed soberly like a Quaker, he rode out from the city to mass houses in East and West Jersey, as far north as Greenwood Lake. As the Revolution drew to a close he moved into the Hudson valley, ministering to Canadian veterans of the American army at Fishkill in Dutchess county, and he founded the first permanent Catholic congregation in New York City.

Farmer was not Manhattan's first Jesuit. After his escape from the Mohawks in the summer of 1643, Isaac Jogues found hospitable refuge there until Governor Willem Kieft arranged safe passage home to France. There were but two Catholics in Nieuw Amsterdam: the Portuguese wife of a Dutch officer and an Irishman from Virginia. A more active Catholic period began after 1664, when New York, and New Jersey together with Martha's Vineyard, Nantucket, and Pemaquid in Maine, became the proprietary colony of James, Duke of York, brother of King Charles II. The Duke became a Roman Catholic in 1672. Two years later Governor Edmund Andros arrived in his colony with instructions that "all persons of what Religion soever" be allowed "quietly to inhabitt within ye precincts of your jurisdiccion."[21] The thrust of the directive was the same as that in the warrant King James granted fifteen years later to George Brent and his partners in Virginia's Northern Neck. It also echoed themes in Lord Baltimore's instructions to the passengers in the *Ark* and *Dove* and in the 1639 enactments of the Maryland Assembly.

For two decades Roman Catholics served Duke James's government with distinction. Anthony Brockholls assisted successive governors as chief councillor and from 1680 to 1683 was himself acting governor. Matthew

Plowman, collector of customs at New York, was a Catholic, and so were Ensign Bartholomew Russell at Manhattan's Fort James and the commandant at Albany, Major Jarvis Baxter. But the "Catholic" period of New York's colonial history really began with the coming, forty years after Isaac Jogues's visit, of Thomas Dongan, the Catholic Irishman who became Governor in August 1683.[22]

There were problems. New York had no representative assembly, a testimony to James's penchant for arbitrary rule. Relations with the Iroquois in the northern reaches of the colony were delicate. There was a danger that their traditional antipathy to the French, the legacy of conflict beginning with Samuel de Champlain, was being mollified by missionary work among them of Jogues's French Jesuit successors. The first problem Dongan handled by having an assembly elected a month after his arrival. To placate Puritans from the Long Island ridings, the assembly's Charter of Liberties and Privileges included provision for church establishment where two-thirds of the voters wished it, but it also affirmed strongly the right to free exercise of religion:

> noe person or persons, which profess faith in God by Jesus Christ, shall at any time be any ways molested, punished, disquieted, or called in question for any difference in opinion or matter of religious concernment, who do not actually disturb the civill peace of the Province.

"All and every such person or persons" should

> from time, and at all times freely have and fully enjoy his or their judgements or consciences in matters of religion throughout all the Province, they behaving themselves peaceably and quietly, and nott using this liberty to licentiousness, nor to the civill injury or outward disturbance of others.[23]

Both the charter language and actual practice in the colony were reminiscent of the Catholic era in Maryland. Dongan welcomed Calvinist Huguenot refugees from France, much as Leonard Calvert accepted Puritan refugees from Virginia. And, although the Charter spoke of religious freedom explicitly only for Christians, it was at Dongan's insistence that Sephardic Jews, who had arrived thirty years earlier in Peter Stuyvesant's time, were first enrolled as freemen of New York and allowed to engage in trade. Opposed by the council, the governor reserved to himself the right to grant licenses to Jews.

Dongan retired when the Dominion of New England, which included New York, was organized in 1688. King James had annulled the Charter in 1686, but left standing the free exercise of religion clause, which remained in effect until Jacob Leisler's 1689 rebellion ended religious toleration in New York until 1806. After 1700 a Catholic priest entering the colony was liable to life imprisonment, while a stiff fine and a spell in the pillory awaited those who harbored him.

Dongan's second problem was the Iroquois. He understood the strategic importance of the northern frontier perhaps better than any other English colonial administrator. Part of his strategy for dealing with the Indians involved replacing French Jesuits with their English counterparts, as he told a group of Iroquois chiefs at Albany in August 1687. Before he left England, groundwork had been laid for the change. The Duke of York consulted English Jesuit officials, who informed Rome that Father Thomas Harvey would go with Dongan to New York, "a respectable city, fit for the foundation of a college." The Jesuits, with considerable innocence of colonial geography, envisioned the college as a headquarters from which "excursions" could be made into Maryland.[24] If Dongan had his way, the excursions would head north rather than south. Harvey was joined by several companions, a chapel and school were opened at Fort James and, as at Newtown in Maryland, Catholic and Protestant boys were educated. But the overthrow of King James's government in 1688–89 put the Jesuits to flight. Not until Ferdinand Farmer came during the American Revolution was a permanent Catholic community organized. The English Jesuit mission to the Iroquois never happened, while that of the French withered and was gone by 1709.

VI

Revolution

The 1763 Treaty of Paris ended Anglo-French rivalry in North America. Little more than ten years later, most of Britain's Atlantic colonies had broken their ties with the crown. Small numbers dictated a minor role in the rebellion for Roman Catholics in the thirteen colonies. They were about twenty to twenty-five thousand, scarcely 1 percent of the two and a half million colonists. At the Declaration of Independence Maryland and Pennsylvania had twenty-three priests, all former members of the Jesuit order which Pope Clement XIV had suppressed in the summer of 1773. Eight were native-born Marylanders, seven were English missionaries, the German states contributed four, and one each came from Ireland, Austria, Luxemburg, and the Austrian Netherlands. Two served the city parish in Philadelphia, four rode circuit in the Pennsylvania countryside, and the rest were in Maryland.[1] The only other priest in the east was at Johnstown in New York's Mohawk valley. Three hundred Catholic Scots highlanders had settled there in 1773 under Sir William Johnson's patronage. Their priest was an Irishman, John MacKenna, and they gave him £46 a year, a house, and a hundred acres of land. Far to the west, there were two more priests. Sébastien Meurin, last of the French Jesuit missionaries in the Illinois country, was at Kaskaskia. His assistant, Québec seminary priest Pierre Gibault, took care of the French settlement at Post Vincennes on the Wabash.

The year 1773 had been catastrophic for the Jesuits. On July 21 in Rome Pope Clement XIV abolished with a stroke of the pen their 233-year-old religious order. Seminarians and brothers became laymen, priests diocesan clergy. They no longer had a corporate existence or superiors of their own. Crushed by the blow, Joseph Mosley wrote from Maryland's Eastern Shore, where for seventeen years he had carried on a lonely ministry:

> When I see so many worthy, saintly, pious, learned, laborious Mission-ers dead and alive have been members, thro' the last two ages, I know no fault we have been guilty of. I am convinced that our labours are pure, upright and sincere, for God's honour and our neighbour's good. What our Supreme Judge on Earth [the Pope] may think of our labours is a mystery to me. He has hurt his own cause, not us. It's true he has stigmatized us thro' the world with infamy, and declared us unfit for our business, or his service. Our Dissolution is known thro' the world; it's in every newspaper, which makes me ashamed to show my face. . . . [2]

Mosley's distress was echoed in distant Belgium. A thirty-seven-year-old Marylander heard news of the suppression at the English Jesuits' "Great College" of Bruges, where he was director of the students' sodality. Father John Carroll mourned that "our so long persecuted, and, I must add, holy society is no more," and wrote that he intended returning home to Mary-land. He had been away for twenty-five years, since he sailed for St. Omer in July 1748 as a thirteen-year-old schoolboy. Carroll's spirits were no higher than those of his colleague on the Eastern Shore, but he wrote:

> In returning to Maryland I shall have the comfort of not only being with you, but of being farther out of reach of scandal and defamation, and removed from the scenes of distress of many of my dearest friends, whom, God knows, I shall not be able to relieve. [3]

Joseph Mosley considered retirement to England, but then in August 1775 told his sister: "discontent or not, I see that I am a very necessary hand in my situation, and our Gentlemen here [his fellow former Jesuits] won't hear of my departure." [4] Not one of the seven English missionaries returned to Great Britain. The other European-born priests all remained at their posts.

The atmosphere in America hardly invited Catholic cooperation with the patriots. Sam Adams felt that "much more is to be dreaded from the growth of Popery in America than from the Stamp Act," [5] and a future Chief Justice of the United States, John Jay, did his best to deny Cathol-ics the rights of citizenship. [6] Harvard College had the Dudleian lectures, the fourth in each series to be devoted to "detecting, convicting and exposing the idolatry, errors and superstitions of the Romish church, "a goal which John Adams thought manifested

> evidence of a strong veneration for the memory of the first settlers, penetrating insight into the purpose and spirit of their policy and an earnest desire of perpetuating the blessings of it to posterity. [7]

Yale provided a different twist. When President Ezra Stiles wanted a professor of French for his college, American diplomat Silas Deane recommended that he solicit funds in France, but recruit the professor in Calvinist Geneva, where the purest French was spoken. His "principles as well as manner," Deane pointed out, "could not fail of being agreeable."[8] The Continental Congress which met at Philadelphia on September 17 took as its own, by unanimous vote, the "Suffolk County Resolves," framed a week earlier in Boston, which denounced the May 20 Quebec Act, "the late Act of Parliament for establishing the Roman Catholic religion in that extensive country now called Canada." This act was "dangerous in an extreme degree to the Protestant religion and to the civil rights and liberties of all Americans."[9] An address to the people of Great Britain, adopted in September 5, spoke of Catholicism as "a religion fraught with sanguinary and impious tenets," which "has deluged your island in blood and dispersed impiety, persecution, murder and rebellion through every part of the world."[10] A "loyal Address" to King George III on October 25 criticized the Quebec Act for establishing "an absolute government and the Roman Catholick religion throughout those vast regions, that border on the westerly and northerly boundaries of the free protestant English settlements."[11]

On the opposite tack, an address to the French *habitants* of Québec urged them to rise above such "low-minded infirmities" as difference of religion to "a hearty amity with us." "Liberty of conscience in your religion," Congress told the *québecois,* was no gift of Britain's parliament. "No, God gave it to you." The delegates at Philadelphia proposed as model for the new American alliance the example of Swiss Protestants and Catholics living together in harmony.[12]

British and American Tory pamphleteers had a field day. Canadians were confirmed in their low estimation of the *bostonnais.* Americans tried to drive a wedge between the *habitants* and their priests and *seigneurs.* They failed and Congress ensured failure when it sent an army to Canada in 1775 commanded by officers like Connecticut's vocal and rabidly anti-Catholic David Wooster. General Washington's order that the army do nothing to "turn the hearts of our Brethren in Canada against us" was often ignored.[13]

Maryland produced the war's most thoughtful and eloquent Catholic spokesman, Charles Carroll of Carrollton, who challenged the distinguished Tory attorney, Daniel Dulany, Jr., in the pages of the *Maryland Gazette.* The debate ran from January to July 1773. Dulany used the *nom de plume* "Antilon"; Carroll was "First Citizen." Their debate was occasioned by Governor Eden's imposition of a schedule of official fees. Really involved was the nature of the British constitution, the underlying issue over which the Revolution was fought. Carroll took what was becoming the American side and is generally conceded to have bettered his opponent. In the process he was brutally reminded what it was to be a Roman Catholic in British America. Dulany rose to rhetorical heights:

> Who is this man, that calls himself a citizen . . . makes his address to the inhabitants of Maryland . . . has charged the members of one of the legislative branches with insolence . . . contradicted the most public and explicit declarations of the governor . . . represented *all* the council but *one* to be mere fools . . . ? Who is he? He has no share in the legislature, as a member of any branch; he is incapable of being a member; he is disabled from giving a vote in the choice of representatives, by the laws and constitution of the country, *on account of his principles,* which are *distrusted* by those laws. he is disabled by an express resolve, from interfering in the election of members, on the *same account.* He is not a Protestant.[14]

With heavy irony Dulany dismissed Carroll's *alma mater.* St. Omer was "the best seminary in the universe," he chaffed, "for the champions for civil and religious liberty," just as "billiard rooms and tippling houses" produced "the most finished patterns of modesty, decorum and animated elocution."[15] Carroll would have none of this. His Catholic co-religionists were charged with Stuart sympathies. He had none. In his view James II's bigotry, despotic temper, "and every other part of his conduct" justified rebellion for the sake of civil and religious liberty. He disliked arbitrary "proclamations" as much as he despised "having a religion crammed down people's throats." "Knaves, and bigots of all sects and denominations I hate, and I despise," he wrote. "I am a warm friend of toleration," he told a friend on another occasion; "I execrate ye intolerating thirst of ye Church of Rome, and of other Churches—for she is not singular in that designing." He did not equate such criticism with disloyalty to his Church and made it clear he would neither leave it nor let himself be driven from it: "I have too much sincerity & too much pride . . . even if filial love did not restrain me." What he did demand, and what Dulany (who "would make a most excellent inquisitor") would have denied him, was freedom of thought and freedom of speech.[16]

Charles Carroll's patriotism led to service on committees of correspondence and in the Maryland state senate. An adviser to the first two Continental Congresses, he was elected to the second congress just in time to sign the Declaration of Independence. His support for General Washington as a member of the Board of War helped defuse the "Conway Cabal." In 1778 there was some sentiment to elect him President of Congress. His abilities and his fortune—estimated at over £200,000—made a strong impression. "He continues to hazard his all, his immense fortune, the largest in America, and his Life," an awed John Adams wrote.[17] For Carroll it was all quite deliberate: "I still think this controversy will be decided by arms," he wrote his father on September 12, 1774, a week after the first Congress opened its sessions. Benjamin Rush called him "an inflexible patriot, and an honest independent friend to his country."[18] His motivations in the 1770s differed not one whit from those he set down a half century later:

> When I signed the Declaration of Independence, I had a view not only our independence of England but the toleration of all sects, professing the Christian religion, and communicating to them all great rights.[19]

There were prominent Catholic patriots. Brents of Virginia served on committees of correspondence and public safety. Three of John Carroll's Brent nephews were with Lafayette in the final campaign against Cornwallis.[20] Colonel John Fitzgerald of Alexandria was Washington's aide-de-camp. Maryland Catholics soldiered in the Charles and St. Mary's county militias—Ignatius Fenwick was a colonel—and in Smallwood's regiment and the Maryland Flying Camp. Daniel Carroll was elected to the Maryland senate and to Congress. He signed the 1777 Articles of Confederation and the Federal Constitution. Even New York, inhospitable to Catholics in the prewar years, counted William Mooney, revolutionary patriot and one of the staunchest "Liberty Boys" despite the fact that the Sons of Liberty did not usually enlist Catholics. Among those foreign officers whose Catholicism was known were artillerist and engineer Thaddeus Kosciusko and Count Casimir Pulaski, Washington's cavalry commander, killed in action at the siege of Savannah.

Philadelphia was a divided city. In 1768 Father Robert Harding congratulated John Dickinson for *Letters from a Farmer in Pennsylvania,* which he thought a fine patriot's defense of "British liberty,"[21] but his fellow-founder of the Sons of St. George, Anglo-Irish businessman Alfred Clifton, recruited among the Catholics of Philadelphia a Tory regiment, the Roman Catholic Volunteers, which led a woebegone existence for a year until Sir Henry Clinton disbanded it in 1778 and merged its remnant with Lord Rawdon's Volunteers of Ireland.[22]

Catholic soldiers fought in the Pennsylvania Line and in Brigadier-General Stephen Moylan's 4th Dragoons. Three of Moylan's brothers were involved on the commissary side. Philadelphia shipping magnate George Meade outfitted privateers and raised money to feed the troops at Valley Forge. His brother-in-law and partner Thomas FitzSimons was an army captain, directed price control, attended the state constitutional convention, and signed the Federal Constitution. On the high seas Captain John Barry won fame on the ships *Lexington, Effingham, Raleigh,*

Delaware, and *Alliance.* He was the first American captain to take a British warship. Of over a dozen St. Mary's parishioners to carry "letters of marque and reprisal" as privateers, the best known was Thomas Flahaven.[23]

The Cauffmans, father and son, reflected Philadelphia's divided loyalties. Joseph, Sr., an Alsatian immigrant and for a half-century prominent in Catholic affairs, was a Loyalist. Joseph, Jr., educated by the English Jesuits at Bruges and medical doctor of the University of Vienna, wrote Benjamin Franklin that he hoped his Catholicism would not bar him from his country's service. He died, at the age of twenty-three tending to wounded Captain Nicholas Biddle when the U. S. frigate *Randolph* exploded off Barbados during a battle with the sixty-four gun two-decker H.M.S. *Yarmouth.*[24] Benjamin Rush has kept alive the name of another parishioner, Nurse Mary Waters, Dublin-born and a Philadelphian since 1766:

> She served the whole war in the military hospitals, where she was esteemed and beloved by all who knew her. She has been a nurse ever since. She possesses a good deal of skill and an uncommon regard to cleanliness. I never saw her out of humor.

Nurse Waters (the Philadelphia city directory called her "doctoress and apothecary") had at one time left off nursing, but was persuaded back to it by Father Farmer, who told her that "her skill in nursing was a commission sent her by heaven, which she was bound never to resign, and that she might merit heaven by it."[25]

The priests in Maryland managed their farms and ministered to the Catholics. John Carroll, living on his mother's estate at Rock Creek, wrote: "I have care of a very large congregation; have often to ride 25 or 30 miles to the sick, besides which I go once a month between 50 & 60 miles to another congregation [at the Brents' plantation] in Virginia." Another letter provided a vignette of the pastor at St. Inigo's: "James Walton, who has as fine land as any in America, is said to make a bad hand at farming. . . . But if he does not succeed in temporals, he is indefatigable in his spiritual occupations."[26]

Life was hardly peaceful. Carroll remembered in 1788: "During the late war the British cruisers landed often at and hovered almost continually around the plantations of the clergy; they pillaged their houses; they drove and slaughtered their sheep and cattle."[27] Father Peter Morris nearly had his head blown off when the British sloop *General Monk* fired a ball through the wall of his first-floor bedroom at St. Inigo's.[28] Farther upriver a landing party from a squadron patrolling the Potomac hit St. Thomas Manor in early April 1781, looting the priests' home and taking

for booty "everything, not sparing the church furniture." They also burned an old house on the property ("Priest Hunter's house"), as Governor
Thomas Sim Lee reported to Lafayette. Counterinsurgency measures
might have been even more vigorous had British commanders known how
deeply the Jesuit plantations were involved in Governor Lee's procure-
ment system for American and French armies. Beef, bacon, and wheat
were sold to the state for inflated currency. Forty new dollars were worth
one of the silver coins in circulation before the war.[29]

On the heavily Tory Eastern Shore, Joseph Mosley labored in solitude.
He covered eight congregations scattered over ten counties in three states
and was grateful for the new "horse chair" which his parishioners, "pity-
ing my distress," bought him. In return, he presented them, at no cost to
themselves, with a new brick church at Tuckahoe, capable of seating over
two hundred. His own room was attached. It measured 16 by 18 feet, "a
cell such as the woman of Sunam prepared for the prophet Elisha, con-
taining just enough space for a bed, a table and a stool."

Mosley was neutral in politics: "A Clergyman's call has little to do with
civil broils and troubled waters," he wrote in August 1775. The Maryland
Assembly which met in February 1777 did not distinguish church and
state so clearly. A law forbade ministers of the gospel to preach unless
they had sworn allegiance to the new government. Mosley delayed; his
diary records of a funeral service: "No sermon, not having qualified by an
oath, to be taken by Law, by all that would preach." He later explained:

> The Roman clergy are a body of men, of which I am an unworthy
> member, so linked, bound and connected together by vow, affection and
> other ties of honour, consistent with which no one of us all would choose
> to act in any affair of real consequence or importance without the knowl-
> edge, consent and approbation of the rest.

The priest had sent an express rider to John Lewis, superior of the
clergy and, at Bohemia Manor, his nearest neighbor, to "know the conduct of the rest of our Clergy." Lewis, he found, was "as ignorant of it as
myself." Discovering finally that the others had taken the oath, he presented himself, but the time limit had run out and a special bill on his
behalf had to be passed. When it was all settled he reported of his
parishioners that "every Roman Catholic took [the oath] in good time,
under my direction, none excepted."[30]

Philadelphia boasted the country's liveliest Catholic congregation. Loyalists and patriots mingled at St. Mary's and St. Joseph's. Ferdinand
Farmer paid a courtesy call on Lieutenant General Sir William Howe
after the British occupied the city in September 1777. The commander-in-
chief offered him the chaplaincy of Clifton's regiment, a post he declined

"on account of my age and several other reasons." Two years later, having sworn to uphold the Commonwealth, he was a trustee of the University of the State of Pennsylvania.[31] His co-pastor, the corpulent Lancashireman Robert Molyneux, a clergyman with "natural talents for elegant life and manners," found work as an English tutor to France's diplomatic agent, Anne-César de la Luzerne,[32] and was probably the priest in vestments "rich with lace" who preached from a "velvet and gold" pulpit on Sunday afternoon, October 9, 1774, when, "led by curiosity and good company," the delegate from Massachusetts, John Adams, came by, together with George Washington of Virginia.

Adam's description of the vespers service he attended recreates with vivid if jaundiced pen the Sunday afternoon public worship of Philadelphia's Catholics:

> I heard a good short moral Essay upon the Duty of Parents to their Children, founded in Justice and Charity, to take care of their interests, temporal and spiritual. This Afternoon's Entertainment was to me most awfull and affecting; the poor Wretches fingering their beads, chanting Latin, not a Word of which they understood; their Pater Nosters and Ave Marias, their holy Water, their Crossing themselves perpetually; their Bowing to the Name of Jesus, whenever they hear it, their Bowings, Kneelings and genuflections before the Altar. . . . The Altar-Piece was very rich, little Images and Crucifixes about; Wax Candles all lighted up. But how shall I describe the Picture of our Saviour in a Frame of Marble over the Altar, at full Length, upon the Cross in the Agonies, and the Blood dropping and streaming from his Wounds! The Music, consisting of an Organ and a Choir of Singers, went all the Afternoon except Sermon Time, and the Assembly chanted most sweetly and exquisitely. Here is everything which can lay hold of the eye, ear and imagination—everything which can charm and bewitch the simple and the ignorant. I wonder how Luther ever broke the spell.[33]

Congress came four times in a body to St. Mary's, twice for requiem masses and twice for thanksgiving services arranged by the French Minister. James Rivington's New York *Royal Gazette* could not let slip the chance to mock President Samuel Huntington of the Continental Congress, who "besprinkled and sanctified himself" with the holy water offered him at the church door, and the members of "this egregious Congress" who, "now reconciled to the Papish Communion," carried lighted tapers in their hands at a mass for Spanish agent Don Juan de Miralles, who had died while visiting the army at Morristown.[34] Dr. Benjamin Rush sent regrets and wrote on the back of his invitation: "Declined attending as not compatible with the principles of a Protestant," but Ebenezer Hazard was more positive. He was happy to see Protestants there and "to find the minds of people so unfettered with the shackles of bigotry." As for the Catholics, their "behaviour in time of worship was very decent and solemn . . . there was not a smiling or disengaged countenance among them."[35]

Wartime Philadelphia offered many congressmen and soldiers their first flesh-and-blood contact with papists known previously only as the French or Spanish bogeymen of the frontier or in the pages of such colonial favorites as *Foxe's Book of Martyrs* or the *New England Primer,* from which little Puritans memorized the "John Rogers Verses":

> Abhor that arrant whore of Rome
> and all her blasphemies;
> And Drink not of her cursed cup;
> Obey not her decrees.

The 1778 French alliance and the entry into the war in 1779 of Catholic Spain also suggested second thoughts about those who belonged to what John Adams called "mother church, or rather grandmother church."

The French Minister brought Congress to St. Mary's, but France's armies and fleets had little impact on the American Catholic community. Regimental and ship's chaplains usually restricted their ministry to their own soldiers and sailors. The Franciscan priest who was chaplain to the French legation in Philadelphia was an exception. When he left for home in 1788, John Carroll recommended Séraphim Bandol to the Pope's nuncio at Versailles:

> He has spent ten years in America. Chaplain of the legation of France and in a position full of perils for a clergyman who does not have the fear of God constantly before his eyes, he has never given bad example or betrayed the holiness of his calling.[36]

The Revolution was also fought in the borderlands of the thirteen colonies. There it came into contact with Catholic remnants of France's old empire: Indians in Maine and the Illinois country, French *habitants* in Québec, fur traders farther west. A unique group were the Catholic Scots highlanders in central New York who followed Sir William Johnson and rallied to the crown.

Most important was Canada. Some Americans hoped to make it a fourteenth rebel state. But the first British governor, James Murray, had been convinced that respect for property rights and opportunity for free exercise of religion would make Québec "in a short time prove a rich and most useful colony." Governor Sir Guy Carleton took the same approach, and in 1774 the Quebec Act retained French civil law, protected feudal land tenure and provided tithes for support of the clergy. Ameri-

can pamphleteers and politicians were beside themselves and lumped the
Quebec Act with the "Intolerable Acts." On the other hand, a delighted
Bishop Jean-Olivier Briand of Québec warmly supported the British regime. In the province itself almost the sole murmurers were English-
speaking Québec and Montréal merchants, many of them recent trans-
plants from New England. The act to them was blasphemy and they
multiplied petitions to king and parliament about the rights of Englishmen. Their preference was for a provincial assembly that excluded the
Roman Catholics who outnumbered them in the population by one hundred to one.

American troops invaded Canada in the summer of 1775. Montréal fell
on November 13, but Québec successfully withstood a siege. By July 1776
the invasion was over and the Americans had retreated south of the
border. Most *habitants* remained neutral, ignoring both their bishop's call
to join Carleton's militia and American urging to enlist in "Congress'
Own" First and Second Canadian regiments. Briand's censure of collabo-
ration with the enemy was more effective than his call to arms. He threatened collaborators with denial of the sacraments. There was no amnesty.
Five months after the Americans left, a German officer attended a service
at Québec city marking the first anniversary of the American failure:

> At 9 A.M. a thanksgiving service was held in the cathedral church and
> Monseigneur [Briand] conducted the service in person; eight unhappy
> Canadians, who has assisted the rebels, had to do public penance in the
> church with ropes around their necks, and to beg forgiveness of God, the
> Church and the King.[37]

Most priests shared the bishop's hostility to Americans, although not all
did. Louis de Lotbinière enlisted with "Congress' Own" regiments and
became the American army's first Catholic chaplain. He was Colonel
Benedict Arnold's candidate to be Bishop of Québec.[38] The Sulpician
Pierre Huet de la Valinière was described in 1779 by Governor Frederick
Haldimand as "a perfect rebel in his heart" and deported to England.[39]
Haldimand also suspected the Jesuits and in 1783 wrote Lord North that
they were "the only order of regular priests who have shown an attachment to the rebels during the course of the war."[40]

It was into this minefield that the United States' first diplomatic mission
to a foreign country stepped gingerly in April 1776. Members were Samuel Chase, Charles Carroll of Carrollton, and Benjamin Franklin. They
has as companion John Carroll, ex-Jesuit, priest, and cousin on his mother's side of Charles Carroll. John Adams spelled out his task: he was "to
administer baptism to the Canadian Children and bestow Absolution on
such as have been refused it by the toryfied Priests in Canada."[41] John

Carroll was a reluctant diplomat. He felt that he could not in conscience urge Canadians to anything more vigorous than neutrality. They had no reason to rebel. The government was one they had chosen, or at least in which they had acquiesced. In Carroll's philosophy rebellion was a last resort, acceptable only when all other avenues failed. He also had practical misgivings about priests in politics:

> I hope I may be allowed to add, that tho I have little regard to my personal safety amidst the present distress of my country, yet I cannot help feeling some for my character: and I have observed that when the ministers of Religion leave their duties of their profession to take a busy part in political matters, they generally fall into contempt; & sometimes even bring discredit to the cause, in whose service they are engaged.[42]

The Canadian embassy was doomed from the start. John Carroll's presence was a problem for his fellow ex-Jesuit, Pierre Floquet, who let him use a chapel and had him to dinner once during his twelve-day stay in Montréal. For that Briand suspended Floquet and ordered him to Québec for a reckoning. The Canadian priest was not a complete innocent. He was already in the bishop's bad books for giving absolution to collaborators. American General Richard Montgomery met him two days after taking the city and found him "a very sensible fellow," to whom he hinted at restitution of confiscated Jesuit property "should this Province accede to the general union."[43] The American commandant, Colonel Moses Hazen, spoke of Floquet as "chaplain" to "Congress' Own," and made him a present of the Jesuit residence at Montréal, which Governor Murray had converted into a prison.[44] Briand's annoyance aside, John Carroll earned none of the contempt or discredit he feared for his part in the mission to Canada, but when Commissioner Benjamin Franklin's poor health dictated early return to Philadelphia, the priest was happy to be his companion.

Contemporary Protestant witnesses were struck by the sacramental emphasis in the Catholicism they observed among Maine's Catholic Indians. Reflecting on his years as Indian Agent, Colonel John Allen wrote in 1791 of the Penobscots:

> they are a very exemplary people . . . zealous and tenacious of the rites of the church, and strictly moral, cautious of misbehaving in point of religion. I have been surprised so little notice has been taken of them in this respect; tho' rude and uncultivated in many other matters, they are truly civilized in this, and it was always observed by the French Gentlemen of the Clergy, which we were favored with during the war that they never saw a more respectable collection in France, and excepting the Cathedral and some particular places of worship, their performances, chants in latin, etc. were in most instances superior to any. . . . they teach their children when able to lisp a word, the service, and as they

grow up become in a manner innate, this owing to the assiduity of the French missionaries—much to their honor.[45]

A more critical observer had still to acknowledge Penobscot religiousness:

> They say that the religion of the Congregationalists is too simple for them and they are in some measure attached to the Roman Catholic religion, on account of its being more ceremonious, repeating their prayers and crossing themselves at morning and evening. They treat the Roman Catholic priests with great respect, and have children baptized. They have no doubt of the power of the priests to pardon their sins and are cheerfully willing to pay the utmost of their ability for so great and necessary an accommodation.[46]

After King George's War (1740–48) most tribes of the Abenaki confederacy moved north into Canada. The Penobscots made a separate peace with the *bostonnais*. When the Revolution began they pledged themselves as allies. Two days after Bunker Hill the great sachem Orono was at Cambridge, to tell the Provincial Congress that "if the grievances under which his people labored were removed they would aid with their whole force to defend the country."[47] The Indians' grievances posed a problem for the Massachusetts patriots. On April 4, 1775, in an unsuccessful effort to wean non-Catholic Oneidas and Mohawks from British alliance, they had used the Quebec Act ploy:

> Brothers, they have made a law to establish the religion of the Pope in Canada, which lies so near to you. We much fear some of your children may be induced, instead of worshipping the only true God, to pay his dues to images made by their own hands.[48]

Now these heirs of the Puritans had to deal with the St. Johns, Micmacs, and Penobscots, whose religion was already that of the Pope. A letter arrived from the Indians in September:

> We have nowhere to look for assistance but to you, and we desire that you would help us to a Priest that he may pray with us to God almighty.

The Council was not really up to the challenge. They answered on October 16, "We are quite willing that you should have a Priest of your own, and worship as you please,"[49] but early in the following July Indian spokesman Ambrose Var was back:

> We want a Father or a *French* priest. Jesus we pray to, and we shall not hear any prayers that come from *England*. We shall have nothing to do with *Old England,* and all that we shall worship or obey will be *Jesus Christ* and *General Washington.*

The Council tried delay and substitution. They were not sure they could find the kind of priest requested; would not one of their own "priests" do?[50] The answer was negative, and the impasse was not resolved until Colonel Allan took a hand. He negotiated with French Consul de Valnais for the services of an Augustinian friar, Hyacinthe de la Motte, who visited Machias in July 1779. Other French priests paid periodic visits to the Indians after that. But the situation remained precarious, as Allan discovered a year after de la Motte's mission. During a conference at Passamaquoddy, the Indians suddenly called a three weeks' recess, announcing that they had to go over into Canada to see their priest "on the business of the church."[51] He was abbé Mathurin Bourg. Lieutenant Governor Richard Hughes at Halifax valued him highly: he had secured for the British only a year earlier a treaty of peace and friendship with the border tribes.[52]

In the far West, Pierre Gibault was soon caught up in the ambitious plans of Lieutenant Colonel George Rogers Clark, who in six weeks during the summer of 1778 drove the British out of the Illinois country and claimed it for Virginia. Gibault accompanied Clark's Rangers at the taking of Post Vincennes and for his services was formally thanked by Governor Patrick Henry and the Virginia House of Burgesses. Bishop Briand had a different reaction. He was no happier with Gibault than with Lotbinière, Valinière, or the Montréal Jesuits.[53]

In central New York's Mohawk valley, over two hundred Gaelic-speaking Scots, mostly Macdonnells of Glengarry in the western Highlands, settled near Johnson Hall in 1773. Their priest was an Irishman, John MacKenna, educated at Louvain, "a man of gigantic stature and prodigious strength," ordained for the Scottish mission and for five years a pastor in Inverness. Refugees from the Revolution, MacKenna and his parishioners fled to Canada. Many of the men enlisted in loyalist units—the Royal Regiment of New York and the Royal Highland Emigrants—and served with distinction in Colonel Barry St. Leger's northern New York campaign of 1777. MacKenna was chaplain to both regiments.[54]

In the tidewater states and on the frontiers, Catholics and their church were involved on both sides in the American Revolution. The turbulent decade worked substantial change in the American religious psyche. It was not that toleration—a decent and practical respect for the opinions of others—became universal. The Federal Constitution had been adopted and the Bill of Rights was about to be framed when the Reverend Jeremy Belknap of Boston wrote to his friend Ebenezer Hazard in praise of John Carroll's personal worth, but hastened to add: "It seems strange that a man of sense should be so zealous in the cause of nonsense."[55] In many states religious restrictions of one sort and another, test acts and the like, remained. Several states supported an established church. But the general picture, as a committee of Catholic clergy wrote to Rome in 1783, was favorable:

in these United States, our Religious system has undergone a revolution, if possible, more extraordinary, than our political one. In all of them free toleration is allowed to Christians of every denomination; and particularly in the States of Pennsylvania, Delaware, Maryland, and Virginia, a communication of all Civil rights, without distinction or diminution, is extended to those of our Religion.[56]

John Carroll made no apologies for the role Catholics played in the Revolution. He was also a strong advocate of general religious freedom, as he told the editor of *The Columbian Magazine or Monthly Miscellany*:

Thanks to the genuine spirit of christianity! the United States have banished intolerance from their systems of government, and many of them have done the justice to every denomination of christians, which ought to be done to them in all, of placing them on the same footing of citizenship, and conferring an equal right of participation in national privileges.

The reasons were simple: "Freedom and independence, acquired by the united efforts, and cemented with the mingled blood of protestant and catholic fellow-citizens, should be equally enjoyed by all."[57] This was Carroll's understanding of what the Revolution was all about.

VII

Organization of a Church

The final peace treaty with Great Britain was signed and awaiting ratification as 1783 began. Steps had to be taken to organize the Catholic Church in the new nation. Above all, a leader was badly needed. John Carroll explained:

> The Clergymen here continue to live in the old form: it is the effect of habit, and if they could promise themselves immortality it would be well enough. But I regret that indolence prevents any form of administration being adopted which might tend to secure to posterity a succession of Catholic Clergymen, and secure to these a comfortable subsistence.[1]

On his own initiative Carroll circulated in 1782 a draft plan for organizing the clergy. Their representatives met three times over the next two years at Whitemarsh plantation in Maryland and worked out a "Constitution of the Clergy," which detailed financial arrangements and a rule of life for priests, including a panel for arbitration and conciliation. The plan separated control of physical and financial assets, which remained with the body of the clergy, from the spiritual authority vested in a bishop or his representative.[2]

Still in question was who would be the "spiritual superior." Since 1773 the office had been held by the Jesuits' last religious superior, Father John Lewis, acting on behalf of the English vicar apostolic of the London District. But in 1783 James Talbot, who now held that office, refused to grant faculties (authorization to preach and hear confessions) to two homeward-bound American priests. The former colonial church was adrift.

Britain's American colonies had known no resident bishop until Briand's installation at Québec, and his mandate extended only to former French territory. The American missionaries' dependence on the London District continued, and both they and the laity resisted efforts to install a vicar apostolic at Philadelphia or to have Québec's bishop pay a pastoral visit to Pennsylvania and Maryland. Bishop Challoner of London suspected the Jesuits' motives. Their attitude, he thought in 1756, was that of men who

> have engrossed the best part of the mission to themselves and who may, not without show of probability, object that a novelty of this kind might give offense to the governing part there, who have been a little hard upon them of late years.[3]

The bishop's suspicions were not totally allayed when a letter from two hundred sixty-five laymen, headed by Charles Carroll of Annapolis, the Signer's father, warned that a bishop in America would

> create great troubles here, and give a handle to our enemies to endeavour at the total suppression of the exercise of our religion, and otherways most grievously to molest us.[4]

He was sure the Jesuits had put them up to it, but he told his agent in Rome: "I plainly see it will be no easy matter to place a Bishop there, although there be so many thousands there that [in the absence of a bishop] live and die without confirmation."[5]

That was the colonial situation. In 1773 Ferdinand Farmer warned off a visit by Briand, explaining that "it is incredible how hateful to non-Catholics in all parts of America is the very name of Bishop, even to such as should be members of the Church which is called Anglican."[6] Proof was ready to hand in declarations like that of prominent Boston preacher Jonathan Mayhew when rumors spread of a possible Church of England bishop for the colonies. "Diocesan bishops," he announced, "are a pernicious set of men, both to church and state," and "people have no security against being priest-ridden but by keeping all imperious bishops and other clergymen who love to lord it over God's heritage from getting their feet into the stirrup at all."[7]

The situation could not be allowed to continue after independence. Two sacraments, holy orders and confirmation, were never conferred in the colonies. Blessed oils needed for certain rites had to be obtained from Europe. Proper church government demanded a superior on the spot. Whether the church in America had matured to the extent that the superior should be a bishop was a separate question. At Carroll's prodding, John Lewis wrote to John Thorpe, an English ex-Jesuit and art connoisseur in Rome, who acted as Roman agent for his English and American brethren. The letter enclosed a petition about church government in the United States. Thorpe felt the Americans asked only for "what is absolutely conducive and perhaps necessary."[8] They explained to Pius VI that

> because of the present arrangement of government in America, we are no longer able as formerly to have recourse for our spiritual jurisdiction to bishops or vicars apostolic who live under a different and foreign government.

"Again and again," the petition ran, "this fact has been urged on us in unmistakable terms by officials of the Republic." They asked that Lewis be confirmed as ecclesiastical superior and allowed to perform certain functions normally reserved to bishops.[9]

Others were also planning. On instructions from Cardinal Leonardo Antonelli of the Congregation for Propagation of the Faith, the pope's nuncio at Versailles approached the French government for advice on American church matters. Rebuffed there, he turned to American Minister Benjamin Franklin, who agreed to consult Congress. The answer from Philadelphia was clear:

> Resolved, that Doctor Franklin be desired to notify to the Apostolical Nuncio at Versailles, that Congress will always be pleased to testify their respect to his sovereign and state; but that the subject of his application to Doctor Franklin, being purely spiritual, it is without the jurisdiction and powers of Congress who have no authority to permit or refuse it, these powers being reserved to the general states individually.[10]

Tempers grew short as matters dragged on. In Rome Thorpe blamed the French: it was nothing new, he wrote, for them to use religion as an instrument of their politics.[11] But from Annapolis Molyneux's onetime English student, French Minister Luzerne, advised his Foreign Minister that American Catholics wanted an American bishop. Suspicious of the Congregation for Propagation of the Faith, John Carroll fumed: "No authority derived from the Propaganda will ever be admitted here."[12] There was an ancillary problem. The American priests had authorized a second letter to the pope, objecting to the appointment of a bishop as their superior. Carroll thought it rudely phrased. It was the work of Bernard Diderick, "a good but wrong-headed Walloon Jesuit."[13] Thorpe was allowed discretion on this latest memorial and elected not to present it, but pleaded that such missives not be sent to Rome, "where the letters of one wronghead can do more harm than the application of ten right heads can redress."[14]

The suspense ended in the summer of 1784 with John Carroll named Superior of the Mission in the thirteen United States of North America. Lewis was passed over because of his age. He was sixty-three. Cardinal Antonelli told Carroll that "it is known that your appointment will please and gratify many members of that republic, and especially Mr. Franklin."[15] In Paris Franklin noted in his journal: "The Pope's Nuncio called, and acquainted me that the Pope had, on my Recommendation, appointed Mr. John Carroll, Superior of the Catholic Clergy in America."[16] It was just eight years since the trek to Montréal and back.

Carroll disliked both the nature of his appointment and the way it was made. He believed "it will never be suffered" that a Catholic ecclesiastical superior, whatever his title, "receive his appointment from a foreign state, and only hold it at the discretion of a foreign tribunal or congregation." Sooner or later,

> some malicious or jealous-minded person would raise a spirit against us, & under pretense of rescuing the state from foreign influence, & dependance, strip us of our common civil rights.[17]

The restricted faculties given him were "too confined for the exigencies of this Country." He was particularly annoyed that he could employ only priests approved and sent by the Roman congregation. America was too big for that. There were

> innumerable Roman Catholics going & ready to go into the new regions bordering on the Mississippi; perhaps the finest in the world, & impatiently clamorous for Clergymen to attend them.[18]

Early in 1785 he complained:

> . . . the Catholics in the Jersies, N.Y., the great Western country bordering on the lakes, & the Ohio, Wabash & Mississippi (to say nothing of many in the N. England States & Carolinas) are entirely destitute of spiritual succours. The Catholics in some of these settlements have been at the expense of paying the passage in of some Irish Franciscans, & providing for their subsistance. These men have brought good testimonials; but I am precluded from giving them any Spiritual powers.[19]

The second problem was the more easily solved. At Rome, Thorpe was assured that the restrictive clauses were only "an old unmeaning formulary," copied by a scribe from documents connected with a mission to Africa.[20] In March 1786, Carroll received faculties "as ample, as for the present, I could wish."[21] The Roman role in picking an ecclesiastical superior for the United States was something else again.

Official word of Carroll's new position came on November 26, 1784, but not until February 27 did he return a formal acceptance, supplemented on March 1 with a "report on the state of religion in the united provinces of federated America."[22] It had three sections: (1) an estimate of the Catholic population; (2) remarks on the quality of religious practice; and (3) the clergy.

There were approximately 15,800 Catholics in Maryland: 9,000 adults (over age twelve), 3,000 children, and 3,000 slaves of all ages ("called Negroes from their color and of African origin"). In Pennsylvania there were 7,000 Catholics, very few of them black. Virginia had 200 in all, visited by a priest four or five times a year. In New York, he was told, there were 1,500 Catholics who at their own expense had brought in an Irish Capuchin priest. Despite the lack of certain information on the Mississippi valley, Carroll understood that there were many French-speaking former Canadians there. The only priest he knew to be in the area was a German Carmelite of uncertain credentials.

Maryland had "outstanding and wealthy families dating back to the first founding of the colony," but most Catholics there and in Pennsylvania were poor farmers. The Philadelphia parish was made up of business and working people. The more stable segments in the Catholic community were faithful to religious practice, but "lacked the fervor which is developed by constant exhortations to piety." In most cases mass and a sermon were available only once every month or two, because of the scarcity of priests and the great distances between congregations.

Among the immigrants "who pour in upon us in large numbers from various European countries," religious practice was poor. "While there are some of our own who do not approach the sacraments of penance and the eucharist more than once a year, usually at Eastertime, hardly anyone is found among the immigrants who observes this duty of religion." Carroll worried about their bad example and about the influence on Catholics of the Protestant community around them. He was also disturbed by "the rather free conduct of the young people of both sexes, which endangers integrity of soul, and perhaps even of body," by "an undue propensity to dancing and other such things," and by the "unbelievable eagerness, especially among girls, to read novels which are brought here in great numbers." Finally, religious education of both children and slaves was neglected. It was left entirely to the priests. The result was that, "since the children [and presumably the slaves] are busy with constant chores and can be with the priest only rarely, most of them usually are uninstructed in the faith and very lax in morals."

There were nineteen priests in Maryland and two in Pennsylvania, two of them septuagenarians and three others approaching that decade of their lives. Others were in poor health and one was on disciplinary probation. The rest worked hard. They were supported by their farms and the generosity of their congregations. Carroll emphasized the need for promoting vocations to the priesthood. He hoped that some might come from the secular colleges of Pennsylvania and Maryland, and planned a seminary to accommodate their theological and spiritual training.

Two final items provide insight into the Catholic community which had developed in Maryland and Pennsylvania. The superior asked authorization to allow marriages between first cousins, explaining that one way Catholics living among a Protestant majority maintained their religious identity was by marriage of close blood relations. He also asked permission for celebration of mass as late as one o'clock in the afternoon. People often travelled thirty miles or more to attend, and the start of mass was frequently delayed for several hours because of the number of confessions to be heard.

If Carroll had been slow in answering Antonelli's letter of apointment, he did not delay in assuming his new responsibilities. Before the summer of 1785 was out, he made the rounds of the Maryland and Virginia missions and by September was on his way north to Pennsylvania and New York. A year later he was busy "from Easter to All Saints . . . with the interruption of only a day now and then, either in travelling from one Congregation to another, or at the confessional or giving Confirmation."[23]

Demands were complex. The Maryland missions continued as they had for a century and a half, but now there was a church in Baltimore, on a lot bought in 1764 from the Charles Carroll family. Many of its parishioners were "French Neutrals," descendants of the Acadian exiles of 1755. Carroll liked them, but had less regard for later French arrivals, commenting in 1789: "I have long thought that almost every man in that kingdom [France] above the rank of mediocrity, and many even of these, are lost to every feeling of Religion." French "traders and others" at Baltimore were, with few exceptions, a scandal, and their contempt for the Church and disregard of religious practice were perverting the Acadians.[24] Things were better in Pennsylvania, where the country missions were prosperous, but disaster struck in 1786. "This year," Carroll wrote mournfully, "proves fateful to our most excellent and incomparable German Brethren." Three priests died in quick succession, including "that great Saint," Ferdinand Farmer of Philadelphia.[25] Two years later Molyneux left Philadelphia to replace John Lewis, who had died at Bohemia Manor. The important Philadelphia parish was in the hands of a pair of young priests. Conflict between German and Irish elements had already begun. In 1788 two separate Catholic congregations were incorporated.

Farther up the Atlantic coast, New York City was no longer the desolate wasteland Carroll saw on his way to Canada in 1776: "no more the gay, polite place it used to be esteemed, but become almost a desert."[26]

On December 4, 1783, the British army took final leave, and General Washington bade farewell to his officers at Fraunces Tavern. Congress fixed on New York as the interim national capital. George Washington was inaugurated first President of the United States on the balcony of Federal Hall at the corner of Broad and Wall streets on April 1, 1789.

New York's anti-priest statute was repealed in 1784 and not long afterwards an Irish Capuchin friar, Charles Maurice Whelan, became the first resident priest. He did not come, as Carroll first thought, directly from Ireland, but had been a French naval chaplain during the Revolution and then a prisoner of war in Jamaica. He was welcomed by a congregation which included foreign consuls Hector St. Jean de Crèvecoeur and Don Thomas Stoughton, importer Dominick Lynch (Stoughton's brother-in-law and partner), fur merchant (and later partner of John Jacob Astor) Cornelius Heeney, and Joaõ Ruiz de Souza, a Portuguese in whose house mass was said. There were also poor immigrants from all corners of the world, as Whelan reported to the nuncio at Versailles:

> The Catholics in these parts are very poor, but very zealous. For the greater part they are Irish. As such they would not be able to build a church nor even to rent a place for saying mass. However, a Portugese gentleman has given them a part of his house for that purpose, and I hope that divine Providence will provide us with another place by next May, since said gentleman cannot let us use his house any longer.

The community was polyglot:

> In this country it is necessary for a priest to know at least the Irish, English, French and Dutch languages, because our congregation is composed of these nationalities, as well also as of Portugese and Spaniards.[27]

Carroll's statement that there were 1,500 Catholics in New York is a puzzle. He had mentioned the figure 200 to Ferdinand Farmer, and in 1786 spoke of 500. The report to Antonelli perhaps included northern New Jersey, where Farmer registered an average of about 140 baptisms a year in the early 1780s. The New York congregation met in a small building in Vauxhall Gardens, near the North River (the lowest section of the Hudson), then moved to a carpenter's shop in Barclay Street.[28] In June 1785 a corporation under the laws of the State of New York was formed, its board of trustees all laymen. Substantial help toward building a church was given by King Charles III of Spain, and the Spanish Minister to the United States, Don Diego de Gardoqui, laid the cornerstone. With a bow to the king, St. Peter's Church opened on St. Charles's day, November 4, 1786.

Whelan's idyll soon ended. The old navy chaplain's manners were rough and he was no preacher. Watching events from Philadelphia, Farmer commented that great preaching, "alas, is all that some want who never frequent the sacraments."[29] There were other irritations. Carroll advised the friar to "make it an invariable rule never to exact any fee or reward for administration of the sacraments." "It never having been practiced in America," he wrote, "I should be sorry to see it introduced." Free-will offerings need not be refused, with the single exception that no gift "on any pretense" might be accepted in connection with the sacrament of penance.[30] But preaching was the major problem. Carroll lamented:

> he is not indeed so learned or good a preacher as I could wish, which mortifies his congregation, as at N. York, & in most other places of America, the different sectaries have scarce any other test to judge of a Clergyman than his talents for preaching: and our Irish Congregations, such as N. York, follow the same rule.[31]

A solution seemed at hand with the arrival, early in the fall of 1785, of a second Irish Capuchin, this time an accomplished orator, Andrew Nugent. By January the two priests were at loggerheads, the congregation divided. Whelan had antagonized Irish leaders like Lynch. He was not, Farmer reported, prudent, eloquent, or learned enough for them and had no idea how to ingratiate himself. Nugent encouraged the hostility. Whelan's enemies wanted him gone. They reminded Carroll how the church suffered from indecisive leaders and hinted at recourse to civil courts or the state legislature. Carroll faced his first full-scale crisis as Superior. A Catholic phenomenon with a peculiarly American twist was born. It became known as "trusteeism."

In his 1785 report Carroll had explained to Antonelli that "strictly speaking, there are no ecclesiastical foundations here." Property in the United States was held, either individually or corporately, by civil title. In March 1786 he elaborated:

> As soon as the laws of England were abrogated freedom of religion was established and we sought in every way to obtain a law permitting Catholic priests to form a corporate body and to hold property in common. In this wise we hoped to bring it about that property acquired from individuals would pass into the perpetual legal right and use of those who labor in the vineyard of the Lord, and thus be assured to religious use.[32]

This was in Maryland. In New York, laymen formed the corporate board and wished to oust the pastor because they did not like his manners or his eloquence. Carroll saw to the heart of the dispute:

> That an opinion was made & propagated, of the Congregation having a right not only to chuse such parish priest, as is agreeable to them; but of discharging him at pleasure; and that after such election, the Bishop, or

other Ecclesiastical Superior cannot hinder him from exercising the usual functions."

If this thesis were accepted, he told the board, "the unity and Catholicity of our Church would be at an end; and it would be formed into distinct & independent Societies, nearly in the same manner, as the Congregational Presbyterians of your neighbouring New England States."[33] The problem was how to conciliate historic Catholic polity, with its bias for hierarchical and clerical control, with a legal system and popular feeling strongly influenced by prevailing American democratic winds as well as by even older English antipathy—long antedating the Reformation of the 16th century—to the claims of Roman and canon law.

Carroll's initial position was a technical one. Until full diocesan and parochial structure was organized in the United States, no "pastor" in the canonical sense could be appointed. He was willing to name the two friars "joint chaplains," and declared that:

> Whenever parishes are established no doubt, a proper regard and such as is suitable to our Governments, will be had to the rights of the Congregation in the mode of election & presentation [of pastors]: and even now I shall ever pay to their wishes every deference consistent with the general welfare of Religion.[34]

Whelan postponed the problem by retiring to his brother's home in Johnstown, New York. Nugent took over the church, but in August 1787 was dismissed by Carroll after charges of a personal nature brought against him by the trustees were substantiated. A difficult few months followed. The friar defied Carroll, who revoked his faculties and suspended him from his duties. Personal intervention failed. Nugent's partisans twice ejected the superior from St. Peter's Church. Nugent was then convicted in civil court of disturbing the peace, and the court held him unfit for pastoral office in the Catholic Church because he did not accept its doctrines. He had in a sermon declared that he did not "recognize the pope or anyone except Christ and the civil authorities of New York."[35] His successor, Irish Dominican William O'Brien, finally brought the troubled church a measure of peace.

Boston's situation was hardly more encouraging. Catholics were unwelcome in colonial times, and the exclusion policy was successful. John Adams boasted that papists and rascally Jacobites—he was careful to associate the two—were as rare in his hometown of Braintree as a comet or an earthquake,[36] and Ebenezer Hazard was sure the happy state would continue: "Superstition cannot acquire many votaries in a country which has been so completely illuminated by the Gospel as New England."[37] Immigration in the late 18th century from France and Ireland, and the comings and goings of French fleets and armies after the alliance of 1778, changed all that.

Boston's first resident priest was the extravagant and flamboyant Claude Florent Bouchard de la Poterie, a naval chaplain whom Admiral de Sainneville was happy to see desert his squadron at Boston in the early fall of 1788. By mid-October, Poterie was saying mass at Louis Baury de Bellerive's home in the West End, and by the end of that month had a small brick church, measuring 35 by 30 feet in School Street.[38] Built for Huguenots and later used by Congregationalists, it was let to the Catholics rent-free, probably thanks to prominent Protestant merchant James Perkins. Poterie quickly made himself well known. Jeremy Belknap spotted him, "dressed in his toga," at one of his religious lectures. Protestants gave donations for the School Street church. The abbé provided music with his church services. Admission was by ticket only, the price up to "the generosity of the purchasers." Sundays were celebrated with morning sung mass and evening vespers and benediction. Benediction was again given on Thursday evenings. Plans were announced for a non-sectarian school, with a Catholic "Academic Boarding School" to follow. Irish were more numerous, French more prominent in the tiny congregation. Elected Irish and French wardens took up the collections and were responsible for church finance and upkeep.

Not until November 19 did Poterie write Carroll about his presence. Carroll sent approval on Christmas eve, but problems soon arose. Poterie promised to keep a register of income and expenses "open for the inspection of the world," but finances got out of control. The abbé's pretensions sat well neither with proper Bostonians nor with his Superior in Baltimore. Carroll rebuked him for a Lenten pastoral letter beginning:

> Claudius Florent Bouchard de la Poterie, Doctor of Divinity, Prothonotary of the Holy Church and of the Holy See of Rome, Apostolic Vice-Prefect and Missionary, Curate of the Catholick Church at Boston in North America . . .

Here and elsewhere in Poterie's broadsheets the Superior found "many passages, highly improper for publication in this country, & of a tendency to alienate from our Religion & disgust the minds of our Protestant Brethren." His sensitivity to the least whiff of Catholic foreign alliance prompted objection to Poterie's practice of including the King of France's name in the bidding prayers of the mass. Carroll notified the abbé that William O'Brien, the priest at New York, had been asked to look into the affairs of the Boston church.[39] But a combination of financial failure (he was served with a writ for non-payment of debts) and other events hastened matters. Poterie was suspended. He did not finally leave the city until

1790, and then only after denouncing "the New Laurent Ricci in America, the Reverend Father John Carroll, Superior of the Jesuits in the United States, along with the Friar-Monk-Inquisitor William O'Brien."[40] Jeremy Belknap had always had his doubts about the abbé. "He is, I believe, but a speckled bird," he wrote to his friend Ebenezer Hazard.[41]

The congregation paid off the debts and a new priest, Louis de Rousselet, was found. His chief problem was lack of familiarity with the English language, and his position was compromised by the advent in January 1790 of New England's first Yankee priest, John Thayer. Many Irish who had dropped away returned to church services, a Catholic library was begun, featuring copies of *An Account of the Conversion of the Reverend John Thayer, lately a Protestant Minister at Boston in North America*, and the young priest launched a vigorous evangelistic effort, including a literary debate with New Hampshire pastor George Leslie in the Newburyport *Essex Gazette*, and a series of articles on Catholic theological teachings in the weekly *Argus*.

Thayer was Boston-born, of Unitarian parents, and had been a classmate at Yale of Noah Webster. He served briefly as militia chaplain on Governor's Island in Boston harbor, then travelled to Europe where he became a Catholic at Rome in 1783. Four years later, after studies with the Sulpicians at Paris, he was a priest with romantic plans to make New England Catholic. These he broached to Benjamin Franklin, who thought him sincere, but not very wise,[42] and to Abigail and John Adams. Mrs. Adams reported that Mr. Adams "took him up pretty short."[43] In London he contacted Bishop Talbot, who had already washed his hands of America and was perhaps unappreciative of the priest's reflections on the English scene. His favorite English correspondent, Charles Plowden, wrote Carroll that Thayer was "of the opinion that twelve good missioners would suffice to convert all this kingdom."[44] He came home to Boston on January 2, 1790.

The Boston congregation numbered some fifty or sixty men and women. Thayer was pleased by the welcome he had from his own family and claimed that "the Governor of the State [John Hancock], whose chaplain I formerly was, has promised to do all in his power to forward my views and favour the work for which I have been sent to Boston."[45] But Rousselet's presence confused matters and provoked a schism which lasted until both priests were gone in 1792. At one point Carroll wrote in frustration that he wished

> all would lay aside national distinctions & attachments & strive to form not Irish, or English, or French Congregations & Churches, but Catholic-American Congregations and Churches.[46]

Reunion of the Irish and French took place with the coming in August 1792 of François Antoine Matignon, former professor of theology at the Collège de Navarre and a doctor in theology of the Sorbonne. He had left France rather than subscribe the Civil Constitution of the Clergy, the body of legislation which in 1791 Pope Pius VI condemned for its "sacriligious" interference in internal church affairs. Thayer took to a wandering ministry, finally leaving the United States to die in Ireland. Rousselet died by the guillotine in a massacre of royalists on the West Indian island of Guadaloupe, October 7, 1795.

Involved with the fate of the Boston church was that of the neglected Maine Indians. In 1790 the Penobscots appealed to the bishop of Québec:

> It is thirty-one years since we have had prayer in our village, because we have had no priest. . . .
> Our heart is sad. Is it not a reason for grief to see men of this age, who have not yet received their First Communion? All our young folk have been baptized only by our own hands: as for our dead, we dig their graves and bury them ourselves. Nor have we anyone to teach us.[47]

Both Rousselet and Thayer visited Maine, but no permanent missionary came until François Cliquart took responsibility for the entire state in 1792. Carroll sought Federal financial help, but President Washington wrote that, while the national government subsidized a Protestant missionary among the western Indians, those in Maine were

> so situated as to be rather considered a part of the inhabitants of the State of Massachusetts than otherwise, and that state has always considered them under its immediate care and protection. Any application therefore relative to these Indians, for the purpose mentioned would seem most proper to be made to the government of Massachusetts.[48]

No funding was forthcoming and in 1794 Cliquart accepted a stipend of £50 per year from Governor Carleton and moved to Canada and the diocese of Québec to work among the St. John's River tribes.

Other areas demanded attention. Carroll was several times balked in efforts to place a suitable priest at Charleston, South Carolina. Most of the South was at best served intermittently and many born Catholics died members of other Christian churches. Efforts to keep pace with the post-Revolution westward movement were only slightly more successful. Western Pennsylvania, Kentucky, and the Illinois country were principal Catholic venues. In 1783 Farmer wrote Carroll that "there is a young man in town from Pittsburgh with a petition to have a visit from a missionary once a year.[49] He represented Catholics led by Felix Hughes and living scattered along or near the Monongahela River, at Muddy Creek, Ten Mile Waters, and Shirtee Waters. Organization of their church life was

hindered by lack of priests. Paul de St. Pierre von Heiligenstein, a Carmelite ex-chaplain with Rochambeau's army, passed through on his way
to the Illinois country in 1785, as did Charles Whelan going to Kentucky
in 1787. For a brief moment in 1794 Carroll dreamed of a monastery of
English Benedictines (he thought a round dozen would do, "including at
least four good laborious lay brothers") in the Pittsburgh area,

> the properest place for a settlement and a school. The situation is so far
> remote from, & as secure as, London, from the Indians. There is a
> continual communication of trade & regular posts from that settlement
> to Baltimore, Philadelphia, & all the trading towns on the Atlantic.[50]

But plans went awry, and not until 1846 did Benedictines from Bavaria
occupy the "Sportsman's Hall" property purchased in 1790 by Dutch Franciscan Theodore Brouwers. In the meantime the larger than life figure of
Dimitri Gallitzin dominated the western Pennsylvania Catholic scene. Son
of a Russian prince and of Countess Amilia von Schmettau (the Princess
Gallitzin of the "Münster Circle" of Catholic intellectuals), he was the first
Catholic priest to make all his theological studies in the United States. His
ministry began in 1799 at present-day Loretto, Pennsylvania, where Captain Michael McGuire, "living on the desk of Alligany," had offered two
hundred acres and a good horse, plus an annual contribution, for the
services of a priest. "This place," a Carroll memorandum noted, "is about
40 miles distant from the Standing Stone. A great number of Catholics
scattered thro this & the neighbouring settlement."[51]

Kentucky was the goal of the second major Catholic thrust westward,
this time by Anglo-Americans from Maryland. Dr. George Hart and the
William Coomes family were there as early as 1775. Basil Hayden
("with whose character and virtue," Carroll wrote, "I am well
acquainted")[52] led a colony of twenty-five families who in 1785 plodded
over Nemacolin's Path to Pittsburgh, then floated down the Ohio to
Maysville, and walked from there to land they had bought on Pot-
tinger's Creek in Nelson County. By 1795 Nelson and Scott counties
would boast eight Catholic settlements.[53]

No priest came until 1787. Then it was Charles Maurice Whelan, fresh
from his New York confrontation with Nugent. Carroll was elated at first
reports and asked Whelan's superior in Dublin if another Capuchin (presumably not Nugent) could be sent as a companion. He held out hopes
that a house of the order might be founded, "which is certainly much to
be desired in view of the great decline in Religious orders in other parts
of the world."[54] But it was not to be. Whelan abandoned Kentucky after
two and a half years. He had nearly landed in jail in a dispute over
payment for his services. He demanded cash, the farmers offered pro-

duce. In 1805 it was English Dominicans led by Colonel Ignatius Fen-wick's son Edward, a native Marylander, who founded a men's religious community in Kentucky.[55]

Carroll was anxious to find a good priest "for the poor souls there [in Kentucky] who in general are virtuous, & some of them eminently so." The only priest available was "a rambling Irish one," whom he preferred not to employ.[56] Not until 1793 did Stephen Badin arrive, a refugee from the French Revolution. He was the first priest ordained in the United States. There were those who found him "cross and crabbed, and he wouldn't let the young folks dance and have a little fun now and then,"[57] but despite a grim 18th-century French spirituality he laid the foundations of church life on which the stern Fleming Charles Nerinckx, Benedict Joseph Flaget (destined to be the first bishop west of the Alleghenies), and John Baptist David built. They found strong support in a Catholic community characterized by solid, undemonstrative English piety, and particularly in two women's religious communities, the Sisters of Loretto, founded by a group of school teachers with Nerinckx as spiritual director, and the Sisters of Charity of Nazareth, whose first superior was Mother Catherine Spalding.[58]

Until the Louisiana Purchase of 1803, the western border of the United States was at the Mississippi. Church jurisdiction was muddled. The right bank belonged to the diocese of Santiago de Cuba until 1787, then to Havana, and finally, beginning in 1793, to "Louisiana and the Two Flori-das," whose bishop lived at New Orleans. On the left bank, Pierre Gi-bault could not return to Canada because of his Revolutionary War ac-tivities, but was still vicar general for the bishop of Québec. Paul de St. Pierre was across the river at Ste. Geneviève, below St. Louis. Carroll named Canadian expatriate Pierre Huet de la Valinière his vicar for the region, which led to conflict with Gibault. The latter's action in securing personal title to church property dating from colonial times caused prob-lems. In 1791 the bishops of Québec and Baltimore heard from Rome that Baltimore's jurisdiction extended to the entire United States. Carroll was finally able to regularize church life in the borderlands of the diocese by sending a trio of refugee French Sulpician priests to take over the western missions in 1792.

During the years when the new nation—as well as the Catholic church establishment—was taking shape, Philadelphia remained the premier Catholic center. It had St. Mary's Church, with its organ and solemn ceremonies, and tiny St. Joseph's Chapel. The two priests were widely respected. Ferdinand Farmer was a trustee of the state university and a member of the American Philosophical Society. Catholics venerated him as pastor to Irish and German alike and as founder of the church throughout New Jersey and in New York's Hudson valley. Robert Molyneux presided over the birth of Catholic publishing in the United States. In 1774 *A Manual of Catholic Prayers* appeared. By 1785 he had coming off the presses "a spelling primer for children with the Catholic catechism annexed" and Joseph Reeve's *History of the Old and New Testament.*

Philadelphia was home also to Mathew Carey, onetime Irish revolutionary and the most prominent publisher of his day. Arriving in 1784 he edited in succession the *Pennsylvania Herald, Columbian Magazine,* and *The American Museum,* the last of which was the most influential news magazine in the country. Driven out of journalism by high postal rates, he turned to book publishing. The initial section of the "Carey Bible," the first American edition of the Douai-Rheims version, appeared in December 1789 and a year later the entire Bible was published. The cost was six dollars to subscribers, seven dollars to others. The subscription list included prominent Protestants and Catholics. John Carroll was a tireless promoter, dunning both priests and laity for subcriptions.[59]

Ferdinand Farmer's death in August 1786 cast the first shadow on the Philadelphia scene. Germans in the congregation were left without a pastor of their own, a lack not made up by the assignment of a thirty-five year old Englishman, onetime Jesuit novice Francis Beeston. Then in October 1787, not one but three German priests came: Lorenz Graessl, a novice in the Jesuits' Bavarian Province when the order was suppressed; and two Capuchin friars, the brothers Johann and Peter Heilbron. Farmer had before his death invited Graessl as his successor; the Heilbrons arrived on their own, but soon won over a substantial number of the German parishioners. During 1788 these Germans formed their own congregation and built Holy Trinity Church. They wanted Johann Heilbron rather than Graessl for their priest. Carroll refused, warning the lay committee of church censures if they resisted. The committee protested censures as "odious and obsolete," but the Superior held his ground. The incident was the first in a series which in the long run considerably weakened the Philadelphia church in the last decades of the 18th century and on into the 19th century.[60]

Church organization was only one area of trouble. Carroll also became a literary apologist. When *Columbian Magazine* published anti-Catholic attacks, he replied in a letter to the editor (not Carey at this time). He did the same when Federalist John Fenno's *Gazette of the United States* suggested that Protestantism deserved establishment as the religion of the republic. He took the gaff of Poterie's anti-Jesuit writings and of a similar screed published at Dublin by Cork priest Patrick Smyth. Closer to home was the controversy in 1784 with fellow ex-Jesuit Charles Wharton, of whom he had written: "He left behind him few of our antient Brethren his equals, none, I believe, his Superiors."[61] Wharton was a kinsman whose company he enjoyed but who now had joined the newly reorganized American Protestant Episcopal Church.

Wharton was a dozen years Carroll's junior. Ordained priest a year before the Jesuit suppression, he was a mathematics teacher at the college in Liège when that blow fell. During the Revolution he stayed abroad, his last post being as chaplain to the Catholics of Worcester, England. He returned in the summer of 1783 to live on his Maryland estate. Carroll reported that "he leads a life clear of all offense, & gives no handle to censure, tho' there are not wanting those who would be glad to find room for it." He did not function as a priest, but was "neither visionary nor fanatick, *un peu philosophe,* but I hope not too much so."[62] By the third week of September 1784, the picture had changed, as Carroll wrote to Plowden:

> You will hear before the receipt of this that I was much deceived in my hopes of Wharton. . . . He has not only renounced his Religion, but has published a pamphlet, which, under the colour of apology, is a malignant invective & misrepresentation of our tenets.[63]

He had just spent the better part of the summer sweltering away at Annapolis on a reply to Wharton. Published in Philadelphia, it showed broad mastery of church history and the church fathers and a good appreciation both of classical theological authors and of more recent Protestant and Catholic controversialists.[64]

Carroll's *Address* involved him in further theological discussions, notably with the English priest Joseph Berington, whose ideas on religious toleration he applauded as

> the only sentiments, that can ever establish, by being generally adopted, a reasonable system of universal Forbearance, and Charity amongst Christians of every Denomination.

It was his hope that "such an unlimited Toleration giving an open Field to the Display of Truth and fair argument may greatly contribute to bring mankind to an unity of Opinion on matters of Religious Concern." Two other topics he urged on Berington, terming them "the greatest Obstacles, with Christians of other Denominations, to a thorough union with us; or at least to a much greater Diffusion of our Religion, particularly in N. America": the "ascertaining of the Extent and Boundaries of the Spiritual Jurisdiction of the Holy See" and "the use of the Latin tongue in the publick Liturgy."[65] Others entered the controversy, including Archbishop John Troy, O.P., of Dublin, fresh from a pastoral letter attacking liturgical vernacularism, and Franciscan Arthur O'Leary, who for good measure tweaked Carroll's nose with an essay laudatory of Pope Clement XIV, suppressor of the Jesuits. The American priest retreated from the battle over liturgical language; the relationship of the pope's authority to that of other bishops preoccupied him all his life.

His pastoral experience as Superior of the Mission, the varied needs and serious problems he encountered, and deepening understanding of the national political experiment in whose launching he and fellow Catholics shared—all contributed to John Carroll's evolving ideas on what should be the structure of the Catholic Church in the United States. So did his profound historical consciousness and appreciation of the age-old Christian tradition. In 1787, arguing with conservative country pastors of southern Maryland who opposed both regularization of episcopal government and funding the proposed academy at Georgetown, Carroll and his supporters reminded them that they lived on "such an extensive continent" that fresh measures were needed to foster church life and growth.[66] Four years later Carroll approached the question from another angle. For well over a thousand years Europe and Latin Christianity had been very nearly interchangeable terms. Now Catholicism was planted in a land with no European center of gravity, no European "metropolitical" connection. Ecclesiological constructs which had grown over centuries in the European context had to be re-thought.[67]

Carroll had a strong sense of the need for and the rights of a national church. Its priests should form "a permanent body of national Clergy," shape their own system of internal government, and choose their own bishop, subject only to papal approval of the man they had picked. They should not be "missioners," working under control of Rome's missionary arm, the Congregation for Propagation of the Faith, but a stable group of priests belonging to the church in the United States. The church should be headed by "an ordinary national bishop," and not a vicar apostolic, a delegate of the pope. He took a dim view of the system of having a titular bishop who exercised authority in the pope's name and not in his own— "a refined Roman political contrivance," he called it. His vision was of a local church in communion with the bishop and see of Rome (a communion which he always emphasized as essential), but internally autonomous, self-perpetuating, and free of the least taint of foreign jurisdiction. Commenting on phrases in the bull *Ex Hac Apostolicae,* in which he was named Bishop of Baltimore, he spelled out practical consequences of his theory in two areas—the choice of bishops, and the control of church property:

> The pope, according to the pretensions, which the see of Rome has always supported, says, he will nominate hereafter. But I conceive that the Clergy will have as good right to say, that the election shall be held

by members of their own body, & that they never can or will admit any
Bishop who is not so constituted. . . .

As to the investing of the Bp with the administration [of church pro-
perty], I never conceived it as any thing more than the expression of
those claims which Rome has always kept up, tho universally disre-
garded; viz: that the pope is the universal administrator, some even have
said, *Dominus* of all ecclesiastical property. . . . [68]

A national clergy, and ways to educate them, were central to his
plans. So was education for lay men and women. The Superior welcomed the small but steady flow of priests ordained from the English
ex-Jesuits' Anglo-Bavarian Academy at Liège. They fitted well, he
thought, with clergy already in America. After Poterie, Smyth, and the
like—that "medley of clerical characters"—he was more cautious about
volunteers. Nor was he anxious to have Americans educated at Mainz or
Rome, where places had been offered. He did finally send two students
to the Propaganda College at Rome, but neither reached ordination.
Carroll's real hopes lay in a seminary in the United States. Negotiations
early in the fall of 1790 led to the arrival in Baltimore the following
summer of four French priests of the Society of St. Sulpice and five
seminarians, among them Stephen Badin. In what had been the "One-
Mile Tavern" they founded St. Mary's Seminary, first institution of its
kind in the country.[69]

Education of a native clergy had top priority, and when Carroll spoke
of his other major project, the academy at Georgetown, it was often
to mention it as a place where future priests might receive preliminary
schooling. In fact, education in itself, for men and women, was for him
something to be cultivated by the church. In 1787, in response to the
southern Maryland pastors who opposed the academy, Carroll said flatly
that the Jesuit order, to which all once belonged, had in its two-hundred
year existence "rendered no service more extensively useful, than that of
the education of youth." His vision was of a school "first in character and
merit in America," its purpose to "diffuse knowledge, promote virtue
and serve Religion." Its goal was the "moral, religious and literary improvement" of students, it would be the "main sheet anchor of Religion"
in the United States.[70]

Carroll worked hard to establish the Georgetown Academy which
received its first student in 1791. He overcame opposition among the
priests, organized fund-raising committees, and personally canvassed the
English Catholic gentry, many of whom gave substantial donations. He
was equally interested, if less successful, in the matter of women's education. When it became clear that the first nuns to come to the United
States would be contemplative Carmelites, Carroll welcomed them for

their contribution to the church's spiritual life, but confessed "I wish rather for Ursulines," a teaching community.[71] Without mentioning it to the Carmelites, he later obtained Pius VI's permission for them to open a school. They refused; he had ruefully to admit that "they will not concern themselves in the business of female education."[72] In 1793 he strongly supported John Thayer's effort to bring teaching sisters to Boston. It was finally an Irishwoman, Alice Lalor, who gathered the community which grew into Georgetown Visitation Convent, home of the first Catholic women's school in the country—apart from the Ursulines' in New Orleans.

Carroll's five years as Superior saw expansion, problems, and challenge. A majority of the priests was convinced that the time had come for the next step. They needed a bishop. Reluctance had two sources: anticipated public hostility to the very idea of such a personage functioning in democratic America and, in the Catholic community, the unaccustomed novelty of a bishop where there had been none for a century and a half. Apprehensions of hostility lessened when no great public outcry greeted the consecration in England in 1787 of William White as the first Protestant Episcopal bishop of Pennsylvania (he had been preceded in the episcopacy of his church by another American, Samuel Seabury of Connecticut, consecrated by Scottish "non-juring" bishops in 1784). His public reception was good and, Carroll noted with approval, his return to his diocese was followed by "greater observance and attention to morals" on the part of his clergy.[73] Opposition among Catholics weakened, and a petition on behalf of the priests went to Rome on March 12, 1788.[74]

The petition to Pius VI asked establishment of a diocese headed by a bishop ordinary, that is, one who would have authority belonging by right to his office, not one who would be a delegate of the pope. He should not be someone set up by a "foreign tribunal" and dependent on it for exercise and duration of office. In plain language, he should not be a vicar apostolic dependent on the Congregation for Propagation of the Faith. The petitoners asked that "at least in this first instance" choice of the bishop be left to the priests having the care of souls in America, and that future procedure for selection of a bishop be determined once the diocese was established. The request was granted on July 12, 1788. Rome left to the priests choice of the city in which the diocese would be located, whether the bishop would be an ordinary or a titular, and authorized them to elect "a person eminent in piety, prudence and zeal for the faith, from the said clergy, and present him to the Apostolic See for confirmation." The election took place at Whitemarsh Plantation on May 18, 1789. John Carroll was chosen by a vote of 24 to 2. He was named first bishop of Baltimore in the papal bull *Ex Hac Apostolicae,* on November 6, 1789. He was consecrated on August 15, 1790, by the Benedictine bishop who served Catholics in the west of England, Charles Walmesley. The ceremony took place in a private chapel at Lulworth Castle in Dorsetshire, the estate of England's largest Catholic landowner, Thomas Weld.

VIII

The Failure of Carroll's Plans

John Carroll's grand plan failed. The Catholic Church did not develop in the United States along the lines he envisioned. There were many reasons. Debilitating economic recession before, during, and after the War of 1812 had its effects. America turned in on itself, sought its roots and found them in one of its periodic nativist binges. On the religious front, a "benevolent empire" of myriad evangelical organizations and societies flourished in the early years of the 19th century, spurred on by a great revivalistic awakening. It was the heyday of Robert Handy's "Protestant America," of Martin Marty's "Righteous Empire," not an altogether comfortable time for Catholics.[1] But American Catholicism's more pressing problems were internal. Now recovered from the trauma of the French Revolution and Napoleon, Pius VII and the curial department which handled American church affairs for him, the Congregation for Propagation of the Faith, were ready and able to exert pressure in the direction of centralization, while in the United States a clergy which would be adequate to the herculean task confronting it had not developed. At the same time, lay leadership collapsed, never really to recover.

One of Carroll's major failures was in securing effective episcopal collaborators. His first choice as coadjutor bishop, Lorenz Graessl, died of yellow fever ministering to the sick during the Philadelphia epidemic of 1793. News of his appointment as titular bishop of Samosata and coadjutor of Baltimore arrived only after he had been some months in the grave. General Bonaparte's Roman Republic and Pius VI's captivity at Valence helped to delay for six years ratification of Carroll's second choice, another ex-Jesuit and onetime missionary in Guyana, Leonard Neale. Neale proved a poor choice. A holy man in the austere tradition, he was an indifferent preacher and writer who as president of Georgetown College from 1799 to 1806 very nearly wrecked the school by a disciplinary approach "not calculated," Carroll ruefully allowed, "for the meridian of America."[2] Although the idea had been to have a bishop resident in Philadelphia, Neale moved to Georgetown after his name was submitted to Rome and he assisted Carroll as regional bishop for Washington and neighboring Maryland and Virginia counties. By the time he began his two years (1815–17) as archbishop of Baltimore, he was sixty-eight years old and living in virtual retirement at Georgetown Visitation Convent.[3]

As early as 1792 Carroll thought of dividing the diocese. By 1807 there was the question of creating several new episcopal seats, which were established in the following year. Baltimore became a metropolitan archdiocese with Carroll as first archbishop. But only in two suffragan dioceses, Boston and Bardstown in Kentucky, was there competent episcopal succession. Ably assisted by Abbé François Matignon, Bishop Jean Lefebvre de Cheverus was strikingly successful at Boston, in a diocese which covered the New England states, but numbered in 1820 only 4,600 Catholics, 750 of them in the Maine Indian missions, with the rest French and Irish immigrants and a few Yankee converts. In 1823 he left for France to become bishop of Montauban and later archbishop of Bordeaux and a cardinal.[4] Two years later he was succeeded by the ablest of the American Jesuits, Benedict Fenwick.[5] In Kentucky, another Frenchman, the Sulpician Benedict Joseph Flaget, reluctantly began what would prove to be a forty-two-year incumbency and firmly established Catholicism in the region.[6]

Developments elsewhere were not so happy. When he recommended Irish Franciscan Michael Egan for Philadelphia, Carroll noted that he lacked robust health and could do with greater firmness of disposition. Egan was ordained bishop in 1810. Within four years he was dead, destroyed by conflicts in the diocese.[7] It took six years to find a successor and then he was the nearly seventy-five-year-old Henry Conwell, vicar-general of the archdiocese of Armagh in Ireland. Irish politics had suggested to Rome the advisability of finding him a foreign see. After considering Madras in southeast India, he opted for Philadelphia. His catastrophic regime completed the demise of that city as Catholicism's American intellectual center.[8] The situation was no better at New York. There Carroll blundered by nominating no candidate. From 1808 to 1815 an Alsatian Jesuit, Anthony Kohlmann, filled in as vicar-general. He built old St. Patrick's Cathedral, opened a Jesuit school for boys and an Ursuline one for girls (neither survived), and successfully fought a court case which won judicial recognition for the secrecy of the confessional. But the diocese suffered from lack of a bishop.[9] That office became in effect an Irish Dominican fief, with candidates urged on Roman authorities from Dublin, from Rome's Dominican theological faculty the Minerva, and from Lisbon's Corpo Santo Irish college, rather than from Baltimore. The first bishop, Richard L. Concanen, O.P., never saw Manhattan. He died in 1810 en route in Naples. His successor, John Connolly, O.P., arrived in 1815, only nine days before Archbishop Carroll's death. Kohlmann's Jesuit superiors had already recalled him to Washington. Connolly was left with three churches, four priests, a substantial debt, and a far from quiescent board of lay trustees controlling the New York City property. Not until the coming in 1838 of Bishop John Hughes did New York Catholic fortunes take a substantial turn for the better.[10]

Carroll's design for local election of bishops worked only in the single instance of his own appointment. Graessl and Neale he picked himself, informing Rome that he had consulted the "older and more worthy priests."[11] There is no evidence of consultation preceding the 1807 choices. Carroll submitted one or more names for each new diocese, leaving final selection to Roman officials. He did express annoyance at Irish interference, asking Archbishop John Troy, O.P., of Dublin how Irish bishops would like it if American bishops made recommendations for Irish sees, but he accepted calmly a series of Roman nominations.[12] By the time of his second successor, Ambrose Maréchal, S.S., the secretary of the Congregation for Propagation of the Faith could flatly inform the archbishop of Baltimore that he had no right to be consulted in the choice of suffragan bishops.[13] It was just thirty years since John Carroll had insisted that a national clergy had the right to choose its own bishops, leaving the pope only the right to veto.

A national clergy was slow in developing. Of the priests available to the bishops, the French Sulpicians, a society of diocesan priests, were the steadiest and most substantial. The worked in seminaries, in back-country missions and on the old French frontiers of the Great Lakes and Illinois country. Their seminaries, the first of which was St. Mary's in Baltimore, educated a growing stream of diocesan clergy, men like Badin, Gallitzin and longtime Washington pastor William Matthews. Immigrant priests, secular and regular alike, proved to be a mixed bag. Some were prominent in church growth, others simply troublemakers. Among religious orders, the Jesuits, who had been virtually the only colonial priests, reaffiliated in 1805 with the remnant of their order still existing in the Russian

Empire by fiat of the Empress Catherine II. Unwilling to lose the services of the Jesuits and not unmindful of a chance to let Rome know her power, the Russian Orthodox empress had forbidden promulgation in her dominions of Pope Clement XIV's decree suppressing the Jesuit order. She ordered the Jesuits to continue working as they were. In 1783 Clement's successor, Pope Pius VI, gave verbal approval to the arrangement. He later allowed ex-Jesuits living in other countries to affiliate with the Russian group. Worldwide restoration of the order followed in 1814. The first new generation included impressive recruits like Benedict Fenwick and was bolstered by foreign additions like Anthony Kohlmann. Besides the Dominicans who moved into the Kentucky wilderness in 1805, another ancient order was established in the United States when Irish Augustinians led by Matthew Carr and John Rosseter founded a community at Philadelphia in 1796.[14] At Bishop DuBourg's invitation, Italian members of the Congregation of the Mission (Vincentians), headed by Felix DeAndreis and Joseph Rosati, later bishop of St. Louis, began an extensive ministry in the midwestern states in 1818. Two years later they opened a seminary at the "Barrens," in Perryville, Missouri.[15] While individual Franciscans, Carmelites, and Capuchins came to America during the post-Revolution years, their communities did not take root until later, with the great immigrant waves.

While religious brothers (the first to settle permanently were the Brothers of Holy Cross at Notre Dame in 1841) contributed substantially to American Catholicism's massive 19th-century institutional growth, the development most distinctively American was the role in educating the young assumed so largely by myriad women's communities. In colonial times a number of Maryland women had joined contemplative monasteries in the Low Countries and France. Driven out by the French Revolution, three of them, with Mother Bernardine Matthews as superior, were among the founders of a Carmel at Port Tobacco, Maryland, in 1790.[16] Ursulines, in New Orleans since 1727, attempted schools in New York City (1812–15) and Boston (1820–34). Visitandines were at Georgetown. Other early ventures included the Sisters of Charity of Emmitsburg, Maryland (1809), whose foundress, Elizabeth Ann Seton, in 1975 became the first native-born United States citizen to be canonized;[17] the Sisters of Charity of Nazareth and the Sisters of Loretto, both 1812 Kentucky foundations;[18] the Religious of the Sacred Heart, led by Rose Philippine Duchesne (declared "Blessed" in 1940), who in 1818 opened an Indian school at St. Charles, Missouri;[19] Kentucky Dominican sisters (1822);[20] and the four black women who at Baltimore in 1829 became the first Oblate Sisters of Providence.[21]

When, late in 1789, the American Catholic community congratulated

General George Washington on his election as first President of the United States, the letter was signed by John Carroll for the clergy and, "in behalf of the Roman Catholic Laity," by Charles Carroll of Carrollton, Daniel Carroll, Thomas FitzSimons, and Dominick Lynch.[22] Lay people had always held significant leadership roles in the community, beginning with the Calverts and Margaret Brent and her brothers. Lay government officials were the backbone of the late 17th-century New York Catholic group. Lay trustees safeguarded Jesuit property in colonial Maryland. When the failure of Rome and London to appreciate the delicacy of the American situation threatened despatch of a vicar apostolic, Charles Carroll of Annapolis and his friends took up the cudgels to avert disaster. The city parishes in Philadelphia and New York counted among their pewholders some of the more prominent merchants of the town. Philadelphian Mathew Carey was a leading figure in the fledgling publishing business. But the early years of the republic saw a significant decline in lay influence on church policy and a significant rate of departure from the Catholic Church among the very families which had been founders of the congregations in the port cities. The Willcoxes of Ivy Mills near Philadelphia remained Catholic. Few others did.

Reasons varied. Catholics married Protestants and joined their churches. It happened among Philadelphia's Meades, Careys, and Caufmanns and New York's Lynches. Protracted battles over local church control at St. Peter's on Barclay Street, in New York City, and Holy Trinity and St. Mary's in Philadelphia, corroded inherited loyalties. Not atypical was the story of Philadelphian James Oellers, an immigrant from Aachen. A businessman, proprietor of Oellers' Hotel, and during the Revolutionary War owner of the privateer *Katharina,* his was in 1782 the largest single contribution (over £75) to the St. Mary's repair fund. Later he offered to found a Jesuit school, if the Jesuits could supply teachers. He was a board member of the Sixth Street orphan asylum when it became the first work outside Emmitsburg of Mother Seton's sisters. But for nearly twenty years, from 1787 to 1806, he was at odds with John Carroll over the affairs of Holy Trinity Church, of which he was a trustee. In 1788 Carroll asked a priest at St. Mary's to keep an eye on "Oillers," and let him know of any "schismatic" or "pernicious" moves on his part. Eleven years later, when Holy Trinity was formally in schism, he wrote to Rome: "The leader is a layman, a shopkeeper, an extremely bold fellow. He has managed all the affairs of Holy Trinity Church, sacred and otherwise, to suit his own fancy." In 1806, when Oellers was on the board of the orphan asylum and thinking of founding a Jesuit college, Carroll was still suspicious. To a priest who considered himself wronged by the merchant he wrote: "I have known Oellers too long to be surprised." His sons, who were entered at Georgetown in 1794, left two years later. His descendants were Protestants.[23]

Lay involvement developed naturally in rural Maryland. The population was homogeneous; priests came from the same small English and American Catholic community as did lay folk. Those who were Marylanders had wide family connections in the province. Services were held in chapels on Jesuit farms or in private homes. Finances were simple. Church goods, and the farms themselves, were owned by Jesuits as a group, with legal title vested in one of their number and passed on by will to others. In special circumstances a lay friend held the title. Mr. Thomas Matthews was legal proprietor of the four-thousand-acre St. Thomas Manor from 1649 to 1662, apparently because it was first acquired during Jesuit quarrels with the Baltimores over Indian land donations. Each Jesuit residence was expected to be self-supporting and if possible to contribute to a general fund for the assistance of poorer stations and payment of travel expenses of missionaries to and from Europe. In 1728 the English Jesuit Provincial asked that the custom be kept of not asking for financial support from the laity.[24] Similar arrangements obtained in the Pennsylvania country missions, which still had help from the Sir John James Fund, dating from colonial days. Only in Philadelphia does regular congregational support seem to have been usual.

The rural model would not work in the urban churches of postwar New York and Philadelphia or among congregations which sprang up in other port cities. The clergy was no longer a tightly knit body of Jesuits or ex-Jesuits. Lay people bought and paid for property, built churches on it, and kept them up. Often enough it was left to them to find a pastor. America's atmosphere, and usually its incorporation laws, favored a congregational style of church polity, as Bishop Connolly of New York explained to Rome in 1818:

> Here no Church, Catholic or Protestant, can possess temporal goods or income to its name. If it is built by public money [i.e. contributions], the congregation must yearly elect trustees to administer the property, and priests as such have no right to interfere with this property.[25]

Polity was not too democratic, however. Normal procedure was that only those who had purchased pews in a church were elected to its board of trustees.

Some factors were constant. In 1821 the trustees of St. Mary's, in Philadelphia, asked relief from "being compelled, as heretofore, to receive, to pay and to obey [priests] who are a disgrace to our religion, to us, to themselves and to those who send them."[26] Preaching ability was a criterion rarely satisfied. National antagonisms were epidemic. Germans wanted autonomy in Baltimore and Philadelphia. The Philadelphians at one point petitioned the state supreme court to forbid any but German sermons in Holy Trinity Church.[27] Irishmen at Norfolk, Virginia, preferred a schismatic bishop to being ruled by a Frenchman. The bottom line was expressed by Dr. Matthew O'Driscoll and the trustees at Charleston, South Carolina, who in 1818 used the following argument with Archbishop Maréchal of Baltimore: since the United States government did not, like European kings, interfere in religious matters,

> that part of the sovereign people of these United States, in communion with His Holiness the Pope . . . think, and hold themselves, *immediately* intitled, to the same benefits and immunities in their religious concerns as are established between the court of Rome and the Sovereigns of Europe, *immediately* negotiating for the interests and religious liberties of their subjects.[28]

Neither Rome nor most American bishops accepted the argument. They understood the age-old European model of intermediate lay involvement through princes. Immediate lay involvement as a consequence of newfangled democratic forms was beyond their comprehension. It was a demand for extension to the United States of the *ius patronatus,* with the sovereign people as "patron," and it was rejected.

Trustee fever, first manifest in the church's body politic at St. Peter's on Barclay Street, in New York City, in 1785, persisted there until the middle of the 19th century. Unable to cope financially with the needs of a parish increasingly peopled by poor immigrants, the St. Peter's trustees filed for bankruptcy in 1844. Five years of conflict followed, climaxed by one board member's threat to horsewhip the bishop if the latter, as he had threatened, came to the church to "expose the delinquency of the trustees." The bishop was John Hughes, master of just such dramatic moments. In a public meeting he faced down the trustees, and then bought the church and named his own committee to manage its affairs. "Episcopal authority," he explained on a later occasion, "comes from above and not from below and Catholics do their duty when they obey their bishop."[29]

Philadelphia's story was the most complicated.[30] There was the frankly nationalistic argument with the German parishioners of Holy Trinity, dating from 1787, in which James Oellers played a leading role. Clerical bit parts fell to wandering friars fleeing the havoc wrought on Europe's monasteries by a quarter-century of revolution and Napoleon, to a secular priest who claimed to be still under the jurisdiction of the archbishop of Mainz and rejected that of John Carroll, and to a Cistercian monk from Rome's Santa Croce monastery. With Leonard Neale's departure for Georgetown in 1799, the last of the ex-Jesuits whose predecessors had begun the Philadelphia congregation was gone. Two decades of struggle for control of St. Mary's Church began under Bishop Michael Egan, O.F.M. (1810–14), and involved three bishops, a procession of migrant priests and many of the city's prominent lay Catholics. Personalities, finances, clerical ambitions, and theories about lay power in the church all contributed to a colossal muddle.

A respected and holy man, Egan was not up to dealing with the complex currents within Philadelphia Catholicism. For six years after his death the diocese was in the hands of an aristocratic German priest, Adolph de Barth de Walbach. He lived at the country mission of Conewago and had the reputation of being "cold" to the Irish. When the venerable Henry Conwell was named bishop in 1820, his recent successful rival for the archbishopric of Armagh could only say that he would not have been more surprised if Conwell had become Emperor of China. Poor health and failing eyesight, combined with an obsession about providing for his personal financial security, were only some of the ingredients in what turned out to be a prescription for disaster.

A central figure in the Philadelphia difficulties was the Irish Dominican William Vincent Harold.[31] Egan's vicar general and apparent choice as successor, he had quarreled with the bishop and gone home to Ireland in 1813. Back again in 1820 he was Conwell's strong right arm in battles with the St. Mary's trustees during the "Hogan Schism," but broke with him over the agreement which the bishop signed with the board in 1826 and was removed from office and suspended from his functions. Two years later he and a Dominican companion, John A. Ryan, lodged a formal complaint with Secretary of State Henry Clay, to the effect that an order from Rome to report to Cincinnati, where Edward Fenwick, O.P., had been bishop since 1821, violated their civil rights. On orders from President John Quincy Adams the question was referred to Minister James Brown at Paris, who raised it with Papal Nuncio Luigi Lambruschini. The latter's reply, emphasizing that the Dominicans were being asked only to fulfill freely assumed obligations, satisfied American authorities, who agreed that the affair was an internal church matter not subject to government cognizance. Harold and Ryan returned to Ireland. The former became provincial superior of the Irish Dominicans from 1840 to 1844.

Other birds of passage included William Harold's uncle James, a Dublin diocesan priest once transported as an alleged revolutionary to Botany Bay. In America he proved to be conspiratorial, money-grubbing, and a malign influence on his nephew, responsible for souring the latter's relations with Bishop Egan and for inciting discord between the bishop and the St. Mary's trustees. Others were the priests Angelo Inglesi and Thaddeus

O'Meally of Limerick. At the height of the controversy, a certain "Friar Rico," purportedly a Spanish Franciscan and canon lawyer though working in Philadelphia as a cigar salesman, contributed his expertise. Most troublesome and at the eye of the storm from 1820 to 1824 was another Limerick priest, William Hogan, a small, foppish (the adjective was applied at the time), handsome young man who set up his own home apart from the house where the priests traditionally lived.[32] He soon established himself as something of a social lion. Conwell disapproved of the life style; he was also annoyed by barbs directed at himself and the former administrator, Father de Barth, with which Hogan spiced his sermons. He ordered him back to the clergy house and, when Hogan refused, suspended him. Mathew Carey, who said Hogan was the most popular preacher St. Mary's had had in years, protested Conwell's action vociferously. The trustees moved to drop priest members from the board, elected Hogan pastor, barred the bishop from the church—it was his cathedral—and addressed a letter to all American Catholics inviting them to join forces in establishment of an independent American church. A somewhat more reflective Carey commented: "If they were Turks or pagans, they could not have done more to bring the Catholic name into contempt."[33]

Bishop Conwell excommunicated Hogan in 1821. The schism came to a head in the April 1822 trustees' election at St. Mary's. Voting was preceded by the hoopla—rallies, placards, throwaway broadsides—of a political campaign. Two elections were held, two slates were chosen, one favorable to Hogan and the other to the bishop and Harold. A brawl took place on Fourth Street, in front of the church. Punches and then bricks were thrown and the police had to break it up. The civil courts upheld the validity of the Hogan ticket's election. The next act in the drama took place in August, with receipt of a "brief" from Pope Pius VII, *Non Sine Magno,* rebuking the trustees for their conduct with regard to church property and the appointment of pastors. An accompanying letter to the archbishop of Baltimore instructed him to see to it that in the United States the powers of trustees were limited and bishops and priests guaranteed whatever was necessary for the free exercise of their ministry. Hogan submitted, then withdrew his submission, briefly left the country, then returned, but in the summer of 1824 found himself turned out by the trustees. He subsequently married twice, managed a circus, became a lawyer, and served in the United States consular service. He was for a time a popular lecturer on the anti-Catholic circuit.

The trustees remained in control, winning the annual election again in 1826. After this Bishop Conwell signed an agreement with them. He was acknowledged senior pastor of the church and his right to appoint priests admitted, but the trustees were to have the right to recommend priests for appointment and the bishop's right to dismiss them was limited. Cases of disagreement were to be referred to a committee, at least half of whose members were lay people. In a separate document, which really nullified their agreement with the bishop, the trustees re-stated their claim to the right of presentation and denied the bishop's right to appoint pastors without their approval.

This "concordat" ended Conwell's tenure as active bishop of Philadelphia. On April 30, 1827, the Roman Congregation for Propagation of the Faith declared the agreement null and summoned the bishop to Rome. Father William Matthews came from Washington as administrator until replaced in 1830 by Rome-trained Francis Patrick Kenrick, who up to Conwell's death in 1842 held the titles coadjutor bishop and apostolic administrator. Conwell lived out his days in Philadelphia, but was not allowed to participate in government of the diocese.

Centers of discontent during the years 1816–20 were Charleston, South Carolina, and Norfolk, Virginia.[34] In both places national differences were a factor, with predominantly Irish boards of trustees opposing French pastors and ultimately the French archbishop of Baltimore. In South Carolina the eloquent though erratic and often intemperate Irish priest Simon Felix Gallagher had the lay trustees on his side in opposition to Abbé Pierre-Joseph Picot de Clorivière, who had been sent by Archbishop Carroll in 1812. A Gallagher ally was Robert Browne, the Irish Augustinian who ministered both at Charleston and at Augusta, Georgia. At Norfolk, the trustees opposed a French priest, James Lucas.

The Charleston and Norfolk trustees, who formed an alliance of sorts during Neale's short tenure, did their homework well. Chief theoretician was Dr. John F. Oliveira Fernandez of Norfolk, whose fellows on the board had names like Reilly, Herron, Moran, Higgins, Mulhollan, and Donaghey. Their basic argument was that pastors had only spiritual powers, while physical administration of the parish belonged to them. The priest was their agent, commissioned by them after appointment by the bishop, an appointment which they reserved the right to reject. They also held that a pastor once contracted to them could not officiate elsewhere without their consent. In defense of their position they cited authorities ranging from Jean Gerson, the conciliarist 15th-century chancellor of the University of Paris, and Paolo Sarpi, a historian known for his hostility to the Council of Trent, to such relatively contemporary ecclesiologists as Göttingen Protestant church historian Johann Lorenz von Mosheim and Auxiliary Bishop Johann Nikolaus von Hontheim ("Justinus Febronius") of Trier, whose 1763 treatise, *The State of the Church and the Legitimate Power of the Roman Pontiff,* was a classic statement on national ecclesiastical autonomy.

The Norfolk and Charleston trustees marshalled arguments out of the American experience as well as from the longer history of the church in Europe. They denounced the system of church government actually in use as un-American, ill according with American democratic ideas. The Holy See's claims in the area of temporal administration were dismissed as based on ignorance and superstition and representing "an uninterrupted system of Machiavellic politics in the Roman Curia." Given this approach, it comes as a surprise to discover the unusual access the dissidents enjoyed to the Congregation for Propagation of the Faith. At crucial junctures they managed to have decisions of both Neale and Maréchal reversed by Roman authorities. The first instance was when Gallagher's Augustinian ally Browne visited Cardinal Lorenzo Litta to plead their joint cause. With no inquiry to Neale (who for his part had not kept Litta, the Prefect of Propaganda, up to date), the cardinal directed that the archbishop lift the suspensions of the two priests. The directive was withdrawn only when Neale sent a full explanation and informed Litta of the scandal his order had occasioned. Neale died on June 18, 1817, before the matter was fully set to rights. By then the story had taken a new twist, with the arrival in Rome of Norfolk trustee John Donaghey. He was there to explain that the best solution for Virginia was to give it an Irish bishop of its own.

Donaghey's mission seemed to succeed. Litta wrote Dr. Fernandez praising his work for the church and agreeing to an Irish bishop, with the trustees' candidate, Thomas Carbry, O.P., as the likely choice. A letter in September 1817 to the new Archbishop of Baltimore, Ambrose Maréchal, S.S., suggested a new diocese for Virginia and requested Carbry's interim appointment as pastor at Norfolk.

Carbry, an Irish Dominican in his late sixties, was a protégé of Archbishop Troy of Dublin and Bishop Connolly of New York, the latter a recent arrival who favored naming a bishop in each of the American states. Maréchal did not name Carbry to Norfolk, nor would he recommend him for a miter. In May 1819 the priest went to Norfolk without the archbishop's authorization. Maréchal was not inactive. He wrote to a friend, Cardinal Antonio Dugnani, complaining of the harm done by Rome's eagerness to listen to troublemakers. He also made a visitation of the diocese, on which he reported in a letter dated October 16, 1818. He stressed the need for native American priests and felt that next most acceptable were Englishmen. Belgians, Frenchmen, and Germans were, in his judgment, "the best of missionaries," and some of the Irish also merited praise. But, he told the cardinals at the Propagation of the Faith, too many Irish priests were drunkards or ambitious schemers and they were at the root of disturbances at "Charleston, Norfolk, Philadelphia, etc., etc." Maréchal was extremely optimistic about Catholic prospects in the United States, but emphasized the steps needed to overcome internal dissensions which were related to the trustee system and the widespread notion that Catholics could choose and dismiss pastors as they pleased.

Maréchal wanted a new diocese based at Charleston and recommended a French-speaking English priest as first bishop. He explicitly ruled out an Irishman or a Frenchman. He was not the only one thinking about a bishop in the southern part of Baltimore's jurisdiction. From New York Bishop Connolly promoted Thomas Carbry's cause, while the Norfolk trustees on January 4, 1819, proposed to Irish Franciscan Richard Hayes that he first seek episcopal consecration from the Jansenist archbishop of Utrecht in the Netherlands and then come to the United States. The embarrassed Hayes, no party to the scheme, quickly reported it to Rome and to the archbishop of Dublin. The trustees memorialized Thomas Jefferson and the members of the United States Congress, denouncing the "foreign interference" of the Holy See in their affairs. Maréchal answered with a pastoral letter explaining the historical and canonical situation. Roman authorities finally produced their solution in the summer of 1820, one hardly calculated to satisfy the archbishop of Baltimore. Dioceses were set up at Charleston and Richmond, both headed by Irish bishops, John England in South Carolina and Patrick Kelly in Virginia. Carbry was ordered back to Ireland. Maréchal was reduced to reading a formal protest at his first meeting with the hapless Kelly. The latter lost no time in exchanging his American see for that of Waterford and Lismore, and retreated to Ireland. The net result was to leave Virginia stripped of priests. But Propaganda had the last word. Maréchal was informed that his protest was out of line: the archbishop of Baltimore had no right to be consulted in the choice of suffragan bishops in his province.

IX

The Era of the Common Man

The Whig leadership that had been the hallmark of the Catholic community since the days of the Carrolls declined in the years leading to civil war. Few Catholics achieved political prominence. Of the generation born during the Revolution, William Gaston—Georgetown's first student—became a congressman and later an associate justice of the North Carolina Supreme Court. He was responsible in 1835 for repeal of the statute in his home state denying Catholics the franchise.[1] Maryland's Roger Brooke Taney, a Federalist turned Jacksonian Democrat, was successively United States attorney general and secretary of the treasury. His contributions to the development of constitutional interpretation during nearly thirty years (1836–64) as chief justice of the United States were impressive, but were overshadowed by his opinion in the Dred Scott case.[2] Later Catholic cabinet members were James Campbell, postmaster general under Franklin Pierce, and the controversial John Floyd, who was Buchanan's secretary of war and then became, until dismissed by Jefferson Davis, a Confederate general. Campbell served as liaison with the government when Archbishop Bedini came in 1853 with plans for a nunciature in Washington. Taney had been one of the attorneys invited in 1829 to formal consultation with the bishops of the First Provincial Council of Baltimore on questions of legal incorporation. They met with the bishops in full session, gave their advice, were thanked, and left the meeting. It was the only occasion in this period when lay people were involved at this level of church government. Their appearance was brief and limited to technical points within their special expertise, a notable devolution from 1789 when the Catholic community felt it appropriate that their joint congratulations to President Washington be signed by the bishop-elect and lay leaders from the church's principal centers.

During his trip to the United States in the early 1830s, Alexis de Tocqueville found American Catholics "very submissive and very sincere." They were "faithful to the observances of their religion . . . fervent and zealous in the belief of their doctrines," yet "they constitute the most republican and most democratic class in the United States." It came as no surprise. Logically, the Frenchman thought, Protestantism promoted independence, while Catholicism emphasized human equality: "It confounds all distinctions of society at the foot of the same altar, even as they are confounded in the sight of God." There were also local factors encouraging the democratic spirit among American Catholics: their poverty, social inferiority and minority status. The Catholic clergy, he noticed, divided their intellectual world in half: "Doctrines of revealed religion" were accepted without discussion, but "political truths" were left to free inquiry.[3]

Tocqueville's summary conclusion was that "Catholics in the United States are at the same time the most submissive believers and the most independent citizens." Between 1790 and the outbreak of the Civil War, those believers and citizens grew from a tiny group of thirty-five thousand at Bishop Carroll's appointment to a community of over three million, nearly a third of whom entered the country in the decade before the attack on Fort Sumter. The old Anglo-American church was swallowed by the church of the immigrants before the century reached its mid-point.

There were many sources of diversity. Catholic immigrants early in the century came mostly from northwestern Europe. The varying cultural strains of their common religion were blended in the American amalgam, though not without difficulty. The sheer numbers of their onslaught—a quarter-million in the 1830s, seven hundred thousand in the next decade, nearly a million in the ten years before the Civil War—overwhelmed the staid old Whig church. Many shed their ancestral religion along with allegiance to European princes, but most retained it. Those who remained Catholics, and their descendants, became American Catholicism.

The number of those who came over to Catholicism from the Protestant churches was perhaps fewer than those who travelled that road in the opposite direction. The importance of the converts was in the quality of their contribution to the life and style of the community. Best known was the widowed Elizabeth Ann Bayley Seton, who became a member of St. Peter's congregation in New York City in 1805.[4] Certainly dramatic was the entrance into the Roman Catholic Church in 1816 of the Episcopalian Barber family of Claremont, New Hampshire: the Reverend Virgil Barber, his wife and children, and, shortly thereafter, Virgil's father, the Reverend Daniel Barber. The younger Barbers separated. He became a Jesuit priest and in 1822 started New Hampshire's first Catholic parish at Claremont. Mrs. Barber and four daughters became nuns, their only son a Jesuit priest.[5] Over the next several decades converts to Catholicism included a half-dozen future bishops, including Archbishops James Roosevelt Bayley of Baltimore and James Wood of Philadelphia.[6] There were priests like Thomas S. Preston, long to be a conservative force in New York Catholic affairs, and Isaac Hecker with his friends who in 1858 founded the Paulist Fathers.[7] A story which set the disciplinary requirements of two Christian churches on collision course was that of Cornelia Peacock Connolly and her husband Pierce, an Episcopalian clergyman in Natchez, Mississippi. They became Roman Catholics in 1835 and in 1844 signed a formal act of separation to allow Pierce to become a Catholic priest. Cornelia decided to become a nun. At Bishop Nicholas Wiseman's invitation, she settled in England, establishing there in 1846 the Sisters of the Holy Child Jesus. Three years later her husband, who had changed his mind about the Catholic priesthood and wished to resume married life, sued in the English courts for restoration of conjugal rights. His action was ultimately unsuccessful.[8]

Vermont-born and raised in upper New York State, Orestes A. Brownson stormed through the Presbyterian, Universalist, and Unitarian churches and planned his own "Church of the Future" before entering the Catholic Church under the guidance of Bishop John B. Fitzpatrick of Boston in 1844. A political and social thinker (an intuitionist who inclined to ontologism in his philosophical tastes), Brownson was by turns liberal and conservative but always controversial. From 1838 to 1842 he edited the *Boston Quarterly Review,* and from 1844 to 1864 and again from 1873 to 1875 *Brownson's Quarterly Review.* His special preoccupations included the role of authority in democratic society, the relationship of church to state and the larger question of Christianity's relationship to society.[9]

Interesting people abounded in what some have seen as an American "Oxford Movement." The Episcopal Bishop of North Carolina, Levi Silliman Ives, became a convert in 1852 and later a moving spirit in such welfare work as the New York Catholic Protectory. Journalists who joined the Catholic Church included John R. G. Hassard, Joseph Ripley Chandler, a onetime Grand Master Mason and later Minister to the Bourbon court of the Two Sicilies under President Buchanan, James A. McMaster, longtime *Freeman's Journal* editor, and Jedediah V. Huntington, editor of *The Metropolitan Record*. Among scientists, Columbia College astronomer William H. Anderson joined the Catholic Church on his return from a United States expedition to the Dead Sea in 1848. Physicians William Edmonds Horner (1839) and Moses L. Linton (1844) were prominent converts. The first was a well-known anatomist, the second founded in 1848 the first American medical monthly, the *St. Louis Medical and Surgical Journal,* and became president (1845) of the initial American Conference of the St. Vincent de Paul Society.

For many immigrants New York City was a way station through which they passed as quickly as possible. Others stayed. Swiss immigrant and restaurateur John Delmonico was a mainstay of Transfiguration parish in the late 1830s, when Cuban refugee and *independentista* Felix Varela was pastor to its largely Irish congregation.[10] A fixture in old New York was the black man called by many "our St. Pierre," the fashionable ladies' hairdresser Pierre Toussaint. Brought as a slave from Santo Domingo in 1787 he impressed Catholics and Protestants alike for over sixty years by the obvious holiness of his life. People remembered that "in sickness and in trouble he was always there." "It is the *whole* which strikes me when thinking of him," a friend recalled, "his perfect Christian benevolence, displaying itself not alone in words but in daily deeds, his entire faith, love and charity." The priest at his funeral in 1853 said simply that there was none in the parish his superior "in devotion and zeal for the church and for the glory of God."[11] A sharper ingredient in the Catholic mix arrived from Scotland in 1819: James Gordon Bennett, ex-seminarian and gadfly of bishops—John Hughes of New York was a favorite target. From 1835 until he received the last sacraments from Archbishop McCloskey in 1872, the editorial columns of Bennett's *New York Herald* relieved a steady diet of acerbic political commentary with pungent observations on the city's Catholic ecclesiastical scene.[12]

The Philadelphia Catholic community was never dull. Mathew Carey concentrated on his career as publisher and political economist. He promoted Henry Clay's "American System" and had time left over for such good causes as the 1830s crusade on behalf of a just wage for the city's working women. His Protestant grandson, Henry C. Lea, became a historian of the Inquisition and of auricular confession. Francis M. Drexel arrived early in the century from Austria to lay the foundations of an investment banking house. Of his sons, only one remained Catholic and he established the trust that long supported the work of the Sisters of the Blessed Sacrament for the Indians and Colored People, which his daughter Katharine founded in 1891.[13]

The ambitious young Austrian banker and the onetime Irish revolutionary publisher were joined on Philadelphia's stage by a throwback to an earlier age in the person of Robert Walsh. Educated at Georgetown and Baltimore's St. Mary's College, he was a well-to-do Federalist in the aristocratic tradition, a disciple of Adam Smith, congenitally hostile to Jeffersonians, Napoléon Bonaparte, and President James Madison. A cultured literateur, he has been described as "instrumental in shaping the neoclassical and Scottish common sense philosophical influence in American criticism of the early national period."[14] Walsh launched the first quarterly review in the United States, the *American Review of History and Politics* (1811–12), was among the founders of the *National Gazette and Literary Register* (1820), and for a decade (1827–37) published the *American Quarterly Review*.

But lay leadership failed. One factor was the snail-like growth and inadequacy of the church's commitment to higher education. Some Catholics, Taney among them, attended Protestant colleges. Others went to Catholic schools, but the standard fell below that of the pre-Revolutionary English Catholic colleges on the continent and European universities attended by Catholic Marylanders and Pennsylvanians. Georgetown meandered along, a sleepy southern school in a sleepy southern town. The granting of its pontifical charter in 1833–a year before the Catholic University of Louvain was resurrected to become a model of the type—could have been the key to creation in the nation's capital of a Catholic university, but that broad level of vision was beyond Georgetown. Funds, too, were lacking.[15] A series of Jesuit ventures misfired: the New York Literary Institution at what became Fifth Avenue and Fiftieth Street; a day college in downtown Washington; the college at Frederick, a town whose future had as premise the fact that it was a day's convenient stage-coach trip from Baltimore.

At Emmitsburg, the diocesan priests' Mount St. Mary's College (founded in 1808) survived, and Archbishop Martin Spalding of Baltimore once thought of it as a site for a university, but it never became a major educational center.[16] The Sulpicians' Baltimore college (founded in 1799) ceased to exist and was supplanted by the Jesuits' Loyola College (1852). Bishop John Hughes opened St. John's College at Fordham (1841) and sold it to French Jesuits who had fled the 1830 revolution to take on a backwoods Kentucky school.[17] In 1843, Bishop Benedict Fenwick, S.J., invited Maryland Jesuits to assume responsibility for the College of the Holy Cross in Worcester, Massachusetts. Eight years later, the Jesuits started St. Joseph's College in Philadelphia, where Augustinians had begun Villanova College in 1842, the same year in which Brothers of the Congregation of Holy Cross led by Father Edward Sorin had dubbed a log cabin in northern Indiana the University of Notre Dame du Lac.[18] Diocesan priests founded St. Louis University (1818) and Mobile's Spring Hill

College (1830), both later Jesuit-staffed. At Cincinnati in 1829 the diocese grandly named its college and preparatory school the Athenaeum of Ohio.

Secondary and tertiary education often fused, as Isaac Hecker indicated in a letter to Orestes Brownson in the summer of 1844, just before both entered the Catholic Church. Hecker had visited Worcester's College of the Holy Cross, where he found that:

> No scholar is taken under 8 years of age. Of the twenty five there are I think no more than 5 or 8 young men, the rest average from the ages of 8 to 12 & 14. . . .

Prayers, daily mass, study in a common hall, recitations, and set periods for recreation made up a day that began at 5 A.M. Coeducation was not thought of, nor even female staff:

> There are no women there for obvious reasons. Protestant slander would be ready on any pretext to injure them & cast suspicion and vile abuse upon them.

Hecker had reservations about the quality of the college's Jesuit professors: they were well but narrowly educated, good in discussing "the Scriptural and historic grounds of their Church," but "as for its philosophic basis they seem to me profoundly ignorant."

> These men have done well to keep & preserve the Church but a new generation must take their place if Catholicism is to be reestablished in the world. . . . These men *seem to me* are wanting [sic] that vital consciousness of divine eternal life and high spiritual aspirations which have animated so many of the children of the true Church. I had to ask them repeatedly if that was the ground on which they based a true Christian life, the lowest and the least that the Church demands of us. . . . Oh my dear friend there must be something deeper, more eternal and invisible than what we see with the outward or sense [sic] that can attract a soul to the Church as she now is in this country.[19]

Education for women had begun with the Ursulines at New Orleans in 1727.[20] Poor Clares and then Alice Lalor and her companions conducted what became Georgetown Visitation Convent. Mother Seton had a school on Paca Street in Baltimore in 1808 and opened the first free parochial school at Emmitsburg in 1810. Boys and girls were admitted. By 1852 there were one hundred academies, seminaries, and institutes for women throughout the East and Midwest, chiefly staffed by women's religious communities. They corresponded to "colleges" for men and like them were geared to more upwardly mobile Catholics. John Hughes expressed their universal purpose when he explained why he started the college at Fordham:

What was our object . . . in this undertaking? It was, that the Catholic parents of this diocese and elsewhere, who could afford it, should have an opportunity of educating their sons with safety to their faith and morals, and yet so as to qualify them to take an honorable part in the more elevated walks of public and social life.[21]

The relatively few affluent Catholics were among the patrons of private church-related schools, but most students came from families which found even modest fees a burden. Reduced tuition for the needy was common practice. Members of the religious communities which owned the schools helped make up deficits by after-school work. They offered private tutoring in art and music or, if they were priests, took on part-time pastoral work in local parishes. For most of the 19th century, secondary and college-level education was largely left to the religious communities. Catholic elementary schools, on the other hand, were primarily a parish responsibility. Their development took place just at a point where American education in general was undergoing reexamination.

Early 19th-century primary education had strong religious overtones. Bible-reading was standard, catechism instruction not unknown. Practice varied.[22] Boston schools were unabashedly Congregational, in a state where Congregationalism was until 1833 the established church. Parents less attached to Puritan ways sent their daughters to school with the Catholic Ursuline sisters in Charlestown. In New York City, church-related schools, including St. Peter's Catholic School (1800), shared in the common school fund from 1795 to 1825. This system broke down under pressure from public school advocates after Bethel Baptist Church in 1822 obtained an amendment to the school law, which allowed the church to use public funds for building purposes.[23] New York specifically exempted religious schools from state inspection, but in Lowell, Massachusetts, instructors were examined and appointed by the public school committee, which prescribed books, exercises, and courses. Lowell also subsidized Catholic schools and then, from 1835 to 1852, integrated them into the city system. Similar plans existed elsewhere, some into the 20th century. But a set of open clashes early in the 1800s, combined with new orientations in the public sector introduced by Horace Mann and others, led the Catholic Church in the United States to the momentous decision to go its own way in a venture in private education unique in concept and magnitude. Toward the end of the century, the bishops of the Third Plenary Council of Baltimore (1884) would phrase it as the wish that "every Catholic child in the land" might have "the benefit of a Catholic school." It was a dream never fulfilled, but in no other nation at any time in history has any non-governmental agency attempted the massive educational program begun in 19th-century America by Roman Catholics.[24]

The initial Catholic position was to "ask in" on systems for allocation of public school funds. At New York in 1840, Bishop John Hughes demanded for Catholics what he considered their just proportion of the common school fund. Since the cutoff of public funds fifteen years before, the situation had become desperate. Eight lay-taught parish schools in Manhattan could not begin to cope with the educational needs of twenty thousand immigrant children, most of them crammed with their families into the lower east side near the East River wharves. Governor William Seward saw the situation as a public welfare crisis and spoke of it in his January message to the state legislature. Because of differences in language and religion, immigrant children were not going to schools run by the "Public School Society." Catholic schools were inadequate and under-funded. Children of newly arrived Irish and German immigrants had one more reason for not attending school and stayed away in droves. Seward wanted public funding of schools "in which the immigrant children may be instructed by teachers speaking the same language with themselves and professing the same faith."[25]

The fat was in the fire, and John Hughes reached for a bellows. He faced formidable obstacles. The Public School Society was a private group of public-spirited citizens who operated on the assumption that schools should reflect the broad Christian tones of their own milieu. "Christian" and "Protestant" were synonymous. Protestant churches indeed differed in matters of polity and ritual, and these "sectarian" differences had no place in the common schools, but it was not difficult for them to agree on a common ground of generally acceptable Protestant hymns, prayers, and religious exercises. The Authorized Version of the Bible was read. It never seemed out of place that history, geography, and literature textbooks ridiculed "Romish" beliefs and practices. The situation, as far as Catholics were concerned, was not bettered when Horace Mann's influence began to be felt. Secretary of the Massachusetts Board of Education for a dozen years beginning in 1837, he was a Unitarian in revolt against Puritan indoctrination. But he also had no time for "that Vice Gerent of Hell the Pope of Rome" and his minions. The Bible, deistic natural theology, and ethics, but under no circumstances "sectarian" dogma, were parts of his formula. His ideas won wide acceptance.

Hughes was not daunted. He had leaflets printed and attracted screaming supporters to public rallies. The bishop challenged representatives from the Public School Society and prominent local ministers to a succession of debates. It was an art form at which he was a past master. The Protestant *Observer* could only regret that "such powers of mind, such varied and extensive learning and such apparent sincerity of purpose were trammeled with a fake system of religion." Hughes needed a dramatic gesture and decided to make it in the 1841 elections in the city for the state legislature. Seward, his ally and ever after his friend, was a Whig. Most immigrant Catholics were Democrats. But Democratic leaders had ignored Catholic complaints about the schools. Working with Whig state boss Thurlow Weed, Hughes entered in the legislative race what he called the "Carroll Hall ticket." Ten Democrats sympathetic to his demands received endorsement. Three others found themselves opposed by an independent candidate. The strategem worked. No independents were elected, but they were effective spoilers. Only the ten Democrats unopposed by a Hughes "independent" won. The message was heard in Albany, and a plan for state control of schools was adopted. The Public School Society did not die without a fight: some of its members moved on to the new Board of Education in New York City and there re-instituted Bible reading. But in wards with heavy Catholic populations local control was established, and many found the new public schools satisfactory and sent their children to them. Hughes had failed to win public funds for church-controlled schools. He and the American bishops headed in another direction. The future they saw was peopled by religious sisters and brothers teaching in parochial schools. Efforts to integrate religious training with the public school system were largely abandoned.

In his 1792 pastoral letter, John Carroll, who had not at first thought separate Catholic schools necessary, stressed the importance of "the virtuous and Christian instruction of youth," and expressed the hope that some of those educated at Georgetown would return home as teachers.[26] At the First Provincial Council of Baltimore in 1829 the bishops announced:

> we judge it absolutely necessary that schools should be established in which the young may be taught the principles of faith and morality, while being instructed in letters.[27]

At the First Plenary Council of Baltimore (1852), the bishops exhorted themselves "through the bowels of the mercy of God" to "see that schools be established in connection with all the churches of their diocese," and that provision for support of competent teachers be made from church revenues.[28] The pattern was set, with much of the impulse coming from the west, where the Second Provincial Council of Cincinnati (1858), representing the Ohio River dioceses, stated flatly:

> It is the judgment of the Fathers of the Council that all pastors of souls are bound, under pain of mortal sin, to provide a Catholic school in every parish or congregation subject to them, where this can be done.[29]

The parochial school became a fixture in parishes throughout the nation, even if the ideal of a Catholic school for every Catholic child was never realized. A major advocate of parochial schools was the Redemptorist John N. Neumann, bishop of Philadelphia from 1852 to 1860. A humble, saintly man, he was canonized by Pope Paul VI in 1977.

Internal church structure on the east coast remained remarkably stable through the first three-quarters of the 19th century. The original diocese of Baltimore became a metropolitan archdiocese in 1808 and retained that role for the southeastern United States until an archbishop was appointed to Atlanta in 1962. After two Maryland archbishops, Carroll and Neale, there was the French interlude of Maréchal (1817–28), who was followed by English-born James Whitfield (1828–34), and then another Marylander, Samuel Eccleston, S.S. (1834–51). Francis P. Kenrick (1851–63) was Irish, but his successor Martin John Spalding (1864–72) came of an old Maryland-Kentucky family, and James Roosevelt Bayley (1872–77) was a convert of English Protestant antecedents. All through this period and into the time of Cardinal James Gibbons (1877–1921), Baltimore played the role of primatial American diocese, although denied the official designation by Rome.

Fifteen other dioceses were established in the East before the Civil War. New York became an archdiocese in 1850 under John Hughes. To the west, the most significant growth area in the century's first quarter was the old Northwest Territory, bounded by the Mississippi and Ohio rivers and the Great Lakes. Along with the southern border states of Kentucky and Tennessee, the region was designated the diocese of Bardstown in 1808. That episcopal seat was moved to Louisville in 1841. By then the real nucleus of church development had shifted north across the Ohio to Cincinnati, where Edward Fenwick, O.P., was bishop from 1821 to 1832 and John B. Purcell for a half-century (1833–1883).

Ohio was a land where cleared forests were turning into rich farmland. Paddle-wheel steamers plied the Ohio River and Lake Erie, flatboats floated down to the Mississippi, the Great National Road reached Columbus by 1833 and Vandalia, Illinois, in 1838. Canals and railroads followed. The country was settled by Revolutionary War veterans, migrants from Virginia and North Carolina, and immigrants from the German states and the British Isles. A population distinctively American developed, self-reliant, wedded to the land, known for sharp business sense. In religion they were heavily Calvinist: Scotch-Irish Presbyterians, New England Congregationalists, Campbellites and Stoneites, Baptists and Methodists.

The frontier was hardscrabble. Some Catholics clustered in the jumble of wooden shacks and budding mansions called Cincinnati. Others eked out a hard living on lonesome farms. With mass vestments and altar supplies bundled into saddlebags, missionary priests rode narrow trails and dusty roads to minister to their congregations. Rewards could be great. John B. Lamy, future Archbishop of Santa Fe, arrived in southern Ohio in 1839 from France. He soon found himself involved in a community in which parishioners took with equal zest to charitable projects and to religious exercises. Not only did they drop other work, he noted, to help raise a church roof, but they also formed a fine choir. From Newark, Ohio, he provided this vignette of church life in the West:

> We have a very good choir of German Catholics with some fair instruments. They sing very well, but almost all in German, except the Kyrie, Gloria and Credo in Latin, till they get some books of church music.[30]

Growth was rapid. Bishop Flaget had found in the vast diocese a handful of French traders and their families, along with the Maryland Catholic pioneers of the Kentucky church. A half-dozen years later Fenwick made a more extensive report from Cincinnati. German and Irish immigrants were arriving. French and Canadian Catholics occupied trading posts from Detroit to Green Bay and Prairie du Chien. Ottawa and Chippewa Indians lived along Michigan's St. Joseph River and around the Straits of Mackinac. Blackbird, the devout Catholic chief of the Ottawa, had been educated by the Montréal Sulpicians. In 1827 he made possible the opening of a school at Arbre Croche, and in 1832 Fenwick sent two American Indian seminarians from it to Rome's Urban College. Of the two, William Maccodabinasse ("Blackbird"), son of the chief, died in Rome in June 1833 of complications from an injury sustained before he left America. August Hamelin, part Indian, part Canadian, gave up his studies because of poor health. Back in northern Michigan, he was elected in 1835 chief of the Ottawa and Chippewa.[31]

Organization followed population growth. Dioceses multiplied: Detroit (1833), Vincennes (1834), Nashville (1837), Chicago and Milwaukee (both 1843), Covington (1853), Fort Wayne, Sault Ste. Marie, and Quincy (all 1857). There were variations on familiar eastern themes. Common schools and a variety of public charitable institutions antedated formal Catholic organization in most older American cities. West of the Appalachians, Catholic hospitals, refuges, and asylums were part of the urban welfare scene from the beginning. It made for a psychological difference. The trans-Mississippi West shared the development. St. Louis, becoming a separate diocese in 1826, was gateway to the Great Plains for church as well as nation. The first bishop (1827–43) was a Vincentian priest from Italy, Joseph Rosati, C.M. Next came an Irishman, Peter Richard Kenrick. Made archbishop in 1847, he did not retire until 1895. Aside from Oregon City (1846) and San Francisco (1853), St. Louis remained the sole archiepiscopal see west of the Mississippi until 1875 when John B. Lamy was named archbishop in Santa Fe and John M. Henni in Milwaukee. New Orleans, where Anthony Blanc, bishop since 1835, was archbishop from 1850 to 1860, was the south-central states' metropolitan see.[32]

European mission-aid societies played a significant role in midwestern church growth. Early bishops were not shy about begging. Edward Fenwick informed Leo XII in 1823 that his diocese of Cincinnati was "the most destitute of all spiritual and temporal resources in the whole Christian world."[33] The pope and some of the Roman cardinals reached into their own purses to help him. DuBourg and Rosati of St. Louis were notably successful in obtaining funds from the Roman Congregation for Propagation of the Faith. But the main source of contributions was a new kind of popular organization which grew up in 19th-century Europe and to a great extent took the place of the largess once distributed among overseas missions by Catholic sovereigns—the mission-aid society.[34]

The senior mission-aid society was the French Society for the Propagation of the Faith, lay-directed and founded at Lyons in 1822. Small regular contributions from a large number of people were pooled under control of lay-directed central committees at Lyons and Paris. These committees allocated funds as they saw fit, but only to overseas missions which submitted detailed reports, including a careful financial accounting. The Roman Congregation for Propagation of the Faith, the pope's missionary department, acted in an advisory capacity, but its suggestions were not mandatory. Bishop DuBourg helped organize the Society, and Bishop Flaget was an influential adviser, but the organization's beneficence extended far beyond Louisiana and Kentucky.

Similar work was carried on by two German-based societies. The Leopoldine Foundation, established during the winter of 1828–29 by Emperor Franz I of Austria and named for his daughter, the Archduchess Leopoldine, Empress of Brazil, focused on mission activity in the United States and Canada. Frederick Résé, later Bishop of Detroit, was instrumental in its foundation, as he was a decade later in persuading King Ludwig I of Bavaria in 1838 to set up the Ludwig's Mission Society, a Munich-based counterpart to the French Society for the Propagation of the Faith. The gallophobe king of Bavaria was anxious to combine support for the church with efforts to preserve "German spirit." The chauvinism did not pass without complaint, but support from any quarter was welcome, and American Catholicism was enormously indebted to these corporate charities, and to a host of individual European benefactors as well.

A tradition of church councils unmatched in Western Catholicism developed in the United States during the 19th century. But the collaborative thrust operated only on the horizontal plane. Priests, "the second order of the hierarchy," were kept firmly in their place. In an 1852 letter to King Maximilian of Bavaria, Benedictine Abbot Boniface Wimmer explained the bishops' attitude:

> The bishop can expect no support from the state against refractory priests, and much less from the Protestant, or better, atheistic state and the democratic inclinations of its citizens. Accordingly, they are naturally distrustful of every attempt to deprive them more or less of their unrestricted power. . . . [35]

Priests generally were no more inclined to share responsibility for conducting church affairs with laity than were bishops to share it with priests. With some understatement, Orestes Brownson noted:

> The modern world is to a great extent laic, and if the laity are not frankly recognized and freely permitted to do whatever laymen can do, we shall find that they will undertake . . . to do more than they have any right to do. . . . [36]

Isaac Hecker later pleaded for a lay Catholic congress, declaring: "The blood must circulate through the limbs, otherwise we [clergy] shall die of apoplexy and the laity of paralysis."[37]

But other sentiments prevailed. Handed a written constitution by one of his congregations, Kentucky missionary Stephen Badin huffed that the clergy were mentioned "only as the obsequious servants of 'Their Mighty Highnesses,' the laity."[38] Philadelphia Bishop Francis P. Kenrick once complained of future Bishop Michael O'Connor's naïveté: "He has not learned how hard it is to uphold sacred rights when laymen meddle in the affairs of the church."[39] John Hughes made the point very clear when he put it to Orestes Brownson: "I will suffer no man in my diocese that I cannot control. I will either put him down, or he shall put me down." On another occasion, in one of their friendlier exchanges, Brownson returned the compliment by informing the bishop that he found him "capricious, tyrannical, unjust, occupied with your own glory, and anxious to discourage every enterprise and talent which did not reflect honor on yourself."[40] Still, American Roman Catholicism, presbyterian in its first century and a half, and with a respectable tradition of lay participation in that colonial phase, in the 19th century entered on a course of development strongly episcopal and, with a peculiarly American twist, papal.

A reforming decree of the Council of Trent ordered that provincial councils—formal meetings of the bishops of an ecclesiastical region—be held every three years. Nowhere was this better observed than in the United States during the middle years of the 19th century.[41] Seven provincial councils of Baltimore were held between 1829 and 1849, and plenary national councils followed in 1852, 1866, and 1884. Prime mover in initiating the series of Baltimore councils was the thirty-four-year-old Cork priest John England, who arrived in Charleston, South Carolina, in 1820 as its first Catholic bishop. The triennial Baltimore meetings were often repetitive, but they contributed to a sense of unity in the growing American church. They also provided the occasion for some forthright statements of identity, as when in 1837 the Third Provincial Council of Baltimore defended American Catholic patriotism, protesting that they did not "acknowledge any civil or political supremacy, or power over us, in any foreign potentate or power, though that potentate might be the chief pastor of our church."

John England also made a substantial, although ultimately fruitless contribution to church government on the local level. He organized in his diocese a system of conventions, one in each state, together with a general convention of "the Church of the Diocese." He was conscious both of the signs of the times and of the Catholic need for continuity with the church's authentic tradition; as he indicated when listing in his *Diurnal* the steps he had taken in preparing his decision:

> having paid great attention to the state of several churches in America and studied as deeply as I could the character of the government and people, and the circumstances of my own flock, as well as the canons and usages of the Holy Roman Catholic Church and having advised with religious men and Clergymen and lawyers. . . . [42]

The conventions met in houses of clergy and laity. They were consultative bodies, with provision made for representation to the bishop in doctrinal areas reserved to his sole competence. The constitution included a statement of Catholic belief, to which all were expected to subscribe. Priests were described as preachers of the doctrine of Christ and ministers of the sacraments. They were to manage church property in cooperation with lay vestries. The constitution worked while John England lived. It did not survive him. No other bishop imitated it. The system remains one of the might-have-beens of American Catholic history.[43]

The first age of the Catholic Church in the United States came to an end in 1851 when Rome-educated Francis P. Kenrick succeeded Samuel Eccleston at Baltimore. Eccleston had presided over five Baltimore councils. His successor, with the title of apostolic delegate, chaired the First Plenary Council of the American church in 1852. Six archbishops and twenty-six bishops met on behalf of a church which counted over one and

a half million members and fifteen hundred priests. There were no startling results. Previous legislation was consolidated and confirmed. As the
nation moved toward the final confrontation between North and South, it
was significant that the council did not say a word on the subject of
slavery.

X

Immigrants Become the Church

Launched in the 1830s, Andrew Jackson's Indian policy effectively eliminated most original native Americans from the United States east of the Mississippi. They were replaced by a new breed, displaced Europeans still seeking, a half-century after independence, a secure national identity. Revolutionary memories had grown dim. Veterans' ranks were thinner each Fourth of July. France's revolution had shocked the sensibilities of some, while others applauded. The buoyant spirit of the frontier, which on Jackson's inauguration day whooped through the White House, had by 1845 found itself an identifying slogan. The Puritan quest for establishment in America of God's new Israel was secularized as America's "Manifest Destiny." Results were tangible. The Gulf Coast and the Florida peninsula had become American in 1821. Negotiation with Great Britain averted war over the Oregon Territory and squared off the nation's northwest corner. War with Mexico yielded the Rio Grande frontier, the Southwest, and California. These formative years of a distinctively American nationality were marked by recurrent boom and bust financial cycles and the battles over tariffs and free trade which have been the bane of school children ever since. All the while, the exploding nation was shaken and ultimately would be torn apart in the epic struggle over slavery, whether new states should be "slave" or "free," the struggle finally whether "slave" ought to be either a word in the American vocabulary or a human fact in the nation's life.

116

Religion and the churches shared in the American identification process. The symbols of civil religion which fell into place were traceably Christian and even Calvinist Christian. Formally organized religion recovered from *fin de siècle* doldrums. Rationalistically inclined New Englanders grouped as Unitarians and Universalists. Some became transcendentalists. Mainline Puritan heirs somehow reconciled Calvinist heritage with the conviction, explicit or implicit, that not all human possibility had disappeared at the fall. Evangelicalism and myriad energetic agencies of Benevolent Empire blossomed. The freshly fashioned gospel of Americanism leaped the continent and opened the "Yale of the Pacific" in Berkeley.[1] It crossed oceans to Burma and the Sandwich Islands, early targets of Protestant missionary zeal. The nation's own mid-continent frontier, where, editor William Stone worried, seven of eight Protestant Kentuckians belonged to no Christian church, developed its own initation rite, the camp meeting down by the riverside. Revivalist religion flourished in a second Great Awakening reminiscent of the evangelical fervor that had gripped the eastern seaboard during the mid-18th century's First Great Awakening.[2]

During the first sixty years of the 19th century, immigration, overwhelmingly from northwestern Europe, was a tremendous factor as the nation's population grew from five to thirty-one million. John Jay had once argued in the *Federalist Papers:*

> Providence has been pleased to give this one connected country to one connected people—a people descended from the same ancestors, speaking the same language, professing the same religion, attached to the same principles of government, very similar in their manners and customs.[3]

That homogeneity was shattered, and the process was painful. The Revolution was made by a people 85 percent British. If only 10 percent were church members, their heritage was overwhelmingly Protestant. But with victory won, anti-Catholicism went into brief remission in early Federal days. John Carroll and Jean Cheverus were respected men. Their portraits were done by Stuart and they moved easily in Baltimore and Boston society. Other straws blew in a gentle wind. Delivering the Dudleian lecture for 1813, President Kirkland of Harvard allowed that "we may . . . abate much of that abhorrence of papists which our fathers felt themselves obliged to maintain and inculcate." He even dared imagine "it may be thought lawful for us to believe in the compatibility of the Romish faith with a capacity for salvation and admit the possible, nay more, the presumptive Christianity of a virtuous and devout Roman Catholic."[4] Ten years later, a Catholic priest, William Taylor, was invited to give the invocation at the opening session of the Great and General Court of the Commonwealth of Massachusetts. It was November 4, 1823, the eve of Guy Fawkes Day, when England and its American colonies had celebrated with anti-Catholic overtones the failure of the conspirators in the 1605 Gunpowder Plot to blow up the Houses of Parliament.[5]

The mood changed in the 1820s. Benevolent Empire and evangelical revivalism were in full swing. The 1825 Dudleian lecturer thought it "an unjustifiable extension of what is termed liberality . . . to view the errors of Rome as unimportant and trivial."[6] Anti-Catholic feeling returned as a fixed feature on the American landscape. The social turmoil of the 1830s helped it along. Industrialization and urbanization—the shaping of a cosmopolitan society—threatened the values of village-green America. That dark specter, the city, loomed evil on the horizon, and it was peopled by teeming hordes of odd-smelling, odd-looking, odd-speaking immigrants. Too many of them ended up in the penitentiary and workhouse. They drank too much, and some even did so on Sundays. A startling percentage were Roman Catholics.

The Reverend Robert Baird, D.D., made his first missionary trip to Europe for the American and Foreign Christian Union in 1835. Six years later he finished the first draft of *Religion in America*. "Of all the forms of error in the United States," he wrote, "Romanism is by far the most formidable." Dissecting the elements in the nation's Catholic problem, he listed the following:

1. The simultaneous efforts which have been of late made by her hierarchy on many of the States to obtain a portion of the funds destined to the support of public schools, and employ them for the support of their own sectarian schools, in which neither the Sacred Scriptures, nor any portions of them, are read, but avowedly sectarian instruction is given. . . .
2. The efforts making by the hierarchy to bring all the property of the Roman Catholic church—church edifices, especially priests' houses, cemeteries [sic], schools, colleges, hospitals, etc., into the possession of the bishops. . . .
3. The disposition, long well known, of some of the leaders of the great political parties, to court the Romanists for their votes at the elections, and the willingness of the hierarchy to be regarded as a "great power in the State," and as, in fact, holding the "balance of power."[7]

Catholic schools, the publicity given to disputes between bishops and trustees, the concentration of wealth and power in clerical and episcopal hands, and the inclination of immigrants, particularly the Irish, to affiliate with big-city political machines, all were early and long-lived complaints against Catholics.

Hostility to immigrants, particularly Irish immigrants, was widespread. In Boston in 1844, Yankee politico Joseph Brickingham regretted the "plenitude of generosity which has induced us to feed the hungry [and] clothe the naked":

> We have warmed to life the torpid viper and the fanged adder to spit their venom upon our dear and blood-bought privileges, our sacred, most cherished institutions.

The result was horrendous:

> Irishmen fresh from the bogs of Ireland are led up to vote like dumb brutes . . . to vote down intelligent, honest, native Americans.[8]

Two prominent preachers emphasized religious aspects of the catastrophe which threatened. The Reverend Lyman Beecher warned in 1834:

> The Catholic Church holds now in darkness and bondage nearly half the civilized world. . . . It is the most skillful, powerful, dreadful system of corruption to those who wield it, and of slavery and debasement to those who live under it.[9]

The father of American theological liberalism, the Reverend Horace Bushnell of North Church, Hartford, summed it up in 1847: "Our first danger is barbarism [the influx of foreigners], Romanism next."[10]

Nativism and anti-Catholicism were not always synonymous, although usually linked. The pope's consul at New Orleans, attorney Charles Daron, advised Cardinal Giacomo Antonelli, papal secretary of state, that in Louisiana antiforeign feeling was not a religious issue. Many leading nativists were themselves Roman Catholics.[11] In 1855 they broke with the nativists' national organization because of the latter's refusal to drop its anti-Catholic stance, although they continued their opposition to recent immigrants.[12] Louisiana-born poet and missionary to the Choctaws Abbé Adrien Roquette made no secret of his nativist views.[13] Other Catholics had similar reservations about their co-religionists. Papal consul-general at New York Louis Binsse complained to Rome of problems caused by Irish addiction to strong drink. Orestes Brownson sensed a deeper malaise in the Catholic body. He wrote to Isaac Hecker:

> And how do you like on trial Catholicity? I grow more and more Catholic and less and less of a Protestant. My great trouble, after the regulation of my own spiritual life, is that the great mass of our Catholics are not Catholics. *Inter nos,* I do not like in general our Irish population. They have no clear understanding of their religion, and though they can fight for it, they do not seem able in general to die for it, and our *Irish* priests are either bent upon making money or else they are Irishmen before they are Catholics.[14]

The 1830s were a lively decade on the religious scene. Tract, Bible, and home missionary societies were part of the Benevolent Empire. The Protestant religious press grew, led by journals like the New York *Observer* (founded in 1823), outspoken, intolerant, ever ready to bait papists. A clutch of Catholic papers took up the gauntlet: John England's *United States Catholic Miscellany* (1822), the Irish-American New York *Truth-Teller* (1825), edited by Father Thomas Levins and featuring the satirical conversations of "Fergus McAlpin" and his cronies, habitués of the "Sheet Anchor" tavern near the Brooklyn navy yard, and the provocatively named *Jesuit,* launched at Boston by Bishop Benedict Fenwick in 1829. In Philadelphia, the future Bishop John Hughes started a Catholic tract society and, in 1833, a newspaper, the *Catholic Herald.*[15]

In a peculiar incident early in 1830, Hughes played an elaborate game with *The Protestant: Expositor of Popery.* Beginning in February, he contributed several articles under the pseudonym "Cranmer," attacking facets of Catholicism. Then on July 3, he revealed himself as "A Catholic," claiming that he had hoodwinked the paper's editors and backers (whom he described as "with the exception of about twenty . . . the clerical scum of the country") by including in his articles "as many lies as possible" about Catholicism.[16] Other debates followed. In a written series published alternately in Catholic and Protestant papers, Hughes took on aristocratic Kentuckian John Breckinridge, a Princeton graduate, a minister in Philadelphia, and son of Thomas Jefferson's attorney general. Heavy pedantry and personal insults were traded in about equal measure. After that exchange in the late winter of 1833, the protagonists met face to face before Philadelphia's Union Literary and Debating Institute in January 1835. Breckinridge remarked that "Popery is the malaria of the nations," and when challenged with the record of Protestant intolerance, replied that "our fathers learned to persecute from the church of Rome." "The principle of the American Constitution," he reminded the Irish-born priest, "is Protestantism." On another tack he commented that convents were "sinks of idleness if not corruption," while Hughes countered that Lyman Beecher, who had helped rouse the people of Charlestown, Massachusetts, against the Ursuline convent there, "wanted money, and like some of his brethren, knew that he could extort more by denouncing Popery than by preaching the gospel."[17]

A similar level was maintained in the 1837 debates between Bishop John B. Purcell and Alexander Campbell of the Disciples of Christ in Cincinnati, on which James H. Smylie has commented:

> The debates reflected mutual distrust. There was no sense of repentance or Christian forbearance on either side. Neither side listened as if it had anything to learn from the other. Each side tried to prove the other

side wrong. Each side had to defend itself against false accusations. Moreover, Campbell's assumption was that the whole matter would be settled by taking a vote among those who attended the debate.[18]

A spate of anti-Catholic writing followed. Yale graduate and portrait painter Samuel F. B. Morse arrived home from three years of European study in 1832. He was the son of a notorious anti-papist, the Reverend Jedidiah Morse of Charlestown, but his own feelings seem to have been largely shaped by an unfortunate confrontation with a papal soldier in Rome which he saw as symbolic of Catholic despotism. A dozen years later he would link Baltimore and Washington by the world's first successful telegraph line, but in 1834 Morse was more concerned with the message in his new book, *Foreign Conspiracy against the Liberties of the United States.* He feared Catholic schools, politicians, and immigrants. He was convinced that the Leopoldine Foundation was the advance agent in the United States of a monarchist-papist putsch. Morse's fears touched many a sympathetic nerve. While east coast Yankees shuddered at the Irish immigrant invasion, in the Midwest it was the Germans, with their schools, clubs, newspapers, and mysterious subsidies from Munich and Vienna, who struck fear into American hearts. The conviction ran wide and deep that Pope Gregory XVI, with royal and imperial help, planned a takeover of the Mississippi valley.[19]

Another anti-Catholic literary genre also flourished. Lurid tales of convent horrors had spiced battles leading to Catholic emancipation in Britain in 1829. American Puritans could now titillate their imaginations with homegrown tales: Rebecca Reed's *Six Months in a Convent* (1835) and Maria Monk's *Awful Disclosures of the Hotel Dieu Nunnery in Montreal* (1836). The first told of stark austerities experienced by a convert from Protestantism among the Ursuline sisters, the second ran to the pornographic, complete with tales of priest-nun rendezvous, murdered infants buried in convent cellars, and the like. Rebecca Reed and Maria Monk became familiar on the lecture circuit, sponsored by ministers like New York City's William C. Brownlee, editor of the *American Protestant Vindicator,* and Samuel Smith, who declared himself an ex-Catholic priest and called his Philadelphia paper *The Downfall of Babylon.* A familiar face surfaced at this time, Bishop Henry Conwell's old nemesis William Hogan, now an anti-Catholic lecturer and sometime cicerone to Maria Monk.[20]

The brewing storm brought violence, most dramatically at Charlestown, across the Charles River from Boston and home of Bunker Hill. John Thayer's legacy to Boston was a convent school run by sisters of the Ursuline community. Originally in downtown Boston, it had moved to an estate in Charlestown named "Mount Benedict." The Catholic school enjoyed heavy patronage from Protestant Bostonians galled by the Congregationalist establishment's control of the city's common schools. The awkward situation burst literally into flames in August 1834. Many factors were involved. Yankee-Irish antipathy was already a fact of Boston life. Insinuations about strange goings-on at Mount Benedict circulated. A lecture stop by Rebecca Reed did not help. Then one of the Ursulines, Elizabeth Harrison (Sister Mary John), left the convent in a fit of mental depression. Though she returned freely after a meeting with Bishop Benedict Fenwick, suspicions escalated. President Lyman Beecher of Cincinnati's Lane Theological Seminary, was in town. In sermons at three churches he denounced Catholicism, harping on a favorite theme: papal plans to take over the Mississippi valley. The Charlestown selectmen went to the convent and demanded admittance. The superior initially refused, reportedly letting drop the remark that the bishop had twenty thousand Irishmen ready to fight if need arose. Eventually town officials were allowed in and came out to say nothing was amiss. Meanwhile a crowd had gathered. The selectmen refused to summon help, declaring that the town's one policeman could maintain order. He could not. The mob evicted the nuns and girls, and then ransacked, robbed, and torched the building. Despite the extremely tense situation, further disaster was avoided. Bishop Fenwick did not loose his twenty thousand Irish. Boston's brahmins held a public meeting at Faneuil Hall to express regret for the incident, a sentiment not shared in the city's poorer wards and never translated by anyone into concrete action. Protestant families sheltered the evacuees on the night of the fire, but Catholics found neither help nor sympathy for efforts to rebuild the convent. Some rioters were eventually brought to court in a travesty of a trial. The attorney-general prosecuted; he could not question prospective jurors about their anti-Catholicism, but defense counsel was allowed to query the bishop and the convent superior about alleged immoralities. One rioter was convicted and pardoned. The state legislature rejected proposals to compensate the sisters; there was greater public sentiment for compensation to those who had been tried.[21]

Philadephia exploded during the spring and summer of 1844.[22] Bishop Francis P. Kenrick had for two years been negotiating with the Board of Public School Controllers about school-time religious observances—hymn sings, religious instruction, and the like—and on the required use of the King James Version of the Bible. Feeling ran high, particularly on the last point, and Kenrick was accused of wanting to exclude the Bible altogether from school use, a charge he consistently denied.

Political squabbles and antagonisms among competing fire companies contributed to the tension. Some volunteer companies were manned by Irish Catholics, others by Orangemen. Rioting broke out in earnest in early May. Sister Mary Gonzaga, stationed at St. Joseph's Orphan Asylum, reported to her superior at Emmitsburg:

> The commencement of the disturbance was chiefly this: Many of the citizens had assembled to adopt some resolutions with regard to political affairs, when some Irish Catholics insulted them and made such a noise that the Speaker could not be heard. One word brought on another until a battle ensued.[23]

The incident occurred when the nativist American Republican Party held a meeting in the afternoon of May 3 in the Irish industrial district of Kensington. Thirty homes and the headquarters of the Hibernia Hose Company went up in flames. Next came St. Michael's Church, the diocesan seminary, St. Augustine's Church, and the Augustinian priests' library. Five thousand books made a grand bonfire. Three policemen were sent to protect the orphan asylum, but Sister Gonzaga was not sanguine. She began her letter with the salutation:

> Perhaps before this letter shall have reached you, many of your poor children and their orphans may be launched into eternity, called to appear in the presence of their God and their Judge without a moment's preparation. We are in the midst of frightful dangers; a great portion of our peaceful city is the scene of a dreadful riot

By May 9 an uneasy truce prevailed. The bishop suspended all Catholic worship for a time. Despite denials from Kenrick and from George W. Biddle of the school board, a grand jury insisted on including among the causes of the riots "the efforts of a portion of the community to exclude the Bible from our public schools." "The imputation," Biddle wrote, "is wholly unfounded."[25]

The second phase of the Philadelphia riots came in July. Some seventy thousand citizens had paraded to honor the Protestant "Martyrs of Kensington." Rumors then spread that weapons were hidden in Southwark's St. Philip Neri Church. A hostile mob collected. Their temper was not improved by the discovery that there were in fact muskets concealed in St. Philip's. They had been supplied by the State Arsenal for self-defense. A militia unit, the Hibernia Greens, mustered to defend the church. Others brought up cannon and a battering ram. More militiamen arrived. After a confused night of shooting, fourteen soldiers and civilians lay dead or dying. Another fifty were wounded. Some of the victims were innocent bystanders caught in the crossfire. Others were militiamen trying to keep the peace. Still others fell among attackers and defenders of St.

Philip's. No religious census of the dead and wounded was taken, but the Catholics were widely blamed for the incident.

Bishop Kenrick was criticized for his passive role in Philadelphia's troubles. No such charge could be levelled at John Hughes in New York. When nativist disturbances threatened to come north, he demanded a meeting with outgoing Mayor Robert Morris, along with his newly elected successor, James Harper of the publishing family. The latter had been supported by a coalition of Whigs and nativist American Republicans. With an allusion that would not be missed to the fires welcoming Emperor Napoléon to Russia's capital in 1812, Hughes coldly informed the public officials that "if a single Catholic church is burned in New York, the city will become a second Moscow." "We can protect our own," he continued; "I come to warn you for your own good." With a parting suggestion that a squadron of cavalry be mobilized as well as an infantry unit, he left them. A planned nativist rally at city hall was cancelled.[26] The city was tense, but it did not burn.

The nativist movement had spilled over into national politics with the formation in June 1843 of the American Republican Party, soon to control both Philadelphia and New York. A year after the Philadelphia riots it reorganized as the Native American Party and met in national convention on the banks of the Schuylkill: War with Mexico was a momentary distraction, but tales of the San Patricio battalion made up of deserters from the American army fueled further doubts about Catholic loyalty. In the postwar years Charles Allen's Order of the Star Spangled Banner devoted itself to excluding Roman Catholics from public office and, they hoped, from the country. It spawned the "Know-Nothing" movement, which took political shape as the American Party. Governors, senators, congressmen and a host of lesser political lights owed their election to Know-Nothing support, which was particularly influential in the northeastern, border and southern states. Ex-President Millard Fillmore was their 1856 presidential candidate. Ironically, he happened to be visiting Pope Pius IX in Rome when nominated. Although he tried to dissociate himself from the party's anti-Catholicism, his "Silver-Gray Whig" supporters were in fact long associated with New York Know-Nothings in opposition to the Seward-Weed faction of the Whigs.[27]

A peculiar interlude began with the arrival at New York on June 30, 1853, of a papal diplomat, Archbishop Gaetano Bedini.[28] His cover story was that he was en route to take up an appointment as nuncio at the court of Emperor Dom Pedro II of Brazil, but his real assignment was to visit the United States, settle as best he might trusteeship disputes like that at St. Louis's Church in Buffalo, and report back to Rome on the state of church affairs in the country. He was also to investigate the possibility of reciprocal diplomatic relations between the United States and the Holy See. There was an American Minister in Rome, but no nuncio had ever been accredited to Washington.[29] Bedini's mission, which began well enough, ended in disaster. He visited east coast cities, met President Pierce and headed for the midwest, where trouble started. An Italian former priest, Alessandro Gavazzi, was a current star on the anti-Catholic lecture circuit. He charged, falsely, that Bedini as papal Governor of Bologna had been responsible for executions carried out there by Austrian military authorities. A gang of toughs blew cigar smoke in the archbishop's face as he sat in a carriage with Bishop O'Connor of Pittsburgh. Mobs protesting the "Butcher of Bologna" converged on the Cincinnati and Wheeling cathedrals. The nuncio had finally to be smuggled aboard the three-master *Atlantic* in New York harbor and spirited out of the country. He never reached Brazil. There was no more talk of a nunciature in Washington. Archbishop Peter Kenrick summed it up: the affair was "a blunder in every point of view."[30]

The mid-fifties were not a comfortable time for Catholics. Incidents multiplied. In October 1854 Father John Bapst, S.J., refugee from the Swiss *Sonderbund* war and parish priest at Ellsworth, Maine, was tarred, feathered, and ridden on a rail in a dispute over Bible-reading in the schools. He survived to become first president of Boston College, but spent his old age confined to an asylum. Memories of the night in Ellsworth haunted him. He would wake up screaming that attackers were climbing through his window.[31]

One of the worst confrontations was in Louisville. Nativist sentiment had been stirred by a lecture visit in January 1855 of Giovanni Achilli, who had been involved in an acrimonious libel suit against John Henry Newman. In April a Know-Nothing mayor was elected. As elections scheduled for August 6 approached, the Whig Louisville *Journal* sounded the call to arms:

> Rally to put down an organization of Jesuit Bishops, Priests, and other Papists, who aim by secret oaths and horrid prejudices, and midnight plottings, to sap the foundations of all our political edifices. . . . So go ahead Know-Nothings, and raise just as big a storm as you please.[32]

They did raise a storm, when they attempted to deny German immigrant Americans the vote. August 6, 1855, became "Bloody Monday" in Louisville history. Over twenty were killed, three-quarters of them "foreigners," and hundreds lay wounded. The city's Catholic bishop, Martin J. Spalding, whose first American ancestor had landed in Maryland just two centuries earlier, in 1657, pleaded publicly for calm:

> I entreat all to pause and reflect, to commit no violence, to believe no idle rumors, and to cultivate that peace and love which are the characteristics of the religion of Christ. We are to remain on earth but a few years; let us not add to the necessary ills of life those more awful ones of civil feuds and bloody strife.[33]

Privately, he confided to the archbishop of Baltimore: "We have just passed through a reign of terror surpassed only by the Philadelphia riots." Tension continued for over a year. "We are quiet here at present," Spalding wrote later, "but it is the quiet of the taut. . . . May God grant us peace."[34]

The Know-Nothing phase of nativism died with the Civil War. The American Party merged with the Whigs and at Baltimore in May 1860 formed the Constitutional Union Party, which nominated Tennessee's John Bell for President. He carried three border states. Slavery was the issue, not Catholicism. But the scars of the prewar years lingered. On August 24, 1855, Abraham Lincoln had said:

> As a nation we began by declaring that all men are created equal. We now practically read it: All men are created equal except Negroes. When the Know-Nothings obtain control, it will read: All men are created equal except Negroes, foreigners and Catholics.[35]

The targets of bigotry do not forget easily. Orestes Brownson sensed this and wrote sadly to Isaac Hecker of

> the real dislike of the American people and character felt by a large portion of our bishops & clergy, and their settled conviction that nothing can be done for their conversion. . . . [36]

The Know-Nothings never controlled the United States, but Lincoln's picture had enough reality in it to drive a deep sense of alienation from the American mainstream into the American Catholic subconscious. Individuals prospered. The Catholic community became, if anything, superpatriotic. As early as 1850 they were the largest single body of churchgoers in the nation. But there still remained a gnawing sense of non-fit. Development of a Catholic tradition authentically American and at the same time authentically Catholic and Roman—John Carroll's dream—proved difficult of achievement. Rome's 19th-century course, as shaped in reaction to France's revolution and continental liberalism, did not facilitate the task. American ideas and concerns did not always translate easily into European idiom and were frequently misunderstood by those whose horizons were bounded by the Adriatic and Tyrhennian seas. On the American side of the water, ancestral memories from two continents mingled: of English and colonial penal laws which ostracized Catholic forebears and of Louis XIV's persecution of Huguenots; of Protestant martyrs at Smithfield under Bloody Mary and Catholic martyrs on the Tyburn gallows under her successors; of Cromwell's massacre of the Irish at Drogheda and the Indian massacre of New Englanders at Deerfield. Evangelical antipathy to the Whore of Babylon was alive and well and heartily reciprocated. American civil religion, grounded in a curious inversion of Calvinism and heavily colored by the Enlightenment, would always be a difficult bedfellow for Christians in communion with the bishop and church of Rome.

XI

Westward the Course of Empire

The Louisiana Purchase doubled the land area of the United States in 1803, adding some 828,000 square miles, all or part of fourteen future states lying in the great plains between the Mississippi River and the Rockies. In 1845 annexation added the Republic of Texas. The Oregon Territory, a United States–British condominium since 1818, was divided in 1846. The future states of Idaho, Washington, and Oregon and the final sliver of Montana were now securely American. That same year war with Mexico started. When it was over the Treaty of Guadalupe Hidalgo and the "Mexican Cession" gave the United States another half-million square miles for its southwestern quadrant. A substantial number of Catholics were incorporated in these annexations, and others migrated west with the nation. Contact was also re-established with Indian tribes, some of which had not seen a priest since the departure of the Jesuits nearly a century before.

Church organization kept pace with the westward movement thanks to bishops like Mathias Loras, appointed to Dubuque in 1837, the same year in which bishops were named for Natchez and Nashville.[1] Loras, a Frenchman who had worked for seven years in Mobile, found three churches and a single priest, the remarkable Samuel Mazzuchelli, O.P., in a territory which reached from the Missouri line to the Canadian border and with parts of Wisconsin and Illinois thrown in for good measure. In twenty years Loras built a diocese renowned for its college and schools and with its own seminary. The French-Canadian population was dwindling and the Catholic Indians had disappeared in government re-settlement projects, and so the bishop promoted German and Irish immi-gration. The approach was in conflict with that of Bishop Hughes of New York, who wanted the Irish to stay in the northeast unless they had the personal means to establish themselves in the west. Hughes consistently opposed "colonization" schemes, believing that they made inadequate provision for the migrants' religious needs and also that settlement by national colonies would retard assimilation into the American main-stream.[2] Loras was not unaware of these problems. In addition, he sensed the potential for conflict between Irish parishioners and the French priests already on the scene, but helped to defuse it by importing an Irish Trappist monastery whose prior, Clement Smyth, O.C.S.O., be-came his coadjutor and then his successor.[3] He also invited from Philadel-phia Mother Mary Frances Clarke and an entire religious community, the Sisters of Charity of the Blessed Virgin Mary, founded there by five immigrant Irish women in 1833.[4] Before his death, Loras saw dioceses at Chicago, St. Paul, and Milwaukee spring up around him, the last to become the country's leading 'German" diocese under Bishop John Mar-tin Henni.[5] In 1850 the rest of the plains as far west as the mountains was lumped together as the "Indian Territory East of the Rocky Mountains," with John B. Miége, S.J., as bishop.[6]

Agriculture with its attendant industries and services was deeply woven into the fabric of midwestern life, whether in isolated farmhouses or in the villages, towns, and cities which dotted the landscape between the Alleghenies and the Rockies. A society developed which was endowed at once with a sense of mobility and freedom and a love of the land. Mid-westerners stressed individual performance but demanded cooperation. They viewed the exotic with suspicion. Less tied to tradition and precent, they tended to be forthright and direct. They were less European, more distinctly American in manners and characteristically pragmatic in outlook, than their compatriots on the east coast. Catholics were part of the milieu and developed their religious style in interaction with it. Ana-lyzing his fellow midwesterners some forty years ago, Thomas McAvoy was struck by what he perceived as a general sense of optimism, poise and security in their Catholicism, traits he attributed in part to the his-toric fact that the Catholic Church had been on the frontier when the first American pioneers arrived. It had grown with the region, rather than intruding on an already established religious pattern.[7]

One group of Catholic midwesterners did not fare so well. In the "Old West," Gabriel Richard at Detroit and Edward Fenwick at Cincinnati had a strong sense of responsibility for the Michigan Indians who until

1763 had been evangelized by French Jesuits. When in 1830 Potawatomi Chief Pokegan asked for a priest "to break the bread of life" for his people along the St. Joseph River, it was Frederick Résé who negotiated for the former Baptist "Carey Mission" there. He arranged for Kentucky veteran Stephen Badin to become the Indians' priest.[8] They built their own church; the congregation grew from twenty to three hundred in three years. Missions staffed by diocesan priests spread through Indiana and Michigan, at South Bend, Chichako's Village, and Chicupi-Outipe as well as north along Lake Michigan's shore toward the Straits of Mackinac. The Slovenian Frederic Baraga was the first priest in sixty years at the Straits. Funded by the Leopoldine Foundation, he arrived at Arbre Croche in 1831, and then moved on to the Upper Peninsula, where he became bishop in 1853. Baraga's missions ranged west to L'Anse on Keweenaw Bay. A linguist who wrote and spoke Indian languages, he published devotional books and a dictionary and grammar of the Ojibwa tongue. He is known as the apostle of the Ottawa and Chippewa.[9]

President Andrew Jackson's Indian Policy was translated into practice during the 1830s. For the Catholic Potawatomi, living peaceably in the Michigan-Indiana area, the day came in 1838. Over eight hundred were rounded up to be removed to their new home on the Sugar Creek in southeast Kansas. The proceedings were marked by chicanery and fraud on the part of whites profiting from the victimization of the Indians. Some Potawatomi resisted. General John Tipton, the military commander in charge of the deportation, advised the Federal Commissioner of Indian Affairs:

> I feel confident that nothing but the presence of an armed force for the protection of the citizens of the State and to punish the insolence of the Indians could have prevented bloodshed.[10]

The "insolent" Indians, whose crime was to live on land wanted by whites, moved out under escort, led by a dragoon carrying the American flag. Mounted dragoons and local volunteers patrolled the column.

Bishop Simon Bruté of Vincennes worried whether to allow Father Benjamin Marie Petit, missionary among the Potawatomi, to go with them to Kansas. He did not want it seen as a sign of support for government policy. In November 1838 the bishop urged the Commissioner of Indian Affairs that the Potawatomi, like tribes in the northeastern states, be left in peace. The impression in government circles was that Catholic authorities were trying "to oppose the intentions of Government for the benefit of these Indians."[11] In the event, this opposition proved unsuccessful. Bruté sent Petit with the Indians. One of them gave him a pony to ride; he celebrated mass along the way, tended the dying, buried the dead, and baptized the newborn. Each evening there were devotions: a chapter of the catechism was read and the Indians prayed and sang in their own language.

In Kansas, a Jesuit priest named Christian Hoecken met them and took up the work left off by his French brethren in 1763.[12] Six hundred and fifty Indians survived. Thirty died along the way, over a hundred fled the column. Benjamin Petit was a casualty. Heading back to Indiana, he took sick and died in St. Louis. In recollections sent to the Lyons Society for the Propagation of the Faith he wrote:

> Amid the pains of exile and the ravages of disease the infant Christian community has received all the aids of religion; the sick have received the sacraments, the grounds which enclose the ashes of the dead is blessed ground. Faith, together with the practice of religious duties, has been fostered; and even in their temporal distresses the Father of these poor creatures, as they name him, has often had the consolation of coming to their aid.

Petit's final prayer for the Potawatomi was that they be at peace, free from "the violence which has wrested them from our midst, from the country, to use their own expression, where their fathers lie."[13]

Sugar Creek was no prize location. The Indians built log cabins, planted corn, and tapped the sugar maples. Some became passable farmers, but the land was poor and by the late 1840s they had to move again, this time ninety miles to a site on the north bank of the Kansas River, which they called St. Mary's. The religious picture was brighter. A log church and priest's house were built with a $2000 government subsidy. Annual payments were made from the federal "Civilization Fund": $300 for the boys' school run by the Jesuits, $500 for the girls' school opened by Philippine Duchesne and three other Religious of the Sacred Heart in 1841. The nuns were warmly welcomed: Mother Duchesne ("The Woman Who Prays Always," they named her) and the three sisters had, on first arrival, to be embraced by all the Indian women and to shake hands with all the men, some seven hundred greetings in all.[14] The Indians put up other log chapels, all dedicated with solemn services. Music, singing, and processions were regular features of Potawatomi devotional life. So were frequent use of the sacrament of penance (one priest heard confessions for eighteen hours on the eve of the feast of Mary's Assumption in 1841) and participation in the eucharist. The Indians also set up a charitable fund to care for their own needy.

Everything was not rosy. Government reports praised Catholic villagers as exemplary, and the schools were highly thought of, but efforts were made to persuade parents to send their sons away from the tribe to schools like the Choctaw Academy in Kentucky. To cultural and religious harrassment was added the plague of brandy. The Indians formed an "Anti-Liquor Brigade" to combat drunkenness and in 1844 drew up a set of regulations with their own constables to enforce them. The subject was a continuing item on council agenda, along with immoral conduct and card-playing. In the attempt to control excessive drinking, Catholic and Protestant Potawatomi joined in ruling that all or part of the government annuity paid each individual should be withheld from notable offenders.

Other plains tribes whom Catholic missionaries approached with varying degrees of success were the Osages, Blackfeet, Grosventres, Winnebago, Sioux, and Kaw.[15] There were both disappointments, such as the failure of the mission to the Miami, whose ancestors had known French missionaries on both shores of Lake Michigan, and encouraging successes, as when Chief Pahuska (George White Hair) led four thousand Big and Little Osage into the church. Jesuits and Sisters of Loretto from Kentucky worked among them. When missionaries reached tribes never before Christian, new problems arose. This was true of the Jesuit mission to the nomadic Blackfeet of the northern Great Plains, begun in 1859.[16] The priests' style resembled that of Jesuit missionaries in earlier centuries only in some respects. True to the classic approach was their insistence on working in the native languages. Missionaries wrote grammars and dictionaries, translated hymns and prayers, produced catechisms. But in 17th-century India Roberto de Nobili had lived the life of a Brahman penitent and scrupulously respected the sensibilities of those he came to evangelize. Mateo Ricci and a succession of Jesuit mandarin-scientists in the waning days of the Ming dynasty became famous and controversial for efforts to express Christian teaching in Chinese thought-patterns and ceremony and for their acceptance of traditional Chinese ritual. Rome had definitively rejected these approaches for China in 1742 and for India in 1744. Those negative judgments were taken as normative elsewhere and so part of the Jesuit tradition was not resumed in the American Indian missions. Native religion was instead treated as superstition, the devil's work. Sacramental life and an educational program relying heavily on boarding schools flourished. A strong religious community was established; the cost was alienation of the Indians' cultural and religious heritage. Three centuries after the modern globalization of Christianity began, the model on the Great Plains was heavy with Europe's culture.

The story of Indian missions in the Pacific Northwest began in St. Louis in 1831 when an Indian delegation from the Flatheads and Nez Perces of the distant Columbia River valley came to ask Bishop Rosati for priests.[17] The moving spirit was "Old Ignace" LaMousse, one of the Catholic Iroquois from Caughnawaga near Montréal who fifteen years previously had intermarried with the Flatheads. Old Ignace made the long trip over the mountains twice more, in 1835 and 1837, but no priest came. Together with three Flathead companions and a Nez Perce, he was murdered by a band of Sioux on his third journey. The Columbia River tribes did not give up. Old Ignace's son, Young Ignace, accompanied by "Lefty Pierre" came again to St. Louis. On the way, at Council Bluffs, they met a Belgian Jesuit named Peter DeSmet.[18] Jesuit superiors at St. Louis agreed with the bishop that he should survey the possibilities, and he made an initial trip to the Rockies in March 1840. A year later he and five companions joined a westward-bound wagon train at Westport, Missouri. One of them was the French priest Nicolas Point, whose collection of sketches and paintings recreates for us the first years of Jesuit work in the northwest.[19] By summer's end they arrived in Montana's Bitter Root Valley. From a base at St. Mary's Mission they worked among Flatheads, Coeur d'Alenes, and Blackfeet. Stations were opened among the Kalispels, Kootenais, Pend d'Oreilles, and others. DeSmet's own stay was brief. He was recalled to a desk job in St. Louis, although seven times in years to come he travelled the Great Plains and Rocky Mountains as a government peace commissioner. But his principal work was as chronicler and publicist of the missions. *Letters and Sketches* appeared in 1843, followed four years later by *Oregon Missions and Travels,* and then came *Western Missions and Missionaries* (1859) and *New Indian Sketches* (1863).

The Oregon country's condominium status was reflected in its Catholic history. The most prominent personality was Québec-born Dr. John McLoughlin, from 1824 to 1846 the Hudson's Bay Company's chief factor at Fort Vancouver on the Columbia.[20] Among the missionaries he welcomed were Dr. Marcus Whitman and his wife Narcissa, who arrived under joint Presbyterian-Congregational sponsorship in 1836 to settle among the Cayuse Indians at Waiilatpu near Fort Walla Walla. Two years later the first Catholic priests came, not from St. Louis, but from Canada.[21] François N. Blanchet was vicar general of the Bishop of Québec. His companion was Modeste Demers. When word came that there were also Jesuits in the Bitter Root Valley, it was too much for Narcissa Whitman. She wrote:

> Romanism stalks abroad on our right hand and on our left and with daring effrontery boasts that she is to prevail and to possess this land. I ask, must it be so?[22]

It was not difficult to confuse religion and politics in the era of "Fifty-four Forty or Fight." Canadians Blanchet and Demers were vigorous representatives of Catholicism along the Columbia and its tributary Willamette and Cowlitz rivers. They worked among Indians and a substantial number of French-Canadian settlers. Hudson's Bay Company factor John McLoughlin openly declared himself a Catholic in 1843. Dr. Whitman was anxious that Oregon be American and Protestant. When he saw the first edition of DeSmet's *Letters and Sketches,* he was deeply concerned and wrote to a friend: "You will see by this book, I think, that the papal effort is designed to convey over the country to the English."[23]

It is a safe assumption that Pope Gregory XVI had only the vaguest notion where Oregon was, but developments suggest that he and the Roman cardinals at the Congregation for Propagation of the Faith were more inclined to place it in Canada then in the United States. Joint plans had been made by the bishops of St. Louis and Québec for Oregon.[24] The latter did not object to the recommendation sent to Rome by the Fifth Provincial Council of Baltimore (1843) that one of three Jesuits be chosen first bishop. DeSmet's name headed the list. But the Canadian bishop also submitted Blanchet's name, in case none of the Jesuits was picked. On December 11, 1843, the Canadian priest was named vicar-apostolic. He set out on a six-months' sea voyage to Montréal for his episcopal consecration. Before debarking at Boston he had touched at Honolulu, rounded Cape Horn, and landed at Liverpool, then recrossed the north Atlantic. He had also come up with a grand plan for diocesan organization of the region. His central concerns were recruiting a native clergy and the establishment by bishops of clear control of the church. He was convinced that inattention to what he saw as these essential ecclesial points had resulted in the fundamental failure of both the reductions, the Indian republics organized by the Jesuits in Paraguay, and the Franciscan missions in California.

Blanchet carried the day at Rome. While American bishops in their triennial Baltimore councils were cautiously planning a second archdiocese at St. Louis, he secured creation in 1846 of an archdiocese at Oregon City, with himself as archbishop and with suffragan dioceses at Walla Walla and Vancouver Island. Additional dioceses in the Oregon Territory were contemplated for Nesqually, Fort Hall, Princess Charlotte, and New Caledonia. That summer the international boundary was drawn at the forty-ninth parallel. Blanchet and his brother, Bishop Magloire Blanchet of Walla Walla, were in American territory, while Bishop Modeste Demers of Vancouver Island remained a Canadian. Walla Walla's diocesan existence was brief. It was abandoned after the Cayuse War of 1847. The bishop moved to Nesqually, which became a diocese in 1850 and remained one until the see was changed to Seattle in 1907.

Catholic growth in the Pacific Northwest was never spectacular. Marcus Whitman had inspired the great migration over the Oregon Trail and those who made the trek included relatively few Catholics. There was from the beginning feeling against them. When Whitman, his wife, and eleven others were murdered in the Cayuse uprising, Catholics were taxed with the atrocity and a bill for their expulsion was introduced in the territorial legislature. It failed of passage, but delivered a message. Anti-Catholic sentiment lingered. Canadian priests of the Oblates of Mary Immaculate community arrived at Fort Walla Walla on the eve of the Cayuse War and later worked among the Yakima and the tribes who lived around Puget Sound. During the Yakima uprising of 1856, the local militia took the opportunity to plunder and burn the missions.[25] But with it all, the Catholic community prospered and became particularly noteworthy for its schools, beginning with Blanchet's St. Joseph's College in 1843. The next year the Sisters of Notre Dame de Namur arrived and pioneer Baptist missionary Ezra Fisher could note that "the Romans are very industrious in attempting to occupy every important point with a school." "The Reverend Mr. Blanchette and his associates," Indian Agent and onetime missionary Elijah White remarked, "are peaceable, industrious, indefatigable and successful in promoting religious knowledge among the Canadian population and the aborigines of this country."[26]

By the time of the Civil War, the frontier advancing from the east stood at Minnesota's western boundary.[27] Moving south, it looped around Kansas and Nebraska.[28] Oklahoma was Indian territory.[29] The first church in Colorado was an open-air chapel on the Conejos River, opened in 1858, the year in which reports of a gold strike on Cherry Creek brought 100,000 would-be prospectors to the territory generally called "Pike's Peak." Care of the region's Catholics was made the responsibility of the bishop at Santa Fe, who sent Joseph Machebeuf to organize the church.[30] To the north, Utah Mormons (Peter DeSmet advised Brigham Young on the location) dreamed of Deseret reaching to the Pacific. Catholics soon became the largest gentile religious group, but did not join evangelistic Protestants in anti-Mormon activities.[31] Arizona was another Indian territory. No priest lived there from the day the Spanish Franciscans left in 1828 until 1858.[32] There were also Texas, New Mexico, and California.

American immigration into Texas[33] began with a Spanish grant to Moses Austin in 1821. The whole area had only four thousand inhabitants. Within a decade there were thirty thousand, mostly *gringos* from the southern United States. Six years later, they were in revolt under Sam Houston's leadership. Defeated at the Alamo, they retaliated at San Jacinto and the Republic of Texas was born. In 1845 it became an American state. Theoretically, all immigrants while Texas was part of Mexico were required to become Roman Catholics, but the law was easily evaded. All but two of the Franciscan colonial missions were in shambles, the Christian Indians scattered. Bleak prospects awaited John Mary Odin, Vincentian priest from the Barrens at Perryville, Missouri, and vice-prefect apostolic of Texas, who landed on the Texas Gulf coast in late spring of 1841 to inspect the church committed to the care of his community just over a year before.[34] He was awed by the treeless land of vast prairies and abundant pasturage—more of it than anywhere else in America, he thought—and by the Comanches who made life miserable for travelers and townspeople alike. He had to travel from Victoria to San Antonio in an armed convoy of covered wagons. The heat was oppressive, food and water were in short supply, and fever rampant. But there were consolations. Although he had to hire armed guards to see him safely through the country, he found the religious fervor of the few remaining Christian Indians remarkable, Mexican Catholics welcomed him, and he discovered seventy onetime Missouri parishioners settled on the Lavaca River. Odin was named bishop and vicar apostolic of the Republic of Texas in 1841 and Bishop of Galveston in 1847. He and the few priests, sisters and brothers who came to help him had to struggle to meet the needs of a small Catholic population scattered in a southern Protestant environment across a vast area of nearly four hundred thousand square miles.

The delegate in Congress from the New Mexico Territory rose on the floor of the House to denounce the "new French bishop" who, with his "imported French clergy," was destroying the Catholic Church in his constituency.[35] His defeated opponent in the 1855 general election was on the floor also, arguing that he had been the victim of electoral fraud and that the New Mexico seat was rightfully his. Mexican-American businessman Miguel A. Otero did not agree with the delegate about church matters either: he told the members of Congress of a church "sunk in the most deplorable conditions of immorality," now being restored to grace thanks to the efforts of the same French bishop and clergy.

Whatever the bemused congressmen made of the ecclesiastical argument, they knew election fraud when they saw it and promptly ousted Delegate José Manuel Gallegos. Otero took his place. Gallegos was a priest, the second (Gabriel Richard was his only predecessor) to sit in Congress. He was also suspended from the church's active ministry. Bishop John B. Lamy had removed him from his parish of San Felipe Neri in Albuquerque in 1853. The immediate charge was that he had been absent without leave from parish duties. He was in Mexico on business for the trading company-cum-general store which he and a female companion ran. The more general complaint was the *parroco*'s thoroughly secular lifestyle. He was one of those priests of whom an American Catholic traveller wrote that they "kept cocks and fit 'em, had cards and played 'em, indulged in housekeepers of an uncanonical age, and had more nieces than the law allowed."[36] The church of New Mexico, in Howard Roberts Lamar's words, was "permissive, simplified, decadent and paradoxically, quite powerful."[37] Gallegos represented it well.

The ex-delegate's situation symbolized the cultural crisis of a people whose church community antedated the *Ark* and the *Dove* by nearly forty years and who were now asked to become, under French auspices, 19th-century *yanqui* Americans. Gallegos touched the neuralgic point when he wrote plaintively to his former bishop at Durango that the "character, language, religion and personal characteristics" of the natives of the territory ill assorted with those of their conquerors.[38] This is not to say that changes were not needed. Religious life had been in a parlous state since the departure of the Spanish friars a quarter-century earlier. A Mexican lawyer, Antonio Barreiro, reported in 1832 that no bishop had seen New Mexico for seventy years. Sacramental life was virtually non-existent:

> The spiritual administration finds itself in a truly dismal condition. Nothing is more common than to see numberless sick folk die without confession and extreme unction, and nothing is rarer than to see the eucharist administered to them. Corpses remain unburied many days, and infants are baptized at the cost of a thousand sacrifices. There are unfortunate ones in considerable number who pass most Sundays of the year without hearing mass. The churches are almost destroyed, and most of them are surely unworthy of being called temples of God.

Tithes were collected, but churches and missions were neglected or abandoned. When priests did function, they extorted exorbitant fees. Mostly they concentrated on business, politics, and the good life.[39] Padre José Antonio Martínez of Taos, depicted under his own name in Willa Cather's *Death Comes for the Archbishop,* was a classic case. He finally died excommunicated and in schism, unable to adjust to the new regime.[40]

Martínez, Gallegos, and many New Mexicans were reluctant United States citizens and church members, brought in by conquest and incorporation, not by choice. Their native religious culture, a somewhat uncertain distillate of Mexican, Indian, and Spanish elements, had suffered from decades of ignorance, neglect, and permissiveness, but was still the bearer of a people's identity. The New Mexico church was now introduced to the stern discipline and Gallic style of 19th-century French Catholicism. Paul Horgan has said of John B. Lamy, who arrived in Santa

Fe as its first bishop on Sunday, August 9, 1851, that he was "an unquestioning perpetuator of the values of almost two thousand years of faith."[41] Over a span of more than three decades the church of Santa Fe took shape under his direction. But underlying cultural conflict was not silenced, only muted. A century and a quarter later, complaints could still be heard of the pioneer priests that "they didn't come to serve; they came to dominate," or that "they were not particularly similar or sympathetic to the Latin temperament."[42] In two thousand years the teaching of faith and values inevitably takes on myriad local cultural overtones. In New Mexico, two of these deeply-rooted and in many ways conflicting interpretations of a common religious heritage were brought into conflict.

Lamy's early years as bishop were largely taken up with problems stemming from the fact that many New Mexican Catholics were suffering cultural displacement in their own land. But his approach found strong support from Catholics like Miguel A. Otero, Colonel Kit Carson, and trader Céran St. Vrain. Vicar-general Joseph Machebeuf claimed that Gallegos's support came chiefly from the dependents of the rich *rancheros* and that only three men in all Albuquerque sided with him in his dispute with the bishop. Lamy forged ahead, enlisting reinforcements from Europe and the United States. Christian Brothers came from France, Sisters of Loretto from Kentucky. They travelled by steamboat up the Missouri to Independence, then by armed wagon train over the Santa Fe Trail, to be welcomed at the cathedral by a band of violins, guitars, and drums. Cultural problems of a church American by incorporation challenged solution, but the diocese and then the archdiocese of Santa Fe stand as a monument to the energy and organizing genius of a bishop who arrived from Auvergne via Cincinnati and stayed for thirty-five years.

New Mexico enjoyed a civilization far older and more stable than that of California. Once the initial shock of *yanqui* occupation was absorbed, *patróns* and *peons* settled back into routine village life. Alien squatters never overwhelmed them. Once the *patróns* got the hang of boss politics North American style (and, Padre Martínez in the van, they were fast learners), they fitted nicely, if somewhat idiosyncratically, into the system. In the church, tension lay just beneath the surface. Generations of Hispanic and Indian people were taught, ruled, preached at, and ministered to by French and then mostly Irish brothers, sisters, and priests. The west coast picture differed notably. California contracted a case of instant Americanization.

Whether San Francisco should be called "a madhouse or Babylon," wrote Italian Jesuit Michele Accolti to Rome on December 8, 1849, "I am at a loss to determine."[43] Irish-born priest Eugene O'Connell was scarcely more complimentary. He wrote to the president of All Hallows College, Dublin, concerning the prevalence of fires in the city by the Golden Gate and added:

> The temporal burnings of which I am speaking naturally remind me of the everlasting ones which they presage to thousands of the citizens of San Francisco unless they stop in their career of iniquity. The rage for duelling, the passion for gambling and barefaced depravity prevail to a frightful degree.[44]

The new bishop of Monterey and all California from Cape San Lucas in Baja to the Oregon line, a Catalan Dominican named Joseph Sadoc Alemany, set out the facts statistically in a begging letter to the Society for Propagation of the Faith at Lyons: his diocese counted forty thousand Catholics, thirty thousand Protestants, and one hundred thirty thousand unbaptized, both Indians and whites. There were forty-one priests, not one a California native, serving twenty-seven churches and eleven chapels. He had three colleges for boys, at Santa Ynes, Santa Clara, and Los Angeles, and two "female academies." These were the Dominican Santa Catalina convent at Monterey (moved to Benicia in 1854), founded by Mother Mary Goemere, a Belgian recruited by the bishop in Paris, and Notre Dame at San Jose (later at Belmont), run by Sisters of Notre Dame de Namur down from Oregon.[45]

Bay Area Catholicism grew rapidly. By 1852 French, Spanish, English, and German congregations competed for the two available churches. Alemany tried to interest first Frederick William Faber and then John Henry Newman in sending priests of their community, the Congregation of the Oratory, but he warned that they must expect to do parish duties.[46] Eugene O'Connell reported the churches "full to overflowing," although one aspect of San Francisco Catholicism puzzled him: the practice, stemming from the *bulla cruciata,* of eating meat on Fridays, even though "the finest salmon in the world" abounded in the waters off the Golden Gate.[47] The bishop gave high priority to education. San Francisco had a small "Bishop's English School," with an Irish ex-seminarian teacher, as well as a tiny seminary at Mission Dolores. In 1853 state funds were made available for schools of all denominations. The practice was stopped two years later. As cultural historian Louis B. Wright discovered: "Certain of the sterner Protestants objected to the law when they realized that Catholic parochial schools were benefiting."[48]

The Jesuits' college at Mission Santa Clara awarded the first bachelor's degree in California history in 1857; two years later its Italian founders opened a second school (today the University of San Francisco) farther up the peninsula.[49] More help came in 1852 when Daughters of Charity from Mother Seton's Emmitsburg community opened an orphan asylum. They were followed in 1854 by Irish Presentation and Mercy sisters.

Nothing matched the Bay Area for institutional growth. As in Boston, the Catholic community was cosmopolitan, but with a decidedly Irish hue. The "cow counties" of southern California had a history different from that of the Mother Lode country to the north and east. The north-south difference in the early American years is typified by two men: the patriarchal Don José de la Guerra, "el gran capitán" of Santa Barbara, and General Don Mariano Guadalupe Vallejo of Sonoma.

In 1848 Bishop Hughes of New York wrote to de la Guerra for information on the California church, addressing him as a person "deeply interested in the advancement of our faith," and "one of the foremost protectors and advisers of the missionaries." He was not disappointed in the informed and thoughtful answer he received. Deliberately and carefully "el gran capitán" traced out the weaknesses of a church still reeling from the destruction a generation before of the Franciscan missions. Priests were the first need. While he appreciated Hughes's suggestion that a Spaniard could be found to be bishop, he would be satisfied if one could be found who was at least proficient in the language. That was essential.[50] Until he died in 1858, de la Guerra remained active in southern California's religious life and politics.

If "el gran capitán" symbolized the ancient legacy of Spain, Vallejo represented the breath of Enlightenment which blew through Spain's one-time colonies early in the 19th century. A free-thinker, unable to fathom dogmas such as papal infallibility, he was nevertheless a Catholic, the patron of the parish church in Sonoma, and a friend and warm admirer of Alemany. At the height of California's Know-Nothing storm in 1854 he urged his nephew (José de la Guerra's son), State Senator Pablo de la Guerra, to remain in the legislature for the sake of "our friendship and our religion."[51]

Alemany became archbishop of San Francisco in 1853 and was succeeded at Monterey by another Catalan priest, Thaddeus Amat, C.M.[52] As the old colonial capital declined in importance, Bishop Amat moved first to Santa Barbara and then to Los Angeles. The town of Nuestra Señora de los Angeles had not been a favorite stopping place for the Franciscan missionaries, one of whom had in 1796 characterized its inhabitants as follows:

> They prefer to hold in hand a deck of cards rather than a plow or a hoe. What little progress is being made must be credited to the population of the neighboring gentile rancherías and not to the settlers. The Indians cultivate the fields, do the planting, and harvest the crops; in short, they do almost everything that is done.

One result was that "because of the bad example set them, and perhaps for their own private reasons, these natives still abide in the shadows of paganism."[53] The situation had improved somewhat, though not greatly, when the bishop arrived. A cluster of single-story adobe buildings straggled out from a central church and plaza. There were a few two-story houses belonging to the well-to-do. Southern California was the land of the great *ranchos,* many considerably augmented in pre-American years when the mission lands were distributed. It was a traditional world of Californios (as the California Mexicans called themselves), Sonora Mexicans, Europeans (Los Angeles boasted a substantial French colony with its own newspaper), and Indians. Economic control rested with landed dons and Yankees who had married into their families and sometimes into their religion. Others remained Protestant; they had a church by 1854. There was also a Jewish community: a long list of Jewish names appears on the roster of Amat's first school. In the early 1850s there were more Indians than whites, but no acceptable structures had replaced the missions in their lives and they were demoralized in the face of a changing society. As the century wore on, Catholic Californios faded from power, but not before they had made a substantial contribution to the region's political evolution and not before a church which had been near extinction at the American occupation was restored to reasonable health.

Between the Bear Flag Revolt in June 1846 and the Cahuenga Capitulation six months later, surprisingly little anti-Catholic animus accompanied the American takeover. Commodore Robert F. Stockton was the major exception. Commodore John Sloat promised to respect the church and its property, and the military government under General Stephen W. Kearny and his successors was benevolent both to the Californios and to their church. But the gold rush sparked by James W. Marshall's discovery in the American River on January 24, 1848, had as a side-effect a sickening outbreak of racial and religious bigotry directed at native Californians.[54]

The Forty-Niners came—a full hundred thousand in the first year alone—some by wagon train and others by sailing ship and steamer around the Horn. They travelled overland through Mexico, by boat on Panama's Chagres River, and along mosquito-infested trails to Panama City. They came from Europe, Central and South America, and Australia, as well as from the east coast and middle western states and from Oregon. Californios and Mexican immigrants from Sinaloa and Sonora joined the pilgrimage, but the Spanish-speaking were not welcomed in the gold fields, whether immigrants or native sons of the golden West. Vigilantes took the law into their own hands. Irish and Australian miners joined nativist Americans to rid the goldfields of the "refuse population" of Chileans, Peruvians, Mexicans—and native Californios. The "greaser" syndrome was born, ironically recalled years later by Grass Valley native Josiah Royce:

> He had no business as an alien to come to the land that God had given us. And if he was a native Californian, a born 'greaser,' then so much the worse for him. He was so much the more our born foe; we hated his whole degenerate, thieving, landowning, lazy and discontented race.[55]

While their onetime tormentor, New Jersey's Commodore Stockton, was seeking the 1856 nativist presidential nomination that eventually went to Millard Fillmore, California Catholics confronted Know-Nothingism closer to home.[56] The *Ignorantes* were anti-Hispanic, anti-immigrant, and anti-Roman Catholic. Supported by vigilance committees and the many Protestant ministers who had moved from New England to northern California cities and towns (Horace Bushnell among them), the American Party swept the 1855 state elections, electing J. Neely Johnson governor and controlling the chief municipal governments. Two years later the electoral tide turned. Change came, when it came, by population rather than by force. California lost its Catholic complexion, and California Catholicism ceased to be mainly Hispanic. State and local laws reflected standard Anglo-American moralities. The Catholic Church became standard American. But in California, although the church lived in a culture obviously and heavily Protestant, it did so among relics and monuments of a Catholic past.[57]

XII

Abolition and Civil War

Some random notes for a letter to Archbishop John Troy of Dublin have survived, written by Archbishop John Carroll in the last year of his life. The slave trade had been abolished in the British Empire eight years before, and the movement led by Thomas Clarkson and William Wilberforce for abolition of slavery itself was gathering momentum. Leaning on economic and humanitarian arguments for slowing down the drive, Carroll wrote:

> Since the great stir raised in England about Slavery, my Brethren being anxious to suppress censure, which some are always glad to affix to the priesthood, have begun some years ago, and are gradually proceeding to emancipate the old population on their estates. To proceed at once to make it a general measure, would not be either humanity toward the Individuals, nor doing justice to the trust, under which the estates have been transmitted and received.[1]

Jesuit Brother Joseph Mobberley was farm manager and general troubleshooter on the Maryland clergy's estates until his death in 1827. He also taught English, Latin, and Greek at Georgetown College, but he was mainly a practical man. In a lengthy essay on slavery, he relied heavily on biblical evidence to support the practice. He certainly had no time for abolitionist Quakers and "Methodistic Ninnyhammers," but he advocated eliminating slavery on the Jesuit farms. His objection was economic: slavery did not pay. He proved his point by a case study of the Jesuits' St. Inigo's farm in St. Mary's County. It would be cheaper to work the farm with "two or three strong men that understand farming," assisted by a half-dozen "apprentice boys." Even better would be to build "good durable houses" on the estate and engage tenant farmers. Expenses for clothing (each slave received summer and winter clothes made on the farm), living quarters, firewood, and food would be eliminated. No land would have to be planted in corn, a staple in the diet of the slaves, whose food ration was two pounds of meat and "one peck and a little heaped" of corn meal per week. Old people received the same; children a half-peck. Each slave family raised a few hundred chickens and cultivated cabbage and cotton, but their chief crop was sweet potatoes. On Sundays and holidays slaves gathered oysters, which they sold—"in defiance of authority," Mobberley noted. Added expenses included medicine and doctors' bills: "In extraordinary cases a Physician was called in, and all possible attention paid to them in their illnesses." Totaling up all these costs, Moberley was sure that slavery was uneconomical, the more so since "slaves are very discontented in their present state of servitude," and the old discipline "is now going to decay." He was no abolitionist. There is no indication that he saw a moral problem in the institution of slavery. But he was convinced the system had seen its day.[2]

A few Maryland Jesuit slaves were sent to Missouri in 1823 to help in starting missionary work for the Indians. The rest were sold off, the final group going to Louisiana in 1838.[3] Jesuits were not the only clerical slaveholders. The practice was common in religious institutions in southern and border states until after the Civil War. Postulants at the Carmel in Port Tobacco, Maryland, brought slaves as part of their dowries. The same was true at Nazareth in Kentucky and elsewhere. House servants and field hands belonged to convents, schools, and seminaries from Maryland to Missouri and throughout the South. Nazareth freed its last thirty slaves ("counting the children") on January 1, 1865.[4]

The Catholic Church related to black people not only in the master-slave relationship. Maryland had more free blacks than any other state. The St. Mary's Seminary Sulpicians opened their basement chapel to a congregation of black Santo Domingo refugees. Sulpician James Joubert was instrumental in founding the Oblate Sisters of Providence. Their St. Francis Academy became a worship center for black Catholics. Redemptorist priests took up the work. One of them, Thaddeus Anwander, C.Ss.R., sponsored a black seminarian, William A. Williams, who studied at Rome's Urban College from 1855 to 1862 before deciding he had no call to ordination. He had been advised that public prejudice in the United States would prevent his functioning as a priest and that he should look to Guinea, Liberia, or Haiti as a field for his labors. When Williams returned to Baltimore he worked with Peter Miller and retired Bishop Michael O'Connor, both Jesuits, in the chapel for black people

which grew into St. Francis Xavier's Church, the first exclusively black
Catholic church in the United States. During Reconstruction Williams
published at Baltimore a journal called the *Truth Communicator,* directed
to freed slaves.[5]

There had been other ventures. John McElroy, S.J., ran a Sunday
afternoon school in 1818 in Holy Trinity parish in Georgetown, teaching
the three Rs and Christian doctrine. By 1827 separate schools existed for
boys and girls. St. Elizabeth Ann Seton herself taught black children at
Emmitsburg. The Ursuline convent in New Orleans was a catechetical
center for a century. The first mission to be established by the Sisters of
St. Joseph outside their mother house at Carondolet, Missouri, was a
school for blacks on Third Street in St. Louis. Sisters of Charity of Nazareth and Sisters of Loretto did similar work in Kentucky. Charles Nerinckx, founder of the Loretto Sisters, tried in 1824 to incorporate a black
women's group in the community but timidity on the part of his bishops
forced abandonment of the idea.[6]

Opponents of slavery found slight support in official church teaching.
Pope Gregory XVI in 1838 condemned the slave trade, but not slavery
itself. American bishops for the most part kept silent as abolitionist fever
mounted. Traditional moral theology gave them no warrant to do otherwise. Additionally, a great many northern abolitionists were the same
people whose nativism led to strong and vocal anti-Catholicism. Lyman
Beecher was typical. Their name was legion. A Know-Nothing resolution
at Norfolk, Massachusetts, uncovered by Ray Allen Billington sums up
their argument:

> Roman Catholicism and slavery being alike founded and supported on
> the basis of ignorance and tyranny; and being, therefore, natural allies in
> every warfare against liberty and enlightenment; therefore, be it
> Resolved, That there can exist no real hostility to Roman Catholicism
> which does not embrace slavery, its natural co-worker in opposition to
> freedom and republican institutions.[7]

Few Catholics argued for abolition. Economic status, particularly of the
Irish immigrants, was a factor. Those struggling for the botton rung of the
ladder can be less inclined to debate in terms of high moral principle.
German-American Catholic immigrants had a better record.

No Catholic bishop spoke for abolition in the prewar years. In 1840
John England explained to Van Buren's Secretary of State, John Forsyth,
that Pope Gregory XVI had condemned the trade in slaves, but that no
pope had ever condemned domestic slavery as it existed in the United
States. The bishop's own fierce antipathy to abolitionists, as well as Forsyth's political use of the pope's letter to tar the Whig presidential candi-

date with a Catholic brush, led England to defend slavery with arguments from scripture and Christian tradition. Even the man who had opened a school for black children on his first arrival in Charleston, and who had been forced by local pressure to close it, and who declared that he was not "friendly to the existence or continuation of slavery," ended by going on record in its favor.[8]

Francis P. Kenrick, Bishop of Philadelphia until he succeeded Samuel Eccleston at Baltimore in 1851, was acknowledged the church's leading theological light. In his moral theology textbook, standard fare in American seminaries, he did no more than "regret" that there were so many slaves, whose liberty and education were so restricted. His emphasis was that the law must be obeyed to avoid chaos.[9] In New York, John Hughes's arguments were personal and pragmatic. His in-laws, the Rodrigue family, had filled him with tales of the horrors of the black uprising which had driven them from Santo Domingo. He remained convinced that, though "this condition of slavery is an evil, yet it is not an absolute and unmitigated evil," since it had brought uncounted Africans to civilization and to Christianity.[10]

Catholic lay people for the most part conformed with the general practice where they lived. Kentucky and Missouri families owned fewer slaves. Slaves were more numerous in Louisiana and Maryland. A Baltimore man, Charles Coles, in 1937 remembered slave days on the Charles County, Maryland, farm of Catholic Silas Dorsey. The pattern had scarcely varied over two centuries. Seventy-five slaves worked thirty-five hundred acres. They were well treated, housed, and fed. The Dorseys conducted regular religious services in a chapel on the farm, and taught the slaves catechism, reading, and writing. Jesuit priests came on holidays and Sundays to offer mass. They baptized slave children and presided at slave funerals. The baptisms were recorded in the family Bible; slaves were buried in the family burying-ground, only their markers were of stone, the family's of marble.[11]

Among early lay leaders, slave owner Charles Carroll of Carrollton in 1797 introduced in the Maryland state senate an unsuccessful bill for gradual abolition. In 1830 he succeeded Bushrod Washington as president of the American Colonization Society. William Gaston, in the year before his election to the North Carolina supreme court, advised up-and-coming leaders of that state, gathered in the Dialectic and Philanthropic Societies at Chapel Hill, that on them would devolve

> the duty which has been too long neglected, but which cannot with impunity, be neglected much longer, of providing for the mitigation, and, (is it too much to hope for in North Carolina?) for the ultimate extirpation of the worst evil that afflicts the Southern part of our Confederacy.

Slavery was to him a hindrance to progress, industry, and enterprise. It impaired the strength of the community and "poisoned morals at the fountainhead."[12]

Another American Colonization Society member was Roger Brooke Taney. Over thirty years before he wrote the Dred Scott decision, Taney had freed his own slaves, except for two he felt were too old. "These two," he wrote, "I supported in comfort as long as they lived." But he did not support the abolition movement. Admitting that manumission had "undoubtedly promoted the happiness" of many blacks, he was convinced that "a general and sudden emancipation" would "bring absolute ruin to the negroes."[13] Taney's attitude was kindly, but paternalistic. His name is forever identified with the cold legalisms of the Dred Scott decision.

The nation's Catholic newspaper editors were less restrained. For the Charleston *Catholic Miscellany,* states' rights were the paramount issue. Louisville's *Catholic Advocate* opposed abolition. It also carried in its classified section reward notices for return of runaway slaves and notices of sale, often with the note: "As they are Catholics, I would prefer selling them to a person of that persuasion," or "I would prefer selling them to a Catholic."[14] The Boston *Pilot* under Patrick Donahoe's editorship argued that abolitionism was a Protestant crusade that was tearing the nation apart.[15] Two years into the Civil War Courtney Jenkins of the Baltimore *Catholic Mirror* was convinced that "there was not a happier people on earth than the slaves," and that emancipation would be "fatal."[16] In New York, the convert-editor of the *Freeman's Journal,* the ever-intemperate and always arch-conservative James A. McMaster, was an out-and-out racist who warned a readership said to include at least a third of the country's priests, as well as a large number of Irish-Americans that they had better look for homes in the West once three and a half million ex-slaves were let loose, thanks to "Massa Linkum."[17]

Occasional rare individuals sided with abolitionists. Jeremiah Cummings, pastor for twenty years of St. Stephen's Church in New York City and a regular contributor to *Brownson's Quarterly Review,* called forcefully for an end to slavery.[18] Brownson himself, no master of understatement, charged it was "undeniable that no religious body in the country stands so generally committed to slavery and the rebellion" as Roman Catholics. During the war he urged emancipation without indemnity. The rebel states had committed suicide, their laws were null, their slaves free. That opinion provoked one of the editor's periodic rows with John Hughes. This time Brownson had the pleasure of telling the archbishop that his views on the civilizing and Christianizing benefits of the slave trade ran counter to those expressed by Pope Gregory XVI a quarter-century earlier.[19] In the border state of Ohio, Cincinnati Archbishop John

B. Purcell issued a call for emancipation of slaves in August 1862, five months before President Lincoln's proclamation. The Archbishop's brother and editor of the *Catholic Telegraph,* Father Edward Purcell, argued the anti-slavery position, informing James A. McMaster and the *Freeman's Journal* that "slavery and the Catholic Church could never get along well together." The church "proclaimed men's fraternity with each other, and their equality before God, and therefore could not be the advocate of slavery."[20] In the far West, Californios and New Mexicans were mostly political allies of pro-slavery Democrats, but slavery was not their issue. They understood class distinctions in their own society; Anglo-Saxon racism was alien. Standing apart from the general position was Francisco P. Ramírez, a Los Angeles Catholic and from 1856 to 1859 publisher of a one-page broadsheet, *El Clamor Público,* which reported news of Californios and advocated their interests. Ramírez was resolutely anti-slavery. His arguments reflected a single-minded political liberalism, and were not grounded in any explicitly religious principles.[21]

In the 1860 presidential election, most northern Catholics probably voted for Stephen A. Douglas. The picture in border and southern states was mixed. Bishop Martin J. Spalding of Louisville regretted that some of his own family supported native son John Cabell Breckinridge, a man "of bad stock, & in wretched disunion company." The bishop himself was for Douglas, although he reconciled himself to the Republican victor in the campaign and was sure, six weeks before the bombardment of Fort Sumter, that "Lincoln has been & will be still further, frightened into moderation and common sense."[22]

If slavery and abolition did not stir Catholic opinion, the breakup of the Union did. Unlike other churches, the Catholic Church did not splinter over the Civil War, but there were strains aplenty between sections of the country and within the North. Northern bishops were generally vociferously patriotic. Newspaper editors were another matter. McMaster of the New York *Freeman's Journal* was openly seditious, telling Irish-Americans that they had "rushed into a fight in which no interest of theirs was at stake." Barred from the mails for attacks on the Lincoln administration, he hurried a substitute newspaper through the presses and was clapped into Fort Lafayette prison.[23] When Archbishop Hughes announced support for conscription, Baltimore's *Catholic Mirror,* whose editor likewise spent time as an enforced guest of the government, denounced him as a "champion of desolation, blood and fratricide."[24] On the other hand, the Union cause had no more loyal supporter than Edward Purcell of the Cincinnati *Catholic Telegraph.*

John Hughes's friendship with President James Buchanan dated back to 1846 and the Mexican War. Both were Ulstermen and in those days that made for a common bond. But the bishop thought the President indecisive: "I cannot imagine a descendant of the Buchanans that I knew in Ireland who, knowing or believing himself to be right, would ever give way," he wrote in March 1858.[25] Hughes's choice in 1860 was another old friend, William H. Seward, veteran with him of battles over funds for New York schools, but he grew to recognize Abraham Lincoln's abilities. Hughes was among the impatient who urged decisive action in the months between Fort Sumter and Bull Run, writing Seward on June 18, 1861:

> I pray you for heaven's sake not to allow it to be a half battle, but one in which whatever the consequences may be, the South will be taught that it is incapable of coping with the North.[26]

Hughes earned the reputation of being a genuine Unionist, yet his views on the central question of slavery did not change. He still hoped that preservation of the Union and abolition could be separated, warning Secretary of War Simon Cameron in October 1861:

> The Catholics so far as I know, whether of native or foreign birth are willing to fight to the death for the support of the constitution, the Government, and the laws of the country. But if it should be understood that, with or without knowing it, they are to fight for the abolition of slavery, then, indeed, they will turn away in disgust from the discharge of what would otherwise be a patriotic duty.[27]

Lincoln's Emancipation Proclamation on September 23, 1862, did not change his mind. He appreciated the President's honesty and patriotism, but told Seward he found Lincoln "deficient in reliance on his own judgement."[28]

Hughes flew the national flag from his cathedral. He encouraged Catholics to serve ("Let volunteers continue, and the draft be made"). He was proud of New York's largely Irish Sixty-ninth Regiment, now once again commanded by Colonel Michael Corcoran, who had been dismissed for refusing to march his men in New York's 1860 parade welcoming the Prince of Wales. But he discouraged expansion of Irish regiments into Irish brigades, fearing as always the ghettoizing of American Catholics. The stance was consistent with his position a decade earlier against Irish "colonies" in the Midwest.

Over the summer of 1861 Hughes exchanged letters on the subject of secession with an old friend, Bishop Patrick N. Lynch of Charleston, and the correspondence appeared in the *Metropolitan Record* that September.[29] Later in the fall, at Lincoln's request, Hughes and political boss Thurlow Weed sailed on an unofficial diplomatic mission to Paris.[30] The archbishop stayed until February and had the opportunity to explain the Union case to Napoléon III and Eugénie. His offer to do the same for Alexander II at St.

Petersburg was declined by the State Department. A chilly reception at Rome, Hughes's next stop, made up for missing February on the Neva. Major papal officials were cool to the northern cause. He stayed in Rome until June and effected some thaw in the climate, then returned home by way of Ireland. His report to the Secretary of State was pessimistic. The terms of comparison he adopted also betrayed what a thorough New Yorker he had become:

> There is no love for the United States on the other side of the water. Generally speaking on the other side of the Atlantic the United States are ignored, if not despised—treated in conversation in the same contemptuous language as we might employ towards the inhabitants of the Sandwich Islands, or the Washington territory, or Vancouvers Island, or the settlement of the Red River or of the Hudson's Bay Territory.[31]

John Hughes's final contribution came in the summer of 1863. It was a tense time. On March 3, Lincoln signed the nation's first conscription act. Men between twenty and forty-five were liable for service, but could be exempted by paying $300 or providing a substitute who would enlist for three years. The act was manifestly unfair to poor whites, which in New York City translated as "Irish." Freed blacks were coming into the city. Irish-black relations were a casualty as the two groups competed for low-level jobs. In the same month in which the draft law was signed, black laborers broke an Irish longshoremen's strike. McMaster's *Freeman's Journal* pandered to anti-black prejudice, warning that emancipation meant more taxes and fewer jobs for the Irish. The draft act was "an outrage on justice and decency," Lincoln another "Caligula." New York's Copperhead Governor Horatio Seymour made things worse by bombastic Fourth of July oratory: "The bloody and treasonable, and revolutionary doctrine of public necessity," which had been invoked by the Federal government, "can be proclaimed by a mob as well as a government." Hughes and Irish-baiter Horace Greeley had words, the *Tribune* editor claiming that by their Democratic politics and anti-abolitionist stance the Irish "have been and are today foremost in the degradation and abuse of this persecuted [black] race." This while heavy Irish casualty lists from Gettysburg were being published. The stage was set for the draft riots of July 13–16. Thousands ran amok, blacks were lynched, an attack made on the black orphan asylum. Greeley goaded Hughes, urging him to control "his people." The archbishop said that he was no "head constable," but he did address a crowd from his balcony after the mob's fury was spent: "They call you rioters, but I cannot see a rioter's face among you. . . . " His effort won praise from the normally anti-Catholic and anti-Irish *Harper's* in an August 1 number which had kind words also for the priests and Irish policemen who had tried to restore order and for the many Irish "stanch friends of law and order" who helped rescue orphans at the black asylum. The riots marked John Hughes's last hurrah. He died shortly after the new year, on January 3, 1864.[32]

Hughes was not the North's only patriot bishop. Cathedral parishioners in Erie criticized their Massachusetts-born bishop, Josue Young, as "the most ultra fanatic that ever New England produced." He did not help matters by declaring a vote for George McClellan in the 1864 presidential race to be a mortal sin, or by locking the church doors so that the congregation could not walk out on his political sermons, or by telling the Irish that they must not, in their pride, think themselves better than blacks.[33] Pittsburgh's Bishop Michael Domenec, C.M., was a confidant of Seward and acted as his emissary to Spain. Bishop John Timon, C.M., of Buffalo, one-time Texas missionary, was another strong Union man.

David Whelan, a Cincinnati priest on loan to the diocese of Mobile, feared the approach of war in the winter of 1860–61. He was sure that "the several Southern states of the cotton sample would be dragged to their deepest misery by a set of wicked politicians."[34] When President Buchanan called for a Day of Humiliation, Fasting, and Prayer to mark the new year 1861, Bishop John Quinlan of Mobile answered with a pastoral letter and Bishop Augustin Verot at St. Augustine with a vigorous sermon later published as *A Tract for the Times: Slavery and Abolitionism*.

Quinlan took a position shared by the vast majority of Catholics in the south:

> While regretting the dismemberment of this great Republic—and heaven knows we would do all we could legitimately to preserve it—we would not purchase Union at the expense of Justice.[35]

Verot blamed the nation's disaster on northern refusal to acknowledge the legitimacy of slavery. He defended slaveholding on biblical, historical, and constitutional grounds. It was "consistent with practical religion and true holiness of life" if attention was paid to the "social, moral and religious improvement" of the slaves. The *Tract* was widely reprinted in English and French. A key element was the call for "a servile code . . . defining clearly the rights and duties of slaves." He was in the van of southerners advocating slavery reform; he thought it would produce

> a most triumphant confutation of the charges which bigotry, ignorance, fanaticism and malice, cloaked under a reverend garb, have for years heaped against Southern institutions.[36]

Southern patriotism was strong. From Moundsville in western Virginia, Father William J. Barry wrote: "With my whole heart and soul I am with the *South and the Right,* now and forever." The Constitution, he charged, "has been shivered into a thousand atoms" by "Republican despotism."[37] Bishops were equally active and outspoken. After the taking of Fort Sumter, Patrick N. Lynch gave over Charleston's cathedral to a solemn *Te Deum,* the traditional liturgy of thanksgiving. In the spring of 1864 he became an official Confederate commissioner to Rome. Only late in 1865 could he return to his shattered diocese, after northern bishops had obtained a pardon for him from President Andrew Johnson.[38] A prominent Confederate agent in Ireland was St. Louis priest John Bannon, who had "gone south" at the war's outbreak.[39] Bishop William Henry Elder of Natchez was briefly confined across the river in Vidalia, Louisiana, for refusal to cooperate with the Union army of occupation in Mississippi. He was a notably conscientious man who worried about the morality of profit-eering (he was willing to concede a 100 percent markup at most), conscription of priests ("more worthy . . . that he bear imprisonment and death itself rather than to be in the shedding of blood"), and violation of the sanctity of oaths. It was the last which brought him into conflict with General Ben Butler, for whom, as Elder ruefully learned, "all who are not with the Federal government are against it and to be treated as enemies."[40]

On the west coast, Archbishop Alemany of San Francisco issued a pastoral letter on February 25, 1861, warning that "we are about to witness the most disastrous divorce that can befall the noblest family, and the most calamitous conflict ever witnessed between brothers." In 1863 he publicly rebuked the violently anti-Lincoln editor of the unofficial Catholic *Monitor,* Thomas A. Brady, for misrepresenting "the principles of the Catholic Church."[41] The Californios were heavily Democratic, and a few of them went east to put on grey uniforms, but most supported the Union. A "native cavalry" complete with lances was formed and saw service in Arizona and New Mexico.[42] Some New Mexicans were attracted by the states' rights aspect of the Confederate cause, but they did not rally to invaders from Texas who occupied Santa Fe and bivouacked around the Loretto convent from March 4 to April 8, 1862. The incursion was interpreted in local terms. "The inhabitants of Texas," Lamy explained, are "making war against us."[43]

The picture in the border states was mixed. German Catholics in St. Louis were pro-Union. The archbishop, Peter Richard Kenrick, and the Irish inclined to the South.[44] Kenrick's initial effort was to remain above partisan strife. He refused even to preach during the first years of the war. Continuing contacts with southern bishops, however, earned him the suspicion of Federal military authorities, and Secretary of State Seward once explored with John Hughes the possibility of removing Kenrick from the sensitive river city. Kenrick became best known for his resistance to the "iron-clad" loyalty oath demanded by Missouri's "Drake Constitution" of 1865. The archbishop's temper was not helped by the known anti-Catholicism of Charles Drake, the constitutional convention's moving spirit, or by the fact that only a single Roman Catholic, St. Louis physician Moses Linton, had been elected among the convention's sixty-six delegates. Penalties for refusing the oath were stiff: a $500 fine and six months' imprisonment, but Kenrick forbade his priests to comply, explaining:

> We cannot permit the Civil Power to interfere with us in any manner in our duties, or to prescribe the conditions on which we may perform them.

Several priests were arrested and a test case was made of the conviction and jailing of Father John Cummings of Louisiana, Missouri. State courts upheld the sentence, but they were reversed and the law thrown out on appeal to the United States Supreme Court.

The Ohio River was a clear boundary. The Purcell brothers, archbishop and editor, and Auxiliary Bishop Sylvester Rosecrans (whose brother commanded a Federal army) were strong Union men. Edward Purcell once challenged the Confederate Bishop of Mobile with a case of conscience: "How do you decide in the Confessional respecting Seceders who have taken the oath to support the Constitution!" No question-mark; an exclamation point.[45] Across the river Covington's Bishop George Carrell, S.J., dropped the *Catholic Telegraph* as his official paper. He wondered what happened to the bishops' agreement at the third provincial council of Cincinnati late in April, 1861:

> they do not think it their province to enter into the political arena. . . . The Catholic Church has carefully preserved her unity of spirit in the bond of peace, literally knowing no North, no South, no East, no West.[46]

Down at the Falls of the Ohio Bishop Martin J. Spalding of Louisville deplored the Purcells' political activism, but was not unwilling to speak out himself. He and his paper, *The Guardian,* were anti-abolitionist in a state with between two and three thousand Catholic slaves, some of them owned by the bishop and diocesan institutions. They made a great effort to identify abolition with Protestantism, *The Guardian* boasting that Catholics did not look to remedy one evil (slavery) by inflicting another (sudden emancipation). The bishop condemned abolitionists as "destructive fanatics." His hope—like that of Bishop Carrell—was that Kentucky might stay neutral, but in 1862 he took, under protest, a loyalty oath to the Union. Increasingly agitated about abolition, he was proud of his restraint when the Rosecrans brothers brought "the odious subject" into his own dining room. Hearing of devastation downriver, he wondered aloud why red-hot Unionist sisters and priests in Cincinnati did not rush to the relief of towns like Natchez. The Purcell brothers and Rosecrans were denounced in three letters in a single month addressed to the Roman official responsible for American church affairs, Cardinal Alessandro Barnabò. They supported "the party of blood," Spalding told the cardinal, and again, "It is certainly a curious thing to see the bishop for War, while his people are for Peace."[47]

Conflicting border state loyalties destroyed the brief career as bishop of Nashville of James Whelan, O.P. A thirty-six-year-old seminary president in 1859 when named coadjutor to Bishop Richard P. Miles, O.P., he succeeded as bishop eight months later. Whelan was a northern sympathizer who had spent most of his active life in Ohio. Tennessee was a southern-oriented state. The situation was intolerable and aggravated by the bishop's obvious friendliness to Union officers including the commander of the Army of the Cumberland, General William Rosecrans. Whelan submitted his resignation in the spring of 1863 and it was accepted in January 1864.[48]

The bishop of Wheeling, West Virginia, Richard V. Whelan, was a southern man who survived in a newly formed northern state. He was also senior bishop in the church province of Baltimore, whose archbishop, Francis P. Kenrick, died on July 3, 1863, just as the battle of Gettysburg was ending not far away. Kenrick, who wrote to Eliza Allen Starr that "from my heart I wish that secession had never been thought of," had tried to be neutral in Baltimore's highly charged climate. His strongest gesture was to read personally Archbishop Carroll's prayer for civil authorities when pro-secession priests on the cathedral staff refused to do so. Some parishioners walked out on him while others "rustled papers and silks."[49] His successor, recommended by John B. Purcell (among others), was the Bishop of Louisville, Martin Spalding.

On both sides, thousands of Catholics took up arms. The "Montgomery Guards" of the First Virginia Infantry donned green and gold uniforms and marched to the basement of Richmond's St. Peter's Cathedral, where Bishop John McGill blessed the pikes they carried. At Bull Run they would confront New York's Irish Catholic Sixty-ninth Regiment.[50] At a mass in the Mobile cathedral, Bishop Quinlan blessed the flag of the "Emerald Guards," Company I of the Eighth Alabama. Of 109 men on the roster, 104 were Irish-born.[51] When Texans threatened the New Mexico Territory, the governor commissioned Colonel Kit Carson and Céran St. Vrain, both parishioners of Taos, to raise troops.[52] French Catholics enlisted in Louisiana regiments.[53] Lieutenant General William J. Hardee, C.S.A., a Georgia Catholic, defended that state while another Catholic, Major General Philip H. Sheridan, U.S.A., made his name in the Shenandoah. Bishops took comfort from General Pierre G. T. Beauregard's attendance at religious services and hoped it might be a sign of better practice to come. The Confederate hero was a Catholic, but also a Freemason. A prominent Charles County, Maryland, Catholic family contributed Rear Admiral Raphael Semmes to the Confederate navy. He captained the C.S.S. *Alabama* during the two-year cruise which cost the Union seventy ships taken as prizes and $6 million in shipping losses. The highest-ranking Catholic in either government, after the aged Chief Justice Taney, was Confederate Secretary of the Navy Stephen R. Mallory.[54]

Over seventy Catholic chaplains, commissioned and volunteer, served the two armies: Jesuits from the French missions in New York and the South and the Maryland Province, Holy Cross priests from Notre Dame, Redemptorists and secular priests from a score of dioceses. The only ministers of any church to be present at Andersonville prison were sent by Bishop Verot and headed by a diocesan priest, Peter Whelan. The diary of Spring Hill College in Mobile noted solemnly that Anselm Usannaz, S.J., returned from a tour of duty at the infamous prison camp "covered with merits and fleas."[55] Between five and six hundred sisters from more than twenty religious communities were nurses in military hospitals. Outstanding were the Emmitsburg Daughters of Charity with two hundred and thirty-two nursing sisters. Mother Teresa Maher and two other Mercy sisters from Cincinnati used skills they had learned in the Crimean War. Their reception was not always the warmest. Superintendent of Women Nurses Dorothea Dix was particularly hostile. At Mobile, Alabama, the chief surgeon turned them away, claiming that he had known sister-nurses in New Orleans and wanted nothing to do with them. Sister Mary Agnes Kelly left a vivid description of the hospital at Pensacola, Florida, where she and others worked with soldiers suffering from tropical fever and measles as well as war wounds. Some had never before seen a Catholic sister:

> When we went into the wards they covered their heads with the blankets and nothing would induce them to uncover them while we were in the wards for three or four days, as they were frightened by our appearance.

The sisters were highly praised for their services to soldiers of both armies.[56]

The American Civil War coincided with Pius IX's loss of four-fifths of the territory of the ancient Pontifical State. While southern American states debated secession in the winter of 1860–61, an all-Italian parliament was being elected. In a kingdom now shrunken to Lazio, with Garibaldians to the south where reassuring Bourbons of the stripe of King Ferdinand Bomba used to be, the pope was the last sovereign prince on the peninsula save for the "Pater Patriae," Victor Emmanuel of Savoy. None of this inclined Roman authorities to sympathy for a Union cause which they saw through European spectacles as "liberal" and oppressive of a traditionalist and conservative South. In 1864, moreover, the pope's last thin reed of a protector, Napoléon III, launched Maximilian and Carlotta on their sad Mexican venture. Pius IX had doubts about Mexico, but he knew that Richmond had a kinder eye for his ally than did Washington.

Rome, like other European capitals in the early 1860s, was a hotbed of intrigue. Confederate agents A. Dudley Mann and James T. Soulter urged the southern cause. Bishop Lynch came to help. It seemed a partial victory when Pius IX addressed a letter to Jefferson Davis as president of the Confederate States of America, but American minister resident at the papal court Rufus King assured Secretary Seward that there was "no political design or significance . . . it was written solely in the interests of Peace and Humanity."[57] King's predecessors, Alexander W. Randall and Richard M. Blatchford, had reported gestures and words of the pope and Cardinal Antonelli friendly to the Union cause. The cardinal was perhaps the preeminent pragmatist of his age—no small feat in an age of pragmatists—and he saw the handwriting on the wall for the South, but Roman policy was to keep both sides at arm's length. Irish Benedictine Bernard Smith wrote to John Hughes from Rome that his efforts as Lincoln's representative had drawn heavy fire. Federal recognition of the Kingdom of Italy had not gone down well, and the pope was said to believe that a reunited United States would be too powerful a nation.[58] British diplomatic agent Odo Russell told the Foreign Office on July 30, 1864, of an audience with Pius IX, who "would not conceal from me the fact that all his sympathies were with the Southern Confederacy and he wished them all success."[59]

In letters sent in 1862 the pope directed the archbishops of New Orleans and New York to make every effort to achieve reconciliation and end the fighting.[60] Response in the South was more enthusiastic than in the North. Purcell and Hughes, the most prominent northern sympathizers, both received further personal messages from Rome exhorting them to work for peace. The pressure from Rome was in part, at least, a measure of the success of Bishop Spalding, who did not limit himself to denouncing Purcell in letters to Roman authorities. In October 1863 Spalding's anonymous "Dissertation on the American Civil War" was serialized in the papal newspaper *Osservatore Romano*.[61] After describing the warm welcome given in northern cities to European radicals like Lajos Kossuth and Giuseppe Garibaldi, he proceeded to the topic of slavery. It was an unfortunate social evil, the legacy of American's Protestant heritage. His solution was a gradualist approach to emancipation. He blamed the war on inequitable tariff structures foisted on the agrarian South by an industrial North. Lincoln's war policies he excoriated: their goal was extermination of the South. Publication of the article had been arranged by Cardinal Alessandro Barnabò, head of the Congregation for Propagation of the Faith. Six months later the pope accepted the Congregation's recommendation and named Martin J. Spalding to succeed Kenrick as Archbishop of Baltimore.

XIII

Reconstruction

When the seventh archbishop of Baltimore came from Kentucky, he brought with him a family tree with deep Maryland roots, a reputation as the Catholic Church's most prolific American apologist, and an amiable disposition which soon won him many friends among priests and lay people, though his amiability was coupled with a stern streak of frontier moralism acquired from Charles Nerinckx. The friendly smiles were interspersed with directives not wholly congenial with easygoing Chesapeake ways. The new archbishop took a dim view of such lay pastimes as waltzing and round-dancing. He frowned on theatricals and parish picnics. He had particularly harsh words for what he called "sporting priests." His politics remained neutralist. He was annoyed because he believed that the Lincoln administration had interfered in the appointment of archbishops for Baltimore and New York, although there is no evidence that this was so. Spalding heard that Bishop Michael Domenec had met with Secretary Seward, and testily inquired of Domenec: "Are some so ill-advised as to wish to bring about union of Church and State?" But the Pittsburgh bishop assured him he had only told Seward "that you never wished to speak on politics and still less to meddle with them."[1]

A great deal of Spalding's introduction to Baltimore involved dealing with politicians. As head of the archdiocese which included the national capital, he was regularly asked to intercede with government officials when difficulties connected with church personnel or property arose. Retired Bishop Michael O'Connor, a friend of Secretary Stanton, helped him with the problem of Bishop Elder's detention in Louisiana. The inspector-general of the army, James A. Hardie, a convert to Catholicism, gave the archbishop regular assistance. It was not always an easy task. When Federal troops ran a defensive work through Cathedral Cemetery on Thunderbolt Road south of Savannah, Bishop Verot protested to the Catholic officer in charge, Major General Quincy A. Gillmore, commander of the Department of the South, and then fired off a sizzler to Stanton, breathing threats of excommunication and muttering of "brutal force" and "infidel ideas." The affair was finally sorted out after considerable spillage of ink, and Verot had won his point.[2]

The year 1865 saw Spalding acting as go-between in a litany of complaints of this kind. A unit of the Protestant United States Christian Commission appropriated a Catholic Church for a school at New Bern, North Carolina; troops billeted in a church at Fort Smith, Arkansas, did $20,000 damage; Bishop Lynch was still in exile while his diocese of Charleston lay in shambles. Then on April 14 John Wilkes Booth shot Abraham Lincoln. Spalding hastened to issue a statement: "A deed of blood has been perpetrated, which has caused every heart to shudder, and which calls for the execration of every citizen. . . . " General Hardie sent a note urging that crepe be hung on all Catholic buildings. Otherwise there was danger of "disorder, destruction of property, riot and perhaps bloodshed."[3] That was avoided, but there was trouble in store for the Catholic community. The conspirators had met in Mrs. Mary Surratt's boarding house in Washington, and that innocent widow was tried, convicted, and hanged. She was a Catholic, as was her son John, who actually was involved in the plot. When he escaped and was discovered hiding out as a volunteer in the pope's own army, anit-papist suspicions were aroused. Another innocent victim was a Catholic physician, Samuel A. Mudd, who, ignorant of what had happened, set Booth's leg for him and ended up in chains at Fort Jefferson on Dry Tortugas.[4]

Spalding also presided over the first general meeting of bishops since 1852. The second plenary council of the Roman Catholic Church in the United States met for two weeks beginning on October 4, 1866, and finished with a solemn session attended by President Andrew Johnson.[5] Mulberry Street, alongside the Baltimore cathedral, was lined with spectators, and people crowded windows and rooftops to watch the procession from Archbishop's House that opened the council. Forty-five archbishops and bishops and two abbots walked in the procession, attended by a phalanx of theological advisers and ceremonial assistants. As they turned the corner onto Cathedral Street and entered the cathedral's main doors, a full orchestra welcomed them with the grand march from *Tannhäuser*. For the music of the morning's liturgy the choir chose Mozart's Twelfth Mass. The bishops represented a church of nearly four million Americans in a national population of some thirty million. Since the last plenary council the number of churches and priests had doubled. The major reason for Catholic growth was evidenced by the council fathers themselves: of forty-seven mitred participants in the opening procession, thirty were foreign-born immigrants.

As in previous American councils, the bishops agreed on a series of internal disciplinary decrees designed to harmonize church procedures throughout the country. What was new in the five hundred thirty-four pages of legislation was a series of statements on theological topics: Revelation, the Church as custodian of Revelation, the doctrine of "outside the Church there is no salvation," the nature and necessity of Faith, Sacred Scripture, the mysteries of the Trinity, creation, redemption, sanctification, the future life, and veneration of the Blessed Virgin Mary. The text relied heavily on recent papal statements, including many of the same documents cited by Pope Pius IX in his 1864 Syllabus of Errors. But the tone was distinctly American, and nowhere was the Syllabus mentioned. The bishops tried to deal with the actual problems of the church on their side of the Atlantic. Their approach was for the most part a more positive one than had been adopted in Rome.[6]

An important item was insistence on collective episcopal authority. The centrality of the bishop and see of Rome to a Catholic understanding of Christianity was underlined but accompanied by a statement on the collegial role of all bishops:

> Bishops, therefore, who are the successors of the Apostles, and whom the Holy Spirit has placed to rule the Church of God, which He acquired with His own blood, agreeing and judging together with its head on earth, the Roman Pontiff, whether they are gathered in general councils, or dispersed throughout the world, are inspired from on high with the gift of inerrancy, so that their body or college can never fail nor define anything against doctrine revealed by God.[7]

The bishops were well aware that most American Catholics lived in the teeming eastern slums. Their predecessors in 1852 had noted:

> Not only have we to erect and maintain the Church, the Seminary and the schoolhouse, but we have to found hospitals, establish orphanages and provide for every want of suffering humanity, which religion forbids us to neglect.[8]

Now there was a new need. The pastoral letter of 1866 was blunt:

> A large number of Catholic parents either appear to have no idea of the sanctity of the Christian family, and of the responsibility imposed on them of providing for the moral training of their offspring, or fulfill their duty in a very imperfect manner.

The result was inevitable:

> It is a melancholy fact, and a very humiliating avowal for us to make, that a very large proportion of the idle and vicious youth of our principal cities are the children of Catholic parents. . . . Day after day, these unhappy children are caught in the commission of petty crimes, which render them amenable to the public authorities; and, day after day, are they transferred by hundreds from the sectarian reformatories in which they have been placed by the courts, to distant localities, where they are brought up in ignorance of, and most commonly in hostility to, the Religion in which they had been baptized.

The solution was foundation of Catholic protectories and industrial schools.[9]

Doctrine and discipline were easier to handle than the crusty and opinionated Archbishop of St. Louis, Peter Kenrick. Spalding had made sure to include him in planning the council, but he still played the obstructionist, punctuating debate with threats to walk out. The agenda was too detailed to suit his taste; he claimed decisions had been reached beforehand and that all that was wanted of the participants was their signatures. He was also angry that several of his pet projects had been shelved. One was standard clerical dress for priests, "many of whom appear to think that the less ecclesiastical their appearance, the more extended their influence." His proposal was something like the Irish "tonsure coat," a sort of cut-down soutane. He also had a complicated solution for church property ownership, involving lay people who would hold title and lease property to bishops. Whatever his reasons, Kenrick nearly caused the council to "go up in smoke," as Verot wrote to Rome. His conduct does suggest, as his biographer has written, "a certain element of sheer pig-headedness."[10]

One serious consequence of internal dissension was the failure to adopt a cohesive and vigorous program for evangelization of the four million freed black people. Specific action plans fashioned by Spalding and recommended by Roman authorities were watered down to the level of pious exhortation with implementation left to local choice. Archbishops Odin and Kenrick-led the opposition, taking the position that all that could be done was being done. A suggestion that one or more prefectures-apostolic—equivalent to non-territorial missionary dioceses—be set up for black people elicited from Kenrick a threat to resign. The proposed collection for support of missionary work among blacks drew from New York's John McCloskey the reply that "in no way was the conscience of the bishops of the North burdened in regard to the black." The council's legislation finally called for religious communities to open schools and other institutions to minister to blacks. It left to local decision the question of separate churches. The council's pastoral letter was decidedly ambivalent: "A new and most extensive field of charity and devotedness" had been opened, although

> we could have wished, that in accordance with the action of the Catholic Church in past ages, in regard to the serfs in Europe, a more gradual system of emancipation could have been adopted, so that they might have been in some measure prepared to make a better use of their freedom, than they are likely to do now. Still the evils which must necessarily attend upon the sudden liberation of so large a multitude, with their peculiar dispositions and habits, only make the appeal to our Christian charity and zeal, presented by their forlorn condition, the more forcible and imperative.[11]

The mixed signals sent by the council were reflected in an evangelization effort that was largely unsuccessful. But northern Catholics were not as unconcerned as Archbishop McCloskey's comment might suggest. Bishop Verot headed "for the oil regions" and collected about $900 in the diocese of Erie, $800 in Buffalo, and $700 in Rochester before finishing a three-week swing with visits to Ohio's major cities. Southern white Catholics were frequently as generous as diminished means allowed. Verot, perhaps the most vehemently pro-slavery of the prewar bishops, developed during Reconstruction an extensive program for ministry to black people. He recruited Sisters of St. Joseph from Le Puy in France to open schools specifically for them. Mother Marie Sidonie Rascle and the first group arrived at the end of August 1866. Before the bishop died ten years later they had seven schools. No other diocese followed his lead to any significant extent and even Verot's efforts appeared minuscule in comparison with those of government and Protestant church-related schools.[12]

The second plenary council's exhortation to black evangelization had little lasting effect. Merton Coulter's judgment is that Catholics "had little success because in fact they made little effort."[13] There were other reasons. Inadequate attention was paid to the subjective side of religion: black people's deeply felt religious needs and how best to meet them. Verot and Lynch made great efforts. But they believed that Catholicism's appeal for blacks lay in the "pomp, variety and symbolism of its ceremonial ritual," in its "Processions and Novenas."[14] They had a limited point. Albert Raboteau has noted how well "ritual use of sacred objects and devotion to the saints" blended with African ritual and understanding of God. But there was more. Catholic worship lacked the "prayer meetings, shouting and spirituals" which were an attractive feature of black Protestantism, "the bodily participation and ecstatic behavior . . . so reminiscent of African patterns of dance and possession."[15] A further problem was communicating a sense of "ownership," or full-fledged membership. Separate churches for blacks grew faster among Protestants than among Catholics, and even where Catholic churches were for both, a separate section, sometimes a "black gallery," was reserved. Most blacks preferred their own churches, where they heard black preachers and played a physically and vocally active part in church worship and management.

The Catholic notion, strong in the 19th century, of the priest as sacral figure set apart had a certain allure, but it was also part of the problem. Given the requirements for ordination, it is not surprising that not until 1888 was the first black priest ordained for work among his own people. He was Augustus Tolton, an ex-slave from Hannibal, Missouri, and he completed his studies for the priesthood in Rome.[16] Black sisters were only slightly more common: Baltimore's Oblate Sisters of Providence, founded in 1829, and the Sisters of the Holy Family, founded in 1842 in New Orleans, continued their work. White communities of priests, sisters, and brothers did not generally accept black candidates until the 20th century. Remarkable exceptions in a dismal landscape were the three Healy brothers, sons of an Irish Georgia slaveowner and his slave wife. James Augustine Healy was chancellor of the Boston diocese and then for a quarter-century, 1875–1900, bishop of Portland, Maine. Alexander Sherwood Healy taught briefly at the regional seminary in Troy, New York, and was secretary to the Bishop of Boston. Patrick Healy, S.J., was president of Georgetown College from 1873 to 1882.[17]

The apostolate expanded with the 1871 arrival of English Mill Hill Missionaries, whose American offshoot became in 1891 the Society of St. Joseph under the gifted leadership of John Richard Slattery. Their first black priest, Charles Randolph Uncles, S.S.J., was ordained in 1891. Others followed: the Society of St. Edmund, Spiritans, the Society of African Missions, the Society of the Divine Word. Diocesan priests and older communities of men and women soldiered on. But after the failed opportunity of 1866 it remained well into the 20th century essentially a missionary effort of whites to blacks.[18]

Other skirmishes reminded Catholics of the complexity of their body in America. On the last day of May 1866, John O'Neill led eight hundred Irishmen of a recently organized revolutionary society, the Fenian Brotherhood, across the Niagara River in a quixotic invasion of Canada. They captured Fort Erie before being beaten back by Canadian militia and cut off by the American army. The steamer *Erin's Hope*, despatched to Ireland itself in 1867, was intercepted on arrival. In a final flourish, the last Fenian invasion of Canada, this time from Vermont, was interrupted by United States marshals who arrested the entire party. American bishops argued about taking action. Few followed the lead of Peter Kenrick who in the summer of 1865 denied Fenians the sacraments in his diocese. An 1870 Roman decree eventually condemned the Brotherhood for the secret oath it exacted, but not until *The Atlantic Monthly* had profited by the chance to resurrect for its readers a sonorous denunciation reminiscent of the days of High Nativism:

> Devotion to an idea, to a constitution, to a flag; respect for law *as* law; sturdy independence and self-reliance; regard for others' rights and jealousy of a man's own,—all these true republican characteristics are most rarely to be found in an Irishman.[19]

American involvement in wider church affairs increased. Five American bishops took part in discussions at the Vatican preceding the pope's doctrinal definition in 1854 that Mary the Mother of Jesus had been conceived free from Original Sin. Archbishop Francis P. Kenrick and Bishop Michael O'Connor criticized loose handling in the draft presented to them of passages from Scripture and the church fathers and reminded the hundred bishops present that the pope's document would be read by non-Catholics whose regard for the church would not be enhanced by seeing texts misused. In line with notions on episcopal collegiality widely accepted in the United States, O'Connor unsuccessfully recommended a clear statement that the pope was making a doctrinal definition with the consent of the college of bishops.[20]

If the 1854 Immaculate Conception definition was a theological event (with political undertones), the gathering of more than three hundred bishops in Rome on June 8, 1862, for the canonization of thirty 16th-century Japanese martyrs was patently a political occasion. Just over a year before, Victor Emmanuel II had been proclaimed King of Italy. What was lacking to his kingdom was Rome as its capital. If any bishops had missed the point of their assembly, Pius IX explained it in a talk the next day in which he denounced the Italian government and stated his determination to defend the temporal power of the papacy, which he considered intimately connected with his spiritual authority. Archbishop Hughes, in Rome on behalf of President Lincoln, was present with fourteen other northern bishops.

The impact in the United States of Pius IX's 1864 Syllabus of Errors, in which Pius had left little doubt about his opposition to most of the chief tenets of 19th-century liberalism, was muted since it appeared during the final winter of the Civil War. But, as Martin Spalding noted, "a howl of indignation" went up in the English and American press, which he attempted to calm with a pastoral letter explaining that Pius IX was concerned with "European radicals," and not with the American Constitution, separation of church and state as known in America, and liberty of conscience, worship, or the press as practiced in the United States. In New York, John McCloskey was not so sanguine when he wrote:

> It is consoling to think and believe that our Holy Father has in all his official acts a light and guidance from on High—for according to all the rules of mere human prudence and wisdom the encyclical [*Quanta Cura*] *with its annex* of condemned propositions would be considered illtimed. . . . [21]

Two incidents in the 1860s threw into relief problems affecting the American church because of its connection with Rome. Paris banker Robert Murphy came to the United States hoping to sell $4 million in papal bonds. The bishops were willing to endorse the existence of the Pontifical State as being necessary under present circumstances, and in the council of 1866 they ordered in all parishes an annual collection for the pope, but they were less than enthusiastic about sale of papal bonds. The situation was not improved when the Baltimore bank to which Spalding with reluctance assigned the task of accepting subscriptions for the loan failed. Also connected with the declining temporal fortunes of the papacy was the effort orchestrated by James A. McMaster of the *Freeman's Journal* to raise a battalion of American volunteers for the papal army. Acutely conscious of legal and other problems, the eastern archbishops moved to quash the project. They were of a mind with Archbishop Purcell, who commented: "Better trust to God, leaving in the scabbard a sword which never established a Church."[22]

The horizontal ties of collegiality which bound American bishops together had obviously worn thin at the 1866 council. Vertical lines of authority in the church were even more frayed. The casual canonical structure prevailing in most American dioceses was a factor. Internal church structures which in Europe assured at least a continental version of due process were missing. The United States knew no cathedral chapters of canons; there were few proper church courts and no parishes in the canonical sense of the term. Priests could not be pastors, only "rectors of missions" whom the bishop appointed and removed at will. The sole appeal from his decisions was to Rome. Some priests had no set salary. They were left to survive as best they might, and situations developed like that which met Archbishop Spalding when he was asked in the summer of 1869 to look into the troubled affairs of the church of Chicago. Some rectors were in their avarice, "not pastors, but wolves," he wrote Cardinal Barnabò at Propaganda.[23]

A restiveness almost epidemic among priests in the 1860s at times broke into rebellion. Thomas O'Flaherty, pastor at Auburn, New York, openly defied Bishop Bernard McQuaid on his arrival in the new diocese of Rochester in 1868. Unfortunately for O'Flaherty, he had not adequately taken the measure of his man.[24] In Cleveland two years later a clerical cabal drove Bishop Amadeus Rappe from office.[25] Chicago provided the most dramatic episode. None of the first three bishops there had lasted five years in office. The first died, the second asked for a transfer to Mississippi, the third retired to England. James Duggan was auxiliary bishop to Peter Kenrick at the age of thirty-two. Appointed to Chicago in 1859, he was in the mid-1860s accused of neglect of duties, absenteeism, and financial extravagance. His accusers included the vicar general, chancellor, cathedral rector, and seminary director. Charges and counter-charges flew. Duggan fled for health reasons to Europe and stayed away for two years. Not long after returning, he was committed to an asylum to spend the next thirty years as a mental patient. His ending was tragic, but the problem remained which Chancellor John McMullen (himself later first Bishop of Davenport) posed: "Whether there be any protection or any right in the Catholic Church above the individual will of the Superior."[26]

Many priests' complaints originated among former students at Rome's Urban College of the Congregation for Propagation of the Faith, including alumni of the new (1859) Roman residential facility, the American College. To his immense annoyance, Archbishop McCloskey was all too aware that New York City was a center for articulate dissent. Veteran pastors like Jeremiah Cummings, Thomas Farrell and Brooklyn's Sylvester Malone found worthy successors in Roman alumni Edward McGlynn and Richard Burtsell. The "progressionists" or "anti-absolutists" did not confine their attention to the arbitrary ways of bishops. They were men of broad social outlook, civic-minded and active in community affairs. Malone liked to say that early Protestant schooling in Ireland had given him a broad perspective on life, and in a description that fit them all, he praised McGlynn as an "advocate of temperance and of every good cause that works for the public good." Down through the years good causes included abolition, the Republican party, the Union, and freed blacks. They opposed parochial schools and refused contributions to help the pope keep Italians from taking the Papal States. McGlynn brought matters to a boil with an article in the *New York Sun* on April 30, 1870, which outlined suggestions looking to "an act (or amendment to the Constitution) to guard against the union of Church and State and to protect liberty of conscience." He urged that public funds not be given to any but common schools. In these there should be no reading of the Bible or of any distinctively religious book, no prayers, worship, or hymn-singing. Public asylums and houses of detention ought not have salaried or unsalaried chaplains, although visits by outside clergymen should be facilitated. McGlynn opposed direct or indirect government subsidy to non-public institutions. His philosophy of priestly ministry stressed

> the paramount importance of doing an apostolic rather than a pedagogic work, of building churches, educating priests, administering the sacraments, caring for the poor, looking after destitute children, and making the best of the public schools, rather than to sacrifice these great things and to entail upon the people the expense of Parish schools.

The New York liberals were all successful pastors, but they soon drew the ire of bishops. Thomas Becker of Wilmington arraigned them on a string of charges: they denigrated devotional practices like saying the rosary, wearing scapulars, venerating relics, and calling on the saints. They would do away with vestments worn by priests celebrating mass and eliminate use of Latin. They questioned the newly defined dogma of Mary's Immaculate Conception and the church's teaching on her Assumption into heaven. They accused the pope of "absorbing all the members and causing atrophy in the Apostolic College." And of course they would oppose the coming definition of papal infallibility.[27] Greeley's *Tribune* for October 23, 1868, pictured an intramural Catholic quarrel pitting entrenched conservatives against a progressive element led by Archbishops Purcell and Spalding. The latter were said to be exponents of "American character" and "American spirit." The alliance was unlikely, and so was the ally who now joined the battle, McMaster of the *Freeman's Journal*. McMaster knew no "American" Catholic church. Catholicism for him was Roman and authority in it was identified with the pope. It was in defense of those positions that he entered the fray. Informing one and all that "a layman *may* be erudite in these matters . . . [since] it is a matter of *knowledge,* not of *ecclesiastical position,*" he did battle for canon law and "the second order of the hierarchy," parish priests. Progressives extolled American democratic ideals and argued for Americanization of church polity. McMaster took the opposite tack: arbitrary bishops needed to be brought more squarely under Roman control. The *Freeman's Journal* featured regular contributions from a Cleveland priest, Eugene M. O'Callaghan, writing as "Jus" and "Ecclesiasticus." The dust finally settled, at least in part because Archbishop McCloskey was correct in judging that most priests feared the tyranny of pastors more than that of bishops, while lay people were more inclined to fault bishops for leniency with their priests than for severity.[28]

Slight expectations were entertained of the role which American bishops would play in the First Vatican Council, which met at the call of Pope Pius IX during 1869–1870.[29] John Henry Newman's brother-in-law Thomas Mozley told the *Times* to expect no original contribution from them.

James Gordon Bennett mourned in the New York *Herald* that "bishops from the land that is foremost in all that material progress which is thought to be leading the nations" would leave it to "their brethren of the less progressive countries to assert the necessity for greater freedom of thought." These estimates had to be revised before the council was long in session.

The very first contact Americans had with the preparations for the council suggested their distinct perspective. Theologian James A. Corcoran of Charleston joined the pre-conciliar commission that dealt with doctrinal matters on December 30, 1868. His lively reports provide a unique record of the commission's work. They also reflect peculiarly American worries: too many doctrinal definitions were contemplated, often "because some Prof. Scratchemback in some German university has written about them in a German philosophical jargon which neither himself nor his readers understand." More serious was the way the relationship of church and state was being handled: Corcoran feared that "the fundamental principles of our (American and common-sense) political system" would be condemned if some had their way. Despite his own Roman education, he also found procedures and the mania for secrecy which enveloped the proceedings irksome.[30]

Vatican I was an essentially European event in a church with a predominantly European membership. Its plans, debates, and documents reflected preoccupation with Europe's 19th-century problems: the impact of Enlightenment and French Revolution, the influence of Kant and Hegel, 19th-century continental liberalism. The Italian *Risorgimento* was quite literally at the gates of Rome. A thousand years of papal sovereign rule in central Italy were in their final twelve months. Since Pius VII's time, a succession of popes had set official Catholicism's face squarely against the political, social, and intellectual temper of the times. The Vatican Council was designed by Pius IX to set the seal on that opposition. Pomp and splendor marked the opening session on December 8, 1869. Less than a year later, General Raffaele Cadorna's Italian army occupied Rome and the twentieth ecumenical council of the Roman Catholic church was quietly adjourned. The last significant session had been on July 18 when, with the overwhelming approval of the council fathers, Pio Nono proclaimed the dogmas of papal jurisdictional primacy and infallibility. A constitution on faith and reason had been adopted three months earlier. Together, the two documents represented the Catholic Church's answer to the 19th century.

On the council's chief preoccupation, a definition of papal infallibility, Bishop Bernard McQuaid of Rochester remarked that "with us in America it was scarcely talked of." Stephen Keenan's *Controversial Catechism,* widely used in English-speaking countries and approved by that thorough ultramontane the late Archbishop Hughes, handled the question this way:

Q. Must not Catholics believe the Pope in himself to be infallible?

A. This is a protestant invention; it is no article of Catholic faith: no decision of his can oblige under pain of heresy unless it be received and enforced by the teaching body; that is, by the bishops of the Church.[31]

Faced with the prospect of formal church acceptance of what they had been teaching was at most a free theological opinion, four-fifths of the forty-nine Americans at the council judged the move to be at the very least inopportune. Their position was rooted in fear that assertion of the pope's infallibility would revive the religious hostility of nativist days, blessedly dormant in the years immediately following the Civil War. Ten bishops disagreed. They were all-out partisans of a definition. Most were Franco-Americans from New England, the Pacific Northwest, and the Gulf Coast, but the group also included the Bavarian-born bishop of LaCrosse, Michael Heiss, and Baltimore-born William Henry Elder of Natchez.

Among the "inopportunists" there was a smaller group whose apprehensions went further. They shared a concern with historical and theological problems which seemed to them serious enough to argue against the definability of the doctrine. It was not a teaching which they found clearly enough in the church's tradition. Some, like McQuaid, could not see how the approach being taken at Rome safeguarded the collegiality of all the bishops so recently reaffirmed at Baltimore. The most outspoken American opponent of the definition was Archbishop Kenrick, who in two pamphlets distributed in Rome questioned the basis in tradition of the teaching.

Infallibility was not the only subject on which Americans spoke out. Kenrick was one of several who raised with the council's managers questions of procedure: the possibility of electing members to the assembly's "rules committee," instead of having them appointed by the pope; the need for time to review the credentials of potential candidates before elections to other conciliar committees; restoration of the time-honored right of initiative on the part of council members to introduce proposals; open committee meetings; adequate press facilities; a hall with better acoustics than the cavernous north transept of St. Peter's basilica. Other American interventions revealed a deep pastoral bias on their part. American bishops called for precision, clarity, and brevity in the council's documents. Kenrick reminded the assembly that their function was not to write theological treatises, but to declare the faith of the church. Verot asked explicit acknowledgement of the good faith of those who did not belong to the Roman Catholic Church. Whelan of Wheeling pointed out that in the contemporary world great care had to be taken in evaluating anyone's religious stance, including the stance of those who could not bring themselves to accept any religion. Both Whelan and Elder urged greater attention to showing the biblical foundation for the council's declarations. The general American thrust was to press for a positive orientation. They wanted positive statements of what Catholics believed and deemphasis on a coercive system of ecclesiastical penalties.

Augustin Verot has been called the *enfant terrible* of the council. His humorous sallies certainly tried the patience of the presiding cardinals and at times of the bishops. But his topics were always serious: the prayer-life of priests, reconciliation between the church and modern science, affirmation of the unity in a common humanity of black and white races. It was more important, he told the council, to declare that black people have souls—there were those in his part of the world who denied it—than to struggle with recondite German philosophical theories about the makeup of the human composite. The most American statement of all was one not actually delivered in Rome. The seventy-year-old Irishman who had by 1870 headed the diocese of Cincinnati for forty years, John Baptist Purcell, announced on his return home that he had deposited among the acts of the council the text of an undelivered address whose theme was the relationship of church and state. Convinced that the American is "the best form of human government," Purcell built to a peroration:

> Our civil constitution grants perfect liberty to every denomination of Christians . . . perfect liberty to them all. I verily believe this was infinitely better for the Catholic religion, than were it the special object of the State's patronage and protection . . . all we want is a free field and no favor. Truth is mighty and will prevail; and as we are here side by side with every sect and denomination of Christians, it is for the people to judge which of us is right, which of us teaches that which is most conformable to the Holy Scriptures. If they approve our religion, they will embrace it; if not they will stay away from it. I believe this is the best system.

By late spring 1870, infallibility had become the focal point of all the council's discussions. The definition, together with that of the pope's jurisdictional primacy, was formally voted and proclaimed on July 18. Twenty-five Americans voted yes. Peter Kenrick, Augustin Verot, and Michael Domenec were among fifty-five bishops who addressed a letter of explanation to Pope Pius IX and then left Rome on the eve of the definition so as not to have to cast negative votes in his presence. Bishop

Edward Fitzgerald of Little Rock was one of the two bishops who voted no in the final tally. The remaining American bishops had already gone home. All of them (and all the bishops of the Catholic Church) eventually accepted the definitions of primacy and infallibility, but not without considerable soul-searching in the case of some. Kenrick was a prime example, but finally he accepted the doctrine of infallibility as an instance of the development of doctrine through the centuries. The bishops from the United States hardly took the council by storm, but they did manage to bring to it something of the ideas and peculiar genius of their own country. Many of the causes they espoused would surface again nearly a century later at the Second Vatican Council.

XIV

The Gilded Age

The international exposition celebrating the hundredth anniversary of United States independence opened in Philadelphia on May 10, 1876. It featured the wonders of scientific discovery. There was no amusement section, and fine arts took a subordinate place. On the national scene the disputed election of the nation's nineteenth President, Rutherford B. Hayes, in November 1876 ended the period of Reconstruction which followed the Civil War. Federal troops were withdrawn from southern states, white supremacy was reestablished and black political strength, which had flourished briefly, was nullified. Racial segregation became the pattern. In 1896 the Supreme Court decided that "separate but equal" facilities for blacks and whites were legal.[1] While one-party white rule by the Democrats controlled the ex-Confederate states, the nation itself, except for the two terms of President Grover Cleveland, was dominated from 1861–1913 by the Republicans, the party of the settled and business classes. Opposition Democrats represented southern and western farmers, working people, and the urban poor. It was the gilded age of the "robber barons." By 1890 the country had four thousand millionaires.

American society underwent profound change. Urban population multiplied sevenfold from 6.2 million in 1860 to 44.6 million in 1910, from 19.8 percent to 45.7 percent of the national total. In 1880 one-quarter of the people lived in cities of over eight thousand inhabitants. Industrial income in 1900 was three times higher than farm income.[2] The "Wild West" of romantic legend flourished. On June 25, 1876, General George Armstrong Custer and two hundred cavalrymen were annihilated at the Little Big Horn River by the Sioux led by Sitting Bull, Gall, and Crazy

Horse. Geronimo led the Chiricahua Apaches in the last large Indian war (1882–86), although scattered battles continued into the 20th century. Two hundred Sioux men, women, and children were massacred by the cavalry at Wounded Knee Creek, South Dakota, in 1890. U.S. marshals, sheriffs, and outlaws—like Jesse James, who was killed in 1882—roamed the prairies.

The era was inspired by the country's conviction of its "manifest destiny" to Americanize and Protestantize the world.[3] For American Protestantism these were golden years of crowded churches and broad influence, a complacent time when God's kingdom on earth and the American way of life became indistinguishable and the Social Darwinist theories of Herbert Spencer provided ample justification for the prosperity and success which increasing numbers of Americans enjoyed. Socio-economic survival of the fittest supported a gospel of wealth in which Horatio Alger was the hero and "acres of diamonds" were there for the digging. It all went on until the liberal theology took another turning and, toward the century's end, theologians like Walter Rauschenbusch and Washington Gladden appeared on the scene. In their social gospel, the kingdom motif meant social and economic change.[4]

Winthrop Hudson has written that "the most spectacular development in American religious life in the latter half of the nineteenth century" was "the growth of the Roman Catholic Church."[5] Immigration transformed American Catholicism. Until 1896, most immigrants had come from northern and western Europe. In a peak year, 1882, 87 percent did so, against 13 percent from southern and eastern Europe. By 1907, 19.3 percent came from northern nations and 80.7 percent from the south and east. Earlier Catholic immigrants were chiefly from Germany, Ireland, and Canada. The newcomers were Italian, Polish, Hungarian, or had their origin in the Slavic lands of the Dual Monarchy. The effect was massive. Over a million Catholics poured into the country in each decade between 1880 and 1920, and over two million in the years 1901–10.[6] Catholic population grew from 6,259,000 in 1880 to 16,363,000 in 1910 in a national population that went from 75,995,000 to 91,972,000.[7] Some Czechs and Germans became farmers, but most Catholics settled in eastern and midwestern cities. In 1890, four of every five people in greater New York City were either immigrants or children of immigrants.[8]

The Irish preferred the East; Germans headed for cities in the Cincinnati-St.Louis-Milwaukee triangle. Italians re-created in city neighborhoods something of the village atmosphere they had left behind. The thesis that the Catholic Church served as primary agent in their inculturation has been challenged. By the time massive Italian immigration began around 1880, the American church and American Catholics were already rather set in their ways, and those ways were too often not the ways of the new arrivals. The situation was not unlike that of Jews from eastern Europe who immigrated in large numbers in the same period and faced integration with a community previously Sephardic and then heavily German. Italian Catholics, and the eastern Europeans who flooded Pennsylvania coalfields and industrial cities across the nation's midsection, met hostile reaction and frequent rejection, not only from old Americans, but from immigrants hardly earlier on the ground than themselves, many of them their coreligionists. Even among this "second wave" of immigrants there were notable differences. Chicago is the ideal laboratory in which to study their impact on city and church alike. It welcomed them all, and they set to work building parishes complete with church and schools. Pastors came from the old countries and from within immigrant groups. Polish sisters from a half-dozen congregations taught in elementary schools and high schools and plans were made for a Polish Catholic university. Other nationalities organized in the same way: Lithuanians, Bohemians, Slovaks, Croats, Slovenes, and Hungarians. "Every group," James Sanders observed, "whatever its size, struggled to build separate parishes and schools—with one notable exception," the Italians, who "distinguished themselves for their disinterest not only in the parochial school but in the Catholic parish itself." The picture was the same elsewhere. Chicago Archbishop James Quigley's complaint to Rome as late as 1913 that "the Italians who come from Southern Italy and Sicily are unexcelled in their ignorance of religion" echoed Wilmington's Bishop Thomas A. Becker, writing thirty years earlier:

> It is a very delicate matter to tell the Sovereign Pontiff how utterly faithless the specimens of his country coming here really are. Ignorance of their religion and a depth of vice little known to us yet, are the prominent characteristics. The fault lies far higher up than the poor people. The clergy are sadly remiss in their duty.

The trend was reversed and Italian-Americans became the strong support of many a 20th-century Catholic parish, but only after there had been a sustained evangelization effort to enlist non-Italian sisters and priests as well as Italian diocesan priests, Servites, Franciscans, Missionaries of St. Charles (founded in 1887 by Bishop Giovanni Battista Scalabrini), and women's communities like Mother Cabrini's Missionary Sisters of the Sacred Heart, who came to the United States in 1889.[9]

Along the Mexican border and in California, Mexican immigrants in increasingly large numbers joined resident Spanish-speaking Catholics incorporated in the United States since the war with Mexico in 1846–48. The "land reforms" of Porfirio Díaz, Mexico's dictator from 1876 to

1911, encouraged emigration: 95 percent of the people were left landless. American policies cutting off the flow of Oriental labor—the 1882 Chinese Exclusion Act and the 1907 "Gentlemen's Agreement" with Japan—made prospects north of the border attractive. Mexicans soon made up 80 percent of the farm work force in the West and contributed 90 percent of the railroad workers and 60 percent of the mine workers.

On the opposite end of the continent, French-Canadian migration southward increased toward the end of the century. The first French parish in New England since the days of Poterie and Rousselet was opened at Burlington, Vermont, in 1850. Irish and French Catholics clashed. The Irish looked down on a group which, despite three centuries of American ancestry, seemed more "foreign" than they. The French posed an economic threat by working longer hours for less pay, and they found Irish customs, such as having to contribute to church support, odd, remarking with some puzzlement that "it costs quite a bit to practice one's religion here." Bishop Louis de Goesbriand of Burlington had other concerns, complaining in 1886 that he found "complete ignorance of religion" among the immigrants, who "knew not either confession or communion and many of whom have been invalidly married before Protestant ministers." A concerted campaign, helped by priests recruited in Québec, reversed the trend. Catholic newspapers and societies were created, and weeklong parish "missions," a Catholic form of revival meeting, were preached. It was not long before Yankee ancestral memories were stirred to recall days when there had been a Catholic nation on colonial borders. Québec nationalist Louis La Flèche, Bishop of Trois-Rivières, did nothing to calm apprehensions when he prophesied in 1889 New England's annexation to Québec. Another Catholic immigrant group, in southern New England and in California, was the Portuguese, many of them from the Azores and most of them initially coming to work as deep-sea fisherman.[10]

The immigrants of the late 19th century marked as "foreign" a church that had come to Maryland in 1634 and to Florida, Maine, and the Southwest even earlier. Catholicism fit awkwardly with established Protestant American patterns. It became preeminently the church of laborer and city-dweller, of ghetto and slum, and kept that image until the post–World War II flight to the suburbs. In many circles, Catholic and otherwise, it keeps the image still. The poverty of Catholic people led their church to concentrate on elementary education and on works of charity. Little time or resources were available for the arts, culture, or higher education.

The church focused immigrant pride and group loyalty. Money that might have begun family fortunes the members of Catholic community

sacrificed for churches, schools and charitable institutions. The Massachusetts laborers earning a dollar a day who pledged fifty dollars each to
support their parish were typical.[11] Catholic life centered in the parish.
Six thousand priests in 1880 grew to twelve thousand in 1900 and seventeen thousand in 1910. They served as advisers and protectors, and they
wielded considerable influence. But rapid growth brought its problems.
When Irish Bishop George Conroy of Ardagh visited the United States
for the Holy See in 1878, he reported that the tumultuous financial situation in the country in combination with the deluge of immigrants had
seriously burdened the church. Its debts equalled half the value of church
property. Pastors had to be picked with an eye to their financial acumen.
It was the same with bishops: "Too often . . . the most valued gifts in the
candidate proposed to the Holy See are properly those of a banker and
not of a pastor of souls."[12]

Under Leo XIII, pope from 1878 to 1903, the church formed much of
its present structure. In 1880 there were eleven archdioceses, forty-seven
dioceses, six vicariates-apostolic governed by missionary bishops, and one
prefecture apostolic headed by a priest. By 1904, two new metropolitan
sees and twenty-six dioceses had been added, and there was four vicari-
ates and a prefecture. In 1875 Archbishop John McCloskey of New York
became the first American cardinal, followed in 1886 by Archbishop
James Gibbons of Baltimore.

The Catholic community had its problems. Orestes Brownson (admit-
tedly in a dour mood) wrote to Isaac Hecker in August 1870 that "the
most lawless & rowdyish and even criminal portions of the population
are Catholics or their offspring." Nearly three decades later Bishop John
Lancaster Spalding regretted that Chicago Catholics were "obliged to
toil seven days in the week without opportunity to cultivate or keep
alive either their mental or religious or moral nature." "They live," he
declared,

> for the most part in hired rooms where, having no proper home, they
> are driven into the street or saloon, where the daily record of crime is
> spread before their eyes to harden and corrupt, where parents have little
> control over the associations of their children.[13]

Proportions are uncertain. Many Catholics, poor and outcast or not, were
genuinely devout. Although they settled chiefly in cities, most retained
their peasant values, bringing to tenement and mill town a conservative
religion centered in the home. They prayed the rosary alone and in family
groups. Religious instruction came in the parochial school if there was
one, or in Sunday School—after 1885 with the help of a series of "Baltimore Catechisms" which remained normative until 1941.

On a more intellectual level Cardinal Gibbons's *Faith of Our Fathers,* first published in 1876, sold thousands of copies. Religious magazines multiplied: *Ave Maria* (1865) was published at Notre Dame by the Congregation of Holy Cross; the *Catholic World* (1865) by the Paulists; the *Messenger of the Sacred Heart* (1866) by the Jesuits; a *Manual of Prayers* authorized by the Third Plenary Council of Baltimore was supplemented by a large number of books of devotional piety. Isaac Hecker founded in 1870 a monthly paper, *The Young Catholic: An Illustrated Magazine for Young Folks,* with his sister-in-law, Josephine Wentworth Hecker, as editor. The Paulists sponsored the Catholic Publication Society, and a number of commercial publishing houses made a living with Catholic books, although it could be a near thing, as Lawrence Kehoe, director of the Catholic Publication Society, admitted in 1886: prayer books and manuals of instruction paid for themselves, but "the best books couldn't be counted on to sell a thousand." Charles Constantine Pise's *Father Rowland* (1829) is generally accepted as the first "Catholic" novel written in the United States. The use of didactic fiction, in novels and in short stories in many of the Catholic magazines, grew steadily through the century.[14]

Liturgical worship was generally plain, more so with the Irish than with the Germans or eastern and southern European immigrants. Typical was Archbishop John Ireland of St. Paul, of whom Paulist priest Walter Elliott wrote: "He is a Celtic American through and through . . . quite content with catacombical public worship."[15] In the East a recited low mass was standard, and early morning was the favorite time for its celebration. If there were hymns, a choir sang them. Congregational participation and sung masses were more a feature of the midwestern German style. The parish mission, a Catholic species of revival meeting held annually or at intervals, was a major feature of parish life. Jesuits on the east cost and in the Midwest, Redemptorists and Paulists were the itinerant preachers of the movement.[16] Paraliturgical services were popular: novenas, or nine-day sequences of prayer, adoration of the eucharistic presence of Christ in the service of benediction and in a periodic intensified "forty hours' devotion," held on a set schedule in the parishes of a diocese. Churches had organizations for men and women. Women joined rosary and altar societies; men belonged to the Knights of Columbus (1882), Knights of St. John (1886), and the Knights of Peter Claver and Holy Name Society (both 1909); for children there were cadet corps and clubs. Catholic societies cared for inmates of public institutions, provided rudimentary life insurance, and paid for burial. Mutual-aid and temperance societies flourished. With a reference to the founder of the worldwide St. Vincent de Paul Society, Thomas Mulry, a New York layman, was called "the American Ozanam" for his work in organizing the St. Vincent de Paul Society to help those in need. Bazaars and picnics helped finance churches which depended totally on parishioners for support.

Bishop Conroy reported to Rome in 1878 that hardly ten in sixty-eight American bishops were distinguished for any kind of talent. The rest "hardly reach a decent mediocrity, and in theological knowledge they do not even reach mediocrity." The problem was not limited to bishops. Sherwood Healy, professor in the Troy seminary in 1868, wrote his bishop: "It is astonishing how young men forget what they learned in the seminary. They study not and become stupid. . . . I cannot think . . . that you know how ignorant are some of our clergymen: you might not sleep easy if you did."[17] There were real problems of leadership. Archbishop John Williams, a genteel Bostonian, was, like his contemporary in Chicago, Archbishop Patrick A. Feehan, well known for a pleasant determination to say nothing as much as possible.[18] Fortunately for the Athens of America, John Boyle O'Reilly, editor of *The Pilot* after 1876, and Patrick Donahoe, the newspaper's liberal owner and publisher, represented a prominent Catholic voice in Boston's civic and literary establishment.[19]

In New York, McCloskey and his successor Archbishop Michael A. Corrigan were symbols of another lasting pattern, association with Irish political machines.[20] The Irish had found their métier in local politics. In ethnically heterogeneous New York City, they formed one-third of the population by 1890 and controlled the political club Tammany Hall which ran the Democratic party. "Honest John" Kelly, who married McCloskey's niece, headed Tammany from 1871 to 1882, and was succeded by another Catholic, Richard Croker, who made some $8 million in public service before his sway ended in 1901. Catholic politicians were frequently generous to church causes. Both Hugh Grant, whom Croker made mayor of New York in 1888, and Peter F. Meyer, Croker's real estate man, were the source of substantial benefactions. But too often they remained remarkably obtuse to the possibility of using political power to achieve fundamental social change. Nor were they much given to the infusion of Christian principles into public life. As Johnny Powers, boss of Chicago's 19th ward put it, "the people of the 19th ward are a people that is governed by the saloons—not by the church." Historian of Chicago Catholicism James Sanders remarks: "Boodle and patronage were their creed. Only the wildest dreamer or the most myopic bigot could see in a Bathhouse John [Coughlin] or a Hinky Dink [Kenna] agents of the Pope."[21]

New York was the diocese of progressive priests like Edward McGlynn and Richard Burtsell. It also remained home to the *Freeman's Journal*, which James McMaster edited from 1848 until he died in 1886, to Patrick

Ford's *Irish World*,[22] and to the *Catholic News,* edited by American Catholicism's premier historian, John Gilmary Shea. Prosperous Catholics founded (1884) the United States Catholic Historical Society, with Shea as first president. The Society in 1899 began publication of *Historical Records and Studies.*[23] In upstate New York the most prominent figure was that most progressive of conservatives, Bernard J. McQuaid, Bishop of Rochester, whose St. Bernard's Seminary (1893) ranked as one of the nation's best.[24]

Philadelphia boasted St. Charles Seminary (1838), the *American Catholic Quarterly Review* (1876–1924), the *American Ecclesiastical Review* (1889–1975, but after 1927 published at the Catholic University in Washington), and the American Catholic Historical Society (1884). Martin I. J. Griffin founded the historical society and for nearly three decades edited, and to a large extent wrote, the volumes of *American Catholic Historical Researches* (1886—1912). The society inaugurated (1887) a historical journal, *Records.* James F. Wood was named coadjutor to Bishop John Nepomucene Neumann, C.Ss.R., in 1857, succeeded him three years later and was named first archbishop from 1875 to 1883. Hostile to secret societies, he found himself in conflict with Irish miners in the "Molly Maguires" crisis which climaxed with the hanging for murder of twenty Irishmen during the years 1877–79. Irish-born Patrick J. Ryan, brought from St. Louis in 1884, achieved better rapport with the diverse elements in the diocese's increasingly ethnically diversified community.[25]

The South's leading Catholic churchman, presiding over an ecclesiastical province reaching from Maryland to Florida and including Washington, D.C., was James Gibbons, vicar apostolic of North Carolina in 1868, youngest father of the First Vatican Council, bishop of Richmond (1872), and for forty-four years (1877–1921) archbishop of Baltimore and titular leader of American Catholics. He was American-born and trained, with a sure instinct for popular spirituality, a conciliationist, the friend of United States presidents—especially Grover Cleveland, Theodore Roosevelt, and William Howard Taft—not a crusading leader, but prudent and a generally progressive influence.[26] John J. Keane succeeded him in Richmond and then become (1887–96) first rector of the Catholic University of America. He was a leader among liberal bishops at the end of the century. Another liberal was John J. Kain, bishop of Wheeling in 1875 and in 1893 coadjutor of St. Louis.[27] Until the end of the century, the dioceses in the deep South with the exception of Catholic sections along the Gulf Coast, remained missionary enterprises.

In St. Louis, Archbishop Peter Richard Kenrick abandoned episcopal functions to a coadjutor from 1872 to 1884. He then picked up the reins again, but he retired in 1895 after fifty-two years as bishop.[28] The last years of Archbishop John B. Purcell at Cincinnati were clouded by the failure of a bank operated by his brother Edward, priest and crusading wartime editor of the *Catholic Telegraph*.[29] William H. Elder of Natchez became coadjutor in 1880 and archbishop in 1883.

German-American Catholicism had its principal seat at Milwaukee under first Swiss-born John Henni and then Bavarian-born Michael Heiss. John Ireland, a French-educated Irish immigrant, became bishop of St. Paul in 1884 and archbishop in 1888. This "consecrated blizzard of the northwest" was eloquent, energetic, and confident of the American dream.[30] Another midwestern progressive, but one who marched to his own drummer, was the philosopher and litterateur John Lancaster Spalding, a member of the old Kentucky Catholic family and educated at Louvain.[31] Mid-America was also the home of active Catholic laymen: conservatives like Arthur Preuss, editor of the St. Louis *Fortnightly Review*, outspoken advocate of German-Americans and translator of Joseph Pohle's *Lehrbuch der Dogmatik*, which in Preuss's English version became standard seminary fare; Condé Pallen, editor of St. Louis *Church Progress* for forty years after 1890, a determined opponent of social involvement by the church. The socially more progressive Henry Spaunhorst was president of the *Central-Verein*, a national federation of parish mutual-aid societies founded in 1855.[32] In addition, there were Henry Brownson of Detroit, son of Orestes Brownson, and William Onahan, Chicago businessman, Democratic politician and leader in efforts to promote Irish Catholic rural settlement.[33]

Missionaries were active in the Rocky Mountains, even in Mormon Utah.[34] Three French bishops were prominent in the Southwest: Joseph Machebeuf, builder over twenty years (1868–89) of the church in Colorado; John B. Lamy, who after a quarter-century as bishop was made Archbishop of Santa Fe in 1875; and his successor in 1885, John B. Salpointe, who in 1869 had become the first bishop in Arizona.[35] A lively and circumstantial account of southwest mission life has been left by a Cincinnati Sister of Charity, Blandina Segale.[36] In California, successive San Francisco Archbishops Joseph Alemany, O.P., and Patrick W. Riordan were hard pressed to keep pace with a developing region where Catholics of the most diverse national origins prospered in business, farming, mining, and politics. In 1902 Riordan became the first successful litigant before the Permanent Court of International Arbitration at the Hague, when a judgment was handed down ordering Mexico to resume payment of annuities due from the "Pious Fund of the Californias," a trust dating back to Jesuit mission days in 1697.[37]

In the Pacific Northwest, the nation's second oldest archdiocese, Oregon City, remained with its suffragans essentially missionary territory with a sizable Indian population.[38] Canadian Oblates of Mary Immaculate made missionary trips in the 1860s and 1870s to Alaska, purchased by the United States from Russia in 1867. John Althoff, a Dutch priest of the diocese of Victoria, B.C., was Alaska's first resident pastor, at Wrangell in 1878. Eight years later, at Wolf's Head Point on the Yukon River, Archbishop Charles Seghers, Bishop of Victoria, was murdered by a lay volunteer mission helper. That same year (1886), Jesuits first came to the mission, followed in 1888 by Canadian Sisters of St. Anne. In 1894, two years before the Klondike gold rush, the prefecture-apostolic of Alaska was assigned to the Jesuits. The first bishop, Joseph R. Crimont, S.J., became vicar-apostolic in 1917.[39]

The island kingdom of Hawaii became American territory in 1898. Picpus priests (Fathers of the Sacred Hearts) had been there since 1827, among them the famous Damien (Joseph) De Veuster, whose ministry on Molokai began in 1873 and ended with his death in 1889, three years after he had himself contracted Hansen's disease.[40]

While most Catholics in the United States were to be found in the lower-income strata of society, some rose to prominence. New York lawyer Charles O'Conor was the "straight-out" Democratic candidate for President of the United States in 1872, running against Ulysses S. Grant and Horace Greeley. He was afterwards primarily responsible for destroying the corrupt Tweed Ring in New York City government and in the disputed presidential election of 1876 served as counsel to Samuel Tilden. Joseph McKenna was President McKinley's attorney general and after 1898 a Supreme Court justice. Edward Douglass White was named to the Supreme Court in 1894.[41] There were Catholics of great wealth like financier Thomas Fortune Ryan, shipping magnate William R. Grace, first Catholic mayor (1880) of New York City and a political reformer, the philanthropic Cudahy brothers who made their money in meat-packing, and John Mackay, with interests ranging from Nevada silver mines to the transatlantic cable.

The Third Plenary Council of Baltimore (1884) ended American Catholicism's organizational era and opened a period of conflict. The principal impetus for a council stemmed from Roman insistence on improved church administration. Conroy's 1878 report to Propaganda listed as major problems the secrecy and favoritism surrounding choice of bishops from a closed circle of episcopal protégés; emphasis on financial rather than pastoral or intellectual ability; and a tradition of autocratic rule by bishops who ignored canon law and resisted establishment of true parishes, in which pastors would have specific legal rights. There were no chapters of canons to act as a brake on the bishop, and diocesan offices were rudimentary. On June 20, 1878, the Congregation for Propagation of the Faith ordered each bishop, with the advice of the priests, to pick a commission for consultation in cases concerning clergymen. The bishops resisted the directive. A spate of books and pamphlets followed, advocating canonical status and rights for parish priests and urging acceptance of ideas of self-government and democracy. The status of priests and the method of selecting bishops were the two chief internal organizational problems of the period.[42]

While eastern bishops were reluctant to have a council, those in the Midwest wanted one. Many of their favorite projects, such as establishment of a Catholic university, were at dead halt, and they preferred national solutions. In 1883 a preliminary meeting of American bishops and officials at the Congregation for Propagation of the Faith in Rome set an agenda. The Americans resisted nomination of an Italian bishop as apostolic delegate, or president, and Archbishop Gibbons presided over a meeting of seventy-two prelates from November 9 to December 7, 1884. Structural changes were made: diocesan chanceries and courts and a quota of "irremovable" rectors were prescribed for each diocese. Priests were given an indirect vote in choice of bishops. A Catholic university was projected, envisioned chiefly as a school for advanced studies in philosophy and theology. Each parish was to open a primary school within two years. A pronounced pastoral emphasis was apparent in the regulation ordering the preaching of carefully prepared, regular, and brief sermons on Sundays and feast days. Preparation of a uniform catechism and manual of prayers was commissioned. Immigrants, blacks, and American Indians were specially commended to the church's pastoral care. The council also urged efforts to encourage Catholics to move out of cities. The reasons given were both material and spiritual.

The Baltimore legislation hardly solved the Catholic Church's problems in the United States. Social and economic changes consequent on industrialization, coupled with recurring financial panics, the scarcity of jobs and growing Catholic urban strength, all helped provoke another nativist outburst.[43] Prestigious journals like *Harper's Weekly* and *Atlantic Monthly* regularly featured anti-Catholic and anti-immigrant articles and cartoons. Just before the national election of 1884, a prominent supporter of Republican presidential candidate James G. Blaine denounced the Democrats as the party of "rum, Romanism, and rebellion." The slur was aimed at Irish Catholics, and probably cost Blaine the electoral votes of New York State and election to the presidency. In 1887 at Clinton, Iowa, Henry F. Bowers founded the American Protective Association (A.P.A.). Members promised never to vote for a Catholic, never to hire one when a Protestant was available, and never to join Catholics in a strike. The organization drew its main strength from rural areas. It achieved its greatest prominence in 1893, when the A.P.A. spread the rumor that a papal decree had absolved all oaths of allegiance to the United States and that a massacre of heretics was planned for September 5, which they mistakenly thought was the feast day of St. Ignatius Loyola, founder of the Jesuit order.[44]

Resentment of foreign immigrants was a major factor in the renewed wave of anti-Catholicism, as was the Church's rapid growth in the 1880s and 1890s, coupled with Catholic insistence on parochial schools at a time when Protestant preference, with some exceptions, was shifting decisively towards secular, state-controlled schools. The Protestant fears enunciated a half-century earlier by Robert Baird were still alive.

XV

Growing Pains in the Catholic Community

The American form of Roman Catholicism which persisted past the halfway mark of the 20th century was shaped by immigrant needs. In an effort more palliative than curative, the church competed and then cooperated with the government in providing hospitals, asylums, orphanages and industrial schools. To an extent the religiously hostile climate of public institutions demanded this approach. Other efforts included "institutional churches" with reading rooms, and athletic facilities. Parish conferences of the St. Vincent de Paul Society multiplied from 235 in 1883 to 428 in 1902.[1] The Catholic Total Abstinence Union (founded in 1872) was a special favorite of liberal churchmen embarrassed by the Irish reputation for heavy drinking. It also accommodated dominant Protestant prejudices against alcohol.[2] In 1894 Bishop John Watterson of Columbus withdrew recognition from any diocesan society which numbered a liquor dealer among its members.[3] Another liberal project, the resettlement of urban Catholics in western farming regions, was unsuccessful. American Catholicism remained an urban phenomenon, with isolated pockets of rural membership, chiefly along railroads and canals.[4] Urban Catholics continued to be slow to combat corrupt political practices, but there were exceptions. Charles Bonaparte, grandson of Jérôme Bonaparte and Elizabeth Patterson, was active in the "Baltimore Union for Doing Good," a branch of the "Union for Practical Progress," and he won a reputation as a fighter against corruption.[5] Cardinal Gibbons condemned child labor and urged a living wage for workingmen, while Bishop George Montgomery of Monterey-Los Angeles advocated compulsory arbitration of labor disputes, imposition of income taxes, municipal ownership of public utilities and nationalization of railroads and communications—all radical positions at the time.[6] As Roman Catholics coped, along with fellow citizens, with the kaleidoscopic problems of the gilded age, they had also to face a series of internal conflicts, some purely domestic, others at least partially reactions to external pressures.

The historic "schools question" had taken several sharp turns since the struggles of the 1830s and 1840s. Penning his *Plea for the West* in 1835, Lyman Beecher thought that

> the conflict which is to decide the destiny of the west will be a conflict of institutions for the education of her sons, for the purposes of superstition or evangelical light, of despotism or liberty.

The alliance of common school and Protestantism, of evangelical light with liberty, prospered. In the mid-1830s Chicago's tykes could choose between Miss Eliza Chappell's school at the Presbyterian church and Mr.Granville Spratt's at the Baptist church. These were the only institutions supported by tax dollars. But by the 1860s a counter-alliance had built up, in Chicago and elsewhere, which included Catholics, Jews, liberal Protestants, Unitarians and Universalists, agnostics and atheists. What was happening in Chicago was symptomatic of developments elsewhere. The time had come in American history when secularization of the public school would proceed one step farther.[7]

President Ulysses S. Grant was a great advocate of the secular public school. In 1875 he suggested an amendment to the Federal Constitution which would make free public schools mandatory everywhere. He also wanted taxation of property held by religious organizations and an absolute prohibition of the use of public money for church-affiliated schools. A constitutional amendment to achieve the last purpose was introduced in the House of Representatives in 1876 by Congressman James G. Blaine of Maine. Clearly, he did not think such aid already prohibited by the First Amendment's "non-establishment" clause. Blaine's amendment passed in the House, but failed narrowly in the Senate. The phrase "Blaine Amendment" came into common use to describe similarly restrictive enactments later included in some state constitutions.[8] In New York, Archbishop Corrigan accepted a restriction of this type and got in return continued state subsidy for non-educational Catholic charitable institutions.[9] Brief Catholic alliances like the one forged in Chicago melted away. The public school took a giant step toward achieving its peculiar destiny in the American firmament. A later Supreme Court justice put it in these words: "The non-sectarian or secular public school [is] perhaps the most powerful agency for promoting cohesion among a heterogeneous democratic people." It became in fact, he said, "a symbol of our secular unity."[10]

Changing educational philosophies had their impact on the Catholic presence in education. Under the influence of philosopher John Dewey, progressive educators insisted that schools attend to the themes of social betterment and cultivation of individual freedom. Charles W. Eliot, president of Harvard University from 1869 to 1909, injected a religious note into his advocacy of the free election of courses by students. He declared that "uniform prescriptions of study in secondary schools" were "impossible and absurd," and noted that an "inflexible plan of studies" prevailed only under religious auspices either in Moslem lands "where the Koran prescribes the perfect education to be administered to all children alike," or "in the curriculum of Jesuit colleges."[11] American Catholics nevertheless continued to emphasize a prescribed curriculum. Their schools were paternalistic and authoritarian. Secular educators charged them with creating a divisive spirit. Against this background, the "school controversy" within the Catholic camp broke out.[12]

In 1884, four of every ten Catholic parishes in the United States had primary schools. The wish of the Third Plenary Council that within two years every parish have a school was never realized and there were signs of a less than solid front on the subject. Addressing the National Education Association in 1889 and 1890, Gibbons, Ireland, and Keane encouraged Catholic schools without condemning state schools. Ireland saw two problems in conducting parochial schools without state support: the expense, and the fact that less than one-half of the Catholic children in the nation were reached by the existing parochial schools. He favored either public support for religious schools, as in England, or state control of Catholic schools during regular hours, with religious instruction after hours. His introduction of the second plan in the Minnesota towns of Faribault and Stillwater provoked an enormous outcry from an alliance of midwestern German and conservative eastern bishops including Katzer of Milwaukee, Corrigan, and McQuaid. Ironically, the plan was known as the "Poughkeepsie plan" because it was already in use in that city in Corrigan's diocese.

Ireland's advocacy made a difference. A pamphlet war began. Belgian moral theology professor Thomas Bouquillon of the Catholic University of America argued for the rights of family, state, and church in education, but Jesuit René Holaind gave primacy to parents and church, with state interest subordinate to these.[13] The archbishop of St. Paul memorialized Rome, calling implementation of the decree on parochial schools of the Third Plenary Council unrealistic and underlining the need for concern about Catholic children in public schools. Rome answered that the Faribault and Stillwater arrangements might be tolerated.[14] In November 1892 papal diplomat Francesco Satolli, meeting with the American archbishops, proposed a fourteen-point plan favorable to the ideas of Ireland and Bouquillon.[15] A May 1893 letter from Pope Leo XIII ended discussion by encouraging Catholic schools but leaving to the discretion of local bishops the conditions of Catholic attendance at public schools.[16]

Parochial elementary schools multiplied. In 1880 there were 2,246, with 405,234 students. By 1900, 3,811 schools had 854,523 students, and in 1910 there were 4,845 schools and 1,237,251 students. Schools were administered by the parish priest under diocesan superintendence. New York named the first diocesan superintendent of schools in 1886, and in 1904 a number of previously existing organizations merged to form the national Catholic Educational Association.[17] Secondary schools grew more slowly. An early example was Roman Catholic High School for Boys, opened in Philadelphia in 1890 and built with $1 million bequeathed by Thomas E. Cahill, who had died in 1879. There were central diocesan and parish high schools as well as private schools which grew out of academies and European-style "colleges" run by religious communities.[18]

At the turn of the century there were sixty-three Catholic colleges. They were peripheral to American higher education, and ran counter to the general trend away from religious control of universities. The first to award academic degrees to women was Notre Dame of Maryland (1899).[19] Most Catholic colleges were built through the combined sacrifices of religious and laity. Some, like Creighton University in Omaha received substantial endowments from benefactors like Edward and John Creighton, American-born sons of Irish immigrants.[20]

Not until 1889 was there a national Catholic university, the fruit of decades of agitation. Papal charters had been granted to St. Mary's Seminary, Baltimore, in 1822, and to Georgetown College in 1833, but neither developed into a university-level theological center. Bishop John Lancaster Spalding promoted the project of a Catholic university at the 1884 council, and material help came in the form of a pledge of $300,000 from a twenty-one-year-old heiress, Mary Gwendolyn Caldwell.[21] The Catholic University of America opened at Washington in 1889 as a graduate school of theology for priests. In 1895 philosophy and social sciences were added. Lay undergraduates were enrolled in 1905. Efforts were made to recruit good faculty, but the institution's history was bedeviled by recurring financial and ideological crises.

Among the problems of the period were secret societies. Many organizations which Americans joined in the late 19th century took inspiration or external forms from the petit bourgeois, vaguely Protestant, Anglo-Saxon form of freemasonry. Fenianism, which had grown in America and spread to Ireland, brought its own special problems. American bishops were cautious about accepting the papal condemnation secured by the Irish bishops in 1870. In 1886 a committee of archbishops found no objections to membership in the Grand Army of the Republic and the Ancient Order of Hibernians. Liberal American bishops urged the Holy See to take a benign approach to organizations of this sort.[22]

The growing labor movement posed special difficulty. Unions needed secrecy to protect their members and they borrowed trappings from the masonic tradition. The first national union, the Knights of Labor (1869), was headed after 1878 by a Catholic, Terence Powderly, and had a majority of Catholic members. Powderly publicly abjured socialism and the Knights avoided violence, but they were blamed for labor troubles that scarred the 1880s, including the May 1, 1886, murder of a dozen policeman in Chicago's Haymarket Square. There were hostile reactions. Baltimore Archbishop James Roosevelt Bayley had damned unions as "communistic." Bishops from western railroad centers, like Kenrick and Salpointe, were apprehensive about strikes. The nation's only black bishop, James A. Healy of Portland, excommunicated men for belonging to the Knights of Labor. In 1884 Québec Archbishop Elzéar Taschereau secured Roman condemnation of the Knights in Canada. The American archbishops voted 10 to 2 against applying such condemnation in the United States and in 1887 Gibbons, Ireland, and Keane drafted a warning to Rome that "to lose the heart of the people would be a misfortune for which the friendship of the few rich and powerful would be no compensation." Vatican officials agreed that Catholics might be Knights so long as any "words that seem to savor of socialism or communism" were eliminated from their constitution.[23] The Knights declined after 1886, yielding to the American Federation of Labor, headed by an English-born Jew, Samuel Gompers, but with a large Catholic membership, a factor which helped steer the American labor movement away from socialism and into a conservative pattern inspired by middle-class values.[24] Labor historian Philip Taft has correctly discounted "Catholic" influence in labor politics, but that should be taken in the sense of clerical interventionism.[25] The real Catholic impact was in the nice harmony between the firm anti-socialist bias of late 19th-century Catholic teaching, re-emphasized with Leo XIII's insistence on the right of private property in *Rerum Novarum* (1891), and the upwardly mobile aspirations of immigrant Catholics, who saw themselves as incipient capitalists, not as members of a proletariat.

That development resulted in a wide gap between the Catholic community and the substantial number of born Catholics who were increasingly prominent in radical causes. Few of the latter bridged the gap to remain church members.

Conflicts within American Catholicism crystallized in the controversy between Archbishop Corrigan and New York pastor Edward McGlynn.[26] The priest's negative opinions on parochial schools and state recognition of religion were well known. In the 1880s he launched a "new crusade" which featured "the very core of all religion"—a theme later prominent among Protestant social gospelers. Baptist social gospel advocate Walter Rauschenbush remembered

> how Father McGlynn, speaking at Cooper Union in New York in the first Single Tax campaign in 1886, recited the words, "The Kingdom come! Thy will be done on earth," and as the great audience realized for the first time the significance of the holy words, it lifted them off their seats with a shout of joy.[27]

McGlynn called for "the fatherhood of one God, the universal brotherhood of man, a Christian community in which all shared in social growth and improvement." He denounced "our so-called Christian communities," which "degraded the teaching of Christ into a mere seven-day code of personal conduct," and begged for distinction "between the ecclesiastical machinery and the ideal church of Christ without spot or wrinkle."[28] Archbishop Corrigan's view of poverty was more eschatalogical than McGlynn's and Corrigan was also closely tied to the Irish-Catholic Tammany political machine, among whose adversaries was economist Henry George, proponent of the theory that only land should be taxed. When George ran for mayor in 1886 McGlynn defied Corrigan's ban and campaigned for him. The archbishop suspended McGlynn and issued a pastoral letter defending private property. Reinstated, McGlynn continued his political activity, was again suspended, and then summoned to Rome. He refused to go. A popular outcry resulted. From Brooklyn Father Sylvester Malone wrote to Pope Leo XIII that McGlynn's rights as an American citizen were being infringed upon in the name of ecclesiastical discipline. McGlynn's refusal to go to Rome resulted in his excommunication. He continued lectures under the auspices of the "Anti-Poverty Society." Corrigan declared attendance at his lectures a sin for Catholics, absolution for which was reserved to himself. In Rome, Gibbons advised authorities to be cautious and not hastily condemn George's theories, which were not original with him, but derived from the ideas of Herbert Spencer and John Stuart Mill.

Many contemporary causes of strife in the American church played a part in the McGlynn episode: the Knights of Labor, the status of priests (Richard Burtsell's articles on "The Canonical Status of Priests in the United States" were appearing in the New York *Tablet*), differences over parochial schools. Corrigan was convinced that Gibbons was interfering at Rome on behalf of McGlynn, and this contributed to the growing rift between conservative and liberal bishops. The McGlynn episode ended when the pope's representative in the United States lifted McGlynn's excommunication and Corrigan assigned him as pastor in the Hudson valley town of Newburgh.

Lay activity quickened.[29] A three-man committee issued a call for a lay congress at Baltimore in 1889. The initiators were Henry F. Brownson, black Catholic editor Daniel A. Rudd, and German-American leader Henry Spaunhorst. Brownson, Chicago businessman William J. Onahan, and St. Louis journalist Peter Foy were the real moving spirits. Liberal bishops were by turns enthusiastic and cautious. They shared many of the lay leaders' progressive ideas. They were less sure about promoting lay autonomy or sharing church management with them. Brownson and Foy were angry with Onahan for giving in to the bishops' insistence on an episcopal advisory committee. With a flash of his father's fire, Brownson criticized the Chicagoan for having "no broad view of what the laity could do for religion if they were encouraged to act freely and spontaneously." Topics at the Baltimore congress included lay action, Sunday observance, problems of capital and labor, insurance, charities, the press, and education. The final resolutions bore a striking resemblance to ideas in the bishops' pastoral letter at the close of the 1884 Third Plenary Council. A euphoric note was struck by Archbishop Ireland, when he urged the delegates:

> Go back and say to your fellow Catholics that there is a departure among the Catholics of the United States. Tell them that heretofore, so to speak, you have done but little, but that henceforth you are going to do great things. Tell them that there is a mission open to laymen. . . . As one of your bishops I am ashamed of myself that I was not conscious before this of the power existing in the midst of the laity and that I have not done anything to bring it out. . . . With God's help . . . I shall do all I can to bring out this power.[30]

A second congress, to include both laity and clergy, was planned for Chicago in 1893 and was to be preceded by a series of diocesan congresses. But local cooperation was not always forthcoming. Cardinal Gibbons was a covert opponent, writing in 1892 to John Ireland:

> With regard to the Congress, we must act with caution. Any overt attempt on your or my part to suppress it would raise a hue and cry, and

the worst motives would be ascribed to us. The best plan is to enjoin on Onahan and our friends a passive attitude that little or nothing should be done to advance the Congress till our meeting in October, and then we would try to kill it, or failing that, to determine that this should be the last Congress.[31]

The Catholic Congress which was held in conjunction with the World's Columbian Exposition at Chicago was notable for the extensive participation of women. Catholic convert Rose Hawthorne Lathrop, the novelist's daughter, who in 1896 would found the Servants of Relief for Incurable Cancer, delivered a ringing exhortation:

> Oh, woman, the hour has struck when you are to arise and defend your rights, your abilities for competition with men in intellectual and professional endurance, the hour when you are to prove that purity and generosity are for the nation as well as for the home. . . .[32]

Bishop James McGolrick of Duluth pleaded for the American Indian, claiming that "the whole management of Indians has been abnormal, with little or absolutely no opportunity for the natural laws regulating social life to operate."[33] Charles H. Butler spoke on behalf of the Colored Catholic Congress. He warned fellow Catholics that "the Negro has been a conspicuous figure in our body politic and like the ghost in Macbeth, 'It will not down.' " The future depended on "whether the proud Anglo-Saxon intends to dispossess himself or mere race prejudice and accord his black brother simple justice." He attacked civic discrimination and segregation in churches and finished with an appeal:

> I here appeal to you, first as American citizens, second as loyal sons of our Holy Mother the Church, to assist us to strike down that hybrid monster, color prejudice, which is unworthy of this glorious republic. We ask it not alone for charity's sake, but as a right that has been dearly paid for.[34]

Other papers dealt with a variety of social problems in the light of Leo XIII's encyclical, *Rerum Novarum*. Among the resolutions was a "Peace Memorial," sent in twenty-five languages to rulers of nations. The memorial protested the arms race in which "Christian nations" were engaged and urged realization that "wars do not settle causes of disputes between nations on principles of right and justice, but upon the barbaric principle of the triumph of the strongest."[35] Archbishop Ryan of Philadelphia declared at the congress that "the Catholic laymen must be understood to speak, not as our mouthpieces, but as free, intelligent Catholic American laymen."[36] But a third congress planned for 1904 died of episcopal opposition.

Between 1889 and 1894 five negro Catholic congresses were held, inspired by Daniel A. Rudd of Cincinnati, editor of the *American Catholic Tribune,* a paper published by and for black Catholics.[37] The 1889 Washington meeting passed a resolution of sympathy "with our brethren of the Emerald Isle, who, like ourselves are struggling for justice." In an "Address to their Catholic Fellow Citizens," they complained that "the sacred rights of justice and humanity are still sadly wounded," and asked for schools, institutions, and societies for blacks, as well as help in eliminating discrimination by labor unions, employers, landlords, and real estate agents. The Chicago congress in 1893 prepared a questionnaire on discrimination to be sent to all the bishops. Grievances would be brought to the pope's attention. The 1894 Baltimore congress again targeted labor unions for discriminatory hiring practices. After that there were no more congresses. American black Catholic congresses and lay Catholic congresses fell victim to the same conservative reaction which spelled the end of the series of international Catholic scholarly congresses held in Europe from 1888 to 1900.

Catholic ministry to the Indians suffered a setback with the "Peace Policy" announced to Congress by President Grant on December 5, 1870.[38] Indian agencies were to be turned over to religious denominations with established missions and to others willing to undertake the work. Catholics had been first on the ground in thirty-eight of the seventy-three existing agencies, but only seven were assigned them. Indian agents had the power to appoint missionaries, to prevent others from coming onto the reservations, and to forbid Indians to leave a reservation to attend services elsewhere. Some eighty thousand Catholic Indians came under control of Protestant denominations. To protect their interests and those of the missions, the bishops named a brother-in-law of General William Tecumseh Sherman, Brigadier General Charles Ewing, as Commissioner of Catholic Indian Affairs. He had the assistance of John Baptist Brouillet, a missionary priest in the Pacific Northwest since 1847. Brouillet was largely responsible for shaping what became the Bureau of Catholic Indian Affairs. Not until 1883, and then only after it had worked to the disadvantage of a Protestant missionary, was official policy reversed, so that Indians enjoyed full religious liberty. Until 1900 Catholic schools shared in Federal subsidies to mission boarding and day schools on reservations. When these subsidies were ended, they were helped from funds collected in the annual nationwide collection taken up in Catholic churches for missions among Indians and blacks, and by substantial benefactions from Katharine Drexel, foundress of the Sisters of the Blessed Sacrament. Use of tribal funds held in trust by the Federal government to support mission schools was authorized by President Theodore Roosevelt, a policy upheld by the United States Supreme Court in *Quick Bear v. Leupp* (1908).

Black Catholics remained a small minority, despite Catholic congresses and Daniel Rudd's newspaper. In 1883 an estimated one hundred thousand were Catholics in a total black population of seven million. Neither the official church nor individual Catholics were outspoken in their zeal for racial justice, with vigorous exceptions like Boston *Pilot* editor John Boyle O'Reilly and Archbishop John Ireland. The latter in 1891 demanded action to "blot out the color line." It was no longer possible to "keep up a wall of separation between whites and blacks." He advocated equal political rights and education, equal opportunity of employment and recognition of social equality. But these views were not translated into effective action for Catholic black people, while the urban nature of American Catholicism minimized contact with the greater part of a black population still predominantly rural. By 1900 blacks were only a minuscule 2 percent of the population of a city like New York. In southern communities black Catholics attended segregated churches and schools or found themselves relegated to church galleries. They approached the communion rail after whites and confessed their sins in segregated confessionals. Some of these external signs of discrimination were missing in the North, but there the realities of Catholic life for black people were in many cases even less pleasant.[39]

Archbishop Ireland's contribution to the history of eastern-rite Catholics in the United States was not a happy one. His harsh reception of Archpriest Alexis Toth and a community of Carpatho-Russians who came to Minneapolis in 1891 led them to seek union with Russian Orthodoxy. It has been estimated that as many as 225,000 Carpatho-Russian and Galician Catholics eventually took the same step after immigrating to the United States. The main issue on which the American bishops chose to challenge the newcomers was that of clerical celibacy. They refused to allow married eastern-rite priests to exercise the ministry. Meeting in 1893, the archbishops resolved

> that the presence of married priests of the Greek rite in our midst is a constant menace to the chastity of our unmarried clergy, a source of scandal to the laity and therefore the sooner this point of discipline is abolished before the evils obtain large proportions, the better for religion. . . .

"The possible loss of a few souls of the Greek rite," the archbishops thought, "bears no proportion to the blessings resulting from uniformity of discipline." Catholics of the Byzantine-Slavic rite, who had begun to settle in American coal-mining regions and factory towns in the last quarter of the 19th century, had to cope with internal divisions, like those which separated Ruthenians and Ukrainians, and to deal also with the prejudices and incomprehension of Latin-rite Catholics and their bishops and priests, who did not easily understand why the newcomers refused to conform to the dominant ecclesial model. In the growth of American Catholicism, insistence on the principle of a single episcopal jurisdiction in a single area had been important to prevent fragmentation and colonialization of the American church by European interests. Neither Western Europe nor the United States ever knew the multiple episcopal jurisdictions common in the Near East and in the Russian and Austrian empires, where Catholics of several rites lived side by side under their respective bishops. The lot of the eastern-rite Catholics was not easy. In 1884 the Archbishop of Lvov sent the priest Ivan Voliansky to begin organizing their churches. He and others who followed remained under Latin-rite bishops until 1907 when a Ukrainian monk, Soter (Stephen) Ortynsky, O.S.B.M., was named Bishop for Ukranians and Ruthenians in the United States.[40]

The century's end saw a general revolt against "hibernarchy," the dominance of Irish priests and bishops in the American church. Of the bishops in 1886, the ancestry was: Irish, 35; German, 15; French, 11; English, 5; Dutch, Scots, and Spanish, 1 each. That was only part of the story. Italian, Slavic, and Hungarian immigrants, as has been seen, kept arriving in increasing numbers. The church they had found in America was too cold and puritanical for their tastes. The situation was further complicated because centuries of persecution had left the Irish, the dominant group in Catholic America, with their own cultural heritage in disarray. Ireland's Gaelic Revival came too late for most of America's Irish immigrants. This cultural lack was one reason why the Catholicism they developed in the American church tended to be narrow, moralistic and bland.

Germans formed the next largest bloc. While eastern and southern immigrants were still struggling to establish their presence in the country and the church, the Germans were long since well-established and were not to be denied their rightful say. A self-consciously strong and vigorous German Catholicism with deep cultural roots flourished. Religious communities of men and women multiplied and were staffed from the homeland as well as from German colonies in America. The Pontifical College Josephinum in Ohio, a regional pontifical seminary, was established in 1888 to train priests for German communities. Germans emphasized parochial schools. They believed that perpetuation of German language and culture went hand in hand with preservation of Catholic faith. Group identity was fostered in benevolent societies federated in a *Central-Verein*. During the decade ending in 1898 the more militant *Priester-Verein* sponsored a series of *Katholikentage,* annual assemblies of German-American Catholics modeled on those held in Germany.[41]

John Jay's ode to American identity in the *Federalist Papers* could never be reconciled with manifestos like the following, issued by the Buffalo *Volksfreund:*

> America is no nation, no race, no people like France, Italy or Germany. We have citizens of a republic, but no nation and, therefore, no national language outside the languages which the immigrated races speak in their families.[42]

Conflict was intensified by the Germans' conviction that Americans were hostile to Catholics. Cincinnati pastor Anton Walburg denounced "Americans" as fanatic, intolerant, radical, dissimulating hypocrites. For the German-American, "denaturalization is demoralization. It degrades and debases human nature. A foreigner who loses his nationality is in danger of losing his faith and character."[43]

Opposing groups of priests supplied local newspapers with polemical memorials between 1878 and 1880 when there was question of a coadjutor for Archbishop Henni of Milwaukee, and the performance was repeated a decade later when Henni's successor, Michael Heiss, died in 1890.[44] In St. Louis, the German Catholic monthly *Pastoral Blatt* in 1884 attacked the system which since 1842 had made German and other "national" parishes dependent on territorial "Irish" parishes. Well-known Franciscan liturgist Innocent Wapelhorst charged that eighteen million Catholics had left the church in the United States, largely through the influence of the public school system. Cologne-born Henry Mühlsiepen, a vicar general of the diocese, and eighty-two priests protested the situation of the parishes to Rome. The question was referred back to the Third Plenary Council of Baltimore and died there, only to be resurrected when the decrees of the council were reviewed in Rome, where German Americans had strong allies among the cardinals.[45]

Several facets of the controversy came together in 1889 in battles over the Bennett Law and the Edwards Law, in Wisconsin and Illinois, respectively. These laws demanded both compulsory education and the teaching of basic skills and American history in English. The laws drew fire from German-American Lutherans as well as Catholics, but the *Chicago Tribune* trained its guns principally on the latter, editorializing that the controversies were

> a contest between the supporters and enemies of the American free schools, between the right of Americans to make their own laws and the claims of an Italian priest living in Rome that he has the power to nullify them.[46]

Tensions had been increased by misunderstandings surrounding the 1883 visit to the United States of Peter Paul Cahensly, a Center Party deputy in the German *Reichstag* and secretary of the St. Raphael Society, an immigrant-aid group founded in 1871.[47] In 1886 Milwaukee priest Peter M. Abbelen brought to Rome a detailed list of complaints about alleged mistreatment of German-American Catholics by those in charge of the church in the United States.[48] Support for the Germans was broadened by the intervention of Albany priest Alphonse Villeneuve at the 1890 Liège international Catholic congress. He claimed that twenty million Catholic immigrants had abandoned the church in America. The same theme was repeated at a meeting in Lucerne of the St. Raphael Society. Premier Honoré Mercier of the Province of Québec joined delegates from several European countries in memorializing Pope Leo XIII on the subject. Catholic losses were estimated at ten million, and specific recommendations were made for stemming the flow: national parishes and schools, broader representation of the nationalities among American bishops, and papal support to train European missionaries for America. After a second memorial upping total losses to sixteen million, Cardinal Gibbons protested interference in American church affairs by "officious gentlemen" in Europe. The issue found its way to the floor of the United States Senate, and President Benjamin Harrison, meeting Gibbons in July at Cape May, New Jersey, where both were on holiday, congratulated him for his forthright stand. The controversy cooled down following Gibbon's receipt of a letter from Pope Leo's Secretary of State, Cardinal Mariano Rampolla del Tindaro. Rome had rejected the memorialists' demands, but American bishops were urged to pay special attention to immigrant needs.[49]

As America's imperial age began, the problems attached to cultural and linguistic assimilation, which had plagued Catholicism for the better part of a century, persisted. A particular virulence attached to these problems in the heyday of Anglo-Saxon self-glorification, when the melting-pot myth reigned supreme and Manifest Destiny expanded to the international scale. The Catholic community's house was divided and its internal identity crisis was to worsen before it got better. And there remained the problem of external image. Long history in America or not, Catholics were perceived as immigrant newcomers, as indeed most of them were. In the face of strident nationalism, they had still to lay claim to an identity as citizens and to legitimate their existence on the American political and religious scene.

European students have catalogued the so-called Americanist episode in the history of the Catholic Church in the United States as a prelude to the predominantly European Modernist crisis in the first decade of the 20th century.[50] It was surely part of the same historical movement, an effort to establish a contemporary identity for an ancient church, but few of the actors or their concerns were the same. Some Americanists knew some Modernists and they shared occasional sympathies, but the movements, which followed one another chronologically, were contiguous rather than continuous. American preoccupations did not run to immanentist philosophy and historico-biblical criticism. Their concern was the church's ability to express itself in and to the contemporary political, intellectual, and social world. They resonated with the social consciousness which gave birth to Protestant social gospel, of which Catholics like McGlynn were indeed precursors. Inspired largely by the thought of Isaac Hecker, who died in 1888, they emphasized individuality and freedom under the guidance of the Holy Spirit as the style of contemporary Christian life. Emphasis on the role of the Holy Spirit was particularly prominent in Keane's theology. At Hecker's prompting, the bishops of the Third Plenary Council had urged greater devotion to the third person of the Trinity. The Americanists stressed the correlation of this theological emphasis with their own stress on the importance of individual initiative.[51] There was a deeply rooted conviction of the basic harmony of American democratic ways with Catholicism. Most of them shared with their Protestant compatriots the vision of Americans as chosen people, the new Israel of God.

Americanist Catholics did not go unchallenged. In the summer of 1870 Orestes Brownson had pronounced the divorce of America and Catholicism in a bitter letter to Isaac Hecker:

> I neither indulge the hopes nor cherish the tendencies I did some six or eight years ago. . . . I defend the republican form of government for our country, because it is the legal and only practicable form, but I no longer hope anything from it. Catholicity is theoretically compatible with democracy, as you and I would explain democracy, but practically, there is, in my judgment, no compatibility between them. According to Catholicity all power comes from above and descends from high to low; according to democracy all power is infernal, is from below, and ascends from low to high. This is democracy in its practical sense, as politicians & the people do & will understand it. Catholicity & it are as mutually antagonistic as the spirit & the flesh, the Church and the World, Christ & Satan.

"Say what we will," he concluded, "we have made little impression on our old American population, & what we have made we owe to the conviction that [the] Church sustains authority, demands government, is anti-radical, anti-democratic."[52] Twenty years later, another former Protestant, New York vicar general Thomas Preston, was no more convinced than Brownson of the compatibility of Catholic religion and American institutions. He denounced "a peculiar kind of Catholicity," marked by religious indifferentism, the desire to separate education from religion, a lack of interest in restoring the pope's temporal power, advocacy of separation of church and state, and the overall, but to him clearly reprehensible, notion that the American form of civil government was best suited to the prosperity of Catholicism.[53]

A series of incidents brought into the open the conflict among American Catholic leaders. They divided into two reasonably discernible camps. Rector of the Catholic University of America from its beginning in 1887, Bishop John Keane was Hecker's spiritual heir. Archbishop John Ireland of St. Paul and Denis O'Connell—Rector of the American College in Rome (1885–95) and then vicar of Cardinal Gibbon's titular church there, Santa Maria in Trastevere—brought the American message to Europe.[54] Gibbons was generally favorable to the Americanists, as was Bishop John Lancaster Spalding, who tended, however, to play his usual lonely hand. The Paulists' *Catholic World* and Notre Dame's *Ave Maria* reflected the views of this school. Conservative opposition was led by Archbishop Corrigan of New York, Bishop McQuaid of Rochester, and the midwestern German-American bishops. They were seconded by the *American Ecclesiastical Review,* edited by Herman Heuser, and by the Jesuits' *Messenger of the Sacred Heart.* Jesuits supported the conservative interest both in the United States and in Rome, where two former faculty members of Woodstock College in Maryland held key positions. Cardinal Camillo Mazzella, S.J., headed the Roman congregation charged with supervision of Catholic educational institutions, while Salvatore Brandi, S.J., was editor of the Roman journal *Civiltà cattolica.* Anti-Americanists could also count on powerful support from the head of the Congregation for Propagation of the Faith, the Prussian-Polish Cardinal Mieczislaw Lédochowski.

In the form of the search for self-identity on the part of a national church, Americanism resurrected questions going back to the days of John Carroll and beyond, and more recently articulated by Isaac Hecker and controverted by such men as Brownson and Preston. In 1890, the Bishop of Portland, James A. Healy, after reading Walter Elliott's biography of the Paulists' founder, worried about Hecker's "spirit of liberty, liberty of spirit if you please," which "led him more than once into words and ways that made his devoted friends tremble."[55] The Americanists raised the possibility of legitimate divergence from European models of church order and the extent to which difference was allowable. It was their fate to do so at a point in world Roman Catholic history when centrifugal action was least welcome. Pope Leo XIII differed from his predecessor in the means he used—revival of scholastic philosophy and political and social constructs he built upon it—but his goals and understanding of the papacy as a monarchical centralizing force in Catholic life were the same as those of Pius IX.[56] Conflict and eventual defeat for nationalizers were inevitable. The process was hastened when progressive European Catholics began to adopt American approaches and ideas.

Bishop Spalding's views on university education for priests had been cited in debate on that subject in the Rhineland as far back as 1885.[57] A dozen years later O'Connell and Ireland were cautiously sounding out the possibility of alliance with progressive German "Reform Catholics" like Franz Xaver Kraus and Hermann Schell.[58] But trouble really erupted with the June 1892 arrival in France of John Ireland, Archbishop of St. Paul. Liberal French Catholics had long been fascinated by American developments, while conservatives had viewed them with scorn. When Ireland arrived he found the Catholic Church in France polarized. Conservatives rejected Leo XIII's effort to rally them to the Republic, the "New Christian" movement was announcing that all ecclesiastical formalities should yield to the desire to be "with Jesus," and there were disquieting scholarly rumblings from the university-level "Catholic Institutes" recently established in Paris and several other French cities. The American archbishop let it be known that he considered the church in Europe, and particularly in France, to be asleep. "The people is king now," he informed a Paris audience, and he urged French priests to learn from their American counterparts the necessity to come down from their ivory towers to meet them.[59] A century before, in 1791, John Carroll had mused apprehensively that "our Clergy will soon be neither Europeans nor have European connexions." The distinctive style developed by that clergy was now being offered, with predictably mixed results, to the church of France.

Each year in the decade of the nineties marked a major stage in the development of the Americanist crisis. Archbishop Francesco Satolli arrived in the United States in 1892, ostensibly to escort a set of the Vatican's ancient maps loaned for display at the World's Columbian Exposition to be held in Chicago from May to November 1893.[60] Like Bedini and Conroy before him, he was also to look into the affairs of the American church. Lédochowski had opposed the mission; it was sponsored by Ireland and O'Connell. Satolli's arrival in New York was arranged in such a way that it seemed he had snubbed Archbishop Corrigan. He lived at the Catholic University, where Keane was rector. The fears of conservatives increased when Satolli made a set of proposals on Catholic education seconding Ireland's approach. Before the year was out he had relieved Edward McGlynn of censure. American Catholicism was experiencing direct Roman rule in a way it had never before known. When the Italian prelate told the American archbishops that his mission was to be permanent, all but Ireland demurred. A letter of protest from Cardinal Gibbons was on its way to Rome when on January 4, 1893, the establishment at Washington of an apostolic delegation was announced. The dream of 1853, a nunciature or papal embassy accredited to the American government, was not realized, but for the first time the pope had in Washington a permanent representative to deal with internal church affairs.

The delegate attended the Catholic congress at Chicago in September 1893, and urged his audience to go forward "in one hand bearing the book of Christian truth and in the other the Constitution of the United States."[61] But there were warning signs. He was not happy with participation by American bishops in the World's Parliament of Religions which was another feature of the festivities on the shores of Lake Michigan. Neither was he happy when the bishops of Peoria and Alton in Illinois spoke out against his office as a foreign intrusion. The year 1894 witnessed the spectacle of a midwestern archbishop (John Ireland) interfering in a New York State election to help defeat a New York bishop (McQuaid of Rochester) in his bid for a seat on the board of regents of the state university. The post was won instead by Brooklyn priest Sylvester Malone, an ally of McGlynn. In full episcopal regalia McQuaid mounted his cathedral pulpit and excoriated the St. Paul archbishop. Reprimanded for that by the delegate, he sent Rome a full report, calling Ireland a political and ecclesiastical meddler, a persecutor of Archbishop Corrigan, and a "false liberal."[62]

Events in 1895 underlined Roman suspicion of progressive American currents. In an encyclical letter, *Longinqua Oceani* (January 6), Leo XIII praised the church's growth in the United States and acknowledged that "thanks are due to the equity of the laws which obtained in America and to the customs of the well-ordered Republic." He was grateful that "unopposed by the Constitution and government of your nation, fettered by no hostile legislation, protected against violence by the common laws and the impartiality of the tribunals," Catholicism was "free to live and act without hindrance," but warned that American-style separation of church and state was not a model for other societies. He went further to express his conviction that the church in the United States "would bring forth more abundant fruit if, in addition to liberty, she enjoyed the favor of the laws and the patronage of public authority." Corrigan proposed a letter of thanks in the name of the American bishops; Ireland asked that any letter be low-key, adding: "The unfortunate allusion to Church & State cannot be explained to Americans."[63] Another straw in the wind came when Satolli in an April speech at Pottsville, Pennsylvania, sang the praises of German-Americans. Early in June, Cardinal Gibbons, head of the bishops' committee for the American College, reached Rome only to learn that, with no consultation of the American hierarchy, officials of the Congregation for Propagation of the Faith had demanded Denis O'Connell's resignation as rector of the college. On September 15 a papal letter rebuked participation in interdenominational congresses like the one at Chicago in 1893.[64]

John Ireland was not fazed. During the episcopal ordination of Bishop Thomas O'Gorman of Sioux Falls at Washington in April 1896, he praised separation of church and state and developed another favorite theme, combining praise for the diocesan priesthood with criticism of religious orders, over which bishops lacked control. The Jesuits were a special target: he thought them responsible for Catholic failures in post-Reformation England and in Japan. The tide, however, was turning against the Americanists. Satolli, who attended O'Gorman's consecration, returned to Rome. He had been named cardinal in November 1895. Back in Italy he joined forces with another ex-American, Cardinal Camillo Mazzella, S.J., to combat "Americanism." In September, Bishop Keane was summarily ousted as Rector of the Catholic University. Satolli, he told a friend, had levelled charges of heteroxody at him "& thro' me against so many others." The former delegate's hostility to Keane was reported to be "like a passion."[65]

The year 1897 saw major explosions. Ireland spoke in May on "Conscience: The Mainstay of Democracy," praising the American form of government and its strong foundation in the good conscience of the American people and their faithfulness to religion and moral law. In the same month Salvatore Brandi's *Civiltà Cattolica* printed an all-out attack on a range of American ideas, and finished by questioning the right of the United States to the title of Christian nation. At the International Catholic Congress in Fribourg, Switzerland, that August, two American papers created a stir. Denis O'Connell's title was: "A New Idea in the Life of Father Hecker."[66] He contrasted pagan Rome, where the emperor's will made law, with American emphasis on inalienable individual rights. He made no claim for the American system as universal model, but pointed out that it worked and that it clashed with neither faith nor morals. He was developing a theme which he had suggested seven years before to Archbishop Ireland: "What is all our canon law . . . but the continuation of the political and disciplinary ideas of the Roman Empire and of the Middle Ages . . . opposed in principle to the ideas governing the progress of events in the U.S.?" The lines were drawn. Conservative blood pressures were not lowered when Father John A. Zahm, C.S.C., of Notre Dame, who as president of the Fribourg congress had invited O'Connell's contribution, spoke on evolution. A year later his book,

Evolution and Dogma, was proscribed by the Roman Congregation of the Index and withdrawn from sale.[67]

The catalyst in the Americanist controversy was the publication in France in 1897 of a French translation of the adulatory biography of Isaac Hecker by Walter Elliott, C.S.P., first published in serial form in *The Catholic World* and then as a book in 1891, with Archbishop Corrigan's *imprimatur.* The translation was under the aegis of Abbé Félix Klein, professor at Paris's *Institut Catholique* and well known in progressive circles. He contributed a preface and Archbishop Ireland an introduction.[68] Hecker came through as a man of action, the ideal contemporary priest, gifted with intelligence, independence, and individuality, all virtues thought characteristic of a good Anglo-Saxon. The French edition went through seven quick printings. Debate, Gibbons heard from France, was "bitter and passionate." As John Tracy Ellis has pointed out, Catholics following Leo XIII's call for *ralliement*—rallying to the Third Republic—hailed the account "as a kind of charter for their program for the French church," while royalists and conservatives "maintained that it contained the seeds of heresy which they characterized under the name of Americanism."[69] French Catholics who associated church with monarchy were not prepared to discuss its compatibility with democracy. American Catholicism was dismissed as neo-Pelagian. Hecker's confidence in a new age of the Spirit was a revival of illuminism. Underlying much of the criticism was the attitude voiced by Abbé Charles Maignen. American "civilization," he wrote, had not yet been born.

The ten-week war during the spring and summer of 1898 in which the United States demolished most of Spain's remaining colonial empire sharpened European antagonism toward Americans. Those feelings were shared in Rome. John Ireland, long active in Republican Party politics, had been asked to use his influence with President McKinley to spare Spain the humiliation of war and defeat. He failed and, along with all the bishops except John Lancaster Spalding, rallied round the flag in America's most blatantly imperialist move since the war on Mexico. The Americanists' credit in Rome sank to a new low.

Cardinals Satolli and Mazzella headed a Roman investigation into the situation of the American church. Salvatore Brandi of *Civiltá Cattolica* served as a consultant. The upshot was the papal encyclical, *Testem Benevolentiae* (January 22, 1899), warning against ideas said to be abroad in the United States and exported to Europe in the translation of Elliott's life of Hecker. Involved were such notions as the demand for relaxation of doctrine if converts were to be attracted in the modern age, depreciation of external spiritual guidance and increased reliance on direct inspiration, emphasis on active rather than passive virtues, and a lack of regard for the traditional vows taken in religious communities. The encyclical met with a predictably mixed reaction. No American bishop contested it. Progressives denied that the reprobated attitudes existed. The archbishops of Chicago, Dubuque, and Santa Fe said nothing. Archbishop Corrigan and Archbishop Katzer were grateful that heresy had been exposed. More had happened than William Clebsch was willing to admit when he dismissed the Americanists as attempting to "fit Catholicism into the live-and-let-live pluralism of the American denominations," and singing "the current songs of the middle-class denominations: progress, social reform and shared religious traditions."[70] William Halsey's comment comes nearer the mark: they "were accused of heresy for espousing the activist individualism, self-confident mystique and optimistic idealism of American civilization."[71] That they did this Margaret Reher has demonstrated in detail.[72] Whether in the process they became heretics or even mildly heterodox is another question. Cultural difference is not the stuff of which genuine heresy is made, although it is sure to provoke ecclesiastical annoyance, and the Catholicism against which the Americanists were measured was heavily freighted with the culture of post–French Revolution Europe. The controversy soon died, but scars remained. In the United States, Ida Tarbell, Lincoln Steffens, and Upton Sinclair held the stage. The muckrakers' era was followed by the disillusionment of the crusade to make the world safe for democracy. American idealism withered. Curiously, American Catholics had been to an extent immunized. Their instinctual American appreciation of the meaning of God, humanity, and the world was scarcely affected by *Testem Benevolentiae,* but the intellectuals among them did become cautious. Something of a deep freeze set in, deepened further in the new century by Roman condemnation of Modernism. American Catholics had known an inchoate moment of native constructive theological thought. They now slipped more or less peaceably into a half-century's theological hibernation.

XVI

The End of the Beginning

The four months' war with Spain from April to August 1898 signaled the debut of the United States as a world power. For diplomat John Hay, it was "a splendid little war; begun with the highest motives, carried on with magnficent intelligence and spirit, favored by that fortune which loves the brave."[1] His spirit was not much different from that of Jesuit army chaplain Thomas Ewing Sherman. The son whose father had given war its classic definition exulted in "the intense pleasure which there is in exposure to danger, one that leads all the world of manhood to concede that fighting is the best fun in the world."[2] As it turned out, General William Tecumseh Sherman's son spent his military career largely in staff duties. San Francisco priest William D. McKinnon's army service was more exciting. Sailing for the Far East with the First California Volunteers, he transferred to the U.S.S. *Charleston* for the taking of Guam, and then resumed his trip to the Philippines, where he was credited with arranging the peaceful capitulation of Manila. McKinnon rapidly worked himself to death organizing schools and relief programs in Manila. He died there in 1902 and is remembered with a statue in San Francisco's Golden Gate Park.[3] Battle deaths during the war were fewer than four hundred, but four times that many died of typhoid and other plagues that swept the army camps. Volunteer chaplains and nursing sisters gave their services at Tampa, principal port of embarkation for Cuba, and elsewhere.[4]

American Catholics supported the war. Some, like Monsignor Denis O'Connell, did so vigorously. The time had come for "that recognition of English-speaking people" owed by the Catholic Church and its Roman authorities. The issue seemed clear. It was a contest between "all that is old and vile & mean & rotten & cruel & false in Europe" and all that is "free & noble & open & true & humane in America."[5] It is perhaps no wonder that Leo XIII and his advisers had their doubts about "Americanism." Alone of Catholic bishops, John Lancaster Spalding joined thirty thousand Boston brahmins and others in the New England Anti-Imperialist League to oppose colonial acquisitions by the United States. Spalding did not mince words. He told a Peoria audience that real service of their country demanded putting love of truth first. He worried aloud about public opinion manipulated by "glaring type and loud shouting" and public policy determined by "the outcry of the mob," rather than by leadership of "our best minds . . . our best men." Pleading for independence of thought and a return to the principles on which the nation had been founded, the bishop warned of the expansionism that took Americans to "islands lying in remote oceans under tropical skies" and he dreaded the inevitable military and naval buildup which would lead the country "gradually to drift into a militarism which must threaten our most cherished institutions." Among prominent Catholic laymen, Mayor Patrick A. Collins of Boston, Massachusetts' leading Irish Democrat, opposed imperial expansion, as did many Irish, although they had supported intervention to free Cuba from Spain.[6]

In the Treaty of Paris, ratified by the Senate on February 6, 1899, Spain gave up Cuba. Puerto Rico and Guam were ceded to the United States, which for $20 million also received the Philippine Islands. Filipinos led by Emilio Aguinaldo were already in revolt against their new masters and it took seventy thousand American troops to put down the insurrection. Spalding reminded a rally in Chicago on April 30 that "we have always believed in human rights, in freedom and opportunity in education and religion, and we have invited all men to come and enjoy these blessings," but in the American tradition these were not "articles to be exported and thrust down unwilling throats at the point of a bayonet." His voice was lost in the chorus of approval for government policies. President McKinley's explanation of American policy to a group of Methodist clergymen has become part of the national lore: "There was nothing left for us to do but to take them all [the Philippines] and to educate the Filipinos and to uplift and civilize and Christianize them."[7] That Christianity had reached the islands a good fifty years before John Smith saw Jamestown was somehow not part of the scenario.

America's arrival on the world stage was dramatic. Secretary of State

Hay announced an "Open Door" policy for China in 1899. One year later American troops joined in putting down the Boxer Rebellion. A year after that the Hay-Pauncefote Treaty made the Caribbean an American lake and freed the British for Europe and *entente cordiale*. Halfway through the next decade, World War I eased the way to hemispheric domination as Latin American trade patterns shifted away from Europe and North American investments flowed south. McKinley's assassination and the accession of Theodore Roosevelt in 1901 had launched the era of dollar diplomacy. Panama was detached from Colombia and gave the United States the Canal Zone. The 1904 Roosevelt Corollary to the Monroe Doctrine asserted international United States police power in the Americas.

The nation felt a sense of greatness. Population rose 21 percent in the decade ending in 1910, from 75,995,000 to 91,972,000. Fifty cities had over one hundred thousand inhabitants. The last frontiers closed when the Indian Territory became Oklahoma in 1905, and Arizona and New Mexico became states in 1912. Social Darwinism yielded to pragmatism, creative evolution, and social engineering. The Progressive Era was born. Humanitarians (Theodore Roosevelt called them "muckrakers") spearheaded reform in government, business, housing and working conditions, wage and hour laws, and education. Roosevelt won a reputation as a trustbuster. His successor from 1909 to 1912, William Howard Taft, was more effective, if less flamboyant.

It was the heyday in American religion of an increasingly anthropocentric Social Gospel, emphasizing divine immanence but above all the realization in time and on this earth—here and now!—of the Kingdom of God. Ethical earnestness replaced doctrinal preoccupation. On the intellectual side, a sense of disenchantment set in—Henry May's "rebellion of the intellectuals" was brewing—as the norms and values that had made America seemed suddenly threadbare and inadequate.[8] The world of thought was no longer principally inhabited by religious professionals; it had become the province of secular philosophers like Charles Peirce, William James, Josiah Royce, and John Dewey. Humanitarianism began to replace Protestantism as America's religion.

The political structure of American Catholicism was still dominated by the figure of Cardinal Gibbons, who, in 1903, became the first American ever to vote in a papal election. Pius X was chosen to succeed Leo XIII, dead at the age of ninety-three. Five years later, a phrase in the papal document *Sapienti Consilio* removed the church in the United States from the mission status and dependence on Rome's Congregation for Propagation of the Faith at which John Carroll had bridled a century and a quarter before.[9] Organizational growth slowed. No new metropolitan sees—archdioceses—were designated by Pius X, pope from 1903 to 1914, although he did establish thirteen new dioceses. Only one was in the East. Eight were located in the Midwest, two in Texas and two in the Northwest. Separate jurisdiction for Byzantine-Slavic Catholics was set up at Philadelphia in 1913.

By 1910 overall Catholic population grew to 16,363,000 and by 1920 to 19,828,000. The net increase from immigration since 1900 was 3,500,000. Catholic growth in rural and smalltown America was assisted by the Catholic Church Extension Society (founded in 1905), headed by Francis Clement Kelley until he became Bishop of Oklahoma in 1924. The society sponsored "missionary congresses" at Chicago in 1908 and Boston in 1913.[10] In his study of Catholic revivalism, Jay Dolan has counted at least thirteen men's religious communities engaged in parish mission work during the 19th century. Further development took place under the aegis of the American Catholic Missionary Union, founded by Walter Elliott in the 1890s. By 1908 thirty mission bands of diocesan priests were involved in a ministry of outreach to neglected Catholic parishes and to others interested in Catholicism.[11] The church's vitality and stability could be seen in the launching of two major ventures, the sixteen-volume *Catholic Encyclopedia* (published from 1907 to 1914), edited by a mixed lay and clerical board, and *America* (begun in 1909), a national weekly journal of opinion published by a staff of Jesuits from all parts of the country. A unique event was the corporate reception into the Roman Catholic Church in 1909 of the Franciscan friars and sisters of the Atonement, Episcopalian communities founded in 1898 at Graymoor, in Garrison, New York, by Paul Francis (Lewis) Wattson and Lurana Mary White. In 1908 they had inaugurated the "church unity octave," an annual week of public prayer for Christian unity.[12]

As the last great wave of immigrants arrived, scions of earlier Catholic generations were making their way in business, and especially in politics. Theodore Roosevelt named Charles Bonaparte Secretary of the Navy in 1905 and Attorney General in 1906. He held the latter post under President Taft until 1909. From 1910 to 1921 the Chief Justice of the United States was a Catholic from Louisiana and a onetime Confederate soldier, Edward Douglass White. On the municipal level, Irish-Catholic involvement in ward politics and identification with the Democratic Party continued. Charles F. Murphy—no one called him anything but "Mr. Murphy"—parlayed a string of saloons into leadership of Tammany Hall after Boss Croker's retirement to Ireland. He dominated New York City from 1902 until his death in 1924. Governor Alfred E. Smith and Senator Robert F. Wagner, Sr. were among those who got their start in Mr. Murphy's machine. Boston, home port to Puritans and then to Yankee merchants, was taken over by a similar crew. Economically, the city was declining. Its financial circles, as in New York, remained in firm Yankee control. But in the 20th century political power belonged to the Irish. John F. Fitzgerald, whose grandson became the thirty-fifth President of the United States in 1961, was elected Boston's third Irish mayor in 1905. The local situation was ready-made for the classic political machine. Unemployment was chronic and disproportionately high. The party in power could dispense patronage and a rough sort of social welfare. It was done in grand, rollicking style in Boston after 1913 when James Michael Curley became mayor.[13]

Ecclesiastical Boston was ruled from 1907 to 1944 by William O'Connell, son of "lace-curtain Irish" parents who had worked their way up through the textile mills of Lowell. Rome-educated and from 1895 to 1901 a very different successor to Denis O'Connell as rector of Rome's American College, he was a social conservative who cultivated a deliberately princely splendor to upgrade the Catholic image. Cardinal O'Connell introduced efficient organization and centralized authority into the somewhat laissez faire church of Archbishop Williams. He was, Donna Merwick notes, "authority's answer to intellectual curiosity." At the same time, his stern political morality contrasted sharply with the practices of some of his flock. During the O'Connell era the convergence of many historical threads out of the area's past made the phrase "Banned in Boston" famous, a symbol of neo-Puritan excess—literary and theatrical censorship exercised by civil authorities under benevolent ecclesiastical eyes.[14]

The Boston pattern recurred with variations over a half-century. New York, Jersey City, Chicago, San Francisco, and Kansas City were among Irish-Catholic Democratic strongholds. Church and city leaders fell into cooperative patterns. The network of family relationships was reminiscent of Maryland before the Revolution. Political influence and a sense of proprietorship were added ingredients. Priests and sisters came of the same families that produced ward leaders. It could happen that surplus desks, otherwise ticketed for the bonfire, found their way into parochial school classrooms. The chaplaincy, with salary, of the police or fire department made a nice perquisite for a deserving pastor. The message was not lightly ignored when Boss Hague of Jersey City took an interest in fund raising for a new diocesan seminary. The phenomenon remained largely Irish. Italians and Slavs were too concerned with sheer economic survival, but in New England some Franco-American Catholics gravitated to the Republican Party and successfully challenged Irish control in states like Rhode Island, where they elected Aram Pothier governor in 1908.[15]

Problems of adjustment were severe. By 1914 Chicago was the world's third-largest Polish city, ranking behind Warsaw and Lodz only. Poles did not mix easily with the Irish, who controlled Chicago's church, nor with the Germans, who had worked out their own accomodation with Irish domination. But there was another side to the coin. Lithuanian parishioners objected that the influence of the Polish sisters in the parish school at St. George's Church was causing their children to follow Polish ways. In Pennsylvania a priest working among Hungarian and Slovak coal miners and their families estimated in 1908 that the church reached only one-sixth of the Catholics among them.[16] Misunderstanding and neglect led to schism. A Lithuanian National Church formed in Chicago in 1906. It was also in Chicago that disputes over ownership of church property and appointment of pastors led in 1897 to formation of the Polish Catholic Church in America, with Anton Kozlowski as bishop. He received episcopal orders from the Old Catholic Church, a group in Europe which had separated from Rome in the aftermath of the First Vatican Council. A year later at Holy Mother of the Rosary Church in Buffalo, Stephan Kaminski became bishop of the Polish Catholic Independent Church in America. By 1907 both groups had affiliated with the Scranton-based Polish National Catholic Church, established in 1900 under the leadership of Francis Hodur, first prime bishop of a church which would later establish a mission in Poland itself.[17] Other national conflicts did not reach the point of schism, but by one estimate scarcely half the Chicago area's substantial Bohemian Catholic population were active church members. St. Procopius Benedictine Abbey and College were founded to become a center of Czech religion and culture. A partial response to deep and widespread Slavic discontent in the Midwest was the appointment of a number of bishops of eastern European origin: Bohemian-born Joseph Koudelka became auxiliary of Cleveland in 1907 and then moved as bishop to Superior, Wisconsin. Paul Rhode, from Prussian Poland, was auxiliary bishop of Chicago in 1908 and later for thirty years bishop of Green Bay. Edward Kozlowski was named auxiliary bishop in Milwaukee. Bishops John Stariha of Lead and James Trobec of St. Cloud were Slovenians.[18]

Many of the conflicts between Catholics of different nationalities revolved around control of parochial schools. In cities across the country a heavy proportion of public school teachers were Catholics—two-thirds of the entering class at Chicago Normal School in 1902 came from three southside Irish Catholic high schools—but the Catholic systems themselves continued to grow at a prodigious rate.[19] There were more children in Philadelphia Catholic schools in 1910 than in the public schools of all but a dozen United States cities. As many as one hundred boys and girls crowded into a single classroom, in the charge of a religious sister who more often than not had only a secondary school education herself. In an age of child labor—18.4 percent of those in the age ten to fifteen group worked—only a quarter finished the eighth grade, and 90 percent of these became common laborers.[20] Professionalism among teachers came gradually. A department of education opened at the Catholic University in 1908, the *Catholic Educational Review* began publication in 1911 and the next year Pope Pius X approved a college for sisters at the University. In a deliberate policy decision, the National Catholic Educational Association in 1911 recommended that secondary schools concentrate on an arts curriculum "for the education of the middle classes." Over seven thousand students were enrolled in Chicago's Catholic high schools in 1910. Secretarial courses were common, but the schools of the "church of the workingman" largely avoided courses in manual training.[21]

Catholics were not prominent in Progressive Era reform movements. Among the bishops, only John Lancaster Spalding gained national recognition when in 1902 President Roosevelt named him to the commission which arbitrated the country's first industry-wide strike, the walkout of 147,000 anthracite coal miners. A majority of the strikers were Catholics and United Mine Workers President John Mitchell had asked for a "high Catholic ecclesiastic" as one of the arbitration commissioners. President Nicholas Murray Butler of Columbia University recommended Spalding for the job and expressed his delight when the recommendation was accepted, telling Roosevelt "there is no better American under the flag and there are few who see more clearly and sympathetically into the social problems of the day." Mitchell, who became a Catholic himself a few years later, was convinced that "Bishop Spalding fought and pleaded harder to secure the redress of the wrongs of the workingman than any other man on the commission."[22]

A growing number of Catholic clergymen made significant contributions to the cause of social reform. They included bishops like William Stang of Fall River, Massachusetts, and Peter Muldoon of Rockford, Illinois.[23] Two outstanding priests were John J. Curran in the Pennsylvania coalfields and Peter C. Yorke in California. Curran had worked for a coal company as a child. By 1902 he was a pastor in Wilkes Barre and an enthusiastic booster of the United Mine Workers among immigrant parishioners. During the anthracite strike he served John Mitchell as consultant. Yorke wore many hats in a career which spanned the waning years of the 19th century and the first quarter of the 20th. He edited *The Monitor* and later *The Leader,* a weekly which promoted the causes of Irish nationalism and of American labor. He edited a series of religion textbooks and wrote on the liturgy, was a regent of the University of California, served parishes in Oakland and San Francisco, and was chancellor of the archdiocese of San Francisco, but was also for a time relieved of his duties in a dispute with the archbishop. A vigorous opponent of the A.P.A., he founded the American Women's Liberal League and the Catholic Truth Society to combat bigotry. During the 1901 San Francisco's teamsters' strike, Yorke was a forceful advocate of collective bargaining, and he played a leading role on labor's side in the 1906–7 street railway strike.[24]

Publisher of a chain of midwestern Catholic newspapers, Humphrey Desmond was an eloquent and thoughtful lay voice. He challenged the Catholic community's priorities, starting from the premise that the church ought not duplicate services provided in the American system by a religiously neutral state. Desmond's proposals for cutbacks in expenditures on Catholic schools and on institutions of "pathological charity" like hospitals, foundling homes, asylums, and protectories fell on deaf ears. He believed that greater resources should be devoted to "half way houses"—temperance societies, young people's clubs and homes, employment bureaus, and settlement houses—than to what he called "end houses." Mary Theresa Elder, sister of the archbishop of Cincinnati, was an outspoken advocate of the same goals. It puzzled her that priests would risk their lives to administer the last rites to the dying while so little attention was paid to opportunities to "govern and guide" the living. Both Desmond and Elder wanted the church to channel its resources to curing the causes of social ills by programs to help immigrants escape the urban squalor in which they found themselves mired.[25]

Desmond's prescription was not accepted, but some Catholic universities did respond to an obvious need by establishing schools of social service. At Washington's Catholic University, sociologist William Kerby was architect in 1910 of the National Conference of Catholic Charities, an umbrella organization to coordinate action in the social service field. There were other signs of growing sophistication. Thousands of middle-class Catholics (over seven thousand in 1905 alone) attended the Catholic Summer School of America at Cliff Haven on Lake Champlain to hear lectures in the sciences and humanities and on current topics. "Muckraking" lectures were popular fare. The school, modeled on the Protestant Chautauqua movement, was the brainchild of Warren E. Mosher of Youngstown, Ohio, editor of the *Catholic Reading Circle Review* until his death in 1906. After a trial run in 1892 at New London, Connecticut, the Delaware and Hudson Railroad donated a permanent home adjoining the Hotel Champlain, where summer schools were held until America's entry into World War II. A notable characteristic of Cliff Haven was the heavy participation of women in its programs both as lecturers and as students. Spinoff schools operated in several parts of the country until the early 1920s: the Columbian Catholic School at Spring Bank near Milwaukee, a

"Winter School" timed to follow Mardi Gras in New Orleans, and the Maryland Catholic Summer School.[26]

Not everyone was equally excited about the summer schools. St. Louis editor Arthur Preuss grumped that "the only kind of lectures appropriate, timely and useful for a Catholic Summer School would be a course of plain everyday catechetical instruction."[27] Catholic conservatives worried more over the "isms" of the day—anarchism, socialism, and liberalism— and focused their energies on what they considered really "Catholic" interests, such as parochial schools. Many refused to see the needs being pointed out by social reformers. In tones reminiscent of Russell H. Conwell's "Acres of Diamonds" speech, Paulist priest William Kress in 1912 wrote off the destitution of the urban poor as minimal and the result of "shiftlessness or intemperance or both combined."[28] He echoed businessman William J. Onahan, who had been convinced that "the labor question is not so much a question of labor as it is of liquor, laziness and loafing."[29]

Despite their disagreements with the Germany of *Kulturkampf* and Bismarck, German-American Catholics kept up a proud interest in the Second *Reich* and thought of sharing its blessings with fellow American Catholics. To the accompaniment of anguished howls from John Ireland and others, a political party modeled on the German *Zentrum* was proposed. Failing that, the German-American Knights of St. John in 1901 led the way in establishing the American Federation of Catholic Societies. The founders denied that the Federation was clerically controlled, but Bishops Sebastian Messmer of Green Bay and James McFaul of Trenton were its ecclesiastical godfathers. Social liberals faulted the Federation for neglecting the causes underlying social discontent, a failure remedied in 1911 when New Orleans attorney Charles Denechaud spearheaded creation within it of a Social Service Commission.[30]

An old German standby, the *Central-Verein,* was reorganized in 1908– 9, complete with central bureau in St. Louis and a bilingual journal, *Central-Blatt and Social Justice.* Its moving spirit was a conservative Chicago reformer, Frederick P. Kenkel. His interests ran more to exploring the fundamental reordering of society than to pinpointing specific remedies, but the vision he projected of an organic, integrated community helped to move the *Central-Verein* solidly in the direction of social commitment.[31] An activist who first cooperated with Kenkel and than ran into conflict with him was Peter E. Dietz, a priest whose meteoric career in labor relations ended with World War I. Impressed by what he knew of Protestant social service agencies, he had founded in 1910 an organization of Catholics who held key positions in the trade union movement called the Militia of Christ for Social Service.[32]

The prewar decades saw the debut of American Catholicism's most significant socioeconomic theoretician, John A. Ryan, a product of Minnesota populism and of the clergy formed in St. Paul under Archbishop Ireland. Ryan's career began in 1906 with a doctoral dissertation described in an introduction by Johns Hopkins University economist Richard Ely as "the first attempt in the English language to elaborate a Roman Catholic system of political economy." In *A Living Wage: Its Ethical and Economic Aspects,* Ryan insisted that employers had an obligation in justice to pay wages sufficient to maintain the worker and his family in decent comfort and argued for a minimum wage of $600 per year (the urban average in 1906 was $571), the eight-hour day, restrictions on child labor and work by women, legalization of picketing, compulsory arbitration of labor disputes, accident and old age insurance, housing programs, public ownership of mines and forests, government control of monopolies, progressive income and inheritance taxes, and government regulation of stock exchanges. Ryan opposed socialism on philosophical grounds, but bluntly declared that "the spirit and traditions of the church" were less favorable to the contemporary pretensions of industrial capitalism than was commonly believed. His overall goal was to promote economic democracy which deemphasized the element of competition and promoted a cooperative approach among the various component segments of the economic world.[33]

American socialists tended to be of the evolutionary variety, committed to achieving goals through political action within the system. They had no notable success. On the national level, the largest vote for a socialist candidate for President came in 1912 when Eugene V. Debs polled fewer than nine hundred thousand votes in a total of over fifteen million. Socialists never controlled any state, although they elected mayors in several cities. They harbored some doctrinaire anti-religionists, but mainline socialists generally limited themselves to economics and politics. There were religious flirtations: the Protestant Socialist Fellowship (1906) and a Catholic Socialist Society (1909) in Chicago. The diocese of Covington, Kentucky, to the undisguised horror of Bishop Camillus Maes, boasted an eloquent apologist for socialism in Thomas McGrady, pastor in Bellevue, just across the Ohio River from Cincinnati. McGrady protested that, although "the early Fathers of the Church were, as a rule, socialists," no one ever taxed them with atheism, as was being done to contemporary socialists. He also sang the praises of such modern heroes as Charles Darwin, Ernest Renan, and Emile Zola. It was too much for Maes. McGrady complained that the bishop "wouldn't let you read the Declaration of Independence because it was composed by an infidel." Their running battle ended when McGrady was suspended, left the active ministry, and retired to California.[34]

More radical than McGrady was his fellow priest and sometime house guest (a sore point with Bishop Maes), Thomas Hagerty. A large man with a great beard, he had been ordained in Chicago, moved first to Texas and then to Our Lady of Sorrows Church in Las Vegas, New Mexico. Attracted by socialist ideas in the course of ministry to exploited Mexican-American railroad workers, Hagerty began to travel for the socialist American Labor Union. When forbidden to exercise the priesthood, he settled at Van Buren, Oklahoma, declaring himself "a Catholic priest, as much a Catholic as the Pope himself." He edited the *Voice of Labor* and in 1903 made a national lecture tour which was marked by increasing stridency. Gradualism was not for him. Denouncing "slowcialism," he announced: "We must have revolution, peaceable if possible, but, to tell the truth, we care not how we get it." In 1905 Hagerty took on the improbable chore of drafting a constitution for the anarchist "Wobblies," the Industrial Workers of the World, a direct-action group with no faith in the political process. He was prominent at the Wobblies' 1905 convention, but soon dropped out of circulation; his clerical past made anarchists uneasy. Friends found him teaching Spanish in Chicago in 1917 under the name "Ricardo Moreno." By 1920 he was on West Madison Street, Chicago's skid row.[35]

Mary Harris ("Mother") Jones was another Wobblies' founder, although she seems to have abandoned the movement after the 1905 convention. Her grandfather had been hanged by the British, her father driven into exile in Canada. One brother became a well-known Canadian priest. She began her American career as a convent-school teacher in Monroe, Michigan, then married an iron molder whom she lost along with their four children when yellow fever ravaged Memphis's poor-Irish "Pinch" district in 1867. She was seamstress in Chicago, "sewing for the lords and barons who lived in magnificent houses on Lake Shore Drive," when the Great Fire of 1871 occurred. The 1886 Haymarket Riot marked a decisive turning point for her. Soon she was winning a reputation as a colorful and passionate labor agitator. She seemed to be everywhere, among railroad and steel strikers and outside southern textile plants, but her main interest was the coalfields and her two biggest interventions were in West Virginia in 1912–13 and in Colorado a year later.

Over ninety when she participated in her last strike, Mother Jones died at one hundred. John D. Rockefeller, Jr. had sent birthday greetings. She reciprocated on John D. Sr.'s ninety-first birthday, but confided: "I wouldn't trade what I've done for what he's done. I've done the best I could to make the world a better place for poor, hardworking people."[36]

The "Miners' Angel" had a salty tongue which she delighted to turn on the institutional church and its ministers—sisters and priests both ("I never saw more moral cowards in my life than those sisters. . . . They are simply owned body and soul by the Rockefeller interests").[37] As she understood it, "Jesus took twelve men from among the laborers of his time (no college graduates among them) and with them founded an organization that revolutionized the society amid which it arose." The church instead preached palliative religion, offering visions of an afterlife, but little for the worker here and now. She criticized the church for its wealth and for abandoning the revolutionary thrust of the Gospel. Christianity for her was revolutionary and redemptive, the labor movement's role to "go down and redeem the Israelites that were in bondage," and lead them from the land of bondage and plunder into the land of freedom. Workers she urged to "pray for the dead and fight like hell for the living."[38] Mother Jones died in 1930, seven months after her one hundredth birthday. She planned her own funeral, received the Catholic Church's last sacraments, and was buried with a requiem mass from St. Gabriel's Church in Washington. President William Green of the A. F. of L. and Secretary of Labor William Doak headed the official mourners. Between ten and fifteen thousand attended the burial service in Illinois. Father John Maguire, C.S.V., President of St. Viator College, Bourbonnais, gave the eulogy. A choir of miners provided the singing.[39]

Benjamin Gitlow observed years ago that "the American Communist movement owes a great deal to the Irish and Irish-American radicals. . . . From the Irish contingent the Communists got organizers, writers, editors, speakers, trade union leaders."[40] Rebel daughter of a rebel father, Elizabeth Gurley Flynn was one. She claimed her family separated from the Catholic Church over its treatment of Father McGlynn.[41] Sally Miller has estimated that one-fourth of the radical immigrants in the final phase of immigration came of Catholic backgrounds, mostly Irish.[42] But the church's role, reflected in its leaders but also overwhelmingly in its active members, was one that Neil Betten has accurately characterized as moderate to conservative.[43] Catholics looked for better working conditions. They concentrated on moderating capitalist excesses. But they remained resistant to socialist blandishments and, with few exceptions, virtually impervious to more radical social promptings. Leo XIII had stressed the right of private property. Few American Catholics needed urging along that line. William Howard Taft was right to single out their community as one of the country's "bulwarks against socialism and anarchy."[44]

Testem Benevolentiae had quieted the Americanists. John Keane became archbishop of Dubuque in 1900 and January 1903 Denis O'Connell became rector of the Catholic University. His tenure there was clouded by financial near-disaster when the university's broker declared bank-ruptcy and two-thirds of the investment portfolio was lost.[45] John Ireland never received the cardinal's hat many had expected him to get. Pius X's election in 1903 and his selection of Anglo-Spanish Cardinal Rafael Merry del Val as Secretary of State finished the last vestiges of liberal influence in Rome. During the Modernist crisis which developed in the new century's first decade, the leading Americanists could not have been more orthodox. In 1908 Denis O'Connell denounced Catholic University professor Charles Grannan to Pius X for liberal exegetical tendencies.[46] John Ireland wrote staunch defenses of the dogmatic authority of church and pope and of the reality of the supernatural order.[47] John Keane had become senile before the crisis really blossomed.[48]

Those preoccupations associated with the phrase "Catholic Modern-ism" in turn-of-the-century France, Britain, and Italy attracted little inter-est in the United States. Philosophical concern with the subject and the postulates of historico-biblical criticism did not rank high on the Ameri-can agenda. Progressives in this country were more likely to concentrate on problems in social, political, and pastoral realms.[49] William Sullivan, C.S.P., knew the European Modernists, but was influenced more by Americanism. He spoke and wrote of a church that championed freedom and progress, and fashioned itself in the mold of the American demo-cratic experience. Disappointed in his hopes, he abandoned Catholicism in 1909 and became a Unitarian minister.[50]

The intellectual preoccupations of the European church did have echoes in the United States. Two Catholic University professors were challenged for holding advanced views in biblical exegesis. In 1907 the nomination of Edward J. Hanna, a professor at St. Bernard's Seminary in Rochester, as coadjutor to the archbishop of San Francisco was rejected because of articles he had written in theological journals and in the *Cath-olic Encyclopedia*. Bishop McQuaid intervened on Hanna's behalf, but it was not until five years later that he was named bishop.[51] A more tragic casualty of the church's ongoing crisis was John R. Slattery, S.S.J., heir to a construction company fortune and from 1892 to 1903 superior-gen-eral of the Josephites. He moved in Americanist circles, was a close friend of Denis O'Connell, and often came into conflict with other mem-bers of the hierarchy in the course of his work for black Catholics. In 1906 he left the Catholic Church and later worked closely with French Modernist Albert Houtin.[52]

The New York seminary at Dunwoodie, Yonkers, was briefly one of the more vibrant intellectual centers the Catholic Church in the United States has known. Under the leadership of James F. Driscoll, studies were brought into greater conformity with the broader American university scene and an exchange program with Columbia University began. The strong faculty included Francis Gigot, an expert in higher criticism and author of introductions to Old and New Testaments; Joseph Bruneau, S.S., a proponent of the apologetic of French philosopher Maurice Blondel; Orientalist Gabriel Oussani; and philosopher Francis P. Duffy, managing editor and moving spirit of the finest American theological journal until then published under Catholic auspices, the *New York Review* (1905–8). The *Review* was ended as a result of pressure applied by the apostolic delegate at Washington, Diomede Falconio, O.F.M., on Archbishop John M. Farley, who had succeeded Archbishop Corrigan in 1902. Duffy turned to pastoral work in 1912. He served in World War I as chaplain to the "Fighting Sixty-Ninth" New York Regiment and later was Governor Alfred E. Smith's theological consultant. A Hollywood movie featured his military career. A statue of Fr. Duffy in battle dress stands at the head of Manhattan's Times Square.[53]

Pope Pius X took sharp action against European Modernism in 1907. A decree of the Roman Congregation of the Holy Office on July 3 (*Lamentabili Sane Exitu*) listed sixty-five condemned propositions concerning church, revelation, Christ, and sacraments said to be culled from Modernist writings. This syllabus of errors was followed by a condemnatory encyclical letter, *Pascendi Dominici Gregis,* on September 7. The situation with *Lamentabili* and *Pascendi* was not the same as eight years earlier with *Testem Benevolentiae.* No identifiably American ideas were directly touched by the new documents, but the effect was chilling. The post-*Pascendi* years in American Catholicism were marked by intellectual retreat and theological sterility. Cultivation of the life of the mind became suspect. A thoroughgoing and immensely effective educational police action isolated the theological reaches of the Catholic community from the contemporary world with which tentative contact had so recently been established. The combination of Americanist and Modernist crises, and particularly the powerful integrist reaction which set in after 1907, effectively put an end for the next fifty years to further development of Catholic thought in authentic American dress.

The emergence of the United States as an international power forced a new role on the Catholic Church in America, itself for so long on the receiving end of missionary efforts.[54] On the day after Dewey took Manila, Ireland had written to Denis O'Connell: "If the pope in the future is to have any world-wide prestige, he must deal as never before with America." O'Connell in his reply depicted Archbishop Ireland as "God's apostle in modern times to Church and to Society." He told him: "You are the only man in America, lay or cleric, who can properly take in or give right initiative to: the design of an American-ordered world."[55] This gradiloquent prophecy was not fulfilled, but Catholics from the United States did become involved in a variety of ways in the affairs of the church elsewhere in the world.

The first American overseas missionary of any denomination was the later second archbishop of Baltimore, Leonard Neale, in Guyana in 1781. He was followed by Bishop Edward Barron, Father John Kelly, and lay catechist Denis Pindar, all of them in Liberia in the early 1840s.[56] Jesuits and Sisters of St. Anne undertook the Alaska mission in the late 1880s. Other 19th-century missionaries included in the Bahamas diocesan priests from Charleston and later from New York, Sisters of Charity, who arrived there in 1889, and Benedictine monks from St. John's Abbey in Minnesota, who accepted responsibility for the Bahamian church in 1891. Midwestern Jesuits went to Belize in Central America in 1893, the same year in which their brethren from the east coast moved into the British island of Jamaica. Holy Family and Mercy sisters also worked in Belize.[57] In 1911 an American community of secular priests, the Catholic Foreign Mission Society (Maryknoll), was founded by James A. Walsh and Thomas Price. It was the first American group designed uniquely for work in foreign lands and the first Maryknoll missionaries left for Kwangtung Province, China, in 1918.[58]

American Catholics inevitably became involved in the nation's new empire. In the Philippines, American-style government and schools were established and Protestant missionaries arrived, including the future ecumenical pioneer, Episcopalian Bishop Charles H. Brent. He deliberately directed his activities to non-Christian tribes, but other Protestant churchmen were less inclined to avoid competition. Secular public schools on the American model became another bone of contention. There was also the Philippine Independent Church, organized during the Spanish-American war by a Filipino priest. An ecclesial counterpart to the national political movement, its initial success was considerable.[59]

A significant weakness of the Spanish regime in the Philippines had been failure to foster a native clergy. The Filipino revolt of 1896 had strong "anti-friar" undertones of resentment against religious orders which controlled 10 percent, and in some provinces 50 percent of the land. Particular targets were the Dominicans, Franciscans, Augustinians and Recollects. The flight of Spanish priests after 1899 had left seven hundred parishes vacant, and a commission headed by William Howard Taft warned that friars could not safely return to their posts. Cardinal Gibbons and Archbishop Ireland were enlisted as intermediaries between the United States and the Holy See. Taft was finally despatched on an official mission to Rome and in 1903 the American government purchased 410,000 acres of "friars' lands" for over $7 million.[60]

American churchmen involved with the Philippines were soon surrounded with ambiguities and torn by conflicting interests. Archbishop Placide Chapelle of New Orleans, apostolic delegate for the Philippines from 1899 to 1901, tried unsuccessfully to defend the friars before the Taft Commission. In 1904 Cardinal Gibbons earned Theodore Roosevelt's ire by stating his hope for eventual Filipino independence; but in 1912, the retiring President Taft persuaded him to canvass bishops in the United States to lobby against independence legislation. From Rome, Cardinal Merry del Val let it be known that he considered Spain's former colony ready for neither political nor ecclesiastical autonomy. In 1903 American bishops had been assigned to Filipino dioceses. Jeremiah Harty, a St. Louis priest who had become archbishop of Manila, confidentially informed Gibbons in 1912 that he thought an independent Philippines would not be viable and would quickly be swallowed up by Japan. But he admitted he would be run out of the country if his anti-independence views became known. The ambivalence persisted.[61] American and other foreign members of religious orders reinforced the Spanish and Filipino clergy, but the church remained caught up in the national identity crisis.

Elsewhere in the former Spanish empire, Guam became American territory when the U.S.S. *Charleston* landed there in 1898 with Chaplain McKinnon on board. The Catholic Church remained in charge of Spanish Capuchin friars until World War II. Before going to Manila, Archbishop Chapelle served as apostolic delegate for Cuba and Puerto Rico. San Juan's fifty-first Spanish bishop resigned in the wake of American occupation, and was succeeded by a Marist priest from New Orleans, James H. Blenk, S.M., a former college president and chairman of the "Winter School" effort. Blenk had been Chapelle's chief aide and later succeeded him as archbishop of New Orleans. An American Augustinian, William A. Jones, O.S.A., president of St. Augustine's College, Havana, followed Blenk in San Juan. The disorganized Puerto Rican church continued to suffer a chronic shortage of priests. In 1908 the United States Supreme Court provided some solace by upholding church property titles dating from Spanish times.[62] Cuba's situation was more complicated. Freed from Spain, the island became a political protectorate and vassal of the United States. American priests were sent to assist the local church, and Bonaventure Broderick, a Hartford priest, served briefly as auxiliary bishop of Havana. American troops were withdrawn in 1902, but reoccupied Cuba from 1906 to 1909. No substantial American church presence endured.

By 1914 Roman Catholicism was well established in the United States with a constituency of multi-national origin. Although their church had been there from the beginning, Catholics were perceived to be somehow more "foreign" than other Americans. Some 85 percent of them in 1920 are estimated to have been descendants of immigrants who had arrived since 1820. Outside of the few traditionally German dioceses in the mid-west, Irish-Americans retained organizational control of the church although other national groups were making themselves heard. World War I was a severe setback for the German-Americans. The nation which renamed sauerkraut "liberty cabbage" was not prepared to tolerate dreams of an American *Deutschtum,* political or eccleasiastical, along the Great Lakes. The age of immigration ended with passage of restrictive and exclusionary legislation in the years 1921-1924. An era in American Catholic history ended with it. The church's period of growth by immigration effectively came to an end with the outbreak of war in Europe in the summer of 1914. The 1920s were a new experience.

XVII

So Certain and Set Apart

In a letter of October 1927 to Wilfred Parsons, S.J., editor of *America,* Mary McGill, associate editor of Indianapolis's *The Catholic Girl,* made this observation about the American Catholic community and how it must strike their fellow Americans: "We are so SURE. That characteristic would hurt me, if I didn't believe. I think I would hate people who are so certain and set apart. . ." The following August, the *National Catholic Alumni Bulletin* reported the joy of Detroit business executive Theodore F. McManus in Catholic culture's "proud and glorious isolation" from the contemporary world. McManus matched words with action. He had a $25,000 kickoff gift ready for a $10 million drive to establish an "American Catholic Foundation" to create "a definite Catholic culture," which would penetrate "every field of research."[1] McGill and McManus were not untypical. There was no lack of problems for America's Catholics during World War I and the Roaring Twenties, but the evidence marshalled by William M. Halsey in his impressive intellectual history of between-the-wars Catholicism, *The Survival of American Innocence,* suggests the overall picture of a community in which assertive, if frequently naïve, self-confidence mingled happily with a remarkable sense of distance from the doubts and disillusionment of the contemporary scene. The American Catholic community throughout its many-layered being grew in self-assurance and acquired a sense of chosen-ness theretofore reserved in America for those with better Puritan credentials. If this resulted in isolation from one or another aspect of surrounding culture, or from the whole congeries, this was for Catholics a source of pride, rather than distress. But before these levels of self-confidence would be achieved, some tests had to be passed. World War I was one of them.

There were two preludes to the war era. One was set principally in the rural midwest and south where few if any Catholics had settled, the other south of the border in Mexico. By 1910 the Populist Party's dream of an alliance between its radical agrarian base and the industrial proletariat in eastern and Great Lakes cities was dead. Thomas E. Watson of Georgia, the Populists' candidate in 1896 for the vice-presidency and in 1904 for the presidency, shifted the focus of his *Tom Watson's Magazine* to the threat posed by "voracious Trusts . . . the Roman Catholic priest-hood . . . and the Knights of Columbus."[2] He was joined by *The Menace* (1911) from Aurora in the Missouri Ozarks, which among other contributions resurrected the bogus 17th-century "cardinal" or "Jesuit" oath, now attributed to the Catholic fraternal order, the Knights of Columbus. One section of the oath, which circulated widely in rural America, read:

> I will, when opportunity presents, make and wage relentless war, se-cretly and openly, against all heretics, Protestants and Masons, as I am directed to do, to extirpate them from the face of the whole earth; and that I will spare neither age, sex, or condition, and that I will hang, burn, waste, boil, flay, strangle and bury alive these infamous heretics; rip up the stomachs and wombs of their women, and crush their infants' heads against the walls in order to annihilate their execrable race . . .

Where such overt action was not feasible, Knights supposedly promised to "secretly use the poisonous cup, the strangulation cord, the steel of the poniard, or the leaden bullet," as ordered by the pope or the superior general of the Jesuits.[3]

This wave of anti-Catholicism included groups like the Guardians of Liberty, whose Chief Guardian was Lieutenant General Nelson A. Miles, hero of the Civil War and of Indian wars and holder of the Medal of Honor. It was soon submerged by American involvement in the European war, to surface again in post-war years. The rural concentration of the phenomenon marked a shift from the eastern urban centers where both Catholic immigrants and religiously tinged nativism had flourished in the preceding century. John Higham has pointed to this shift as evidence of the secularization of American nationalism in more sophisticated circles.[4]

Trouble meanwhile was brewing below the Rio Grande and would involve both the United States and the Catholic Church. When the 1911 overthrow of the Porfirio Diaz dictatorship was followed by persecution of Mexican clergy and restrictions on the church, Cardinal Gibbons of

Baltimore worked with President Woodrow Wilson and Secretary of State William Jennings Bryan to try to ease the situation. He kept in touch with Mexican and American bishops and did his best to mute Catholic criticism, which was always ready to hand in *America*, edited by Richard H. Tierney, S.J., and in *Extension*, where editor Francis Clement Kelley worried over refugee problems created by the Mexican upheaval. By March 1915, Gibbons's patience was sufficiently exhausted that he publicly took to task both President Venustiano Carranza and his rival, Francisco ("Pancho") Villa. In August, the Baltimore cardinal suggested the advisability of American armed intervention, arguing that it had benefitted Cuba some years before. Gibbons's efforts brought nothing but frustration. When in October Wilson recognized the Carranza government, a torrent of Catholic wrath descended on him. The American archbishops lodged a formal protest against restrictive clauses in the Mexican constitution adopted at Querétaro on May 1, 1917. By that time the United States was already at war with the Central Powers and Mexican problems faded from American view.[5]

The Archduke Franz Ferdinand was murdered at Sarajevo on June 28, 1914. Pius X died that same summer on August 20, and Europe was at war when Cardinals O'Connell of Boston and Gibbons of Baltimore sailed on the S.S. *Canopic*. They arrived in Rome on September 3, just too late to take their places among the cardinals, including New York's John Farley, who elected as pope Giacomo della Chiesa. He took the name Benedict XV.

In its early stages the war aroused no particular enthusiasm among Catholic Americans. Italy, homeland of many, was not party to the conflict until May 1915. Italian-Americans were pro-Allies. Poles did not rush back to report to Russian, Austrian, or Prussian armies and like Czechs and Slovaks became involved instead in pro-Allies independence activities. The Irish had no reason to favor either side, though hatred of Britain led some to support the Central Powers. Irish independence advocates sensed that their cause was not among Allied war aims. Woodrow Wilson made no secret of his scorn for "hyphenated" Americans whose hearts were anywhere across the ocean except perhaps in England. Five years later at the Paris Peace Conference he remarked that he had been approached on the subject of Irish independence. His reply was frank:

> My first impulse was to tell the Irish to go to hell, but, feeling that this would not be the act of a statesman, I denied myself this personal satisfaction.

More American Catholic periodicals leaned to support of the Central Powers than to support of the Allies. Church leaders were strong supporters of the official neutrality position adopted by the government. Perhaps the last thing by which American Catholics, "hierarchy, priesthood, and press," were inclined to be influenced was the factor suggested by Wilson historian Arthur Link: "the Vatican's friendship for the Hapsburg dynasty." Despite what Lyman Beecher once thought, the Hapsburgs had never bulked large in American Catholic thinking. Ethnic loyalties were really the operative factor, and the cauldron of anti-Wilson sentiment had been superheated by the Mexican imbroglio. Gibbons, O'Connell in Boston, and Messmer in Milwaukee all disavowed it, but there was strong and emotional opposition to the President in many Catholic quarters when Charles Evans Hughes challenged Wilson for the White House in 1916. Francis Clement Kelley had contributed to the ill will by publishing a tract on Mexico called *The Book of Red and Yellow,* subtitled "Blood and a Yellow Streak."[6]

Unpleasant *Kulturkampf* memories had faded and German pride was strong among Catholics as well as Protestants in America. German-Americans had prospered; they were looked on as respected citizens. Unafraid to speak their minds, they felt no need to hide their identity or their highly partisan views on the European war. Catholic German-Americans were happy that *America* editor Tierney seemed friendly to the Central Powers, and they were angry with the Paulists of the *Catholic World,* where editor John Burke, C.S.P., tried to be neutral and even declared in 1915: "War is by no means a Christian tradition. Indeed our very profession of Christian means that we are pacifists." There were those who faulted his "Recent Events" column, however, as tilted toward the Allies.[7] German-American Catholics had a strong and very national sense of religious community, strengthened in city after city along the Great Lakes by religious houses peopled with women and men exiled in the after-shock of the long-ago *Kulturkampf.* These had been joined by émigré Germans and by American recruits, many of them trained in convents and seminaries clustering just over the *Reich*'s borders in countries like Holland. In rural America, German and German-American Benedictines and secular clergy provided similar strength. Although only the war and their massive rush to the colors finally changed laws which barred members of many religious orders from returning to the Fatherland, the enforced alienation had not extended into the financial realm. More than one religious community in the United States suffered severe losses after 1918 when Imperial German bonds and bank notes went the way of the empire that had issued them. Until United States entry into the conflict, support for the German cause was strong in German-American Catholic circles. The annual meeting of the *Central-Verein* held in Pittsburgh on August 8, 1914, two days after Liège had fallen, began with the singing of "Die Wacht am Rhein" followed by "Deutschland über Alles" and the cheer "Deutschland lebe! hoch! hoch! hoch!" The organization's historian, Philip Gleason, has remarked that after the war it "would never again be a 'German-American Catholic' organization in quite the same proud, bold and fruitful way that it had been before 1914."[8]

As war came on, American Catholic bishops supported the "Preparedness Movement." Gibbons endorsed universal military training. He thought it would promote discipline, improve the character and physical condition of young men, and instill in them proper ideas of obedience to lawful authority.[9] Once Congress had declared war on Germany (April 6, 1917), the cardinal issued a statement declaring that "the members of both Houses of Congress are the instruments of God in guiding us in our civic duties." His friend Theodore Roosevelt telegraphed his appreciation for a "noble and patriotic appeal for loyalty."[10] Two weeks later, the nation's assembled archbishops informed President Wilson that

> we are all true Americans, ready as our age, our ability, and our conditions will permit, to do whatsoever is in us to do, for the preservation, the progress and the triumph of our beloved country.[11]

The Catholic community participated in home front activities: Liberty Loan and Red Cross drives, United War Work, sale of war savings stamps. Efforts at fund-raising for Ireland rapidly became as complex and noisy as Irish domestic politics. But Catholic response to appeals for Belgian Relief was good. In October 1917 Cardinal Gibbons accepted the chair of the "League of National Unity," an organization dedicated to stirring up people of all creeds, classes, and occupations to prosecute the war to the finish. Gibbons made no secret of his own views. He wrote President Wilson on October 6, 1917, of the "folly and grave disobedience of unjust and ill-tempered criticism of national policies." For him, the government alone had adequate perspective to "judge of the expediency of national affairs." When Wilson proclaimed Sunday, October 28, 1917, a day of prayer for the success of American arms, the cardinal took as his sermon theme the citizen's paramount duty of obedience.[12]

There were Catholic conscientious objectors to military service in World War I: four in a total of 3,989.[13] Despite John Burke's *Catholic World* editorial, a survey in 1917–18 uncovered no identifiable pacifist Catholic priest or bishop in the country.[14] A million Catholics were among the 4,791,172 who served in the armed forces. Ranking Catholic officer was Admiral William Shepherd Benson, a convert to Catholicism and the first person to hold the position of Chief of Naval Operations. Cardinal Gibbons exaggerated when he told British Ambassador Earl

Reading that Catholics in uniform ran to 35 percent in the army and higher in the navy, but the Catholic community—between fifteen and eighteen million in a total population of one hundred five million—did have a higher proportion in service than its numbers warranted.[15] Service people's needs were looked after by commissioned chaplains (the number soared from 28 to 1,525) and by the Knights of Columbus, who maintained huts ("Everybody Welcome, Everything Free") consisting of recreational facilities, offices, and chapels at two hundred fifty centers overseas and three hundred sixty stateside, staffed by two thousand "secretaries" and twenty-seven thousand volunteers.[16] During the influenza epidemic in the fall of 1918, scenes reminiscent of the Civil and Spanish-American wars were replayed as nursing sisters and chaplains from Catholic hospitals did volunteer duty at military bases like Camp Meade.

In 1917 the Catholic Church in the United States had no national organization. The last plenary council had been held in 1884 and no permanent secretariat existed. Only the annual gathering of the archbishops, who since 1890 had met as an unofficial consultative body, served as a vehicle for unified action. Wartime demands overwhelmed this non-structure. Efforts of Catholic agencies had to be coordinated. The Knights of Columbus were already in the field. Some of their secretaries had seen service with General Pershing's troops in the Mexican border campaign of 1916–17. The American Federation of Catholic Societies was disorganized. It barely survived the war years. The *Central-Verein* had its own special problems. With approval from Cardinals Gibbons, O'Connell, and Farley, a meeting was called at Washington for August 11–12, 1917. The organizers were John J. Burke of the *Catholic World,* Paulist founder of the Chaplain's Aid Association; Lewis O'Hern, also a Paulist and the bishops' liaison with the government for appointment of chaplains; Catholic University sociologist William Kerby, founder of the National Conference of Catholic Charities; and former U.S. Commissioner of Labor Charles P. Neill, a member of the government's Commission on Training Camp activities. One hundred fifteen delegates from sixty-eight dioceses and twenty-seven societies picked Burke to head the National Catholic War Council (NCWC). He was to be assisted by an executive council of delegates from each church province, the Knights of Columbus, and the American Federation of Catholic Societies. Burke lost no time in establishing contact with the War Department and with parallel Protestant and Jewish agencies. He became permanent chairman of "The Committee of Six," designated an official advisory body by Secretary of War Newton D. Baker. Other members were Robert E. Speer, Chairman of the General War-Time Commission of the Churches of the Federal Council of Churches; that Commission's Secretary, William

Adams Brown; John R. Mott of the YMCA; Episcopal Bishop James deWolf Perry; and Colonel Harry Cutler of the Jewish Welfare Board.[17]

Formation of the War Council was a major organizational step for the Catholic Church in the United States. For the first time in its history an institutional commitment was being made to social and political action. Second thoughts suggested a firmer base for the venture, and an administrative committee of four bishops was named to oversee the council's activities. Bishop Peter J. Muldoon of Rockford was chairman; committee members were Bishops Joseph Schrembs of Toledo, William Russell of Charleston, and Patrick J. Hayes, Cardinal Farley's auxiliary in New York and newly named ecclesiastical supervisor of Catholic military chaplains. The Knights of Columbus retained a degree of autonomy in the new structure. Louisville industrialist Patrick H. Callahan directed their efforts. Burke headed the NCWC committee on "Special War Activities," with seven subcommittees reporting to him: men's activities; women's activities; chaplains; Catholic interests; historical records; reconstruction; and finance. The council won official government recognition; it promised a million canvassers to the interdenominational "United War Work" campaign which raised $188.6 million —the largest single collection to that date in world history. The NCWC's share was $32.6 million.[18]

During the world war, Cardinal Gibbons had on several occasions to cope with Pope Benedict's desire to become involved in the peace process. Gibbons's actions showed that he understood clearly the truth of what Patrick Hayes—by 1924 archbishop of New York and about to be made cardinal—wrote bluntly of Woodrow Wilson: "He certainly was not sympathetic to us."[19] Gibbons was slow to respond to the Pope's August 1, 1917, peace note. He conceded Benedict's idealism and defended his approach as the only hope for peace. But he made no effort to see Wilson about it, which was just as well in the light of French Ambassador Jules Jusserand's later recollection of the President's "ill-humor at Benedict's wanting to 'butt in' (his own words)." Similarly, in October 1918, when Pope Benedict cabled Gibbons to plead personally with the President for an Austrian armistice, the cardinal chose instead to send Wilson a letter. Nor, despite continuing pressure at home and from abroad, would he take up with the President the matter of the Holy See's exclusion from the peace conference under article 15 of the London Treaty of 1915, or the "Roman Question," the problem of the Vatican's international status.[20] He did discuss these problems with the British ambassador, Lord Reading, and with British Foreign Secretary Arthur Balfour.

Gibbons was far from hostile to the papal initiatives; he simply knew the reception they would get in Washington. When criticism of Pope Benedict's allegedly pro-Central Powers bias mounted, the Baltimore cardinal penned a vigorous defense, "The War Policy of the Pope," which appeared in February 1918.[21] Relations between the White House and Archbishop's House on Charles Street, which were certainly cooler than they had been in previous Republican presidencies, did not stand in the way of Gibbons's later support of the Treaty of Versailles and League of Nations. According to presidential secretary Joseph Tumulty, the administration's leading Catholic figure, this support was not shared by Cardinal O'Connell and Archbishop Hayes.[22] While Woodrow Wilson sat in the White House, American Catholic forays into international diplomacy largely ended in blind alleys. Indeed, on the one occasion when an American, Father Francis C. Kelley of *Extension* magazine, succeeded in achieving a significant breakthrough—the arrangement of a meeting on the Roman Question between Italian Premier Vittorio Orlando and papal diplomat Bonaventura Cerretti—Wilson's quarrel with the Italians and Orlando's subsequent departure from Paris ended all hope of an agreement.[23]

The wartime NCWC left a lasting mark on the Catholic Church in the United States. Large groups of organized lay people represented the church in the public forum on an unprecedented scale. The Knights of Columbus were the most visible Catholic presence in the American Expeditionary Force and in army camps around the nation, but the NCWC women's committee made its own contribution. Under its aegis a National Catholic School of Social Service was opened in Washington and after the Armistice alumnae were despatched overseas. "Father Burke's Girls" had to agree in writing not to drink, smoke, or use "paint or powder," and they had to wear the council's uniform. Their efforts were so successful that Raymond Fosdick of the Commission on Training Camps asked for reinforcements.[24] Cooperation among the organizations serving the troops was a "first" in American religious history. Occasional conflicts and competitiveness between the YMCA and the K of C were inevitable, although Mott and Callahan, the respective chiefs, got on well and handled problems with reasonably good humor. Both groups mingled religious and social purposes. Government and church funds were used indiscriminately in both areas without public outcry. Catholics, Elizabeth McKeown has found, generally emerged from the experience persuaded that unity was their strength and that divided Protestantism could not provide the nation adequate spiritual and moral leadership. They also found in the interdenominational experience a sense of acceptance as part of the American religious scene that had escaped them previously.[25]

The institutional commitment to social action symbolized by the NCWC also found expression in a detailed social action policy statement written by John A. Ryan and issued in the name of the council's administrative committee. "Social Reconstruction: A General Review of the Problems and Survey of the Remedies" was issued by the NCWC administrative committee on February 12, 1919. It came to be known as the "Bishops' Program of Social Reconstruction." Ryan had prepared it after studying a number of plans suggested by religious and secular groups in Britain and the United States. He intended to suggest "those reforms that seem to be desirable and also obtainable within a reasonable time," and "a few general principles which should become a guide to more distant developments." For the returning veteran, Ryan urged retention of agencies like the United States Employment Service and War Labor Board. He was concerned about housing, and maintenance of wage scales even where they had risen past minimum levels needed for "living" wages. He urged vocational training, minimum wage laws, various forms of social insurance, and control of the cost of living, which had risen 73 percent since 1913. He opposed child labor, "this reproach to our country," and, in the absence of other methods, advocated taxing it out of existence. Women had gone to work in industry in large numbers during the war. Ryan was cautious here. He wanted them freed from "any occupation that is harmful to health or morals." "Women should disappear as quickly as possible from such tasks as conducting and guarding street cars, cleaning locomotives, and a great number of other activities for which conditions of life and their physique render them unfit." But on one point he was adamant: "Those women who are engaged at the same tasks as men should receive equal pay for equal amounts and qualities of work."

Ryan thought workers should share in industrial management, perhaps along the lines of shop committees developed in English Quaker circles. He did not foresee adoption in the United States of collectivist socialism, which "would mean bureaucracy, political tyranny, the helplessness of the individual as a factor in the ordering of his own life, and in general social inefficiency and decadence." But the American system stood "in grievous need of considerable modifications and improvement." There were three chief defects: (1) inefficiency in production and distribution of goods; (2) insufficient incomes for the great majority of wage earners; and (3) unnecessarily large incomes for a small minority of privileged capitalists. Ryan's agenda for handling these problems included emphasis on cooperatives and co-partnership, increased income for labor, and abolition or control of monopolies, so as to restore competition. Above all, "a reform in the spirit of both labor and capital" was needed. The document closed with the words: "This is the human and Christian, in contrast to the purely commercial and pagan, ethics of industry." Reactions varied. By the end of February, Cardinal Gibbons had yet to read "the article." The Benedictine Bishop of Bismarck, Vincent Wehrle, declared that socialist agitators were now claiming the NCWC as their ally. President Stephen C. Mason of the National Association of Manufacturers thought it a plot to spread "partisan, pro-labor union, socialistic propaganda under the official insignia of the Roman Catholic Church in America." Upton Sinclair believed he had witnessed a "Catholic miracle."[26]

The War Council's initials were bequeathed to a permanent postwar organization, but not without some anxious moments. At Gibbons's celebration of his fiftieth anniversary as bishop, Archbishop Bonaventura Cerretti, the pope's representative, urged the American bishops to joint action with the Vatican in efforts to secure a just and lasting peace and to apply Christian ethics to problems of education and labor. This led to plans for an annual meeting of all the bishops of the country and appointment of a standing committee of five of their number to oversee general Catholic activities and interests. Benedict XV approved on April 10, 1919. The National Catholic Welfare Council came into existence. The initial years were rocky. Bishop Charles McDonnell of Brooklyn, a protégé of Archbishop Corrigan, objected that the council infringed upon local episcopal authority. An attempt in 1921–22 to have the NCWC suppressed was nearly successful. American opposition was spearheaded by Cardinals O'Connell and Dougherty, "our two redmen," as Bishop Louis Walsh of Portland whimsically called them. He hoped they would "feel the heavy hand" for their efforts. They and allies in Rome disliked the national church structure that was being set up. The editor of the *American Ecclesiastical Review* had perhaps not helped matters when he enthused at the council's founding:

> with the predominant American spirit of individual freedom, of recognition of individual rights, or the absence of tyrannizing traditions and of officialdom and bureaucracy, the promise of frank and fearless discussion and open action is bright.

Obituary notices for "Americanism" had clearly been premature. Nor did the approach assort well with the mood of those in Rome and in America who lived in a perpetual world of Modernist-Integrist intrigue. "They still see Modernism in everything and are afraid of every movement," the general of the Jesuits, Wlodimir Lédochowski, warned American bishops who came to plead NCWC's cause at the Vatican. Benedict XV died on January 22, 1922. His successor, Pius XI, authorized the NCWC's dissolution on February 25, but rescinded his decree four months later. The reprieve carefully delimited the organization's scope and stressed its non-conciliar, non-legislative character. To make this clear, the designation "council" was changed to "conference." John Burke had gotten President

Warren G. Harding to intervene with the Holy See through the American ambassador to Italy, but the chief architect of salvation was the Bishop of Cleveland, Joseph Schrembs, who went himself to Rome to see the affair through.[27]

Americans somehow found time during the war to deal with agenda left over from the Progressive Era. Prohibition, Woman Suffrage, and Child Labor were all debated. Amendments dealing with the first two were added to the Constitution by 1920. A child labor amendment was finally submitted to the states in 1924, but never ratified. The American Catholic community was involved under each heading.

Temperance and even total abstinence were favored causes of late 19th-century American Catholic liberals. Joan Bland, historian of the Catholic Total Abstinence Union of America (CTAU), described the movement as the "incarnation of Archbishop Ireland's ideal of a prosperous, civic-minded American Catholicism."[28] The Catholic approach leaned toward moral suasion rather than prohibitory legislation, although John Lancaster Spalding was an exception and Montana Senator Thomas J. Walsh was an active "dry" during his twenty years (1913–33) in the Senate. Uneasy with the fanaticism of the Anti-Saloon League, many Catholics tended to be suspicious and apprehensive as the campaign for prohibition developed. After announcing to the CTAU's 1891 convention that he was "a temperate man, but not a temperance man," Cardinal Gibbons warned of the dangers of hypocrisy and the impossibility of policing prohibition. He did not, he advised the delegates, see total abstinence as "essential to morality." As the day of reckoning drew near, he told the *New York Times* in April 1917 that he "would regard the passage of a federal prohibition law as a national catastrophe, little short of a crime against the spiritual and physical well-being of the American people."[29] National catastrophe became reality on January 16, 1920.

Apart from individuals like Senator Walsh and tiny groups like the Catholic Prohibition League, Catholics reacted for the most part negatively to the new state of affairs. Cultural traditions in ethnic enclaves made prohibition seem absurd. Labor agitator Mother Jones articulated the anger of many working people when she complained that a middle-class morality had been foisted on them. Their social club—the neighborhood saloon—was gone and the only club left for them was the patrolman's billy-club.[30] On the darker side, the hoodlum element discovered new jobs in the flourishing illegal liquor traffic. Many of the names appearing on police blotters and in sensational gangster stories sounded "Catholic." Negative public perceptions of the urban Catholic dating back to the Irish in colonial Philadelphia were reinforced. Teachers of moral theology helped very little. Some wove tangled webs of casuistry about the obligation, or lack of it, to obey "purely penal laws." The administrative committee of the NCWC maintained prudent silence. John A. Ryan told readers of the St. Louis *Fortnightly Review* in 1916 that he favored prohibition where it could reasonably be enforced, since liquor's "disutility" outweighed its utility. By 1925 he admitted that when a law is disobeyed more often than not, it loses it force and in 1927 he conceded that the experiment was a debacle.[31] Except in a negative sense, prohibition was never a Catholic issue. One problem that did arise, when Oklahoma's 1917 "bone-dry" law prevented the purchase of sacramental wine, was resolved by state supreme court decision that such wine did not fall "within the spirit nor within the intention" of the law. That norm was generally accepted, although only in 1926 was a procedure—filing Form 1412—set up on the federal level to enable priests to obtain wine for mass.[32]

The Nineteenth Amendment, passed by Congress on June 5, 1919, was ratified little over a year later, on August 26, 1920. It forbade discrimination at the ballot box "on account of sex." Catholics were popularly identified as opponents of woman suffrage. They were blamed for its defeat at the state level in Massachusetts in 1915, although the issue had been brought to a vote by a Catholic governor, David I. Walsh. Cardinal O'Connell and the other bishops carefully avoided official commitment of the church on the issue, but prominent priests had spoken on behalf of anti-suffrage groups. Novelist Katherine Conway, editor of *The Pilot,* continued with great vigor its anti-suffragist tradition reaching back to the days of John Boyle O'Reilly. Issues were further entangled when Margaret Sanger and the National Birth Control League entered the lists on the suffragists' side in the 1915 vote to amend the Massachusetts constitution. Those urging a "no" vote included Catholic anti-socialists David Goldstein and Martha Moore Avery. They saw the ballot for women as somehow connected with the "red menace."[33] In Baltimore, Cardinal Gibbons was a known opponent. He had supported women's admission to The Johns Hopkins Medical School in 1891 and when he spoke of the need for just wages he meant for both men and women, but he feared confusion of sex roles and diversion of women from their proper sphere in the home.[34] In this he did not differ much from Mother Jones, who despite her own peripatetic existence believed strongly that women belonged at home with their children and not at the ballot box.[35]

Catholic advocates of woman suffrage in Massachusetts multiplied during the governorship of David I. Walsh, the commonwealth's first statewide Catholic officeholder. Both he and the proposed amendment to the state constitution were defeated in the 1915 general election, but Catholic names became more prominent in the suffrage movement: labor leader

Mary K. O'Sullivan; Teresa Crowley; Margaret Foley; and Evelyn Scanlan, the last who was president of the Margaret Brent Suffrage Guild, named for Maryland's vocal 17th-century proponent of women's rights. Among Catholic Bishops, Austin Dowling of Des Moines became the best known suffragist.[36] Once the Nineteenth Amendment had been ratified, Cardinal Gibbons urged women to vote, "not only as a right, but as a strict social duty."[37] John A. Ryan, who had looked on woman suffrage "with neither fear nor great hope," took much the same line, expressing the hope that women would shame their menfolk by a "constructive" use of the franchise.[38]

A last item of Progressive Era legislation went without final disposition until the New Deal years. Catholic congressman and labor leader Edward Keating co-authored in 1916 a law forbidding interstate commerce in products of child labor. The Keating-Owens Act was declared unconstitutional by the Supreme Court in 1918 and a similar second legislative effort met a like fate in 1922. In 1924 Congress sent the states a constitutional amendment empowering the federal legislature to "limit, regulate and prohibit the labor of persons under eighteen years of age." It was the work of Senator Thomas J. Walsh of Montana. John A. Ryan had advised him on it. But it was to a considerable extent thanks to Cardinal William O'Connell of Boston that, as Ryan's biographer put it, "the Twentieth Amendment that was finally ratified made whiskey legal, not child labor illegal." Although Catholic social liberals were wholehearted supporters of the child labor proposal, O'Connell was violently opposed to "this soviet legislation." It was "nefarious and bolshevik." He complained to the Chancellor of the Catholic University, Archbishop Michael J. Curley, of John Ryan's "radical," "queer crooked," "socialistic," and "false" views and regretted the harm he and others were doing "the University and the Catholic position which is certainly not theirs." The cardinal's blood pressure was not lowered when, on the eve of a Massachusetts referendum, Edward Keating, now editor of the railway brotherhoods' journal *Labor,* flooded Boston with one hundred thousand copies of an issue carrying an article by Ryan favoring the amendment. The child labor amendment failed in Massachusetts and never won enough states for ratification. The main reason for widespread opposition among Catholics was fear that federal control of child labor represented an opening wedge for government invasion of individual and parental rights, leading to the undermining of family life and loss of free choice in the area of education.[39]

XVIII

Catholicism Unbound: The Church of the Twenties

Reflecting on "Religion's Limitations," the twenty-seven-year-old pastor of Detroit's Bethel Evangelical Church wrote in 1920 that

> the Christian church deceives itself in believing that the revival of religious sentiment during the war . . . will secure it that glorious destiny of prestige and power which religious leaders are so confidently and so unanimously predicting.[1]

Reinhold Niebuhr's pessimism was borne out by the event, but the church's decline was not for want of trying on its part. Eldon Ernst has written the history of the abortive Interchurch World Movement, conceived in high hope by men of the caliber of John R. Mott and Robert E. Speer and helped by personal involvement of others like John D. Rockefeller, Jr. The idea was to capitalize on the optimistic spirit of unity and cooperation of Protestants during the war and mount a crusade to finish the democratization and Christianization of the world. By 1920 the Movement had collapsed. Ernst concluded that its "single most important impact" was to demonstrate that

> crusading Protestantism—indeed Protestantism-in-general—was losing its traditional hold on the American people as a whole and on the social

234

and cultural tone of the nation . . . The long-developing pattern of a
rising urban, secularized, religiously and culturally and racially pluralistic
population . . . had begun to come of age after World War I.[2]

Robert Handy has summed up Protestant response: it ranged "from determined opposition to an eager acceptance of most of the values and
patterns of modernity."[3]

The situation was different with the nation's more than seventeen million Roman Catholics. They emerged from their first extended experience
of inter-religious cooperation with newly heightened self-confidence. No
opportunity was missed to trumpet the patriotic extent of American Catholic contribution to the war effort. Such Catholic war heroes as King
Albert of the Belgians, Cardinal Mercier, and Marshal Foch visited the
United States and were toasted by Catholic bishops and Catholic universities. At the same time, Woodrow Wilson's world had never been quite
home to Catholic Americans and they were less shattered than many
others when it dissolved. On the negative side, Protestants of what Robert Handy has called the "determined opposition" bracketed them as the
enemy during the next decade, lumped together with Jews, blacks, and
modernity in general. The Catholics' problem was not limited to yahoos.
Moderate people like Charles G. Marshall wondered how a "loyal and
conscientious Roman Catholic" could reconcile his religious convictions
with "the principles of civil and religious liberty on which American
institutions are based."[4]

The Catholic community suffered from an internal cancer too. It remained prey to institutional narcissism which drained energies into narrowly focused crusades for what were deemed church interests, and inhib-
ited cooperation with campaigns in the broader interest of society. That
coin had another side. From Abolition to Prohibition and Woman Suffrage, crusades in the Puritan-Evangelical tradition had all been touched
with a barely concealed—sometimes quite open—nativism that warned
Catholics off. The new secular moralists were hardly more congenial.
Still, Catholics' isolation in the twenties had a touch of pride about it
and—again Robert Handy—they were by and large spared the "debilitating effects of the spiritual depression of 1925–1935 that so affected
Protestants."[5] John Burke's successor at the *Catholic World*, James M.
Gillis, C.S.P., summed it up when he wrote in 1922: "We Catholics are
more hopeful for modern civilization than are they who built modern
civilization."[6]

Though by no means all, many who came from the Catholic milieu
shared Gillis's confidence in the possibilities of the time. American Catholicism's poet laureate of the moment, Sergeant Joyce Kilmer, had

been killed in action on the western front. His legacy was patriotic and upbeat: he found beauty in the "exhilaration of star-shells and the tattoo of machine guns," and hoped that poetry back home was reflecting "the virtues which are blossoming on the blood-soaked soil of this land— courage and self-abnegation, and love and faith."[7] On a more gentle note, for sixty years until the eve of her death in 1950, Philadelphia essayist Agnes Repplier brought "into thousands of homes . . . learning and elevation, purity and refinement, 'fair thoughts and happy hours' "[8] But there were other Catholics, both converts and born Catholics, who loomed far larger in the literary mainstream and whose histories posed in a new form the conundrum of how to reconcile Catholic perception of humanity and world with America, now a rapidly secularizing America.

Among born Catholic writers of the era, Theodore Dreiser and John O'Hara avoided significant intersection with the Catholic experience. Convert Ernest Hemingway knew Catholicism principally in its extra-American forms. But James T. Farrell spelled out in painful detail the stultifying southside Chicago culture that had numbed his youth. Still, his experience of the church was, in Dennis Flynn's words, "a focus of his art," and he never managed to sever ties with the southside Irish Catholic world.[9] F. Scott Fitzgerald was pure lace curtain. Thomas Curley resents him for it. He did not know "the kind of lower-middle-class, big-city Catholicism that Farrell knew."[10] But that was not all there was to know. In his ledger, opposite his twenty-first year, he wrote, "last year as a Catholic," but Henry Piper, who notes this, adds: "Like James Joyce, Fitzgerald continued to be influenced by Catholic values long after he had left the Church itself."[11] Two years later, he claimed that Catholicism was "scarcely a memory," then added: "No, that's wrong, it's more than that."[12] A Catholic sense of sin, good and evil, heaven and hell, did not leave him. Reconciliation with the church's contemporary reality was something else again. Original sin, a God who "knows my most secret thoughts, words and actions," as the *Baltimore Catechism* has it, and the fleeting nature of this present life were themes repeated by Eugene O'Neill, wrestling with religious faith in his plays and with alternating doubt and belief in his life.[13] However much or little religious ties affected their artistic imagination, no literary giant of the twenties managed to live peaceably within the Catholic community. For some it did not exist; for Farrell, Fitzgerald, and O'Neill at least, the ties were never quite broken. George Shuster pointed out in 1930 that artists of the twenties saw themselves as "makers of images." They did not find in the American representation of Catholicism, because it was not easily found there, a possibility of the freedom they felt must be theirs in interpreting world and humanity.[14]

Catholic population in the United States went from nearly eighteen million in 1920 to over twenty million by 1930. With the introduction of the quota system, the flow of immigrants slacked off. The 1924 Reed-Johnson act deliberately aimed at cutting the number from southern and eastern Europe, which in 1914 accounted for three-quarters of the total flow. Pressure for restrictive legislation was not without religious overtones. Martin Marty has noted that "moderates throughout the nation were no less disturbed than [Ku Klux] Klansmen about the threat that America would go Catholic by immigration."[15] In the Catholic community, energies previously devoted to coping with religious needs of immigrants were diverted to consolidating and stabilizing institutional structures. Immigration did not stop entirely, but was a less all-consuming preoccupation. Europeans kept coming, if in limited numbers, and there were no quotas on hemispheric migration. Only with the Depression of the 1930s were steps taken to limit the number of Mexicans entering the country, including forcible "repatriation" of five hundred thousand people, half of them said to have been American citizens.[16]

Institutional development was extensive. In his first ten years in Philadelphia, Cardinal Dennis Dougherty opened ninety-two parishes, eighty-nine parish schools, three diocesan high schools, fourteen academies, a women's college, and a preparatory seminary. Other ventures included a diocesan retreat house, orphanages, a school for the deaf, and other special institutions and hospitals.[17] Across the nation Catholic education grew on all levels. One hundred thirty colleges and universities in 1921 became one hundred sixty-three by 1928, enrolling between one-half and two-thirds of all Catholic college students, as against one-third in 1921. Nearly half the faculty were priests and members of religious communities. The latter gave services gratis, receiving only room, board, and minimal expenses. Diocesan priests were paid on scales lower than those for lay colleagues. Lay professors themselves received minimum wages. Catholic high schools nationwide went from 1,552 to 2,169 in the same seven years. Sisters, brothers, and priests on their staffs numbered 11,543, lay teachers 1,943.[18] Parish grade schools increased proportionately. By 1930, 89 percent of Chicago's suburban parishes had their own school, although these were more popular in the industrial suburbs than in newer areas, and did not match urban parish schools in the percentage of total school population which they enrolled. Catholic grade schools in Chicago educated 27.9 percent of the city's children.[19] A significant factor in school growth during the 1920s was development within religious communities and on a diocesan basis of normal schools for sister- and brother-teachers. The age was passing when men and women with a high-school, or even only a grade-school, education were given a brief introduction to life in religious community and then sent out to teach.[20]

University-level education was supported by dioceses—Newark's Seton Hall dated back to 1856—and by men's and women's religious communities. The largest single commitment was that of the Jesuits, whose six provinces in 1930 educated 44,536 students in twenty-six colleges or universities and 14,852 in thirty-six high schools across the country.[21] In northern Indiana, Notre Dame began its climb to true university status in 1919.[22] Washington's Catholic University remained the responsibility of all the bishops. George Mundelein, a New Yorker sent in 1915 as archbishop to Chicago and made cardinal in 1924, encouraged education at all levels, including colleges for men and for "the bright, promising, ambitious daughters of the mechanic, the tradesman, the man who works for his daily bread."[23] By 1928 he dreamed of amalgamating women's and men's colleges into a single Catholic University of Chicago, the jewel of which would be the seminary of St. Mary of the Lake, fourteen spacious Georgian buildings situated on a thousand acres in northern Illinois. Mundelein secured a papal charter authorizing the seminary to grant doctorates in theology and the Jesuits were to supply the faculty, but neither they nor the Dominican order accepted the cardinal's invitation to move their own seminaries near his.[24] The Catholic University of Chicago never materialized although the seminary still exists. The Ku Klux Klan protested the renaming of Area, Illionis, the town in which St. Mary of the Lake was located. In late 1924 it "became the first [village] on American soil to capitulate to the Vatican" when it changed its name to Mundelein. *The Fiery Cross* wondered if Washington, D.C., might not be changed to "Piusville or St. Patricksburg."[25]

The financing of splendid parks like the one at Mundelein was possible because Catholics in most walks of life shared handsomely in the nation's prosperity. Some exhibited the characteristics Tocqueville attributed to "manufacturing aristocracy." They were wealthy, a few fabulously so, and made substantial gifts to Catholic and other philanthropic causes, but there was little about them to suggest any specifically Christian sense of ethical or social responsibility. One prominent Catholic businessman answered an invitation to a conference on Catholic social teaching: "What did Leo XIII know about digging subways with steam shovels?"[26] Other wealthy Catholics were remarkably spiritual people, knowledgeable about theology and the church's social teaching. There were good Christians, some rogues, and a great many in between.

Pius XI's papacy (1922–39) saw a liberal distribution of papal honors and titles. Cathedral ceremonies began to feature American entrepreneurs and politicians dressed in the Renaissance ruffs of papal chamber-

lains and the 19th-century court uniforms of papal knights. Martin Maloney, "the man who lighted Philadelphia," got his start when he illuminated the Centennial Exposition of 1876. He died in 1929. His summer
home on the Jersey shore was modeled after Dublin's Leinster House and
he lies buried in a nearby memorial church. A papal marquis in 1903,
Maloney "outranked all other laymen in America,"[27] at least until Gene-
vieve Garvan Brady become a papal duchess. Her husband, utilities magnate Nicholas F. Brady, was a knight of the Supreme Order of Christ, an
honor usually reserved for Catholic heads of state.

A great deal of Comstock silver passed through Catholic hands. In San
Francisco, banker, onetime reform mayor, and former United States
Senator James D. Phelan left much of a $10 million fortune to Catholic
institutions when he died in 1930. Buildings at California's Catholic colleges and seminaries commemorate other benefactors, including Edward
and Carrie Betzhold Doheny. Oilman Doheny's fortune came from Mexican and southern California fields. In 1927 he was acquitted of having
bribed Secretary of the Interior Albert B. Fall, but his lease on the Elk
Hills oil reserves was cancelled. Most of John J. Raskob's estate went to a
foundation for Catholic activities. When he agreed in 1928 to head the
Democratic National Committee, he had behind him a meteoric career in
munitions with the duPonts and at General Motors. Charles M. Schwab's
fortune was once estimated at $200 million. Of an old Pennsylvania Ger-
man Catholic family, he was the first president of U. S. Steel, developed
Bethlehem Steel, and during World War I was director-general of
shipbuilding.[28]

John Keane died in Dubuque in late June 1918. He had been seven
years retired. The following september, John Ireland, still active in St.
Paul, and Cardinal John M. Farley, Corrigan's successor in New York,
died within a week of each other. With their passing, upper echelons in
church administration entered a period of stable leadership. Only four of
fourteen archdioceses changed hands in the 1920s, Baltimore in 1921,
Dubuque in 1929, and Cincinnati and Oregon city in 1925. San Antonio
became an archdiocese in 1926. Archbishops were distinguished for lon-
gevity. When he died in 1951, Dennis Dougherty was two weeks shy of
his forty-eighth anniversary as bishop. He began at Nueva Segovia in the
Philippines in 1903 and finished with thirty-three years in Philadelphia.
John J. Glennon came within three months of reaching his fiftieth episcopal anniversary. He died in 1946, three weeks after receiving a cardinal's
red hat; he had been archbishop of St. Louis for forty-three years. All-
time dean of American bishops is Edward D. Howard (1877–   ), consecrated in 1923 and archbishop of Oregon City (which changed its name
to Portland in 1928) from 1926 to 1966.

Cardinal Gibbons died on March 24, 1921. Maryland Catholicism was two hundred eighty-seven years old the following day. James Gibbons presided over forty-four of those years. He was the last archbishop of Baltimore, in a line reaching back to John Carroll, to exercise *de facto* primacy among fellow bishops. That function shifted elsewhere, to the pope's apostolic delegate, to the American cardinals (four during this period, in Boston, New York, Philadelphia, and Chicago), and in diffused fashion to the NCWC and its administrative board. Pope Pius XI's strong personality and style made a difference. Aided by revolutionary advances in transatlantic communication and transportation, he and the Roman congregations exercised a more immediate influence in American church life than had been possible in previous generations. A universal Code of Canon Law, with final interpretation of its prescriptions reserved to Rome, became operative in 1918.

The four American cardinals were American-born, but only Patrick J. Hayes, New York's "Cardinal of Charities," had missed a Roman education. On the local political scene, his headquarters on Madison Avenue was referred to as "The Powerhouse," but he had no extensive national influence. William O'Connell of Boston, Dennis Dougherty of Philadelphia, and George Mundelein of Chicago symbolized the increasingly heavy percentage of American bishops drawn from the ranks of students who had lived at Rome's North American College on Via dell'Umiltà while studying at one of the papal university faculties. All three were ordained in Rome; O'Connell returned there for six years to serve as rector of the American College. The cultivation of *romanità*—Roman ecclesiastical spirit—became an important pursuit in clerical and some lay circles. In a tiff over NCWC's sophisticated approach to legislation dealing with federal involvement in education, Cardinal O'Connell read John Burke a lesson on the subject in 1926. Burke pleaded that he was acting with approval from Archbishop Austin Dowling of St. Paul, chairman of the Conference's Department of Education. O'Connell brushed that aside as due to Dowling's lack of Roman training: "To know the Catholic Church and to have those Catholic traditions that enable one to keep the faith intact, one must have been to Rome: have had international experience." Dowling failed the test. His education was wholly American and had for that reason left him inadequately grounded in Catholic principles. He was too easily led to compromise. Catholics in the United States, O'Connell insisted, had always to be on guard, always suspicious of the government: "America is a Protestant country, expressive of Protestant traditions, not Catholic."[29]

Dennis Dougherty was fifty-two years old and fifteen years a bishop in the Philippines and then in Buffalo when he came to Philadelphia in 1918 to succeed genial, easy-going Edmond F. Prendergast. "It would be diffi-cult to exaggerate," Philadelphia historian Hugh J. Nolan has written, "the influence that Rome had upon Cardinal Dougherty."[30] A formal man whose word was law, he was a demanding administrator. "Bear in mind," he warned the editor of the diocesan newspaper before a circula-tion drive, "that what we want is results."[31] As "God's bricklayer"—his own phrase—he presided over rapid institutional growth and at the same time took effective interest in diocesan programs for black and Chinese Catholics and in the work of Katharine Drexel's Sisters for blacks and Indians, and in elimination of racial discrimination in Philadelphia. "Car-dinal Dougherty was firm man, but he was at his firmest in this matter," Nolan remembers.[32] In analyzing the signs of his times, he was not in-clined to look beyond surface phenomena. In his eyes, leakage of church members was caused by scarcity of priests, marriages with those of another religious tradition, membership in secret societies, and atten-dance at public schools. To remedy the last, he made clear to reluctant pastors that failure to operate a parish school constituted cause for re-moval from office. He was enthusiastic for higher education of the clergy, but with a somewhat narrow vision. More were assigned to study canon law than were needed to manage the archdiocesan courts. All future teachers went either to Rome or to Catholic University. He "seemed to think a doctorate in theology from Rome enabled a priest to teach any subject . . . from biology to American history."[33] The Roman connection was everything. Dougherty summed it up at his episcopal silver jubilee in 1928 when he said: "After God I owe what I am to the Holy See."[34]

The third "Roman" cardinal was George H. Mundelein, who was ap-pointed archbishop of Chicago in 1915. His tenure got off to a chilling start when a cook with anarchist inclinations poisoned the soup at the new archbishop's installation banquet, to the discomfiture, but not lasting harm, of the guests. Mundelein was not fazed. He found a city where Catholics were failing to exert influence proportionate to their number, which was estimated at upwards of 30 percent of the population, and quickly made himself known as a vigorous advocate of Catholic interests, not unwilling to exercise political muscle. In March 1917, little over a year after his arrival, bills adverse to Catholic orphanages were intro-duced in the legislature at Springfield. Mundelein asked Speaker of the Illinois House David Shanahan to "bury those bills in the wastebasket or in a committee where they cannot be resurrected."[35] When that legislative resurrection came to pass in 1920, he mobilized the other Illinois bishops, the state Knights of Columbus and various ethnic groups to apply political pressure. He took the matter up with Chicago Mayor William Hale ("Big Bill") Thompson and with Illinois Governor Frank O. Lowden. He had already settled with Thompson what he considered the inequitable composition of Chicago's Board of Education, which had five Catholic members out of twenty-one. When vacancies occurred in the spring of 1917, Mundelein sent the mayor the names of two Catholics "for appointment as members of the Board of Education." "I have selected these names with a great deal of care," he added, "both as to their personal qualifications and their fitness for the position." Anthony Czarnecki and Richard Gannon became members of the Board.[36] Mundelein's influence grew steadily. By the time of his death in 1939 he was the Catholic bishop closest to Franklin D. Roosevelt.

On the east coast, Gibbons's successor at Baltimore and as Chancellor of the Catholic University was Michael J. Curley, an Irish-born, Roman-educated priest who had come to the United States in 1904 as a missionary to Florida. Not the conciliator his predecessor was, Curley was more careful of the details of diocesan administration, but projected an outspoken, conservative, and defensive public image. Archbishop Henry Moeller of Cincinnati was, in Thomas McAvoy's judgment, "a solid churchman, as were most of his numerous suffragans."[37] The suffragans included Joseph Schrembs, transferred to Cleveland from Toledo in 1921, a man of superior intellect limited only by the narrow possibilities of his location. John T. McNicholas, O.P., who in 1925 succeeded Moeller in Cincinnati, a diocese founded by another Dominican, Edward Fenwick, became in later years a national spokesman on church affairs. Sebastian Messmer was Archbishop of Milwaukee from 1903 to 1930, and John W. Shaw held the same position in New Orleans from 1918 to 1934. In St. Louis, John J. Glennon's long episcopate (1903–46) was plagued with national quarrels and problems of anti-black racism. San Antonio (Arthur Jerome Drossaerts, 1918–40) and Santa Fe (Albert T. Daeger, O.F.M., 1919–32) stood at the head of church provinces with large Mexican-American populations. In the Pacific Northwest, Edward D. Howard in 1926 succeeded Alexander Christie, who had been archbishop of Oregon City since just before the turn of the century.

By 1917 when John J. Cantwell arrived at the onetime *pueblo* of Nuestra Señora de los Angeles as bishop, cities were overgrowing *ranchos* in southern California and suburban sprawl was not far behind. Los Angeles was a city of a half million people. Californio culture had disappeared from public view, although romantic revival sparked by Helen Hunt Jackson's novel *Ramona* (1884) resurrected jollier aspects on festive occasions. But Mexican-Americans were only too aware that not all those who celebrated *fiestas* were enamored of the people who invented them. During World War I and the twenties, thousands of *braceros* came to work in the fields of the San Joaquin and Imperial valleys. They mingled uneasily with Anglos moving in from the East. The diocese (archdiocese in 1936) was heavily staffed with priests recruited from Irish seminaries. When Cantwell died in 1947, the population of Los Angeles stood at two million.[38] In northern California, San Francisco's most prominent citizen was Archbishop Edward J. Hanna. After surviving accusations of modernism at St. Bernard's in Rochester, he came to California as Archbishop Riordan's auxiliary in 1912 and succeeded him in 1915. For the first sixteen years of its existence he presided over the NCWC's Administrative Board. President Franklin D. Roosevelt named him chairman of the National Longshoreman Board and he mediated the 1934 San Francisco general strike. In 1935 he resigned his positions and retired to a Roman monastery where he lived until his death in 1944.[39]

It was not surprising that Roman authorities balked at permanent status for the NCWC. Stable national and multi-national conferences of bishops are a standard feature of worldwide Catholicism in the 1980s; the idea was a distinct novelty in 1920. The tendency to centralize church government and teaching in Rome, the church's "monarchization" as Roger Aubert called it, which was so prominent a feature of the 19th century, was still in full career. It would grow, not diminish, under two strong and vigorous popes, Pius XI (1922–39) and Pius XII (1939–58). The achievement of Bishop Schrembs and the others who put across the American case at Rome in 1922 was considerable.

There was widespread awareness of the need to counter on both theoretical and practical planes the rapid secularization of society that was the legacy of war and the collapse of the old European system. The Catholic bishops of the United States had a long way to go. Before the war, Peter Dietz had hoped that the annual meeting of the archbishops would respond to findings of the Commission on Industrial Relations (set up in 1912 by the federal government), of which Kansas City attorney Frank P. Walsh was a member. But a half dozen years later, John A. Ryan had sadly to report that the number of bishops with pronouncements on social issues to their credit could be counted on the fingers of one hand, and that the number of priests who had spoken out was proportionately no greater.[40] The new decade promised brighter prospects. Ryan's program for social reconstruction, known to the dismay of some and the joy of others as the "Bishops' Program," appeared on February 12, 1919, and was followed on September 26 by the first pastoral letter from the entire American hierarchy since 1884. The long pastoral repeated some of the program's ideas and sounded as their theoretical base themes drawn from the social teaching affirmed by Pope Leo XIII at the turn of the century: the divine origin of humanity and society, the demand for justice as the

foundation of social order, the need for cooperation and mutual dependence of capital and labor in shaping that social order.[41] Liberals like
Frank Walsh were delighted that the bishops recognized an identity between "true religion" and "economic democracy,"[42] but no proposal in
the 1919 program was enacted into law during the twenties, and in 1929
John A. Ryan, responding to criticism of NCWC's Social Action Department, admitted:

> The first obstacle confronting the department is the fact that neither
> the bishops, the priests, nor the laity are convinced that our industrial
> system should be reorganized in this radical fashion.[43]

Even after Pius XI's approval, the NCWC was not universally welcomed. There were social projects aplenty in Philadelphia, but in the
judgment of the historian of his years in Philadelphia Cardinal Dougherty
"wanted no directives other than those from Rome regarding the administration of his archdiocese and he dealt directly with Rome, whose
leaders he knew well."[44] In Boston, Cardinal O'Connell had long since
taken characteristically vigorous action. He did not need outside help.
David O'Brien has the story. On succeeding Archbishop John Williams in
1907, O'Connell found "that the myriad of social agencies were riddled
with duplication, decaying facilities and intolerable debts." It was not
long before he "phased out unsupported programs, replaced pious but
incompetent officials, centralized administration under his direction, and
placed diocesan agencies on a sound financial footing."[45]

The Conference was not a national church government, but did serve as
an information clearing house and assumed a certain representative function. Its active divisions like the Social Action Department helped church
and nation bridge the years between the Progressive Era and the New
Deal. Until his death in 1927, Bishop Muldoon of Rockford was chairman. His most important decision was the choice of John A. Ryan to
head the department's industrial relations section. Militant labor activist
Peter Dietz had hoped for the position, but he was a man impatient with
talk of co-management, profit sharing and worker co-ownership—all
ideas prominent in European social thought and in line with Leo XIII's
emphasis on harmony ("*concordia*") as the key to improved industrial
relations. Dietz's abrasive tactics and close identification with the unions
put off some bishops. He was recalled to his diocese.

Ryan was at the NCWC from 1919 to 1945 and in charge of all aspects of
the social action department from 1928 on. He headed the Washington
office, while a lay labor arbitrator, John A. Lapp, worked out of Chicago
and directed programs in social service and education for good citizenship.

The times were not good for social theorists and activists. Ryan's biographer, Francis L. Broderick, has pointed this out: "The decade was an age of retreat when holding actions, limited counter-offensives and prayer were the only recourse." The War Labor Board, with Frank P. Walsh as co-chairman, had insisted on the idea of a living wage; the Railway Labor Board dismissed it as "a bit of mellifluous phraseology."[46] Ryan could plead that the state was bound to protect the weak, since the rich could care for themselves, but the "Catholic seat" on the Supreme Court was held from 1922 to 1939 by Pierce Butler—the "monolith," Oliver Wendell Holmes called him, because of his regular votes upholding government restrictions on individual liberties and striking down government regulation of business. Frederick Kenkel of the *Central-Verein* and Louisville corporate executive Patrick H. Callahan helped organize regional and national meetings of the Catholic Conference on Industrial Problems, but had little success in interesting employers in programs on Catholic social teaching. More fruitful was the work of John A. Lapp and Rose J. McHugh in surveying areas of neglect in diocesan planning and improving social services. Lapp's division of the social action department also promoted "Americanization" programs both for adults and in parochial schools.

During the 1920s the National Council of Catholic Women was more active than its counterpart, the National Council of Catholic Men, which became known as sponsor of the weekly "Catholic Hour" on radio in 1930. The NCCW devoted considerable energy to educating social workers and after 1921 supported the National Catholic School of Social Service in Washington. A substantial venture in social action was the National Catholic Rural Life Conference. Founded in 1923, it concerned itself with the welfare of the less than 20 percent of American Catholics who lived in rural areas. The leading spirit of this endeavor was Edwin V. O'Hara, parish priest in Eugene, Oregon, and later a bishop.[47] Several agencies cooperated with the Rural Life Conference, notably the Church Extension Society, the *Central-Verein,* and the American Board of Catholic Missions. The National Council of Catholic Women contributed to vacation schools for young country people. But the overall picture remained bleak. Aaron Abell's judgement was that:

> By the mid-1920s the Catholic minority in the United States was an obstructionist influence so far as labor legislation was concerned. . . . In effect, if not in so many words, Catholics shelved the Bishops' Program until a period more propitious for its application arrived.[48]

Reasons for failure of the postwar liberal Catholics' dream are many. The principal one was simple enough: widespread lack of support among bishops, priests, and laity. A writer in *Commonweal* could suggest that

American Catholics transcend themselves "to strive for sanctity rather than settle for the comfort of a secured universe," but as William Halsey has soberly pointed out in *The Survival of American Innocence* this sort of desire to "test the boundaries of experience" was not prominent even in the rarefied atmosphere of *Commonweal*'s pages.[49] Catholics were bedeviled by external and internal pressures. To a great extent these blinded them to the import of the larger secularist challenge of the times.

The most blatantly anti-Catholic group in the country during the first half of the twenties was the Ku Klux Klan, four to five million strong at its peak and spread throughout southern, midwestern, and middle Atlantic states. The Klansmen had a long enemies' list, but John Higham has concluded that Catholics stood at the top of it.[50] Some incidents lent a sense of *déjà vu,* reminding Catholics of the Know-Nothings their grandparents knew and the A.P.A. of their parents' generation: Alabama passed a convent inspection bill, Governor Sidney J. Catts of Florida announced that the pope was planning to invade Florida and transfer the Vatican there. Other episodes reminded Catholics that it was not only the Klan that had doubts about them. In the fall of 1924, essayist, poet, and Harvard alumnus John Jay Chapman protested the election of a Catholic as a fellow of his *alma mater.* "The outspoken purpose," he wrote, "of the Roman Church is to control American education." Among the Harvard overseers, however, only novelist Owen Wister agreed with Chapman's demur. For Wister, the Catholic Church was "an organized power alien to American ideals."[51] In January *The Christian Century* took up the cudgels on behalf of taxation of all religious institutions as "a rational means of removing that menace to democratic civilization," the Roman Catholic Church, which had the allegiance of "many who do not wish to think for themselves, those who wish to commit their spiritual interests to the arbitrament of a self-constituted authority." In tones reminiscent of Jonathan Mayhew, and also of Robert Baird, the *Century* reminded its readers that:

> It is doubtless correct to say that no other one cause has been so prolific
> of decay and wreck among civilizations as the ensconcing of priesthoods
> in the arbitrary or irresponsible control of property.[52]

Barrels of ink have been spilled over the question of whether it was his religion affiliation that caused Alfred E. Smith to lose the Democratic presidential nomination in 1924 and the presidential election in 1928. The most recent study by Allan Lichtman is apodictic: "Of all possible explanations for the distinctive political alignment of 1928, religion is the best."[53] A battle over repudiation of the Klan deadlocked the 1924

Democratic convention and denied the nomination both to Smith and to his chief opponent, William G. McAdoo (who had been nominated by Senator James D. Phelan). Smith's Catholicism was certainly no secret in the 1928 campaign. Neither were his brown derby, Fulton Fish Market accent, Tammany background, "wet" proclivities, or views on finance. Neither was the prosperity the country thought it was experiencing in Republican hands. But the fact remains that the New York governor's candidacies became for his co-religionists one more reminder, and on the highest level of their political sensibility, that they and their church were an object of mistrust and suspicion to an uncomfortably large number of their fellow citizens.

In November and December of 1924, first John Ryan and then Patrick Callahan dealt in print with "Tactics for Catholic Citizens." Their plea was quite simple: Catholics should involve themselves with general reform groups in society and not limit their exertions to narrowly conceived partisan issues.[54] In light of the frequent enough association of anti-Catholicism with reform movements—an association that had hardly disappeared now that reform was being secularized—this was a tall order and one to which few Catholics would respond. Ryan tried. At Roger Baldwin's invitation, he joined the American Civil Liberties Union and served on its national board. Catholics of the right were scandalized by his associates and by the causes to which he lent his name. He, on his part, did not hesitate to challenge what he perceived as the illiberalism of those same associates on such topics as the problems of Mexican Catholics. Ryan's broad commitment to and involvement with the secular world and its needs won him a hearing, if not necessarily agreement, when he spoke on church-related topics. He spoke out on birth control. He addressed the Foreign Policy Association in Boston on the Lateran Treaties. And in an invited article in the *Nation,* he discussed Cardinal Merry del Val's denunciation of "that moral pestilence known as liberalism," to "very nearly every tenet of which," according to the Cardinal, Catholicism was "unalterably opposed."[55]

On June 1, 1925, in *Pierce v. Society of the Sisters,* the United States Supreme Court struck down as unconstitutional an Oregon law compelling all children between the ages of eight and sixteen—with a few exceptions—to attend public schools. The law, adopted by referendum in 1922, was to have gone into effect on September 1, 1926. Its principal sponsors were the Scottish Rite Masons. The law's constitutionality was challenged by the Sisters of the Holy Names of Jesus and Mary and by a non-sectarian school, Hill Military Academy. The state argued that private schools were unnecessary and divisive. Counsel for Oregon faced the church-state issue squarely. There was danger that children might be taught "that the claims upon them of the religion to which they belong are superior to the claims of the United States." "Between church and state," he continued, "we insist that the state has the prior and paramount right to direct the education of the children of the state." The Supreme Court's opinion was unanimous: the state had the right "reasonably to regulate" all schools, but it could not make attendance at public schools compulsory. Private schools were "a kind of undertaking not inherently harmful, but long regarded as useful and meritorious." The consequence was clear:

> The fundamental theory of liberty upon which all governments in this Union repose excludes any general power of the state to standardize its children by forcing them to accept instruction from public teachers only. The child is not the mere creature of the state; those who nurture him and direct his destiny have the right, coupled with the high duty, to recognize and prepare him for additional obligations.[56]

Pierce has been hailed as a Magna Carta for Catholic education in the United States. The case attracted wide interest and support, with *amicus curiae* briefs attacking the law's constitutionality filed by the Protestant Episcopal Church, the Seventh-Day Adventists, and the American Jewish Committee. More controversial was another trend of the 1920s, the push for Federal aid to education. At their meeting in September 1919, the Catholic bishops took a stand against the Smith-Towner bill then before Congress, a measure which looked to creation of a federal department of education and federal financial aid to public schools.

This issue could be viewed either in the context of the wider community or in terms of narrower Catholic concerns. Cardinal Gibbons could see advantages to centralization: "It would be more satisfactory to deal with a few intelligent men in Washington than . . . with so many petty, narrow officials of each state." His chief educational adviser, Edward A. Pace of Catholic University, noted that centralized control would improve standards and work more effectively against discrimination. The controversy simmered. In 1922, John Burke prepared a release for the NCWC Administrative Board:

> The growth of bureaucracy in the United States is one of the most significant after-effects of the war. This growth must be resolutely checked. Federal assistance and federal direction are in some cases beneficial and even necessary but extreme bureaucracy is foreign to everything American. It is unconstitutional and undemocratic. It means officialism, red tape and prodigal waste of public money. It spells hordes of so-called experts and self-perpetuating cliques of politicians to regulate every detail of life. It would eventually sovietize our form of government. . . .

Not all Catholics wanted to base their arguments on such broad lines. The Jesuits at *America* worried lest "guardians of our Catholic interests" betray the church. Archbishop Curley was all for vigorous counterattack. Archbishop Glennon demanded the "constitutional and equitable" aid due Catholic schools. Archbishop Mundelein saw federal aid as a threat to parochial schools, but one that could be warded off by "united opposition on the part of Catholics. . . . We may be a minority, but we are a minority to be counted with." Cardinal Dougherty told graduating seniors at Villanova: "We give notice that we will never permit our Catholic schools to be controlled by a clique of politicians in Washington. . . . We are obliged to contribute to the imperfect schools of the state and have given our heart's blood to keep up the Catholic schools."[57] It was during these discussions that Cardinal O'Connell reminded John Burke of the difference between the "Roman" and the "American" mind.

The bishops were not the only ones disturbed by the prospect of a larger government role in education. Tremors swept through the Catholic educational establishment. The palpitations reached university level. Since John Carroll in the 1790s abandoned his plan for chaplaincies at secular universities and concentrated instead on the academy at Georgetown, Catholic colleges had sprung up across the country. But most Catholics still attended state or Protestant schools. In 1906, conservative Archbishop of Milwaukee Sebastian Messmer had opened a formal chaplaincy at the University of Wisconsin in Madison. In the following year, "The Newman House" for Harvard students opened in Cambridge with Archbishop William H. O'Connell as patron. A Federation of Catholic College Clubs was organized in 1915. In January 1920 the NCWC formed a special bureau to look after the religious interests of Catholic students in secular institutions. After a lengthy study of the question, John Whitney Evans has concluded that the Newman Movement was considered in church circles "a valid expression of Catholic higher education."[58]

The Conference of Catholic Colleges, chaired by Georgetown's John A. Conway, S.J., had in 1907 circularized the bishops about rising Catholic enrollment at non-Catholic schools, and a year later Archbishop O'Connell lent support to Boston College's drive for a new campus with the dictum: "No Catholic community can be content without a Catholic college"[59] The issue became more heated in the 1920s. Jesuits spearheaded the attack: some as college administrators and, writing for *America*, Paul Blakely, Wilfrid Parsons, and John LaFarge. NCWC releases spoke of "titanic struggles" and a "momentous crisis." They focused on the Catholic center at the University of Illinois and its successful, articulate chaplain, John A. O'Brien. In 1919 the university senate had author-

ized academic credits for religious studies sponsored by outside foundations, provided instructors, facilities, and standards were of university
level. Supported by Bishop Edmund M. Dunne of Peoria, O'Brien set
out to build a chapel, library, lecture halls, and dormitory. His premise
was that religious education was what made a Catholic college different,
and that the same end could be achieved at a secular institution by a
well-organized "Catholic foundation."

Jesuits, led by ex-Marquette University President Herbert C. Noonan,
disagreed. Noonan claimed that Henry S. Pritchett of the Carnegie Foundation (the same who later condemned Notre Dame and the University of
Southern California for their involvement in "the football industry") once
told him that "Elihu Root and I believe that you Jesuits have the principles upon which the prosperity of our nation depends." Noonan focused
the debate on the issue of moral training. Catholic colleges must keep up
the intellectual side, but "our moral pre-eminence is our greatest
asset. . . . It is our duty to direct the thought of the nation, to develop
leaders and not trailers." He was a combative type, concerned that prudence not become "a euphonious name for cowardice," and he worried
about some of his own brethren: "Vivid pictures of Jesuits in the watch-
towers . . . have become blurred in the past twenty-five years . . . replaced by men cowering in the cyclone cellar until the storm has spent its
fury." Soldiers of that ilk, "who shirk the battle, may be kept usefully
employed behind the firing line."[60] John A. O'Brien felt the accumulated
wrath. Archbishop Curley called him a modernist and forwarded a dos-
sier on him to Rome. He was attacked in *America, Civiltà cattolica,* the
papal newspaper *Osservatore Romano,* and at the 1926 annual meeting of
the National Catholic Educational Association, where the college and
university division voted that attendance by Catholics at secular institutions was "not at all desirable, but at most tolerated." Unfortunately,
only the University of Notre Dame among Catholic schools was able
during the 1920s to begin an endowment program that in that respect
eventually ranked it among the more substantial American universities.

Catholic interests in Mexico during the ten-year presidency of Plutarco
Elías Calles (1924–34) consumed a great deal of ink and energy. Calles
used a violent anti-clerical campaign to mask his failure to effect needed
social reforms. Mexico's bishops retaliated by closing all churches for
three years. They themselves went into hiding or exile. Militant Catholics
with the battle cry "Long live Christ the King!" launched the "Cristero"
rebellion (1926–29). Miguel Pro, S.J., shot without trial on trumped up
charges of plotting an assassination, became a folk hero. The Coolidge
administration reacted cautiously, trying to curb the United States's inter-

ventionist impulse. Led by *America,* Catholic magazines kept up an insistant drumfire of criticism of the Mexican government and of United States policy toward that country. American bishops were sympathetic to the plight of Mexican Catholics—some, like Droessarts and Curley, emphatically so—but they limited themselves to denouncing government persecution and to offering hospitality to refugees. They drew the line at supporting armed revolt. So did Nicholas F. Brady when oilman William F. Buckley brought a leader of the Mexican National League for Religious Defense to him. Brady was not interested in financing armed rebellion. A measure of peace was finally established in 1929, following negotiations involving American Ambassador Dwight W. Morrow, Mexican authorities, John J. Burke, NCWC legal counsel William F. Montavon, and Dean Edmund A. Walsh, S.J., of the Georgetown School of Foreign Service.[61]

The Mexican crisis was an instance in which Catholics' concentration on a special interest threatened to set them at cross-purposes with positions more generally perceived as in the national interest. What the more militant pilloried as callous disregard of the plight of Mexican Catholics, other Americans saw as commendable restraint on the part of a United States government trying to live down its interventionist image in Latin America. An even sharper and more direct conflict between Catholics and the American majority was occasioned, paradoxically enough, by the views of liberal John A. Ryan in *The State and the Church,* a volume co-authored with Fordham Jesuit Moorhouse I. X. Millar. Published first in 1922, it was widely used as a textbook in Catholic colleges. In his discussion of the nature of the state, Ryan relied heavily on the continental European tradition, as developed in Pope Leo XIII's encyclical letter *Immortale Dei* (1885) on "the Christian Constitution of States." None of the rich insights developed among American Catholics from the time of the Baltimores through that of Charles and John Carroll and down to his own early patron, John Ireland, was allowed to intrude. James A. Corcoran had brought better contributions to Vatican I's preparatory commission in the winter of 1868–69. Ryan repeated clichés derived from Europe's experience and framed in terms of Europe's politics: the state's obligation to make public profession of religion, recognition in principle of the Catholic religion as that of the state; toleration of religious dissidence only if it were practically unavoidable and scandal could be avoided. The underlying principle was that "error has not the same rights as truth." Expedience could demand religious toleration where its opposite was not practicable, but Ryan admitted that in his scheme of things religious proscription could also be both feasible and expedient. In theory, although he dismissed it as a real possibility, he could envision a time when religious dissenters would be required to worship as inconspicuously as possible, forbidden the right to propagandize, and denied tax exemption. He was convinced that in all this he was only honestly enunciating divinely ordained "principles of eternal and unchangeable truth." He would not do otherwise "in order to avoid the enmity of . . . unreasonable persons."[62]

Charles G. Marshall, an Episcopalian attorney in New York City, had in mind Ryan's explanation of Catholic teaching on church and state when he addressed "An Open Letter to the Honorable Alfred E. Smith," in April 1927 number of *Atlantic Monthly*.[63] Smith was a candidate for the office of President of the United States. Marshall asked if his Roman Catholic religious beliefs were reconcilable with the Constitution and with American principles of civil and religious liberty. Challenged to take a stand with respect to *Immortale Dei,* Smith's initial reaction was: "Will somebody please tell me what in hell an encyclical is?" In his later answer to Marshall, he rephrased it: "I, a devout Catholic from childhood, never heard of them [the papal documents referred to by the attorney] till I read your letter." In the May issue of *Atlantic Monthly,* Smith, with the help of Francis P. Duffy, Joseph M. Proskauer and Belle Moskowitz, stated his position:

> I believe in the worship of God according to the faith and practice of the Roman Catholic Church. I recognize no power in the institutions of my Church to interfere with the operations of the Constitution of the United States or the enforcement of the law of the land. I believe in absolute freedom of conscience for all men and in equality of all churches, all sects, and all beliefs before the law as a matter of right and not of favor. I believe in the absolute separation of Church and State and in the strict enforcement of the provisions of the Constitution that Congress shall make no law respecting an establishment of religion or prohibiting the free exercise thereof. I believe that no tribunal of any church has any power to make any decree of any force in the law of the land other than to establish the status of its own communicants within its own church. I believe in the support of the public school as one of the cornerstones of American liberty. I believe in the right of every parent to choose whether his child shall be educated in the public school or in a religious school supported by those of his own faith. I believe in the principle of noninterference by this country in the internal affairs of other nations and that we should stand steadfastly against any such interference by whomsoever it may be urged. And I believe in the common brotherhood of man under the common fatherhood of God.[64]

Smith's reply did not allay everyone's fears. The 1928 campaign was a field day for bigots, and the American Catholic community sustained deep hurts that would be long in the healing. Among the disillusioned were the liberal editors of *Commonweal*, Michael Williams and George Shuster. In spite of their disappointment, they did not fail to reflect that it was not only the legions of Methodist Bishop James E. Cannon, Jr. who were disturbed by the prospect of Alfred E. Smith in the White House. Charles Marshall, *Commonweal* editorialized, had spoken "the doubts and difficulties which beset many minds," and he had not been answered.[65] The close of the first postwar decade left American Catholics puzzled. There was among them the growing conviction that they were the last defenders of that objective moral order and reliance upon reason which they saw as the root of the American experience, yet they had received for their pains only stinging rebuff.

Their fellow Americans still demanded of the nation's Catholic citizens that they establish the compatibility of their religion with American democratic ideals, laws, and practices. There was ample evidence that suspicion of them along those lines was widespread. The job of rebutting accusations had not been helped by publications like John Ryan's. Some Catholics were discouraged in the aftermath of the election. Not Paulist Father James Gillis, editor of the *Catholic World*. In an editorial in the December 1928 issue, he proclaimed for all to hear: "We shall not wither up and blow away."[66]

XIX

We Shall Not Wither
Up and Blow Away

American Catholics did not easily shake off the alienation and discouragement fostered by the message they seemed to be receiving in 1928. But there were plenty of distractions as the stock market crash of 1929 was followed by worldwide economic depression. Individual Catholics and church institutions shared the general distress. Average earnings in the nation dropped 33 percent. In 1933 unemployment stood at thirteen million, one-quarter of the work force. Some Catholics joined fellow Americans on breadlines, sold apples on street corners, and huddled around WPA bonfires at public works projects. Others, Joseph P. Kennedy among them, built fortunes. The old political leadership faded off to the right. Denied the Democratic presidential nomination in 1932 at Chicago, by 1936 Alfred E. Smith was supporting the Republican nominee. He and John J. Raskob were active in the Liberty League, fighting the Wagner-Connery Act's protection of unions and Franklin D. Roosevelt's "soak the rich" tax policies.

Smith, Raskob, and others represented a conservative element in the American Catholic mix never absent since the days when most Catholics were Federalists and then Whigs in the republic's early days. During the 1930s they vied with leaders ranging from the nation's prime reactionary demagogue on the far right, through social democratic and ruralist partisans in firm control of the permanent machinery at the NCWC, to a utopian fringe wielding influence that belied its small numbers. Publications and movements reflected the spectrum. Fresh lay leadership sprouted in New Deal agencies and in upper ranks of the unions, particularly in the CIO.

In these years the underlying quest of American Catholics for a unifying, integrating principle on which to build a vision of America and their special role in it acquired a significant new dimension. Philosophy, specifically that stemming from the neo-Thomistic revival begun in 1879 by Pope Leo XIII, had been the dominant discipline. It was not routed, but by 1940 a strong if friendly rival was in the field.[1] With liturgists providing the major impetus, Catholic social doctrine, already strongly colored by Thomistic philosophy, began in some quarters to assume a decidedly theological cast. Deeper appreciation of St. Paul's understanding of the church as Christ's mystical body was the key, as Carl P. Hensler, a founder of the not-so-radical Catholic Radical Alliance of Pittsburgh, explained when he spoke of

> the doctrine most capable today of supplying a synthesis of the social implications of Christianity. The Mystical Body of Christ, as studied in the corporate worship of the Church, is a living system of social sanctification. May it be the dynamic that will hasten the solution of the natural antagonism between the individual and society.[2]

The predominance of philosophy was by no means reversed. It survived in academic circles and served to shore up the continuing Catholic conviction of being a people "certain and set apart." A thirty-four-year-old professor at the Catholic University of America, Fulton J. Sheen, struck just the right note in his 1929 call to the National Catholic Educational Association to "educate for a Catholic Renaissance," in which people's faith would be "vitalized"—fired to become a living reality at the core of their being—and "integrated" with the rest of their lives. The premise was that Catholicism represented a coherent system grounded in reason that perfectly met the needs of modern society and the spiritual longings of modern humanity.[3] The NCEA listened carefully. Its college and university department in 1935 declared that "the Catholic college will not be content with presenting Catholicism as a creed, a code, or a cult. Catholicism must be seen as a culture." Graduates would not merely be trained in Catholic doctrine, they "will have seen the whole sweep of Catholicism, its part in the building up of our western civilization, past and present. . . . " Finally, "they will have before them not merely the facts of the natural order but those in the supernatural order also, those facts which give meaning and coherence to the whole of life."[4] The dream was not new. After describing the arrival of Thomism on the American scene, William Halsey put it in perspective: "When Catholics peered at the universe, they saw, not flux and contingency, but harmony, order and law."[5] They pictured themselves as final defenders of reason and objective moral order in a world adrift from it moorings. Midway through the decade, philosopher John O. Riedl reminded his fellows:

> Scholastic philosophers are somewhat unique among present-day philosophers. They still believe in Truth, in reality, in God, in the power of the human reason to know real things, in an immortal soul, an after life and the power of man to guide his own destiny. Oddly enough, they base their belief in these fundamental verities on the authority of reason alone. . . . Outside scholasticism there seems to be nothing but intellectual chaos and despair.[6]

There were disagreements among Catholic intellectuals. George Bull, S.J., of Fordham University had no interest in "the impossible task of being Catholic in creed and anti-Catholic in culture." For "100 percent" Catholics like Bull, compromise with the pragmatic would in which they lived was unthinkable. He explained what Catholic "totality of view" meant for him: "It is the simple assumption that wisdom has been achieved by man, and that the humane use of the mind, the function proper to him as man, is contemplation and not research." "Research," he concluded, "cannot be the primary object of a Catholic graduate school, because it is at war with the whole Catholic life of the mind."[7] Others, even at Fordham, were more open to the larger American scene. Bull's senior colleague, Moorhouse I. X. Millar, S.J., was one of many who labored to trace American democratic ideals back to medieval (and therefore Catholic) roots. It was the season of essays demonstrating the influence of Aquinas, Bellarmine, and Suarez on Mr. Jefferson of Monticello. On occasion, the dialogue penetrated closer to the heart of the matter, probing deficiencies in the characteristic American Catholic perception of reality. George Shuster of *Commonweal* worried about a Catholicism which "clenches its fist against beauty and mystical insight" while giving too much weight to numbers, moralism, and apologetics. Catholicism was for him profoundly incarnational, and he feared what he perceived as the "terrible contempt" of many Catholics "for thought and loveliness."[8] There were less tormented voices. On the eve of World War II, Fordham philosophy professor Robert Pollock was challenging students to "total repossession of our tradition." His brand of "integral Catholicism" was a far cry from that advocated on Rose Hill by George Bull. Pollock called for Christian commitment to involvement in society, and abandonment of the Platonic dualism which for many Catholics had neatly compartmentalized and sealed off their religion from the real world in which they lived.[9]

Along with these philosophical developments, other changes that were to have long-term effects were taking place in Catholic colleges. "Religion" in those institutions had long been the chief concern of an administrator charged with supervising the piety and morals of the students. John F. O'Hara' tenure as prefect of religion at Notre Dame is a classic example. He heard confessions, counseled, was an advocate of frequent reception of the Eucharist, even outside the context of the mass, and served as censor of books.[10] When, in the early 1920s, a young English literature professor named George Shuster put D. H. Lawrence's *The Rainbow* on a reserve shelf for one of his classes, the prefect of religion personally removed and tore it up.[11] When "Religion" or "The Evidences of Religion" were taught in the classroom, what was meant was for the most part a form of philosophical apologetics. At Catholic University, John Montgomery Cooper pioneered in the scientific study of religion. A milestone was the publication in 1933 by Gerald Ellard, S.J., of a textbook, *Christian Life and Worship,* portraying Christian life as vital union with Christ and his mystical body, the church, which has for its corporate worship the mass.[12] American liturgists—Virgil Michel, O.S.B., William Busch, Martin Hellriegel, German refugee Hans A. Reinhold, Godfrey Diekmann, O.S.B., William J. Leonard, S.J., and Gerald Ellard—were deeply concerned with the social dimension in the Christian community's understanding of itself, and in its worship.[13]

Further theological development came during a 1939 symposium sponsored by the National Catholic Alumni Federation. The topic was the role of theology as unifying force and inspiration of an integral Catholic culture. A young priest recently named to the theological faculty at Woodstock in Maryland, John Courtney Murray, S.J., urged development of a theological course geared to the "liveability of the Word of God," to help people relate their beliefs to the world of their daily lives. His emphasis was Christological; his approach suggested familiarity with the kerygmatic theology of the Innsbruck Jesuit faculty which would be fundamental to modern catechetical development, and also with the "return to sources" in Scripture and Tradition which was a significant feature of the "New Theology" movement among contemporary French Jesuits and Dominicans. Meanwhile at Catholic University, theologians Joseph C. Fenton and Francis J. Connell, C.Ss.R., advocated a lay theology program more nearly akin to the current seminary curriculum of apologetics, dogma and moral theology, while Dominicans plumped for wider use of Thomas Aquinas's *Summa Theologica.*[14]

Among more visible signs of Catholic presence were periodic "reviews of the troops." New York's St. Patrick's Day parade had long since become a powerful Catholic manifestation, with the archbishop taking the salute from the steps of the cathedral. In Chicago, memories were still vivid of the "red train" which carried papal representative Giovanni Bonzano, eight other cardinals and a dozen bishops to the spectacular Twenty-Eighth International Eucharistic Congress in the summer of 1926. Cardinal Dougherty's celebration of the sesquicentennial of American Independence was held in Philadelphia's Municipal Stadium, under a baldachino modeled after that at St. Peter's in Rome. When Maryland commemorated the tercentenary of the *Ark* and the *Dove* in 1934, the Georgetown University band, followed by three hundred Jesuits from Woodstock, dressed in cassocks and wearing birettas, led a military-style parade of one hundred thousand priests, brothers, sisters, and lay people into Baltimore's stadium. Observers were impressed as "group after group of retiring nuns came swinging into the stadium with the free step of Red Cross nurses on parade." At the consecration, the central point of the Mass, there was "the roll of drums . . . the shrill of bugles . . . the clank of sabres . . . and the roar of cannon," as a ten-gun salute was fired.[15]

Less spectacular events included Summer Schools of Catholic Action (SSCA), begun in 1931 by Daniel A. Lord, S.J., editor of *The Queen's Work,* the organ of the Sodalities of the Blessed Virgin Mary in the United States. Over a quarter-century Daniel Lord revived the dying sodality movement. His forte was youth groups. Meeting on university campuses, in convention hotels, and at summer camps in Texas, the Midwest, and on the east coast, the SSCA offered thousands of young people intensive weeks of prayer, liturgical participation, lectures, and social life. A generation sang the lilting marching song:

> An army of youth, flying the standard of truth,
> We're fighting for Christ the Lord.
> Heads lifted high, Catholic Action our cry,
> And the cross our only sword. . . .

Lord was a playwright with fifty plays, twelve musicals, and six pageants to his name. He wrote thirty books, and by the mid-1960s his more than three hundred fifty booklets and pamphlets had sold over twenty-five million copies.[16]

The pageantry, the ebullient popular spirituality, the beginnings of liturgical awakening, broad social concern, and the philosophical self-confidence that underlay it all masked a serious deficiency in American Catholicism. Reading habits were not the problem, but only symptomatic of it. Three centuries after the *Ark* and the *Dove,* and even longer after Pedro Menéndez de Avilés and Samuel de Champlain, no significant body of writing could be said to represent American Catholic thought. Contemporary agonies produced nothing in American Catholicism comparable to *Moral Man and Immoral Society.* In a phenomenon noticed also among

Australian Catholics by their historian Patrick O'Farrell, Catholics in the United States remained cheerfully colonialized when it came to seriously reflective religious thought.[17] Intellectuals read Mauriac, Claudel, Bernanos, and sometimes Bloy. Maritain became a favorite philosopher. Eric Gill was popular in Catholic Worker houses. Hilaire Belloc and G. K. Chesterton fed controversialist fires and Christopher Dawson's broad strokes projected, as R. C. Zaehner later wrote, "the security of his faith and his deep embeddedness in the classical tradition of rationality and . . . excellence." For "Catholic" novels, Americans turned to Sigrid Undset, Evelyn Waugh, and Graham Greene. From America's past, Willa Cather, herself not a Catholic, offered *Death Comes for the Archbishop*. Little, if any, serious theological reflection emerged from the American experience, certainly nothing accepted as comparable to the imports.

Boston activist editor Francis P. Lally claimed the 1930s as the first decade when "we can really speak in realistic terms of a widespread Catholic social consciousness and with it a willingness not simply to adapt to the community life but also to work to transform it."[18] Many factors conspired to make that happen. Though still smarting from the election of 1928, Catholics were in other respects confident. They had available a coherent body of social thought. Leo XIII's 1891 encyclical letter on the condition of the working class, *Rerum Novarum,* was reinforced and expanded by Pius XI's *Quadragesimo Anno* of May 15, 1931, on reconstructing the social order. Of the twelve major proposals in the 1919 Bishops' Program, all but one became law under the New Deal.[19] Catholics found congenial the administration which Franklin D. Roosevelt inaugurated on March 4, 1933, particularly in its earlier days. John A. Ryan wrote in *Commonweal* in October 1934: "Never before in our history have the policies of the federal government embodied so much legislation that is of a highly ethical order. Never before have government policies been so deliberately, formally and consciously based upon conceptions and convictions of moral right and social justice."[20] John J. Burke, C.S.P., of the NCWC, cooperated with the new administration, helping interpret Catholic questions and on occasion drafting replies for the President.[21] Initial support from the bishops was encouraging. Cardinal O'Connell welcomed Roosevelt in somewhat the same terms Pius XI had used of Mussolini when the Lateran accords were reached. Bishop Karl Alter of Toledo thought the inaugural address breathed the spirit of *Quadragesimo Anno.* Cardinal Mundelein credited Roosevelt with "more friendly sympathy to the Church and its institutions than any occupant of the White House in half a century." Auxiliary Bishop William D. O'Brien of Chicago, veteran of many years of work for Catholics in poorer parts of the country through the Catholic Church Extension Society, wrote that "Almighty God raised up FDR—the Apostle of the New Deal."[22]

An experienced New York politician, Roosevelt had earned good credentials from Catholics in his home state. As President he missed few opportunities to cultivate the Catholic vote. He and some of his advisers—notably Henry A. Wallace—were not hesitant to compare their programs with suggestions found in papal social documents. George Q. Flynn has pointed to the variety of sources from which New Deal policies came—reform movements of the Progressive Era and the Social Gospel movement, among others—and has stated the obvious conclusion that "the New Deal would have developed even if the popes had not spoken," but it did the collective and somewhat bruised Catholic ego no harm to hear candidate Roosevelt declare at Detroit on October 2, 1932, that *Quadragesimo Anno,* which he has just quoted, was "as radical as I am . . . one of the greatest documents of modern times."[23]

Further balm for the bruised ego came with a stream of appointments of Catholics to high office: James A. Farley and Thomas J. Walsh to the cabinet; Robert H. Gore as governor of Puerto Rico; and Detroit Mayor Frank P. Murphy to be governor-general of the Philippines. A special report from Manila to *Christian Century* reported satisfaction with the last appointment. In contrast to some former residents of Malacañan, Murphy "at least went to church on Sunday" and he was a faithful Bible-reader.[24] A strong liberal, he held many positions during the Roosevelt years: last American governor-general and first high commissioner in the Philippines, governor of Michigan, attorney general of the United States, and from 1940 to 1949 associate justice of the Supreme Court. William Leuchtenberg calculates that one-quarter of the judicial appointments made in the Roosevelt years went to Roman Catholics, a sharp increase over the ratio under his three predecessors, where the average had been one in twenty-five.[25] Government service was not limited to lay people. John A. Ryan sat on several commissions. The biographer of Francis J. Haas thinks it "quite possible" that the Milwaukee priest "held more important government positions than any other priest of the time, or perhaps of all time." Haas served on the NRA Labor Advisory Board and as labor representative on the National Labor Board and was chairman of the Fair Employment Practice Committee until named bishop of Grand Rapids in 1943.[26]

Economic disaster demanded a closer look at free-enterprise capitalism. The more most Catholics looked, the less they liked what they saw. Responses varied. At one pole were radical personalists like Catholic University sociologist Paul Hanley Furfey and the Catholic Worker communities inspired by Peter Maurin and Dorothy Day. Father Charles E. Coughlin of the Shrine of the Little Flower at Royal Oak, Michigan, and

his National Union for Social Justice occupied the far right. During the early years of the New Deal, the traditional alliance of Catholics and organized labor took on new dimensions: church leaders and thinkers found union counterparts congenial—"their own kind." Widespread personal approval of Franklin D. Roosevelt, however, did not always translate into approval of big-government policies. There was a degree of wariness about eastern liberal braintrusters.

Never really admitted to the club, Catholics mixed uneasily with the heirs of American reform politics and the practitioners of Niebuhrian Realism. They welcomed, on the other hand, formation in 1935 of the Committee for Industrial Organization.[27] Catholic membership in the industrial unions was estimated at 30 percent and representation in the leadership at 40 percent. The leaders were a new breed. Three of five members of the executive board, chosen in 1938 when the Committee became the Congress of Industrial Organizations, were practicing Catholics knowledgeable about papal social teachings. They were Philip Murray, who succeeded John L. Lewis as CIO president in 1940 and held that position until his death in 1952, Secretary-Treasurer James Carey, and General Director John Brophy, the immigrant from Lancashire who boldly announced: "The labor encyclicals are a call to action—let us have action!"[28] Relations between CIO leaders and the NCWC's Social Action Department were excellent.

Opposition to labor unions and the CIO in Catholic circles ranged from Mayor Frank Hague of Jersey City, who mustered one hundred thousand of the faithful in Journal Square in an "Americanization Day" rally against communist influence in labor's ranks, to editor Edward Koch of *The Guildsman,* an opponent of the "multiplied egoism" of American labor-management relations. Koch believed that the only genuinely Catholic approach was organization according to functional groups of all those—workers and managers—involved in a given industry.[29]

The corporatist vision, expressed by Leo XIII and urged by Pius XI, had roots deep in the pervasive class-consciousness of European society. Designed to seize the middle ground between individualistic free enterprise and socialism, corporatism derived a touch of glamor from its linkage with the not thoroughly understood, but romantically perceived, medieval guild system. Concrete suggestions for its application to the American scene varied. At one point, Charles E. Coughlin wanted wholesale constitutional change, with the population organized in vocational or trade bodies which would elect a house of representatives. The representatives would choose the President. A senate composed of one representative of capital and one of labor from each state completed the picture. The government would have authority to regulate supply and demand, limit profits and output, settle labor disputes, guarantee employment, tax incomes, and "counsel and guide" workers in dealings with industry. Strikes and lockouts would yield to compulsory arbitration.[30]

Within the social action department of the NCWC, there was theoretical disagreement, John A. Ryan was a statist, though not in Coughlin's league. He saw the pragmatic necessity of increased government involvement. His longtime assistant and, in 1945, his successor, Father Raymond A. McGowan, was more hopeful that the collective bargaining process would bring capital and labor to industrial democracy and partnership in ownership, control, and profits.[31] The state, as Pittsburgh activist priest Carl Hensler told the Steel Workers' Organizing Committee, had the role of providing "the framework of liberty and order" within which this could happen.[32] After his election as CIO president in 1940, Philip Murray, referring explicitly to papal ideas about vocational/occupational groups, proposed establishment of industry defense councils to include representatives of labor, management, and government. On the other hand, Leo P. Brown, S.J., of the Jesuits' Institute of Social Order at St. Louis did not think that Murray's scheme corresponded to "the integration built around a community of action and interest which the encyclicals have in mind."[33]

During the 1920s the bishops produced only a single joint letter, on Mexico in 1926. They returned to that theme in 1933 and 1934. Letters in the 1930s focused on social issues. As causes of the world crisis, the bishops singled out selfish greed and the inversion of priorities which put money ahead of human rights and dignity. In "Church and Social Order" (1940) they endorsed the social action department's projects with the exception of its advocacy of a child labor amendment, and set out a code of social ethics. The letter warned of the "anonymous character" of modern wealth and of the social irresponsibility spawned by that anonymity.[34] The NCWC, headed by Cleveland priest Michael J. Ready, after John Burke's death in 1936 continued its activities, adding a committee on catechetics in 1934 and a youth department in 1940. In 1935 the social action department produced a pamphlet prepared by McGowan and Ryan, *Organized Social Justice*. A reprise on the 1919 Bishop's Program, it emphasized the need of occupational groups to have corporate structure and regretted that moves in that direction under the aegis of the NRA had been foreclosed by the Supreme Court.

Leadership passed to the Midwest and its Rome-trained archbishops. Principal staffers at the NCWC were from the midwest; midwestern bishops, priests, and lay people provided much of the imaginative planning that gave life to the Catholic body in difficult times. Chicago, under the socially progressive lead of Cardinal Mundelein, led the way. On the school front, James Sanders has recorded the extraordinary efforts of Chicago's Catholics which led to a situation by the end of the decade in which:

> no schools closed or shortened their school year. The elementary school enrollment declined less than did the public school; and ended the decade with a higher percentage of the school-age children than ever before. Further, the gains made were in the middle class. The high schools, after a few faltering years, managed to keep up, too, and ended the decade without losing ground to the public schools despite the greatly increased percentage of youngsters attending high school. Catholic education in Chicago had weathered the Depression, and Catholics felt they were sitting once more in the catbird seat.[35]

Chicago Catholics gave the CIO strong support. Auxiliary Bishop Bernard Sheil, founder in 1930 of the Catholic Youth Organization, lent his support to organizing efforts among packing house workers and in a strike against the Hearst newspapers.[36] Reynold Hillenbrand, Rector of St. Mary of the Lake seminary from 1935–1944, educated a generation of Chicago priests to a sense of liturgy, community, and social involvement. An extraordinary number of movements developed among priests and laity: the Christian Family Movement, Young Christian Workers and Young Christian Students, a Catholic Interracial Council and a Labor Alliance, the Cana Conferences for married couples. Samuel Stritch, who moved from Milwaukee to Chicago to succeed Mundelein in 1940, continued the progressive approach.

Detroit, Father Coughlin's home grounds, had a conservative bishop, Michael J. Gallagher, from 1918 to 1937. Edward A. Mooney, once a papal diplomat in India and Japan, succeeded him in a diocese hit harder than most by the Depression, where feelings ran strong about the recent rash of sitdown strikes in the auto industry. The sitdown strikes had been enormously successful as a dramatic technique. But Governor Frank Murphy, who successfully negotiated an end to them, lost his reelection bid in 1938, and the CIO's militancy and tactics shocked the innate conservatism of many Catholics. Charges of communism and sovietization sounded on the right, while even such progressives as John A. Ryan and young sociologist Joseph Fichter doubted the wisdom of workers occupying plants. Jerome D. Hannan, a future Bishop of Scranton, was one defender. Another was Benedictine liturgist Virgil Michel, whose liturgical ministry was inspired by deep conviction of the social nature and implications of Christianity. In response to conservatives who worried about the implications of the sitdown for the security of private property rights, Michel asked if a worker's job were not a form of property right for him.[37]

Archbishop Mooney was a strong union man who supported the CIO and urged active participation in its unions. Labor schools and the Association of Catholic Trade Unionists flourished under his firm but encouraging hand, and a newpaper, the Michigan *Labor Leader* (later *Wage Earner*), was published in the diocese.

Two other pro-labor archbishops were John T. McNicholas, O.P., of Cincinnati, who educated priests for involvement with labor, and Robert E. Lucey, a Californian who became bishop of Amarillo in 1934 and archbishop of San Antonio in 1941. Lucey was an outspoken defender of labor unions and the CIO, writing in 1935 that "devotion to the laboring classes automaticaly includes the union." He found irony in the position of those who professed devotion to papal social ideals while demanding that moral reform precede unionization. Many of them were in fact hand in glove with reactionary forces in the nation. Workers, he wrote, "must be organized and set free."[38]

There were activist labor priests throughout the country. Some, like Buffalo's John P. Boland, were heavily involved in government work. He founded a diocesan labor college where workers could learn social theory, labor law, public speaking, and organizing techniques, served on a regional panel of the National Labor Relations Board, and was named chairman of the State Labor Relations Board by Governor Herbert H. Lehman. In New York City, John P. Monaghan was inspiration to a generation of priests, founded a speaker's bureau and a social action school, and helped to found the Association of Catholic Trade Unionists. Jesuits founded labor schools in several east coast cities. New Orleans priest Jerome Drolet worked with the National Maritime Union. In Pittsburgh, Charles Owen Rice and Carl P. Hensler, militant supporters of industrial unionism, founded the Catholic Radical Alliance in 1934. They worked with the Steel Workers' Organizing Committee; Rice became known as "the chaplain of the CIO" because of his close association with leaders like Philip Murray and John Brophy.

Labor leaders, workers, priests, and bishops took many roads in the struggle for solutions to economic and social dilemmas. Catholic ruralists sometimes parted company with the majority. Agriculture for them was not just another business to be cured by large doses of consolidation and centralization. They wanted, in Leo XIII's words, "a share in the land," not as tenants or farmhands, but as owners. In Iowa, Father Luigi Ligutti, increasingly prominent in the National Catholic Rural Life Conference, dreamed Jeffersonian dreams of small, family-owned farms. Other ruralist leaders included NCRLC founder Edwin V. O'Hara, bishop of Great Falls since 1930; his successor at the NCRLC, Edgar Schmiedler, O.S.B.; Bishop Aloysius J. Muench of Fargo; and John C. Rawe, S.J.[39]

No one in farm or city was untouched by the Great Depression, but life went on and old parish patterns persisted. Men belonged to the Holy Name Society; the St. Vincent de Paul Society functioned as something of a Catholic salvation army; women gathered in rosary and altar societies. Parish missions flourished and millionaires' mansions became retreat houses as the weekend retreat movement developed. With Prohibition repealed, the 19th century temperance crusade revived; many bishops demanded that priests-to-be pledge total abstinence from spirits for five years after ordination and that boys and girls receiving the sacrament of confirmation do the same until they were twenty-one. On another moral front, John LaFarge's New York Catholic Interracial Council in 1934 took over the *Interracial Review,* founded at St. Louis by William M. Markoe, S.J. Interracial councils blossomed around the country.[40]

The most far-reaching Catholic venture in public morality was the establishment in 1934 of the National League of Decency. The movie industry's Motion Picture Production Code (1930) had been framed by Catholic trade publisher Martin J. Quigley and Daniel A. Lord, S.J., but by 1933 was generally considered ineffective. The Legion of Decency classified new film releases as "morally unobjectionable" either for adults or for all, "objectionable in part," or "condemned." The lists were publicized; all Catholics in the nation were asked once a year to promise to abide by the ratings. Outside Catholic ranks, the Legion attracted both praise and blame, but it was effective. By 1938, 93 percent of all new films were classified in one of the two highest categories. Not all Catholics were satisfied. In June 1934 Cardinal Dougherty, declaring that "perhaps the greatest menace to faith and morals in America today is the moving picture theatre," called for a complete boycott of all movies by Philadelphia Catholics. The boycott had still not been lifted when he died in 1951.[41]

The emergence of lay groups committed to lives of Christian perfection was a sign of spiritual growth. Committed to prayer and caught up in the liturgical movement, they witnessed against the pervasive individualism and materialism of American society by their lives of voluntary poverty and service. While others debated reform of the socio-economic structure, their understanding of faith demanded love in action, a contribution not only of resources and know-how, but of self. Reaching out to others in service of the most elementary soup-kitchen kind, they also created centers where many of the exciting ideas in American Catholicism began.[42]

Among the leading theoreticians of this new personalism were Catholic University priest-sociologist Paul Hanley Furfey and Virgil Michel, the Benedictine liturgical theologian and social philosopher from St. John's Abbey in Minnesota. Groupings included the interracial Friendship

Houses, introduced into the United States in Harlem (1938) by Russian-born Baroness Catherine de Hueck, and various expressions of the Catholic Worker movement. Furfey made no secret of his Gospel literalism. In *Fire on Earth* (1936) he wrote of "supernatural sociology"—Christianity made manifest by voluntary poverty and active self-giving in spiritual and corporal works of mercy.[43]

Describing the "new social Catholicism" for Richard Deverall and Norman McKenna's *Christian Front* in 1936, Furfey wrote: "The Liturgy is the perfect expression of the new social Catholicism. The new movement is founded upon faith and the Liturgy is the public expression of our faith."[44] To the liturgical awakening of the 1930s, Virgil Michel brought awareness of the social dimension of Christianity. He was troubled by an "un-Christian" capitalist system founded on "greed, selfish egoism, and heartlessness." Michel's intention in liturgical renewal was to promote human and Christian solidarity. Fellowship grounded in oneness in Christ would become the basis of truly Christian life and attitudes.[45] The public worship of American Catholics at the time was characterized by limited understanding of its specifically public and communal nature, coupled with a strong strain of spiritual individualism. The future Cardinal O'Hara's practice at Notre Dame only reflected common piety: one "went to Mass"; one "received communion." The sense of participation in a community's eucharistic celebration was missing. Salvation was conceived as an individual effort. The church, a juridical institution, supported the individual's union in grace with God by its sacraments and sacramentals and by making crystal clear what "you had to do" to avoid hell or an uncomfortable term in purgatory. Little room was left for the idea of church membership as incorporation into the Body of Christ, an organic union with Christ and all other Christians. Many men and women lived lives of deep prayer; they gave to charity; but too often in a lonely way.

Michel had a straightforward understanding of Christianity: "Not paper programs, not highsounding unfulfilled resolutions once renewed the world, but new and living men born out of the depths of Christianity."[46] The enemy was within, in church members' surrender to individualism and materialism and in resultant social apathy. The antidote, promoted by active participation in the community's worship, was development of a spirit of love and mutual sacrifice that issued in personal commitment, a free giving of oneself to others.

The Catholic Worker movement, which began in New York City and soon had dozens of affiliates throughout the country, was inspired by the French peasant-philosopher Peter Maurin and by Dorothy Day, a Catholic convert whose interests had included the suffragettes and the

IWW.[47] On May Day of 1933, the first issue of the penny-a-copy *Catholic Worker* was on sale in Union Square. Its message was that bourgeois capitalist culture is essentially un-Christian. Human beings do not love, but rather use, one another and rationalize it as rugged individualism. The answer to modern humanity's dilemma is in a communitarian revolution (" . . . basically a personal revolution. It starts with I, not they"), and an emphasis on creative and manual work by people living and working together. Day spoke of "a harsh and dreadful love" that implied willingness to give to those more in need, poverty both voluntary and real, pacifism, non-violence, and personalism that demanded genuine personal involvement.

In the pages of the *Worker,* newsnotes about people in the movement mingled with scholarly essays from Europe, the stern spirituality of Pittsburgh priest John J. Hugo, and accounts of Dorothy Day's pilgrimages. One trip took her to Governor Frank Murphy's office—he was a subscriber—and to San Quentin to see anarchist Tom Mooney. Maurin's "easy essays" were featured:

> If the Catholic Church
> is not today the dominant social, dynamic force,
> it is because Catholic scholars have failed
> to blow the dynamite of the church.
>
>   . . .
>
> It is about time
> to blow the lid off
> so that the Catholic Church
> may again become the dominant social force.[48]

A profound sense of communication with the church remained a hallmark of the founders. Day explained in *The Long Loneliness* that she loved the church "not for itself, because it was so often a scandal for me," but as the "Cross on which Christ was crucified." Following Munich theologian Romano Guardini, she held that "one could not separate Christ from His Cross, and one must live in a state of permanent dissatisfaction with the Church":

> The scandal of businesslike priests, of collective wealth, the lack of a sense of reponsibility for the poor, the worker, the Negro, the Mexican, the Filipino, and even the oppression of these, and the consenting to the oppression of them by our industrialist capitalist order—these made me feel often that priests were more like Cain than Abel. "Am I my brother's keeper," they seemed to say in respect to the social order. There was plenty of charity, but too little justice.

"And yet," she added, "the priests were the dispensers of the Sacraments, bringing Christ to men, enabling us to put on Christ and to achieve more nearly in the world a sense of peace and unity."[49]

Maurin had been appalled by the complexity and impersonality of life in the modern world, by the prevalence of greed and by the low value placed on the human individual, who had been made in the image and likeness of God and redeemed by Christ. In answer to the secularist divorce of material and spiritual, he proposed to reclaim values discounted by the industrial revolution and mass production. The Catholic Worker program prescribed round tables of workers and intellectuals and the opening of hospitality houses, so that Catholics might fulfill their personal responsibilities to the poor. Most important was the agrarian ideal: establishment of farm communes in a "green revolution." One model which Maurin held up was the *kibbutzim* in Palestine. John Cort, an early Worker, remarked that he tended to identify Christianity "with handicrafts and subsistence farming."[50]

The personalities and movements prominent in the Catholic social activism of the 1930s regularly crossed paths with the Workers. Pacifist and conscientious objector groups drew strength from them, as would tax-resisters and anti-war groups of a later generation. Worker houses kept up a dialogue with those committed to the system, as when John A. Ryan came to talk about the child labor admendment. When Jerome Drolet was forbidden by his bishop to offer the opening prayer at a convention of the communist-infiltrated National Maritime Union, Drolet wrote the *Catholic Worker* of his trouble.[51]

Intellectual activists Richard Deverall and Norman McKenna headed an early spinoff of the Worker movement. In January, 1936, the first issue of their *Christian Front* appeared in Philadelphia. Initially, they were committed to a stark understanding of Christianity as separated by a vast chasm from either Marxism, fascism, or capitalism. Eventually, however, they moved toward the center and became advocates of the liberal welfare state. In 1939 the paper's name became *Christian Social Action* and it was moved to Detroit and Archbishop Mooney's patronage.[52] It remained strongly pro-labor and was allied with the Association of Catholic Trade Unionists (ACTU), an organization founded in New York in 1937 by union organizer Martin Wersing, Harvard alumnus John C. Cort, and others, with John P. Monaghan as chaplain. The ACTU's concern with labor's role in industry and the Catholic interest in labor pulled it away from mainline Workers, whose bias ran to voluntary socialism and rural-agrarian solutions. Out of the ACTU, which became a strong force in combatting both racketeering and the communist influence in unions, grew the Catholic Labor Defense League (1938), made up of attorneys who volunteered time and expertise in labor causes, and also Pittsburgh's Catholic Radical Alliance.[53]

The Worker community in Chicago developed a life of its own. It began with meetings at the home of Dr. Arthur G. Falls, a black physician. At his suggestion the woodcut on the *Worker*'s masthead—the work of artist Ade Bethune—was altered to include the figure of a black man. Young Chicago recruits included Edward Marciniak and John Cogley. A house of hospitality opened in 1937 and from 1938 to 1941 the group published the *Chicago Catholic Worker*. Moderate in approach, they prospered as part of the generally liberal world of Chicago Catholicism, in the company of socially conscious priests trained under Reynold Hillenbrand, community organizer Father John Egan, pro-labor Bishop Sheil, and pro–New Deal Cardinal Mundelein.[54]

Conservative blood ran strong in the main arteries of American Catholicism. By 1936, Franklin Roosevelt still had the support of Mundelein, John A. Ryan, and "social democratic" Catholics, but looked as if he might be in trouble with Catholic voters as a whole. Father Charles E. Coughlin, who supported a third party in the presidential race, was one threat. There were others, both doubters and outright opponents. Big government and the perceived erosion of constitutional principles were one issue. Failure to control unemployment was another. Overshadowing everything was the specter to which many Catholics ascribed the nation's problems: communism, domestic and foreign.

Constitutional issues bothered Frederick C. Kenkel, veteran editor of *Central-Blatt and Social Justice,* who saw Roosevelt's planned economy as the imposition of state socialism. Patrick Scanlan, lay editor of the *Brooklyn Tablet,* and James M. Gillis, C.S.P., of the *Catholic World,* had the same worries. Alfred E. Smith told the American Liberty League that the choice was plain: one could have either communism or constitutional government. Ignatius W. Cox, S.J., of Fordham refused to accept this simple dichotomy. He believed that Governor Smith should look to Smith's own rugged individualism for the "cancerous growth" in "our immoral economic order." But many others stressed communism. In addition to Father Coughlin, Brooklyn priest Edward Lodge Curran of the International Catholic Truth Society leaned heavily on this argument. Erosion of Roosevelt's Catholic support was not nearly so great as some had expected. An estimated 70 to 80 percent of the nation's Catholic voters cast ballots for the Roosevelt-Garner ticket in the November elections.[55]

The communism issue did not die with the 1936 elections. The civil war that had broken out in Spain the previous summer helped keep it alive. So did the considerable communist presence in a number of CIO unions.

A particularly painful incident occurred in 1938 when *Our Sunday Visitor,* the national weekly published by Bishop John F. Noll of Fort Wayne, attacked labor leader John Brophy as being no Catholic, but a communist sympathizer. Charges of communism were also lodged against Brophy before the House Un-American Affairs Committee. Friends rushed to his defense, including Fathers Ryan, Rice, and Hensler, but Bishop Noll, withdrawing the aspersion on Brophy's religion with ill grace, remarked that it was "difficult to believe that you have the mind of the Church, which is certainly opposed to cooperation with communists."[56] Nor were others convinced. *America* editorialized that "in the opinion of some, the CIO is infested with Communists and in some localities ruled by Communists . . . no Catholic who has the cause of labor at heart can stand by in silence."[57]

A series of events helped to alienate Catholics, set many more firmly in the anti-Communist mold and reopened fissures that had begun to close between them and other Americans. Numbers of Catholics moved to an isolationist perspective as the country began to edge in the opposite direction. The problem spots were the USSR, Mexico, and Spain. During the 1932 campaign, Roosevelt carefully avoided committing himself on diplomatic relations with the Soviet Union. Once in office, he moved to restore the link broken by Wilson when the bolsheviks overthrew Kerensky in 1917. USSR President Mikhail Kalinin was included among the heads of state to whom Roosevelt sent a message on disarmament in May 1933. By fall Roosevelt was negotiating with Foreign Affairs Commissar Maxim Litvinov the agreements which were exchanged on November 16. Catholics were understood to be opposed to recognition of the Soviet regime because of its militant atheism and persecution of religion. Alfred E. Smith and Frank P. Walsh among others took an opposite tack, but the *Central-Blatt and Social Justice* warned that the "resurrected hordes of Genghis Khan will put an end to European civilization."

Edmund A. Walsh, S.J., head since 1919 of Georgetown's School of Foreign Service, spearheaded the attack of the forces opposing recognition. Walsh headed the papal relief mission sent to Russia in 1922 and had subsequent high-level experience in Mexico and Iraq. He was first president of the Catholic Near East Welfare Association. His principal expressed reason for opposition to Roosevelt's plans was the Soviet goal of world revolution. Catholic papers, with James Gillis of the *Catholic World* and Patrick Scanlan of the *Brooklyn Tablet* in the van, pounded that theme and added the Soviets' militant atheism and record of persecution of Christians. Roosevelt met with Walsh in October and seems to have talked him over to his side. The November 16 agreements provided for Soviet abstention from propaganda and interference in American affairs—a promise promptly broken—and for freedom of worship for American citizens in the Soviet Union. Since then, American priests of the Assumptionist congregation have been stationed in Moscow. In the diplomacy of 1933 American Catholic protests had little effect, but seeds of suspicion about the tilt of the administration had been planted. Scanlan, Gillis, and many others were not satisfied by the November 16 exchange. More to their liking was the sharp condemnation of atheistic communism in Pius XI's encyclical letter *Divini Redemptoris,* issued on March 19, 1937, five days after the pope had taken on Naziism in another letter, *Mit brennender Sorge.*[58]

After a few years' peace, persecution of the church in Mexico resumed in the early 1930s.[59] An incident in July of 1934 provided fuel for American Catholic attacks on United States policy. Ambassador Josephus Daniels gave a speech in which he praised the contribution to rural education of former President Calles. The ambassador's relations with the Catholic Church had been cordial when he was Wilson's Secretary of the Navy but he now came under a torrent of abuse. Catholic newspapers, the Catholic Daughters of America, the Ancient Order of Hibernians, Holy Name societies by the dozen, the National Council of Catholic Women, and others deplored his praise of the notoriously anti-clerical Calles, who still held effective power in Mexico. In November, the bishops issued a pastoral letter detailing the extent of the persecution, which concluded:

> No man's voice should sound an uncertain note. We cannot but deplore the expressions unwittingly offered, at times, of sympathy with and support of governments and policies which are absolutely at variance with our own American principles. They give color to the boast of supporters of tyrannical policies, that the influence of our American government is favorable to such policies.[60]

If the American pubic and secular press had "fuller knowledge of the actual conditions in Mexico," the bishops wrote, they would realize that "we are pleading not only the cause of the Catholic Church, but the cause of human freedom and human liberty for all the nations of the world." But public opinion did not shift, and American Catholic criticism became more strident. Archbishop Curley of Baltimore was a vocal critic. The Knights of Columbus, headed by Supreme Knight Martin H. Carmody, mounted a vigorous campaign, with Carmody warning Roosevelt in October 1935 that he could not escape responsibility for failing to act on behalf of "bleeding Mexico." Others tried to achieve a sense of balance. Archbishop McNicholas publicly disavowed Carmody's claim to speak for "all Catholics"; Father John Burke and Auxiliary Bishop Francis J. Spellman of Boston, a newcomer to the national scene, became involved.

President John F. O'Hara, C.S.C., of Notre Dame, who was an expert in Latin American affairs, invited Roosevelt to accept an honorary degree at a convocation in December honoring the establishment of the Philippine Commonwealth. Cardinal Mundelein made it a point to attend and to praise the President. But the stridency of some Catholics on the one hand, and insensitivity to the problem on the part of the American government and general public on the other, were troubling factors.

The civil war which broke out in Spain in the summer of 1936 opened wide the division between Catholics and other Americans.[61] Popular Catholic feeling was not as one-sided as some thought, but support for Franco's Nationalists was virtually unanimous in nearly two hundred fifty Catholic publications in the United States and among bishops and opinion makers. The difference between Catholics and Protestants was notable. In a December 1938 Gallup poll, the findings were:

	Pro-Nationalist	Pro-Loyalist
Catholics	58%	42%
Protestants	17%	83%

Few Catholics openly favored the Madrid regime. One was Frank P. Walsh, head of the Lawyer's Committee for Loyalist Spain. George Flynn has pointed out Walsh's insistence that it was a secular matter and that he did not speak as a "Catholic layman." He wrote to a friend: "The idea that I should speak as a 'Catholic layman' or attempt to advise Catholics upon any matter or even to address them as such upon a public matter, is as abhorrent to me as it is to you."

Only two national publications had doubts about where Catholic support belonged. The *Catholic Worker* was both pacifist and wary of fascism. Pro-Nationalist Catholics pointed to the bloodbath in which, according to Hugh Thomas, 75,000 died in the summer of 1936 and a total of 85,940, including 7,937 bishops, priests, brothers, nuns, and seminarians, were murdered in Republican areas in the course of the war.[62] The *Catholic Worker* invited Catholics to look at a fascist country, like Hitler's Third Reich to "see just how much love the Catholic Church can expect" from such a regime. *Commonweal*, since 1924 a last representative of the once flourishing American Catholic tradition of independent lay journalism, argued the complexity of the situation and suffered financially for its pains. Editor George Shuster was forced out by his colleagues on the staff. "It now dawned on me," he said ruefully years later, "that for Catholic New York the world outside the United States was either Communist or Fascist, and that therefore they had opted for Fascism."[63] *Commonweal* did not undergo complete conversion to either side: one reason for the ouster in

1937 of founding editor Michael Williams was that he had involved the magazine's name in a pro-Franco rally at Madison Square Garden. Columbia University historian Carlton J. H. Hayes, one of a group of New York intellectuals who, if not pro-loyalist, were no more pro-Franco, played a leading part in Williams's exit.[64]

Far more typical was the holy war waged against "sovietized" and "red" Spanish Republicans by Gillis's *Catholic World* and Talbot's *America*. Right up to the eve of World War II, the fissure between Catholics and most other Americans continued to widen. On July 1, 1937, the Spanish bishops headed by their primate, Cardinal Isidoro Gomá y Tomás of Toledo, circulated a letter "to the Bishops of the Whole World." They were pro-Nationalists, they detailed martyrdoms at the hands of Republicans, and they claimed theological justification for a rebellion "to save the principles of religion." Only Cardinal Vidal y Balaguer of Tarragona in Catalonia and the Basque bishop of Vitoria, Mateo Mugica, refused to sign.[65] In October, one hundred fifty prominent Protestant Americans published a critical rejoinder to the Spanish bishops' effort to justify revolution against legitimate government. A week later, one hundred seventy-five Catholics responded, asking if the Protestant remonstrants really supported a government which persecuted Christians. On November 15, the American Catholic bishops in a joint letter to the Spanish hierarchy regretted that "some Christian leaders unwittingly have allowed themselves to be the sponsors of principles which, if given wide sway, would destroy the very last vestige of Western civilization."[66]

Incidents multiplied. Catholic funds for Spanish relief were channeled to Nationalist sources; other Americans gave to Loyalist charities. Plans to bring Basque children to the United States foundered on Catholic opposition. Massachusetts Senator David I. Walsh and Representative John McCormack agreed with Cardinal O'Connell that the anti-Franco Catholic Basques were being used as communist pawns. Attempts to lift the embargo on sale of arms to belligerents failed, to the chagrin of Interior Secretary Ickes and first lady Eleanor Roosevelt, and Catholic pressure was blamed. The rift with the eastern liberal establishment widened. Passions generated in debate over Spain left a residue of bitterness which strained the fragile entente which had been achieved between Catholics and other Americans in the early 1930s. The Catholic body itself became more of a monolith. There was discontent with the rightward shift—muted among New York intellectuals, open among Catholic Workers. But no one produced a protest to match the burning passion of anti-Nationalist Georges Bernanos's excoriation of the "hangmen of the so-called Spanish Crusade," or Jacques Maritain's denunciation of Nationalists who in religion's name murdered the poor, "the people of Christ." American Catholics continued to be perceived as uncomfortably comfortable with authoritarian solutions to the world's problems.[67]

One Catholic who made no secret of his preference for authoritarian solutions was radio priest Charles E. Coughlin, pastor of a suburban Detroit church, the Shrine of the Little Flower at Royal Oak, Michigan.[68] His audience peaked at ten million listeners; he had his own political organization, the National Union of Social Justice (1934), and his own newspaper, *Social Justice,* (1936), which was sold after Sunday masses outside churches across the country. As early as 1933, *Commonweal* worried about Coughlin's populist demagogy. George Shuster complained that "men who have studied least are listened to most." John A. Ryan wrote an article for *Catholic Charities Review* on "Quack Remedies for a Depression Malady."[69] And each Sunday afternoon, in millions of homes, life came to a standstill as radio sets were tuned to the mellifluous voice from Michigan. In the late twenties and early thirties, Coughlin was pro-labor and reformist, a New Deal supporter. But as he saw his inflationist remedies ignored he became increasingly the spokesman for the alienated middle class of small business people, property owners, and civil servants. Big business and high finance were the villains, the "godless capitalists, the Jews, Communists, international bankers and plutocrats." He moved away from the A. F. of L. and was hostile to the CIO, but retained a personal labor following. By 1936 he had formed a natural, but quite unhistorical, alliance with the kind of Protestant fundamentalists who had been the most bitter enemies of Roman Catholics throughout the nation's history. They discovered community in black-and-white mindsets which allowed no room for trifling differences, and in the need to find scapegoats for problems beyond their comprehension. American tradition allotted Catholics the scapegoat role. With Father Coughlin participating the script had to be changed. Jews and bankers filled the bill nicely.

After the 1936 presidential elections, in which he backed Union Party candidate William Lemke, with Thomas C. O'Brien of Massachusetts as vice-presidential running mate, Coughlin became increasingly anti-democratic. Attacks on Jews increased, although he stoutly denied being anti-Semitic. He was involved with the storm-trooper-like Christian Front, which began in 1938 and forced Richard Deverall's labor paper to a quick name-change. He found both strong opposition and strong support. Cardinal Hayes had Father Joseph N. Moody write a pamphlet debunking anti-Semitic canards of the kind being published in Coughlin's *Social Justice.*[70] Cardinal O'Connell could not abide Coughlin, but Mayor James Michael Curley, whose knowledge of Boston no one has ever denied, called it "the strongest Coughlinite city in America."[71] Brooklyn, with Scanlan's *Tablet* setting the pace, was another such center. A Gallup poll in 1938 found the following division on Coughlin:

	Approve	Disapprove	No Opinion
Protestants	19%	31%	50%
Catholics	42%	25%	33%
Jews	10%	63%	27%
No Religious Choice	19%	28%	53%[72]

Until the election of 1936, the radio priest enjoyed the tacit support of Innsbruck-educated Bishop Michael J. Gallagher of Detroit, a friend of Austrian Chancellors Ignaz Seipel and Englebert Dollfuss.[73] The atmosphere changed with Archbishop Mooney, who did not support the radio priest. Coughlin left the air briefly in 1937, then returned until government pressure forced him from public life after American entry into World War II.[74] In a sensitive coda, David O'Brien called him "one of the decade's most colorful and controversial figures and the most famous of the American 'social Catholics.' " Many who subsequently parted company with him testified that he had provided their first inspiration to social thought. "People today have no idea of Father Coughlin's impact in awakening the social conscience of America," was Richard Deverall's recollection.[75] The fears, prejudices, and insecurities he dredged up from the American Catholic subconscious are an important if dark side of the picture that emerges in their collective biography.

As war approached there was a large isolationist streak among American Catholics. There were pacifists also—Dorothy Day split the Catholic Worker movement in June 1940 by demanding adherence to that tenet—but it was not always easy to distinguish the two. John LaFarge at *America* believed that only "a physical attack on our shores justified involvement.[76] The New York *Catholic Worker* remained uncompromisingly pacifist and in 1941 sponsored a Catholic conscientious objector camp at Stoddard, New Hampshire. The five-hundred-member Catholic Association for International Peace worked to keep America out of war and to end war everywhere. They understood that greater access to and redistribution of world resources was the key.[77] Catholics had fought relaxation of neutrality laws in the case of the Spanish civil war embargo. They were generally not inclined to lower barriers for England once war broke out in September 1939.

Corporatist Edward Koch of *The Guildsman* was still looking forward to Axis victory and establishment of a "new Christian social order" as late as April 1941.[78] Non-intervention was advocated for a host of reasons. James Gillis and Fulton Sheen argued that Europe was paying for past sins.[79] Catholic congressmen were notably reluctant for the United States to become involved. Among the bishops, McNicholas, Curley, Francis J. Beckman of Dubuque, and Gerald Shaughnessy, S.M., of Seattle were leading isolationists. Catholics opposed the arms embargo, the 1940 Selective Training and Service Act, and the 1941 Lend-Lease Act. Roosevelt sought Vatican help in dealing with American Catholic anti-communism, a problem with respect to the alliance he was forging with the Soviets.[80] This Catholic opposition was not unanimous. On the other side, Alfred E. Smith was persuaded to give a speech to try to break down Irish prejudice against the British.[81] Archbishop Lucey and John A. Ryan were charter members of the Committee to Defend America by Aiding the Allies. Bishops Edwin V. O'Hara, Joseph P. Hurley of St. Augustine, and James H. Ryan of Omaha, as well as Archbishop Schrembs of Cleveland, supported Roosevelt's actions. Cardinal Mundelein was his strongest ally. Mundelein died in October 1939, a day after completing work with presidential adviser Thomas G. Corcoran on a pro-administration radio address. Bishop Bernard Sheil delivered it for him.[82]

Roosevelt found a strong new ally in Francis J. Spellman, Hayes's successor as archbishop of New York and ecclesiastical superior of Roman Catholic chaplains in the armed forces.[83] The archbishop provided words used by the President at the first drawing in the new draft lottery on October 29, 1940: "We really cannot longer afford to be moles who cannot see, or ostriches who will not see."[84] A year later, Germany had invaded the Soviet Union and gallons of ink had been spilled over Lend-Lease to the Soviets. While Roosevelt assured Stalin that a billion dollars' worth was on the way, the bishops issued a letter on "The Crisis of Christianity." They condemned Nazism and Communism, repeated Pius XII's call for peace and, "recognizing the liberty of discussion and even of criticism" guaranteed by democracy, urged "respect and reverence for the authority of our civil officials, which has its source in God."[85]

Two weeks after Pearl Harbor, Archbishop Mooney wrote President Roosevelt in the name of the bishops to pledge "wholehearted cooperation" with the war effort. Roosevelt replied:

> We shall win the war and in victory we shall not seek vengeance but the establishment of an international order in which the spirit of Christ shall rule the hearts of men and of nations.[86]

The bishops' joint letter in 1942 spoke of the "positive duty of a nation to wage war in the defense of life and right." "Our nation," they continued, "now finds itself in such circumstances." They condemned the "premeditated and systematic extermination" of subjugated peoples like the Poles, and declared their "deep sense of revulsion against the cruel indignities heaped upon the Jews in conquered countries and upon defenseless people not of our faith."[87]

By 1943 the bishops had turned their attention to "The Essentials of a Good Peace." Proclaiming the primacy of divine sovereignty and moral law, they discussed the needs of young people and of families and then the "Constitutional Rights of the Black Man":

> We owe it to these fellow citizens, who have contributed so largely to the development of our country, and for whose welfare history imposes on us a special obligation of justice, to see that they have in fact the rights which are given them in our Constitution. This means not only political equality, but also fair economic and educational opportunities, a just share in public welfare projects, good housing without exploitation, and a full chance for the social advancement of their race.

"When given their rights in fact as in law," the bishops said, black Americans "will prize with us our national heritage and not lend ear to agitators whose real objective is not to improve but to destroy our way of living." After urging priests and people to "a neighborhood spirit of justice and reconciliation," the letter—with an eye to conditions spotlighted by the June Zoot-suit riots in Los Angeles—turned to the needs of Spanish-speaking Americans:

> They also have a right to expect the full enjoyment of our democratic institutions and that help in social life which is accorded to others. . . . The sincerity of our Good Neighbor Policy . . . will be attested by our attitude toward our fellow citizens of Latin-American origin or descent.[88]

The 1944 letter urged elimination of hatred and greed and attention to principles enunciated in the 1941 Atlantic Charter. It closed by quoting Roosevelt's "we shall not seek vengeance" letter to the bishops in the days after Pearl Harbor.[89] By 1945 a pessimistic note sounded. "The war is over, but there is no peace in the world." The pattern emerging from big-power conferences was "disappointing in the extreme." It represented compromise without a plan. "Profound differences in thought and policy between Russia and the Western democracies" must be faced. The Soviets were gobbling up eastern and southeastern Europe, their Asian policy was an enigma. The bishops had reservations about the United Nations, where permanent Security Council members had "a status above the law." They also pleaded for mercy for defeated enemies:

> The inhumanities which now mark the mass transference of populations, the systematized use of slave labor, and the cruel treatment of prisoners of war should have no place in our civilization.[90]

Archbishop Mooney's December 22, 1941, letter to President Roosevelt promised that, "with a patriotism that is guided and sustained by the Christian virtues of faith, hope and charity," the bishops would "marshal the spiritual forces at our command to render secure our God-given blessings of freedom." The personal contribution of American Catholics was considerable. Estimates put Catholic members of the armed forces in the war years at between 25 and 35 percent of the total. Between Pearl Harbor and VJ Day, 3,036 military chaplains saw service.[91] Among 11,887 conscientious objectors, there were 135 Catholics, some of them assigned to forestry camps at Stoddard and Warner, New Hampshire, sponsored by the Catholic Workers' Association of Catholic Conscientious Objectors.[92]

On Christmas Eve of 1939, Franklin D. Roosevelt wrote Pope Pius XII that "it would give me great satisfaction to send to you my personal representative in order that our parallel endeavors for peace and the alleviation of suffering may be assisted."[93] A link was restored which had been broken in 1868, when "Black Republicans" embarassed President Andrew Johnson and insulted Pope Pius IX by refusing to appropriate funds to maintain the United States minister-resident at the papal court. Roosevelt was sensitive to the mixed feelings which his action would evoke. He sent similar messages of concern, but no special representative, to President George A. Buttrick of the Federal Council of Churches and President Cyrus Adler of Jewish Theological Seminary. The personal representative who arrived in Rome in February 1940 was Myron C. Taylor, a Protestant and retired board chairman of U.S. Steel who held the Vatican post until 1950. He visited the Vatican periodically, and from 1941 to 1944 his assistant, Harold H. Tittman, lived in Vatican City with formal diplomatic rank as chargé d'affaires.[94] Pope and President corresponded throughout the war.[95]

Taylor was unpaid; the mission's expenses were met from a special White House fund. Roosevelt gave him the rank of ambassador "for social purposes," but did not submit the nomination to the Senate. At the Vatican Taylor was, with minor differences, treated as a diplomat. Roosevelt insisted that he was not. The appointment caused the inevitable stir in the United States. Opponents were unable to comprehend the Holy See's special status in international law, which was established at the 1815 Congress of Vienna, and presented arguments out of their own absolutist interpretation of the non-establishment clause of the First Amendment to the Constitution. Most Catholics were less doctrinaire about the First Amendment, although equally without understanding the diplomatic fine points. As late as 1948, even Archbishop McNicholas could be found using quite irrelevant arguments from the British king's status in the Anglican Church and from the pope's civil sovereignty over Vatican City State to defend the arrangement.[96] One who paved the way for the Taylor mission was Francis J. Spellman. Returning home in 1932 after a seven-year stint in the papal secretariat of state, he became archbishop of New

York in the spring of 1939. Together with Bishops John F. O'Hara, C.S.C., and William T. McCarty, C.Ss.R., he superintended the religious work of chaplains in the armed forces and began a career of visits to the armed forces overseas that ended only with his death in 1967.[97]

Those services which had in World War I been largely provided by the YMCA, the Salvation Army, and the Knights of Columbus, fell to the United Service Organizations (USO), which in 1941 included among its constitutive associations the National Catholic Community Service. Other service organizations were formed. As far back as 1934, there had been a Catholic Committee for Refugees and Refugee Children. In 1940 the bishops formed the War Relief and Emergency Committee, and in 1942 the War Relief Services of the NCWC was established, to care for the needs of refugees, stateless persons, the needy in unoccupied Allied countries, merchant seamen, and Axis prisoners of war. In 1955 it became Catholic Relief Services, an organization which in the twenty years following the decade and a half of depression and war had distributed more than $1.25 billion in relief supplies throughout the world.[98]

XX

Cross and Flag

For the Catholic community in the United States, World War II was another in a long series of rites of passage. Catholic patriotism was unalloyed. Church leaders supplied encouragement. For San Diego Bishop Charles F. Buddy, "the cross and the flag" were the "highest symbols of glory."[1] Three weeks after II Corps's disaster at Kasserine Pass, Archbishop Spellman was in Tunisia to reassure the troops that they were "the sacred instruments of the triumph of our cause," and that "in serving your country in a just cause, you are also serving God."[2] Although the reservations of some persisted—Bishop O'Hara of the "Army and Navy Diocese" would not participate in "public conferences with Protestants and Jews"[3]—the war years saw the effective beginning of the acceptance of religious pluralism later analyzed by Will Herberg.[4] The high moral pitch deliberately cultivated by President Roosevelt contributed. Spokesmen for religious groups cooperated. Fulton J. Sheen, a popular radio orator since the early 1930s, declared that the war was not primarily a political or economic struggle against the Axis, but "a theological one," in which the enemy was "anti-Christ."[5] The bishops' joint statement, "Victory and Peace," issued in November 1942, pictured the United States as allied "in deadly conflict" against nations "united in waging war to bring about a slave world—a world that would deprive man of his divinely conferred dignity, reject human freedom and permit no religious liberty."[6] Remarkably similar examples of religious-patriotic rhetoric issued from Protestant and Jewish sources. Differing traditions had found a common theme.

Seeds of future schism were, however, already in the ground. Such

Catholic apologists for the Roosevelt administration as Postmaster General Frank C. Walker, Wyoming Senator Joseph C. O'Mahoney, and Supreme Court Justice Frank Murphy could not wholly set at rest the uneasiness among Catholics over the Soviet alliance. The Vatican's unyielding anti-communist stance fueled ancient British antipathies to Rome and was grist for the mill of American liberals always leery of papists. The Holy See's establishment of diplomatic relations with Japan in February 1942, during the high tide of Japanese Pacific conquest, compounded the problem and weakened Vatican influence with the Allies.

Soviet armies moved westward in 1943 and 1944, bringing in their wake persecution of Latin-rite Catholics and forcible incorporation of eastern-rite Catholic jurisdictions into the Orthodox Church.[7] American Catholics grew increasingly apprehensive concerning the political and religious fate of Poles, Lithuanians, and other peoples behind the Iron Curtain. The bishops' letter of 1945 reflected that anxiety. The 1946 letter too was set against the background of "the conflict between Russia and the West which has so long delayed the making of peace." Concerns expressed included the Soviet totalitarianism which had replaced that of the Nazis, inhumane treatment of POWs and DPs, deportations, and the "ruthless herding of uprooted people."[8] Religious persecution remained a festering sore. Within five years of VE Day the names of Alojzije Stepinac, Jozsef Mindszenty, Josef Beran, and Josyf Slipyi—Croatian, Hungarian, Czech, and Ukrainian bishops—were linked in a new litany of martyrs venerated by American Catholics.

Addressing the Catholic Association for International Peace in 1956, inventor, industrialist, and prominent Catholic layman Thomas E. Murray, a member of the Atomic Energy Commission, denounced the "totalization of war" practiced by the Allies during World War II. For Murray it was immoral, "a regression toward barbarism." He had in mind three policies: obliteration bombing, the demand for unconditional Axis surrender agreed to at the 1943 Casablanca conference, and the atomic bombing of Hiroshima and Nagasaki.[9] These were areas in which Catholic moral tradition challenged prevailing American assumptions. Opinions were by no means unanimous, but strong currents questioning the nation's posture ran through the Catholic community. A year before the war ended, John C. Ford, S.J. published a negative analysis of "The Morality of Obliteration Bombing."[10] He later concluded a similarly negative treatment of "The Hydrogen Bombing of Cities" with the dictum, couched in the clinical jargon of Catholic moralists, that "no proportionate reason can be assigned for 'permitting' the extinction of the human race."[11]

It was reported that 53.5 percent of Americans approved of the bombing of Hiroshima and Nagasaki, and the American bishops and most diocesan papers remained silent on the subject. Most leading Catholic journals, however, reacted negatively.[12] *America* waffled, claiming that the moral issues were too complex for quick judgments, but Dorothy Day's perception was sharp and clear: "We have created destruction."[13] In a rare display of agreement *Commonweal* and Patrick Scanlan's *Brooklyn Tablet* joined in criticism. At the *Catholic World,* editor James M. Gillis, C.S.P. thought the United States responsible for "the most powerful blow ever delivered against Christian civilization and moral law."[14]

Distinctive Catholic attitudes were discernible in other areas. Three months before the first Allied bombs fell on Rome, a national sample in the spring of 1943 indicated that 37 percent of Americans would approve of the bombing as a military measure, as against 24 percent of Catholic Americans.[15] In the following year, two months before the Allies would level the ancient Benedictine abbey on Monte Cassino, a poll showed three-quarters of the population approving the bombing of historic buildings and cities on military say-so, but the approval rate among Catholic respondents was somewhat lower, with 64 percent in favor and 28 percent opposed.[16] A more profound division was exposed by reaction to both the Casablanca conference's demand in January 1943 for unconditional Axis surrender, and the tenor of plans for postwar reconstruction originating at the meeting of American, British, and Soviet foreign ministers at Moscow in October.

Roosevelt's good friend, Archbishop Spellman, was becoming apprehensive. He could not see how unconditional surrender would lead to the "peace with justice" of which Pius XII so often spoke. The near-starvation conditions existing in Italy under the military rule of the Allied Control Commission seemed a harbinger of worse to come, especially when in the fall of 1943 Secretary of State Cordell Hull and Foreign Economic Administrator Leo T. Crowley called Spellman home from a battlefront trip to add his influence on the side of the starving Italians.[17]

Crowley, who directed the Lend-Lease program for the final two years of the war and had often been Roosevelt's go-between with Catholic bishops, was also involved in the aftermath of Treasury Secretary Henry Morgenthau's plan to dismember Germany and turn it into a primarily agricultural and pastoral country. The President and Churchill had initialed this plan at their September 1944 meeting in Québec, but within a month Roosevelt had reconsidered. Morgenthau's diary records that Crowley was then asked to work out his own economic policy for Germany.[18] The treasury secretary's diary indicates that fears were growing in some circles about the extent and nature of Catholic influence in the postwar European settlement. Doubts were cast on the effectiveness of diplomats who were Catholics, like Robert D. Murphy and James Dunn.[19] Mrs.

Roosevelt let it be known to Morgenthau and the President that she thought it was a mistake to send a Catholic as adviser to the military government in Germany.[20] Powerful forces in the liberal wing of Roosevelt's coalition feared disruption of their plans for Europe's future. Antagonisms were being revived that would persist well into postwar years.

While these matters of European policy were being debated, Franklin Delano Roosevelt signed on June 22, 1944, the "Servicemen's Readjustment Act," the "GI Bill of Rights." Its impact on American Catholic community has been permanent. Subsistence allowance, tuition, and supplies would help veterans to take advantage of educational opportunities. One of the great levelling processes in American history was under way, and its effects were greatly felt among Roman Catholics. By 1952, some 7,600,000 World War II veterans, about one-half of those eligible, had received some form of education or training under the act. Catholics attended universities in unprecedented numbers. A second element helping to effect major change in the community was the impact of financial and status gains which labor had made during the New Deal years. A study reported by Liston Pope in 1948 suggested that "Catholicism has more middle-class members than popular generalizations have assumed."[21] Upward mobility in education, financial standing, and occupation noted by later investigators was already well established in the immediate postwar years.

The equally massive influx of GIs who chose to attend Catholic colleges and universities permanently changed the style of virtually all those institutions. Traditional seminary-type discipline crumbled. Its absence was cheered or mourned, but rarely compensated for by fresh and distinctively Catholic approaches. Many administrators failed to comprehend that university-level education not only demanded such expensive facilities as research libraries and laboratories, but was also basically non-self-supporting. Catholic intellectual (as opposed to pietistic) identity was in most institutions tenuous at best, as Robert M. Hutchins told the midwest regional unit of the National Catholic Educational Association in 1937.[22] As a consequence of reckless postwar expansion, the flickering identities of unendowed schools were extinguished. Reliance on tuition, low faculty salaries, large-scale exclusion of lay people from administrative positions, and the unpaid service of men and women members of religious communities staved off the inevitable for a time; but by the mid-sixties, the church's education establishment had awakened to find that it had, in varying degrees and with some exceptions, secularized American Catholic higher education in return for government subsidy.

From 1940 to 1960 the Catholic community grew from twenty-one million to an astounding forty-two million members. It flourished, in Robert

Handy's words, "in the genial atmosphere of religious revival."[23] The birth rate was high, immigrants joined the church, converts were numerous. American religion's Indian summer, the Eisenhower years (1953–61), featured the dramatic popularization of religious philosophy by Fulton J. Sheen, television's first significant Catholic star. Thousands read his books—*Peace of Soul* (1949) and the five-volume *Life Is Worth Living* (1953–57) among them. Fulton Oursler had died in 1952; his *The Greatest Story Ever Told* and *The Greatest Book Ever Written* remained popular. Thomas Merton's *The Seven Storey Mountain* (1948) introduced Americans and most American Catholics to an exceptional religious writer and poet and to the life of the Trappist monks.

Handy has noted among Catholics in the postwar years less tendency to the social activism that had marked the 1930s, although Catholic Worker groups flourished. There was greater emphasis on biblical and theological reading, and a small but active liturgical movement prospered.[24] Publications multiplied. *Commonweal* was in the hands of a new generation of Irish-Americans, replacing the Ivy League founders. Prominent Catholic publications included the *Register* chain of Catholic weeklies, begun by Denver priest Matthew Smith, and *Our Sunday Visitor,* founded in 1912 by John F. Noll, who from 1925 to 1956 was Bishop of Fort Wayne. Noll also wrote the enormously popular pamphlet, *Father Smith Instructs Jackson,* widely used in convert work and in religious correspondence courses. Diocesan papers multiplied, but few had the spice of the *Brooklyn Tablet,* edited by the redoubtable Patrick Scanlan. In the midwest, the German *Der Wanderer* had become the conservative English weekly, *The Wanderer,* still published by the Matt family. New Catholic periodicals appeared, all of them in tune with contemporary theological movements: *Integrity, Cross Currents, Jubilee.*

One of the classic statements about American Catholic bishops was made at the ninth annual convention of the CIO, opening in Boston on October 13, 1947. Archbishop Richard J. Cushing announced:

> In all the American hierarchy, resident in the United States, there is not known to me one bishop, archbishop or cardinal whose father or mother was a college graduate. Every one of our bishops and archbishops is the son of a working man and working man's wife.[25]

A decade later, Boston College sociologist John D. Donovan's scientific study substantially supported Cushing's generalization. Donovan found in 1957 that 5 percent of the bishops' fathers were college graduates and another 5 percent had attended college. Over 50 percent fell into the occupational categories of small businessmen, clerks, salesmen, foremen, or minor executives, 27 percent owned their own small businesses, and 17 percent were unskilled laborers. As against 1897, when 66% of the bishops were foreign-born and 1927, when 23 percent were foreign-born, 96% of the 1957 American bishops were native-born Americans, nearly three-quarters of them from the more heavily Catholic northeastern and north central sections of the country.[26]

The principal national figure among the bishops until his death in 1967 was Archbishop Spellman of New York, close personal associate of Pius XII, who named him cardinal in 1946, and friend of Presidents from Roosevelt to Johnson. His Christmas trips to United States forces abroad became an annual tradition. He became involved in United Nations negotiations concerning the future of Palestine, and was known for strong and frequently expressed anti-communist views. Though he was a published author and a poet, he rarely preached in his cathedral. One of his few appearances in the pulpit of St. Patrick's was to condemn the movie *Baby Doll* in 1956. Five years earlier he had been involved in the argument over the "sacrilegious" nature of Roberto Rossellini's film, *The Miracle* which ended in the Supreme Court's decision that New York state censors could not ban films on that ground.

There were other national figures. The church of Chicago knew a cultivated leader during the nineteen years (1939–58) when Nashville-born Samuel A. Stritch was archbishop. He died in Rome, where he had gone to take up an appointment as head of the Vatican's Congregation for Propagation of the Faith. Boston's Cardinal O'Connell had been succeeded in 1944 by Richard J. Cushing, who for over a quarter-century built an unsurpassed reputation for charitable benefactions throughout the United States and abroad. He founded the Missionary Society of St. James the Apostle, as association of diocesan priests who serve in Latin America. Cushing received his cardinal's hat from Pope John XXIII in 1958. He became nationally prominent during the brief presidency of John F. Kennedy (1961–63); he delivered the inaugural invocation from a smoking rostrum and presided at the assassinated President's funeral in Washington's St. Matthew's Cathedral.

Cardinal Mooney (he received the title in 1946) died in 1958, after twenty-one eventful years as archbishop of Detroit. Farther west, Joseph E. Ritter succeeded Cardinal Glennon at St. Louis in 1946. He too became a cardinal, in 1961. An outspoken progressive, he pioneered in school desegregation. Asked for guidance in the spring of 1947 by the Loretto sisters at Webster College, he returned a straightforward answer: "Admit any qualified Catholic student, irrespective of color."[27] He established that policy for all Catholic schools with a directive issued the following August, and in September the archbishop warned dissidents that they risked excommunication if they opposed the policy by court action.

In Philadelphia, John F. O'Hara, C.S.C. was made cardinal by John XXIII in 1958, having succeeded Dougherty in 1951. O'Hara, former Notre Dame president, had become Bishop of Buffalo after serving with the Military Ordinariate during World War II. His tenure in Philadelphia lasted until 1960, two years after he became cardinal. O'Hara was vitally interested in the growth of Philadelphia's school system. A notable economic conservative, he supported William F. Buckley, Jr., in founding the *National Review*. At the same time, O'Hara was proud of and strongly supported the efforts of Dennis J. Comey, S.J., founder of St. Joseph's College Institute of Industrial Relations and since 1952 impartial arbitrator of labor disputes in the port of Philadelphia.[28]

Baltimore, which was always the political center of the Catholic Church in the United States, had receded in influence after the death in 1921 of Cardinal Gibbons. His successor, Michael J. Curley, was given the additional title of archbishop of Washington in 1939. When he died in 1947, jurisdiction was divided. Francis P. Keough came from Providence to Baltimore, and a New York priest with an extensive social-work background, Patrick A. O'Boyle, became Archbishop of Washington. During World War II, he had been executive director of NCWC's War Relief Services. Made a cardinal in 1967, he retired as archbishop in 1973.

Elsewhere in the country, Robert E. Lucey, noted for his efforts in social reform and race relations, was archbishop of San Antonio from 1941 until he retired in 1969. Joseph F. Rummel spent twenty-nine years (1935–64) as archbishop of New Orleans. Two bishops were considered scholarly leaders in the church: Fulton J. Sheen, national director since 1950 of the Society for Propagation of the Faith and briefly (1966–69) bishop of Rochester, and Boston-born John J. Wright, bishop of Worcester and then of Pittsburgh before becoming a cardinal and head in 1969 of the Roman Congregation of the Clergy, charged with supervision of priests throughout the world. On the west coast, the first cardinal was James Francis A. McIntyre, who had left a career on Wall Street to enter the seminary. After eight years as assistant to Archbishop Spellman, he became archbishop of Los Angeles in 1948 and cardinal in 1953. He retired in 1970.

In the last years of Pius XII (pope from 1939 to 1958), the Catholic community prospered in the United States. Between 1912 and 1963, the country's Catholic population had nearly tripled, from 15,015,569 to 43,851,538. Between 1954 and 1963, almost half of this increase was accomplished—over twelve million. Reflecting on the state of the church of Philadelphia at Cardinal Dougherty's death, Hugh Nolan has painted a nostalgic but accurate picture:

The Catholics of that era were a joyous group positive of their identity, proud of their church and of their priests and of their schools. There
was a truly strong parish spirit. Most Catholics in a parish knew one
another: the school pulled the parishioners close together as the children
played and competed together on the various parish teams; parishioners
often socialized together and in many instances their children intermarried. Most parents wanted to give their children a better education than
they themselves had, and greatly preferred the Catholic colleges. . . . [29]

Seminaries and convent motherhouses blossomed across the nation to
handle large numbers of applicants. The silent Trappists peaked at over
one thousand monks and nuns in 1956. The summer of 1956 saw 408
young men begin their training as Jesuits. By 1965 their religious order
had 8393 American members, nearly a quarter of its world membership,
and 900 of these Americans were serving as the largest single contingent
from their country in missions overseas. Other communities experienced
similar development. In 1954 there were 158,069 religious sisters, the
mainstay of the church's extensive system of schools, hospitals, and charitable institutions. Their numerical peak year was 1965, when they totaled
181,421. The 8,752 religious brothers of 1954 had grown to 12,539 by
1966. Seminarians increased from 32,344 in 1954 to 48,992 in 1964. The
46,970 priests of 1954 had become 59,892 by 1966.[30]

The Catholic community in these halcyon days was increasingly better
educated, but not particularly well organized nationally. Monsignor
George Higgins and Father John F. Cronin, S.S., carried on the tradition
of NCWC's social action department, but with not quite the impact of
their predecessors in the 1930s. "In matters of social and political movement," Thomas McAvoy has commented, "the Catholic body was generally inert."[31] The causes that did stir it were few: anti-communism, Catholic education, birth control. Sociologists reported Catholic church attendance high. A national sample by the University of Michigan Survey
Research Center in 1957 found 67 percent of Catholic men and 75 percent
of Catholic women attending mass regularly, and another 14 percent and
13 percent respectively, attending often.[32] National Opinion Research
Center staffers concluded that Catholic church attendance ran at about
70 percent.[33] A survey carried in the *Catholic Digest* in 1953 found strong
evidence of personal devoutness and acceptance of church teachings. Only in two areas were the percentages of those agreeing with standard
teaching appreciably lower: while 99 percent believed in the existence of
God, 89 percent in Christ's divinity, and 85 percent in personal immortal-
ity, only 51 percent accepted that divorced persons who remarried were
"living in sin," or that "mechanical birth control" was wrong.[34] A significant change occurred with the population shift to suburbia. New parish

and school structures had to be worked out, as a third dimension was added to the urban and rural Catholic polities that had developed since the days when the community was restricted to rural Maryland, Pennsylvania, and Virginia and the single city parish in Philadelphia. An organization helpful in bridging the gap was the flourishing Christian Family Movement, which in 1957 claimed twenty-five thousand units located in one hundred fifty dioceses and in all but six states.[35]

A pervasive moralism characterized American Catholics of the 1950s. What William Clebsch has described as the concern for "living rightly . . . the quest for a clean heart"[36] promoted religious privatism in a professedly communitarian church. Moral theology, curiously immune to the influence of Christian history and dogma and heavily influenced by the legalistic approach of canonists and the abstractions of scholastic philosophers, dominated the scene. On the popular level, long lines at Saturday afternoon and evening confessions gave impressive witness to the phenomenon. Legalism, too, loomed large, reflected in and assisted by the willingness of churchmen (Pius XII in the van) to legislate the tiniest minutiae of church observance. Moralism was confused with religiousness, ethics with theology. Efforts at promoting specifically community worship were inspired by the liturgical periodical *Orate Fratres* (it became *Worship* in 1951), but individualistic Christianity still predominated among American Catholics.

Postwar upward mobility among Catholics was notable in the legal and medical professions and in business generally. Corresponding growth of a religiously informed lay leadership was not so noticeable. Frank Murphy, an Associate Justice from 1940 to 1949, was the Supreme Court's sole Catholic between the 1939 death of arch-conservative Pierce Butler and the appointment in 1956 of William J. Brennan, Jr. Four Catholic cabinet members served under Truman and two under Eisenhower. Legislators who were Catholics included Senators Brien McMahon of Connecticut, chairman of the Joint Committee on Atomic Energy until his death in 1952; Patrick A. McCarran of Nevada, who gave his name to the 1950 Internal Security Act and the 1952 Immigration and Nationality Act; Dennis Chávez of New Mexico; and Robert F. Wagner, Sr., author of the Railroad Retirement Act (1935), the National Labor Relations Act (1936), and the National Housing Act (1937). Wagner served New York in the Senate from 1927 to 1949; he became a Catholic in 1946 and died in 1953.

Under executive order from President Harry S. Truman, the federal government began in the summer of 1947 a "loyalty check" of its employees. Nearly five million investigations were conducted with meager results, but the season of anti-communist purge had opened, punctuated by spy trials,

prosecution of Communist Party leaders under the Smith Act and passage over Truman's veto of the McCarran Act in 1950, which demanded registration of communist and communist-front organizations, forbade employment of communists in defense-related industry, and provided for their internment in time of national emergency. The Berlin blockade and airlift (1948), loss by Chiang Kai-shek in 1949 of China's mainland and the subsequent expulsion or imprisonment of foreign missionaries, including Americans, by the new regime there, and the outbreak of war in Korea in 1950 heightened tensions.[37]

In the atmosphere of cold war Catholic credentials looked impeccable. Even before the Teheran and Yalta conferences they had been apprehensive about the Russian alliance. The plight of co-religionists in eastern Europe forcused that apprehension. In his first magazine article after receiving the cardinal's *galero* at Rome in February 1946, Francis J. Spellman had announced that "Communism Is Unamerican," and promised that he would engage in "no conspiracy of silence" on the subject.[38] In this he was one with Pope Pius XII, for whom coexistence with bolshevism was out of the question. During the heyday of Christian Democratic governments in Western Europe, the pope became a strong advocate of the NATO collective security approach. His 1956 Christmas message deprecated suggestions of dialogue with the Communist east:

> What is the use of discussion without a common language? And can it be useful when the interlocutors have neither objectives nor moral values accepted by the two parties; which excludes any form of co-existence in security?[39]

On the home front, deteriorating relations among former allies once more exposed divisions between Catholics and the eastern liberal establishment. In less than a year, New York Catholics raised $4 million—twice the amount needed—to finance Archbishop Stepinac High School in White Plains, named for the Croatian bishop imprisoned in Tito's Yugoslavia on charges of wartime collaboration with the Axis. For Spellman, the archbishop's sole crime was "fidelity to God and country."[40] The National Council of Catholic Women asked the secretary of state to intercede for the "saintly" Stepinac, victimized by Yugoslavia's "atheistic communistic forces." Mrs. Eleanor Roosevelt, chairman of the American Committee for Yugoslav Relief, wrote in response to a request for help: "I am sorry but I fear that I cannot help you as you suggest. I understand the Archbishop took part in political affairs and the government now in power has jurisdiction in such matters."[41]

Mass rallies and other actions on behalf of persecuted Catholics behind the Iron Curtain continued. New York Jesuits named a school on Koror

Island in the Carolines after Hungary's Cardinal Mindszenty and three thousand Fordham University students joined in public recitation of the rosary on a day of prayer set aside for him by Cardinal Spellman.[42] The Catholic War Veterans and the Knights of Columbus were particularly active anti-communists, as was Fulton Sheen in his lectures and in books like *Communism and the Conscience of the West* and *Philosophy of Religion,* both published in 1948,

Catholic anti-communism was not limited to the political front. The ACTU had since its origin in 1937 been concerned with communist influence in labor unions. In the mid-forties it had concentrated largely on that issue. Philip Murray and John Brophy led the movement to expel communist-dominated unions from the CIO in 1949–50. The more than one hundred Catholic labor schools in the United States prepared union members to contest control of their locals with communists and labor racketeers. The 1954 film *On the Waterfront* spotlighted the ministry to New York longshoremen of Jesuits Philip A. Carey and John M. Corridan of lower Manhattan's Xavier Labor School.[43]

Catholic periodicals and newspapers were unanimous in the anti-communist crusade, even though Patrick Scanlan's *Tablet* and *Commonweal* differed in their reasons and in the remedies they contemplated. According to sociologist Joseph Fichter:

> The crucial difference between conservative and liberal Catholics has been their stance on moral intervention in society. The conservatives want a hands-off policy, arguing that civil rights, social welfare, public housing, minimum wages are *political* matters outside the scope of religious authorities. Liberal Catholics, of course, believe that these are all moral problems about which church people should be deeply concerned.[44]

Catholicism's public face during New Deal years by and large smiled on liberal programs, even if frowns were occasionally seen in some quarters. Conservatives, however, were now more influential. Liberal Catholics argued from the corpus of Catholic social thought and shaded their arguments with the latest developments in French theology. They were also conscious of the main emphases of Western liberal thinking. *Commonweal* staffer William Clancy claimed for them an identity as

> a type of Catholic whose world-view is marked by an enthusiastic acceptance of certain ideals for which liberalism has waged its great battles— maximum human freedom under law, social progress, and democratic equality.[45]

Louis Francis Budenz was a popular lecturer on communism, and one with special credentials. Born a Catholic, from 1935 to 1945 he had belonged to the Communist Party and edited the party's newspaper, the *Daily Worker*. Monsignor Fulton Sheen reconciled him with the church and Fordham University gave him a faculty appointment. In the spring of 1950 he told the Tydings subcommittee of the Senate Foreign Relations Committee of his belief that Johns Hopkins Professor Owen Lattimore, a specialist in far eastern affairs, had been a party member. Budenz made capital of his Catholicism as evidence of *bona fides*. Not all Catholics were convinced. Declaring that "my ancestors brought the cross to this hemisphere; Louis Budenz has been using it as a club," New Mexico's Senator Chávez denounced his testimony against Lattimore as unfair and untrue. Father George Higgins of the NCWC seconded the senator, urging that Budenz make it clear that the Catholic Church was not "a sort of international FBI," and that its opposition to communism was coupled with "a radical program of social justice." Others reacted differently. Chávez was tagged by some as a "bad Catholic" and himself under communist influence. Fordham's president called him a "modern Pharisee." The Los Angeles archdiocesan paper rebuked him for abetting "the joyous howls of all the atheistic conspirators."[46]

The bishops' annual letter dated November 18, 1951, "God's Law: The Measure of Man's Conduct," pilloried moral corruption in American life and prescribed strong remedies for the restoration of the nation's moral tone. The statement was widely reprinted in the secular press and won praise from Protestant religious leaders. Presbyterian Stated Clerk Eugene Carson Blake lauded a "forthright and able contribution . . . at this time of alarming moral slackness." *Christian Century* commented: "Sophisticates can sneer the bishops' statement does not rise above the a-b-c's of morality. . . . That may be its greatest significance—that the times call for getting back to the a-b-c's."[47] A passage under the heading "Morality and Politics" came in for special attention:

> Those who are selected for office by their fellow men are entrusted with grave responsibilities. They have been selected not for self-enrichment but for conscientious public service. In their speech and in their actions they are bound by the same laws of justice and charity which bind private individuals in every other sphere of human activity. Dishonesty, slander, detraction, and defamation of character are as truly transgressions of God's commandments when resorted to by men in political life as they are for all other men.[48]

It is difficult not to see in the final sentence a reference to the manifestly un-Christian political style of the junior United States senator from Wisconsin, Joseph R. McCarthy.[49]

McCarthy, a lifelong practicing Catholic and a graduate of Marquette

University, was innocent of any apparent knowledge of the church's social teaching. His style was populist; he was a consummate pragmatist. In
a 1946 Republican primary he had ended the career of veteran Wisconsin
Senator Robert M. LaFollette, Jr.[50] A speech to the Wheeling, West
Virginia, Republican Women's Club on February 9, 1950, brought Mc-
Carthy to the national scene with charges that the State Department was
infiltrated with communists and their dupes, two hundred five of them.
The traitors were "bright young men who are born with silver spoons in
their mouth," favored with the "finest homes, the finest college educa-
tions, and the finest jobs in the government that we can give."[51] For the
next five years, in senate hearings, lectures, and radio and television
appearances, he pursued Americans he deemed subversive. His style was
aptly described by Auxiliary Bishop Bernard J. Sheil of Chicago to an
audience of United Auto Workers as "a monstrous perversion of morality" to justify "lies, calumny, the absence of charity and calculated de-
ceit" in the name of anti-communism.[52] McCarthy was long on charges,
and free in publicizing them, but short on facts and documentation.

Owen Lattimore was the first individual target. McCarthy produced
Louis Budenz as his star witness before the Tydings subcommittee.
Charges against the State Department and Lattimore were dismissed, but
there was fallout. Maryland Senator Millard E. Tydings had survived a
"purge" attempt by the redoubtable Franklin Delano Roosevelt. He was
defeated for reelection in the same year in which his committee labeled
Joseph Raymond McCarthy a fraud and a liar. The legend of the Wisconsin
senator's national power grew as other opponents fell by the wayside,
although closer political analysis has suggested that the picture was not as
simple as it seemed.[53]

McCarthy's targets included Adlai Stevenson during his 1952 run for
the presidency against Dwight D. Eisenhower, the Democratic party for
"twenty years of treason," and General of the Army George C. Marshall,
World War II chief of staff, Ambassador to China, architect of European
recovery, Secretary of State and of Defense, and in 1953 recipient of the
Nobel Peace Prize. On June 14, 1951, McCarthy suggested that Marshall
was somehow involved in the communist "conspiracy of infamy" that had
kept the world off balance since the waning days of World War II. President Eisenhower, who had maintained his distance, was finally moved to
action in June, when he condemned "book burners" and then in July
1953, when he associated himself with condemnation by the National
Conference of Christians and Jews of an attack by a McCarthy staff
member on the nation's Protestant ministers. The final act but one in the
tragedy featured the "Army-McCarthy" hearings, televised from mid-
April 1954. Support for the senator eroded. By summer, the "Joe Must

Go" movement was in full swing. A select senate committee empaneled to examine his conduct recommended that he be censured. The full Senate used instead the term "condemn" in its resolution of December 2, 1954, which passed by a vote of 67 to 22. McCarthy died on May 2, 1957.

The received wisdom is that fellow Catholics widely supported Senator McCarthy's "crusade." Seymour Lipset has summed up conclusions reported by Nelson W. Polsby:

> His report indicates that McCarthy received disproportionate support from Catholics, New Englanders, Republicans, the less educated, the lower class, manual workers, farmers, older people and the Irish.[54]

Surely one of the more curious coalitions in American history! Lipset also reported that McCarthy "drew disproportionately from Catholics of recent immigrant background."[55] Overall Catholic support for the senator ran 7 to 9 percent ahead of national and Protestant support. Neither Catholic nor Protestant support was inconsiderable in the early days of his campaign. Jews and blacks inclined to opposition. In September 1954, Catholic support, which had been dropping during the televised hearings, stood at 40 percent. But Protestant approval had taken a drastic nosedive, down to 23 percent from a 49 percent high the previous January. This represented the widest spread between the two religious groups.[56] Geographic factors which are still inadequately explored also entered in.[57] McCarthy's Catholic support was relatively weak in southern and western states, with southern California an exception. Cardinal McIntyre did not speak out, but his newspaper, *The Tidings,* was vocally pro-McCarthy. One of the senator's major appearances was at a 1954 St. Patrick's Day dinner in Chicago, but sentiment there was moderated by the generally liberal climate of the church under Cardinal Stritch.

Support in the metropolitan New York area, orchestrated by the *Brooklyn Tablet* and marshalled by groups like the Catholic War Veterans and the Knights of Columbus, was strong. Cardinal Spellman issued no pronunciamentos, but in August 1953 said of McCarthy: "He is against communism and he has done and is doing something about it." The cardinal's presence at a New York City police department breakfast the following April, at which the senator spoke, was widely interpreted as heartfelt approval, although he confined himself to applauding the main speaker, shaking his hand, and declaring: "Senator McCarthy has told us about the Communists and the Communist methods. I want to say I'm not only against communism—but I'm against the methods of Communists."[58] Discussing the political problem that McCarthy represented for Congressman John F. Kennedy, Donald F. Crosby concluded that "in no part of the Union, so it seemed, did Joe McCarthy have a more enthusiastic following than in Kennedy's Massachusetts." Neither Archbishop Cushing nor *The Pilot* was committed. Cushing announced that there was no "Catholic attitude on McCarthy." Still, the Bay State boasted the highest proportion of McCarthy supporters. During the Army-McCarthy hearings, Boston reported the highest percentage of viewers of any city, and it was the only one in which a majority of those viewers sided with the senator in his epic battle with Boston brahmin Joseph L. Welch and his army clients.[59]

Among Catholic journals, *Commonweal* was consistent in opposition to Senator McCarthy.[60] The *Catholic Worker* ignored the issue, except for a single complaint about the oppressive atmosphere his activities had generated. The Workers were already established as opponents of the Smith and McCarran Acts and had received from the pulpit of St. Patrick's Cathedral a tongue-lashing directed at the "so called idealist Christian left" by a priest who declared that "there's no place in the Church of Christ for religious centaurs, for collaborators, equivocators, appeasers, temporizers, straddlers, deluded professional liberals, carpetbaggers . . ." It was a painful moment for those who believed they could reject the atheism and materialism which they found both "in Marxist thought and in bourgeois thought," and at the same time respect the freedom and protest the imprisonment of "Communist brothers."[61]

McCarthy could generally count on good press in Catholic publications. Notable advocates were Patrick Scanlan of the *Brooklyn Tablet,* James M. Gillis, C.S.P., of the *Catholic World,* and columnist Richard Ginder of *Our Sunday Visitor.* Notre Dame's *Ave Maria* lent strong support. *America* was at first cautious, but editor Robert Hartnett, a man of strong social reform tendencies, was incensed by the slander and fakery of McCarthy's 1952 assault on Stevenson. Until ordered by Jesuit superiors to drop the attack in the spring of 1954, *America*'s editors kept up steady criticism of the senator's arguments and lack of documentation. Jesuits across the United States were bitterly divided on the issue. In June their superior general, the Belgian Jan B. Janssens, intervened to order the magazine's staff—all Jesuits—to avoid discussion of "merely secular or political matters." In September 1955 Hartnett retired from his editorship.[62]

The McCarthy episode stirred violent emotions within the Catholic community and affected its relations with other Americans. After Bishop Sheil's UAW speech in April 1954, a torrent of abuse descended on him. The situation was further confused when, in September, he abruptly resigned as director-general of the Catholic Youth Organization, which he had founded. It seems clear that his action was prompted by financial problems within the CYO, but many accepted the wholly unlikely theory that Cardinal Stritch had demanded his resignation because of his speech of five months earlier.[63] A clutch of Catholic politicians, all Democrats, was outspoken against McCarthy: a young congressman from Minnesota named Eugene J. McCarthy; Truman's secretary of labor, former mayor of Boston and governor of Massachusetts Maurice J. Tobin, a civil libertarian who denounced the climate of slander, terror, and thought repression; and Democratic National Committee Chairman Stephen Mitchell. Hunter College President George Shuster, Columbia University chaplain George Ford, and John A. O'Brien, who had collaborated on the National Council of Christians and Jews statement which roused President Eisenhower to action, were other critics. But they represented a minority. If at various stages along the way, many Catholics were indifferent to the senator and his concerns, a substantial 40 percent continued to support him as the drama moved to resolution in the fall of 1954. Many have kept on supporting him.

Events of the McCarthy era worsened Catholic-Protestant relations. In the letdown after the unified effort of wartime days, old suspicions and fears revived. Theologian John Courtney Murray noticed something else: the "new nativism" was not so much Protestant as it was naturalist, operating on the premise that democracy demanded a naturalist, secularist philosophy.[64] Incidents kept tempers at the boil. President Truman's abortive attempt to nominate General Mark W. Clark as ambassador to the Holy See provoked criticism from the watchdogs of church-state separation.[65] The problem of support for parochial schools entered a particularly acrimonious phase. In 1947 Methodist Bishop G. Bromley Oxnam and others organized Protestants and Other Americans United for the Separation of Church and State. Paul Blanshard became a spokesman; his *American Freedom and Catholic Power,* issued in March 1949, was in a sixth printing by August.[66] The somnolescent Federal Council of Churches yielded in 1950 to a more vigorous National Council of Churches, which successfully incorporated Orthodox bodies. Such liberal Protestant ecumenists as Charles Clayton Morison of *The Christian Century* were considerably less anxious to relate to Roman Catholicism. Catholic rituals and practices, the church's authority structure, its Roman relationship, its presumed "softness" in matters of church-state separation, all suggested arm's length rather than the right hand of fellowship as the suitable approach to Romans.[67] The crisis of McCarthy days reinforced stereotypes. Ancestral memories on both sides were refreshed. It became difficult to sort out fact from fiction, reality from appearances. The fiction and the appearances exacerbated the situation.

The General Assembly of the Presbyterian Church in the United States held in October 1953 issued "A Letter to Presbyterians, Concerning the

Present Situation in Our Country, and in the World." It was chiefly the work of the Moderator, John A. Mackay of Princeton Theological Seminary. The "Letter" warned that "treason and dissent are being confused," and "attacks made upon citizens of integrity and social passion which are utterly alien to our democratic habits." "The majesty of truth," Mackay wrote, "must be preserved at all times and at all costs." He had never concealed his distaste for Roman Catholicism, and inclusion of buzzwords like "Inquisitions," and a reference to the "uncorroborated word" of those who had transferred allegiance "from one authoritarian system to another" were not missed.[68] The church's Stated Clerk Eugene Carson Blake, who had praised the 1951 Catholic bishops' statement, commented in 1953 that the "Roman Church has been and still is, industriously spreading the false propaganda that the only safe church, fully anti-communistic, is the Roman Church."[69] There were other incidents, as when the Deans of St. John the Divine and Washington cathedrals, James A. Pike and Francis B. Sayre, Jr. (Woodrow Wilson's grandson), exchanged pulpits to ask the same question: why had the Catholic Church not formally condemned McCarthy?[70] The strict separationists at the *Christian Century*, fearing a McCarthy presidential candidacy, demanded that the Catholic bishops repudiate him.[71] Replies to all this came in kind and dialogue was postponed.

In an article reminiscent of Robert Baird's analysis almost exactly a century before, Methodist minister Alson J. Smith in the fall of 1947 suggested in *American Mercury* three factors contributing to "The Catholic-Protestant Feud": (1) Myron Taylor's mission to the Vatican; (2) the Catholic drive for conversions among blacks and in rural America; and (3) Catholic support for legislation to make public funds available for parochial schools. The last, a worry also of Baird in the 1840s, was "the most important issue between the faiths."[72]

In 1949 there were 10,183 Roman Catholic elementary and high schools in the country, with 2,607,879 enrolled pupils.[73] By the end of the next decade, some 5,600,000 students, 11 percent of the total school population, were in private schools, 90 percent of them Catholic.[74] Private educators were faced with sharply escalating capital and operating costs. In the case of the Catholic schools the problem was compounded by a diminishing work force of teachers who contributed their services for near-subsistence wages. The education story of the 1950s had several chapters: division among Catholics on the acceptability of government funding; an unsavory and divisive interfaith controversy; and ongoing development in interpretation of the First Amendment to the Federal Constitution.

Philadelphia's Cardinal O'Hara opposed acceptance of government subsidy by Catholic schools. He was convinced that support through taxation would be more costly for Catholic parents than if they paid their own bills, because of "the waste of public funds that goes on in public school construction and operation," and he saw that state control inevitably followed state money. He held, however, that "parents are entitled to any sort of relief that is given to parents of public school children." This he understood as "health and welfare service," not as educational subsidy.[75] Other bishops thought along the same lines, but it was not the approach taken in 1949 by the education department of the NCWC.

Appearing before the House Committee on Education and Labor on June 3, 1949, Father William E. McManus laid out a carefully reasoned argument that "every school to which parents may send their children in compliance with the compulsory education laws of the State is entitled to a fair share of the tax funds."[76] This was true whether the school was public, parochial, or private. He further argued that the federal government must limit itself to its obligation to equalize educational opportunity for all Americans. He was apprehensive about government interference in school management; that was "mainly a local or community responsibility." And above all the primacy of parental rights and duties in education—as declared in the 1925 Oregon School Case decision—must be protected. Paul Blanshard later recalled that "nothing did so much to frighten non-Catholics" as McManus's testimony. It sounded to him "like a message from the Dark Ages."[77]

Federal aid to education was soon engulfed in bitter controversy. Cardinal Spellman's ire was focused on one of the proposals before Congress. It was sponsored by North Carolina Congressman Graham Barden and contemplated federal aid exclusively for public schools. The cardinal's rhetoric tended to be purple and he did not avoid personalities. He argued for the "primacy of the citizen's right of conscience," and that no one should be penalized for exercising that civic right in the area of educational choice. But his suggestions that his opponents were "bigots," his terming them "unhooded Klansmen," the title of an address he delivered at Fordham University ("The Barden Bill—Brewer of Bigotry"), none of these was conducive to civilized discourse. Nor, on the other hand, were headlines like the following, culled by the cardinal and filed for use in a commencement address: "METHODIST BISHOPS ATTACK CATHOLICS," "BAPTIST CONVENTION TOLD WALL BETWEEN CHURCH AND STATE IS BEING ATTACKED," "PRESBYTERIANS CONDEMN CATHOLIC DEMANDS." When Spellman declared that "once again a crusade is being preached against the Catholic Church in the United States . . . against the Catholic Church as a social institution, as a cultural force in the United States," a trio of prominent Protestants rejoined that their attack was rather on "the political activities of members of the Roman Catholic hierarchy," who, "as representatives of a foreign power," were trying "to break down our United States Constitutional guarantee of separation of church and state."[78]

The most distasteful episode in the brouhaha began when Eleanor Roosevelt entered the lists with her column, "My Day," for June 23, 1949. Conceding that "it is quite possible . . . that private schools . . . may make a great contribution to the public school system" and admitting that she had not read the Barden bill, she asserted her own strict-separationist constitutional views on aid to education. Two more columns followed. On July 21 Cardinal Spellman wrote the former first lady. In his letter, emotional appeal and attack mingled with constitutional argument. The letter reflected, as had the Roosevelt columns from an opposite perspective, the mutual inability to empathize so characteristic of brahmin-Catholic relations since colonial days. But Spellman overstepped himself badly. He closed his letter by telling Mrs. Roosevelt:

> I shall not again publicly acknowledge you. For, whatever you may say in the future, your record of anti-Catholicism stands for all to see—a record which you yourself wrote on the pages of history which cannot be recalled—documents of discrimination unworthy of an American mother!

On August 4 Cardinal Spellman phoned Mrs. Roosevelt and asked her to go over with him a "clarifying statement" on school-aid which he issued the next day. She agreed it was "clarifying and fair." Spellman was forced into tactical retreat. Anson Phelps Stokes may have overstated the case when he concluded in his massive study of *Church and State in the United States* that:

> Cardinal Spellman's statement was of epoch-making importance as far as church-state relations in the United States are concerned. It was the first time that the hierarchy, represented by one of its most prominent members . . . recognized publicly that direct aid for the support of parochial schools was, under existing constitutions, laws and Supreme Court decisions, unconstitutional.[79]

The battle over state aid to parochial schools was just beginning.

Beginning in the late 1940s, for over thirty years two schools of constitutional interpretation have locked horns on the question of government aid to church-affiliated schools.[80] One side, heavily Roman Catholic, reads the Constitution as allowing some accommodation between church and state. Advocates of this view appeal to the historical origin of the nonestablishment clause of the First Amendment (designed to prevent a single national state church), to the same amendment's free exercise clause, and to the Fourteenth Amendment's equal protection clause. This approach adopts the philosophical principle of distributive justice; it reflects the presupposition lying behind William McManus's 1949 congressional testimony. Historically it accepts the thesis that in America church-state separation was conceived in cooperation and not, as in Europe in the aftermath of the French Revolution, in hostility. The opposing side, a broadly based band of secular humanist, Protestant, and Jewish individuals and groups, holds, with variations, that the non-establishment clause mandates maintenance in education and in other areas of American life of the "wall of separation between church and state" of which President Thomas Jefferson wrote to the Danbury, Connecticut, Baptist Association on New Year's Day of 1802.

Everson v. Board of Education (1947), in which the Supreme Court upheld a New Jersey statute which authorized municipalities to reimburse parents for costs in using regular bus lines to transport children to non-public schools, made constitutional history. For the first time, the Supreme Court read into the due process clause of the Fourteenth Amendment the First Amendment's non-establishment clause. Whatever prohibition was contained there now applied to states as well as to the national government. The bussing statute itself was upheld in a 5–4 vote on the "individual benefit" theory: no religious institution, but individuals—the children—were the immediate beneficiaries. Opinions in the case set the direction for the future. Justice Hugo Black in his dissent stated that the non-establishment clause commanded no support for any or all religion. Justice Wiley Rutledge argued from James Madison that the First Amendment meant uprooting all relationships between religion and the state. His was a dissenting opinion: he held that aiding children in any way to get a religious education was not a public purpose. The "wall of separation" metaphor, used also in *Reynolds v. United States,* the 1878 decision which disallowed polygamy, was resurrected and enshrined in constitutional theory. Contrary to *Bradfield v. Roberts* (1899), "establishment of religion" and "a religious establishment" came to be taken as practically synonymous. Understanding of the clause as simply prohibiting an established church receded.

In *McCollum v. Board of Education* (1948), the court disallowed by an 8–1 margin religious education in public school buildings. In a concurring opinion, Justice Felix Frankfurter enunciated his dictum that the public school is "a symbol of our secular unity." The court in *Zorach v. Clauson* (1952) upheld "released-time" religious education programs outside public school buildings, with Justice William O. Douglas declaring that "we are a religious people whose institutions presuppose a Supreme Being."

Subsequently the Supreme Court has heard a series of cases dealing with prayer and Bible reading in public schools, issues on which some otherwise separationists switch sides, and some cases concerned with government subsidy for various auxiliary services and teacher and program development. Over the years the court has gradually refined its criteria, from the individual benefit theory in *Everson* to examination of legislative purpose and effect, the extent of government entanglement, a program's potential for divisiveness, and, more recently, its effect in furthering religious activity. A deliberate distinction has been made between programs aiding colleges and universities and those geared to the lower grades. On the theory that college students are less susceptible to indoctrination than are their younger siblings, criteria are more lenient for higher education.

The Catholic community's emergence as a highly visible element on the American religious scene has been a cause of other episodes. Jesuit poet and essayist Leonard Feeney was spiritual leader of a group which met at Cambridge's St. Benedict Center, a chaplaincy frequented by Harvard and Radcliffe students. Some of its members, both there and across the Charles River at Boston College, came to interpret St. Cyprian's adage, "Outside the church there is no salvation," as denying salvation to all modern non-Roman Catholics, excepting only catechumens who had expressed the explicit intention of entering the Catholic Church. In a letter addressed to Archbishop Cushing on August 8, 1949, the Roman Supreme Congregation of the Holy Office rejected this rigorist view. Father Feeney was formally dismissed from the Jesuit order in 1949 and excommunicated in 1954. Before his death he and some followers, who lived a communal form of life at Harvard, Massachusetts, were reconciled by the bishop of Worcester.[81]

John Tracy Ellis, professor of American Catholic history at the Catholic University of America, was not the first to offer a critical analysis of intellectual failings in the American Catholic community. In 1925, George N. Shuster had sparked lively controversy with his negative answer to the question "Have We Any Scholars?" A New York layman weighed in with criticism of Catholic colleges for "complacency in mediocrity." In return, they met with an avalanche of criticism from that anti-intellectual element which was just as commonplace in American Catholicism as in Protestant evangelicalism.[82] In 1937 Robert Hutchins expressed puzzlement over the failure of Catholics in the United States to cultivate their inherited cultural tradition. Cambridge political scientist Denis W. Brogan wrote bluntly: "In no Western society is the intellectual prestige of Catholicism lower than in the country where, in such respects as wealth, numbers, and strength of organization, it is so powerful."[83] On May 14, 1955, Ellis gave a talk to a meeting of the Catholic Commission on Intellectual and Cultural Affairs, at Maryville College in St. Louis.

Printed in *Thought*'s fall number that year, it opened the floodgates.[84] His tone was that of a committed churchman; his analysis telling and devastating.

Ellis searched the Catholic community's history for the reasons for its intellectual failures, pointing to its initial status as a persecuted and excluded minority with the burden of inherited hatreds, as well as the struggling makeup of its immigrant membership during the major period of its development. Catholics, too, had shared in what Orestes Brownson termed "the grand heresy of the age," the prevailing anti-intellectualism of Americans who, as Tocqueville put it, "do not fear distinguished talents, but are rarely fond of them." On a more practical level, Ellis pointed to the rarity of Catholic homes with a cultured or scholarly atmosphere, repeated failure to develop adequate funding for higher educational institutions and the ruinous competition in which those institutions indulged, the absence among many Catholic professors of love of scholarship for its own sake, toleration of "intellectual sloth" on supposedly spiritual grounds linked to an eschatological bias in theology, and over-emphasis in Catholic education on morality, to the disparagement of intellectual development. Reactions were predictably divided. Sociologist Thomas F. O'Dea and polymath Walter J. Ong, S.J., took up the topic with zest. Gustave Weigel, S.J., wrote "American Catholic Intellectualism—A Theologian's Reflections."[85] One former president of Notre Dame, John Cavanaugh, C.S.C., escalated the rhetoric by asking "Where are the Catholic Salks, Oppenheimers, Einsteins?" while the diocesan paper of his predecessor, Cardinal O'Hara, published an editorial disparaging the "fogbound" intellectual, buried in his books and "considered profound because no one understands what he is saying." "Are we to belittle," the writer asked, "the tremendous contribution of the great body of the good, sound citizens as we go about searching for a poet laureate?"[86] That Ellis had not in fact done this was beside the point.

As the Second Vatican Council (1962–65) moved into its final session, at which the Declaration on Religious Freedom he had helped to frame was incorporated in the tradition of the universal Catholic Church, John Courtney Murray gathered his thoughts on "The Problem of Religious Freedom." he began:

> The problematic of religious freedom is concrete and historical. Its construction begins with a scrutiny of the "signs of the times." Two are decisive. The first is the growth of man's personal consciousness; the second is the growth of man's political consciousness.

To support this formulation, Murray appealed to Pope John XXIII's 1963 encyclical letter, *Pacem in Terris*, with its assertions that "freedom, not force, is the dynamism of personal and social progress," and that "in a particular way freedom is felt to be man's right in the order of his most profound concern, which is the order of religion."[87]

In 1945, just twenty years before, Archbishop Edward Mooney of Detroit had encouraged Murray to interest himself in the problem of church-state relations which had bedeviled the Catholic community in the United States since the time of John Carroll and had been at the root of so much division between Catholics and other Americans.[88] Three years later, in a statement for the NCWC administrative board, Archbishop McNicholas had vigorously affirmed Catholic loyalty, without trying to reconcile his practical position with the commonly accepted Catholic theory which had been outlined by John A. Ryan in *The State and the Church* (1923). McNicholas's statement read:

> No group in America is seeking union of church and state; and least of all are Catholics. We deny absolutely and without any qualification that the Catholic bishops of the United States are seeking a union of church and state by any endeavors whatsoever, either proximate or remote. If tomorrow Catholics constitute a majority in our country, they would not seek a union of church and state. They would then, as now, uphold the Constitution and all its Amendments, recognizing the moral obligations imposed on all Catholics to observe and defend the Constitution and its Amendments.[89]

This scarcely satisfied Paul Blanshard. In the same statement, McNicholas had referred to the pope as ruler of a sovereign state (correctly, but without relevance to his argument about envoys to the Holy See); he favored aid to parochial schools, and was, on other grounds, a favorite target. The editor of the *Register* newspapers did not help matters by hinting that things might change should Catholics become a majority.[90] American Catholic theologians were at the time divided in a scholarly debate which occupied the pages of *Theological Studies* (John Courtney Murray, S.J., editor) and *The American Ecclesiastical Review* (Joseph Clifford Fenton, editor). Monsignor Fenton, dean of the School of Theology at the Catholic University of America, and Redemptorist Father Francis J. Connell, who had been first president of the Catholic Theological Society of America, opposed Murray on behalf of what they understood to be perennial and unchangeable Catholic doctrine. Their ideal was that there should be one religion and that it should work hand in hand with the state—one caring for society's temporal good and the other for its spiritual good. Catholicism should be "professed" by the state. In the present condition of the world (and of the United States), concessions must be made out of expediency, but that did not detract from the ideal.

Murray's opponents had a powerful and sincere Roman supporter in Cardinal Alfredo Ottaviani, operating head of the Supreme Congregation of the Holy Office, charged with supervision of Catholic orthodoxy throughout the world. After Murray, on March 25, 1954, in an address at Catholic University, suggested that Ottaviani's position on church and state was not consonant with that expressed in a talk by Pope Pius XII the previous December 3, he entered a difficult period during which the Jesuit superior general required that he submit all his writings to Rome for prior censorship. For several years he published nothing on church-state relations. He was ignored during preparations for Vatican II, except once when Archbishop Lawrence J. Shehan of Baltimore asked his advice on a proposed document on church and state. Murray criticized it: it was written in the "traditional" formulas. In the spring of 1963, Murray, Gustave Weigel, S.J., liturgist Godfrey Diekmann, O.S.B., and the young Swiss theologian Hans Küng were banned by the rector of the Catholic University at the urging of Apostolic Delegate Egidio Vagnozzi, from lecturing there. That same April, however, at Cardinal Spellman's request, Pope John XXIII named Murray a *peritus,* or official theological expert, at Vatican II. Finding on his arrival that the subject of religious liberty had been dropped from the agenda, Murray was instrumental in persuading the American bishops, with Cardinal Spellman leading them, to demand its restoration. Had it not been for the American intervention, the topic would have been discarded.

John Courtney Murray understood, as biographer Donald Pelotte wrote, that "man's quest for understanding is not static and unchanging." His great contribution was to alert American Roman Catholic theologians to the role of historical sensitivity in their discipline. The so-called traditional position on church and state had exalted certain temporal embodiments of the relationship and set them up as universal ideals. James A. Corcoran and a majority of the American bishops at Vatican I in 1869–70 sensed this. It was left to Murray to find theological words for it. He did not apotheosize the American system, as some earlier Catholic Americanists were accused of doing, but he appreciated its merits and its emphasis on the rule of law. The "care of religion" which older theorists ascribed to the state he saw adequately fulfilled by the state's care of the freedom of religion. His thinking was alien to the secularist trend in the nation and in the Supreme Court's non-establishment decisions. He believed in a "concordia," a harmony between church and state which allowed for cooperation. Secularism he rejected as at the root of the nation's crisis: it was "built on destroying the traditional concept of man and setting in its place a positive new ideal—a humanism without God." His one requirement of the state for the church was freedom; his explanation of the human right to religious freedom started from the assertion of individual human dignity and its necessary consequences.[91]

Charles H. Butler had demanded of the 1893 Columbian Catholic Congress "whether the proud Anglo-Saxon intends to dispossess himself of mere race prejudice and accord his black brother simple justice." In 1950 law or custom dictated segregation by race in large areas of American life, and most churches meekly acquiesced in the situation. The Federal Council of Churches had in 1946 formally renounced segregation as a violation of the Christian gospel. Adverting to wartime urban racial tension in their 1943 joint pastoral letter, the Catholic bishops urged the nation's obligation to recognize the political, educational, economic, and social rights of black people. But most blacks were still constrained to worship apart from white fellow Christians. There were bright moments. In February 1944 one thousand St. Louis University students joined Jesuit archaeologist Claude H. Heithaus in a protest against racial discrimination.[92] California Jesuit George H. Dunne wrote in Commonweal on "The Sin of Segregation."[93] In New Orleans Louis J. Twomey's bulletin, Blueprint for the South, pioneered in promoting interracial relations. But John Courtney Murray thought that "the values at stake seem to be social, not moral," when there was question of black students attending a prom,[94] and President O'Hara of Notre Dame explained the university's prewar policy of not accepting black students on the ground that a tenth of the student body came from southern states and that more good would be done by explaining Catholic teaching to them than by chancing their withdrawal.[95] Black Catholic Alice Renard had sadly to report in January 1947 that "clergy and institutions can practice race discrimination with impunity."[96]

World War II hastened one of the most dramatic population shifts in American history.[97] At the turn of the century, 90 percent of American blacks lived in the south and only 27.7 percent in cities. By 1960 the demography had changed: 53 percent still lived in the south, but 20 percent were in the north central region and another 19 percent in the northeast, both long areas of Catholic concentration. A decade later, 70 percent of black Americans lived in cities. Among Catholics, the diocese of Lafayette, Louisiana, counted in 1970 the largest absolute number of blacks: 80,237. Chicago was second with 80,000, some of them creoles of ancient southern Catholic lineage, others products of the convert movement that had in 1947 so disturbed Protestants like the Reverend Alson J. Smith. Chicago's first non-Indian settler was a black Catholic, Baptiste Pointe du Sable, in 1795. Two centuries later pioneer black priest Augustus Tolton founded St. Monica's parish there for black Catholics in 1890–

93. The major increase for Chicago followed World War II. Education was an attraction, and Catholic schools were unabashedly used for proselytizing. Door-to-door evangelization by lay people, sisters, and priests was effective. So was the generally perceived Catholic atmosphere of the city and the fact that jobs in industry and in the myriad agencies controlled by the Cook County Democratic machine were in the gift of Catholics with a natural sympathy for co-religionists.[98] Successive decades saw growth of the black Catholic population in the South and in Chicago and other northern and western cities. The 297,000 in 1940 became a half-million in 1960, 837,000 by 1970, and 916,854 in 1975.[99]

A five-year legal campaign ended in 1954 when, by a unanimous vote, the Supreme court in *Oliver Brown et al. v. Board of Education of Topeka*, reversed the "separate but equal rule" laid down in *Plessy v. Ferguson* in 1896. The Civil Rights Revolution was under way. Not directly touched by the court case, the Catholic Church in the United States was caught up in the revolution. Until 1954 the general rule had been to follow local patterns in the South. Northern practice was more varied, but separate churches for black Catholics were usual in larger cities. There were few black priests. Liberal Chicago ordained its first in 1947 and added only eight more by the mid-1970s. The aftershock of *Brown* was felt throughout the Catholic community. Developments of the 1960s would introduce still other dynamics.

Catholic activity among New York blacks, particularly in Harlem, was considerable in the 1930s and 1940s. The pastor of St. Aloysius Church boasted in 1943: "Ten years ago the Catholic Church was known in Harlem or was sneeringly referred to as the 'white man's church.' today it needs no advertisement, and is known as a potent instrument of good in our Negro community." In twelve years, Father William McCann had baptized six thousand converts. The Catholic Interracial Council, Baroness De Hueck's Friendship House, and the Catholic Workers helped to create a climate better than elsewhere. Cardinal Spellman made his views clear soon after his arrival from Boston in 1939. Dedicating a new Harlem school, he announced: "There are no schools for Negroes. There are no schools for whites. There are only schools for all children." At another school opening, he said: "This is not a Negro school. This is a Catholic school which any Catholic child who is qualified may enter." Official policy was clear, and considerable efforts were made to implement it. But the nature of New York City, where a host of groups has always had to struggle for entry-level jobs, and where survivors of earlier immigrations have pre-empted job- and living-areas, complicated the situation.[100]

Archbishop Ritter desegregated St. Louis Catholic institutions in 1947. Washington's Archbishop O'Boyle did the same in the northern part of the diocese in a gradual process from 1948 to 1952. Southern Maryland, heavily Catholic since 1634, was more difficult. Some churches had triple segregation: whites, blacks and part-Indians known as we-sorts. Desegregation was introduced in 1956. One mission church was closed permanently when parishioners reacted by ostentatiously refusing financial support.[101] Southern born and bred Bishop Vincent S. Waters took vigorous action when he wrote to the people of his diocese in 1953:

> There is no segregation of races to be tolerated in any Catholic church in the diocese of Raleigh. . . . The Church does not propose tolerance, which is negative, but love, which is positive. If Christ said love our enemies, we certainly can love our friends. These are our friends and members of our own body. . . .

In 1959, the Catholic journal *Jubilee* could still write that "with the exception of North Carolina (a liberal oasis)," only two parochial schools out of a possible 745 "in the hard-core racist states of the Deep South" were integrated.[102] Archbishop Joseph F. Rummel, who had been in New Orleans since 1935, had one of the most difficult struggles. He understood segregation to be a moral question, but was frustrated in his attempts to eliminate it in Catholic institutions by resistance deeply rooted in Louisiana's history and culture. Not until 1962 did his effort finally succeed with the assistance of Coadjutor Archbishop John P. Cody and only after the archbishop had excommunicated three lay leaders in Plaquemines Parish, including the local political boss, for their resistance.[103]

The Civil Rights Revolution continued into the 1960s. Picking up where their 1943 statement had left off, the Catholic bishops issued in 1958 the pastoral letter, "Discrimination and the Christian conscience," in which they stated baldly that "the heart of the race question is moral and religious."[104] The next decade would be a crucial one for the nation and its Catholic citizens. Pope John XXIII called an ecumenical council, at which Americans had the next largest representation after Italy. The nation's first Roman Catholic President was elected and, three years later, assassinated. Catholics became widely involved in civil rights actions and, in response to the Vietnam War, a "Catholic Left" took shape. The church, its people, and its ministers, were about to take a new turning.

XXI

A Revolutionary Moment

In an address to chaplains of the Christian Family Movement at Denver in July of 1960, Gustave Weigel, S.J., who had just been named one of the first consultors of the new papal Secretariat for Promoting Christian Unity, spoke on the church as the "People of God," among whom lay people differed from priests and bishops with respect to function, but were not subordinate in membership:

> The world is new. The situation of 1960 is revolutionary. It is quite unlike the world of 1900. Consequently, the relationship of the action of the laity and hierarchy must be seen in the light of the new world. We are living in a revolutionary moment.

Weigel saw that "world society and our own institutions are changing."[1] The revolution began for American Catholics on an upbeat. It was the season of Pope John XXIII, elected in the fall of 1958, and of President John F. Kennedy, elected in the fall of 1960.

The new President's father, Joseph P. Kennedy, was a Harvard graduate who had made a fortune from interests which ranged from investment banking to shipbuilding and real estate. After brief stints as chairman of the Securities and Exchange Commission and the United States Maritime Commission, he was appointed ambassador to the Court of St. James's. He was Roosevelt's special ambassador at the 1939 coronation of Pope Pius XII.

A World War II navy veteran, John F. Kennedy had a thirteen-year career in both houses of congress behind him when he was elected president. He had narrowly missed his party's nomination for vice president in 1956. Religion was used as an argument against him, as it would be four years later. Among the highlights of the campaign that tested finally the acceptability of a Roman Catholic for the nation's highest office were an interview with Kennedy published in the March 1959 issue of *Look* magazine, the victory over Hubert H. Humphrey in the May 1960 primary in West Virginia despite that state's tiny Catholic population, and an appearance before the Ministerial Association of Houston, Texas.[2]

Nothing in Kennedy's record suggested that he was constitutionally suspect. Indeed, some had reservations on opposite grounds. Presbyterian scholar Robert McAfee Brown thought the *Look* article revealed "a rather irregular Christian," and Lutheran Martin Marty feared Kennedy was "spiritually rootless and almost disturbingly secular."[3] These criticisms were different from those of New York's Norman Vincent Peale, Boston's Harold Okenga, and Philadelphia's Daniel A. Poling, ministers leagued in the newly organized National Conference of Citizens for Religious Freedom, who argued that the candidate's religious affiliation rendered him unfit for the presidency. They were charged with opening "floodgates of bigotry" in an interfaith rejoinder signed by prominent Protestants, Orthodox, Jews, and Catholics, headed by Union Theological Seminary's Reinhold Niebuhr and John C. Bennett.[4] Kennedy had already been helped by an open letter to pastors signed by Dean Sayre of Washington Cathedral, POAU leader Bishop Bromley Oxnam, and eleven others, who wrote that, "quite apart from what our attitude toward the Roman Church may be," it was unjust to discount a candidate simply because he was a member of it.[5]

Many members of the National Conference of Citizens for Religious Freedom were known to be conservative Republicans. That was not the case with President Ramsey Pollard of the Southern Baptist Convention. Dr. Pollard insisted "I am not a bigot" and announced, apparently without hope of success that "all we ask is that Roman Catholicism lift its bloody hand from the throats of those that want to worship in the church of their choice." His boast was that "my church has enough members to beat Kennedy in this area if they all vote like I tell them to."[6] To an extent they did, but Kennedy managed a narrow win in November. His popular plurality nationwide against Richard M. Nixon was 112,881. The vote in the electoral college was 303 to 219. Analysts noted both gains and losses attributable to the religious issue. Theodore Sorensen thought it was the strongest factor working against his candidate, apart from Republican party loyalty.[7]

John F. Kennedy's election lessened the psychological defensiveness that had historically marked the Catholic American. One result was the bridging of the chasm which had long made Catholics feel unwelcome in general philanthropic endeavors. While vocations to religious communities and seminaries continued to increase until the mid-1960s, a growing number of younger Catholics became secular American missionaries in the Peace Corps and later in VISTA and similiar programs. At the same time, the papacy was charting its own new course which radically altered the parameters by which the American Catholic community measured itself and the world around it.

Pope John's personality, his naturalness, homeliness (in several senses of the word), and unpretentious common sense approach attracted most Americans, Catholic or not. Only gradually did they begin to sense the sea change occurring in the papacy's appreciation of world problems and its prescriptions for them. The pope's first encyclical, *Ad Petri Cathedram* (June 29, 1959), lamented that "there still remains too great a difference in the distribution of wealth" and laid blame for this on "the concept of the right of private property, which is at times defective and downright unjust, held by those who are interested only in their own benefit and convenience." He condemned "despicable layoffs from work," and demanded that employers not only pay just wages but regard workers "as fellow men or more specifically as brothers."[8] A pattern was set which marked the social teaching of John XXIII and his successor, Paul VI (1963–1978), in the letters *Mater et Magistra* (1961), *Pacem in Terris* (1963), *Populorum Progressio* (1967), and *Octogesima Adveniens* (1971).[9]

Both popes continued to challenge the atheistic materialism and totalitarian ways of world communism. But they abandoned ritual denunciation and initiated dialogue with communists. Salvos were directed with greater force at western cultural imperialism and liberal capitalism, "a system . . . which considers profit the key motive for economic progress, competition as the supreme law of economics, and private ownership of the means of production as an absolute right that has no limits and carries no corresponding social obligation" (*Populorum Progressio*, n. 27). Both popes considered the gap between developed and underdeveloped nations the major social crisis of the age and called for broad changes in the distribution of wealth. Popes John and Paul intended the Catholic Church to be neither religious prop for capitalism nor social stabilizer for authoritarian right-wing regimes. For those who expressed their Catholicism largely in terms of emotional anti-communism or uncritically accepted the assumptions of the American and Western economic system, an era had ended even before the Second Vatican Council began.

American participation in the council which met in Rome each fall for four successive years from 1962 to 1965 was considerably more extensive than at Vatican I nearly a century before.[10] At the earlier council only James A. Corcoran had served as an American member of the preparatory commissions; forty-three Americans now shared in organizing the agenda for Vatican II. Another twenty-three served on committees during the sessions and over sixty were official *periti* or experts. When the termagant Scots minister Dr. John Cumming asked if those separated from Rome might have the council floor in 1869 to present their views, Pius IX was unequivocal: Cumming "must certainly recognize that the church cannot permit the reopening of a discussion of errors which she has already examined with care, judged and condemned." Perhaps the pope remembered the doctor's earlier suggestion that England's Catholic bishops be loaded on a 120-gun Royal Navy ship-of-the-line and exported, "duty free," to Italy.[11] At Vatican II a different approach was adopted. Nineteen American Protestants were among the fifty-two delegate observers representing other Christian churches at the council's 1964 session. At Vatican I, news reports had been frequently confused, often jaundiced; secrecy was obsessive. At Vatican II, a mysterious American using the name Xavier Rynne broke that barrier in a series of "Letters from Vatican City," first published in *The New Yorker.* By mid-point in the first session, the American bishops had set up a regular press panel in which bishops, *periti,* and professors from Roman universities participated. The bishops themselves met each week, often to hear theological presentations on topics to be discussed in the council hall.

Cardinal Spellman made 131 of the 341 oral and written American interventions at the council. He and Cardinal Albert Meyer of Chicago were among the council's presidents, with Cardinal Lawrence J. Shehan of Baltimore replacing Meyer, who died in 1965. A biblical scholar, Meyer achieved a reputation as the Americans' intellectual leader. Other notable American contributors were Cardinal Ritter of St. Louis and Archbishop Paul J. Hallinan, who was outstanding for his work on the liturgy decree. Three American lay people and a religious sister were official observers: Sister Mary Luke Tobin, S.L., of the Conference of Major Superiors of Women; Executive Director Martin H. Work of the National Council of Catholic Men; President Catherine McCarthy of the National Council of Catholic Women; and James J. Norris, assistant executive director of Catholic Relief Services and president of the International Catholic Migration Committee. Norris, who had worked in the areas of relief, refugees, and migration for thirty years, addressed the council on November 5, 1964. His topic was the global dimension of poverty and hunger.[12]

The council was good copy and its activities were widely reported in the secular press and in news magazines. Interest heightened as it became clear that disciplinary and doctrinal statements formulated by the preparatory commissions under Roman guidance faced rough going on the council floor, in some cases being returned to committee for near-total revision. Items from a *Commonweal* series in the summer of 1962 were talked about: freedom of thought in the church; emphasis on its prophetic as well as priestly and institutional reality; the priesthood of the laity and the laity's role in development of doctrine; religious liberty and renunciation by the church of privileged status; consequences of human solidarity in Christ's Mystical Body; common responsibility for all the peoples of the world; Christian unity; dialogue and real communication between people and pastors; cultural adaptation of worship forms, including introduction of vernacular languages; diminution of pomp and pageantry; emphasis on bishops as informed teachers and witnesses of faith, rather than rulers or administrators; confrontation with the "deinstitutionalized Catholic"; recognition that a serious gap existed between clergy and laity on birth control, with statistics showing Catholic practice not substantially different from that of other Americans.[13]

Americans at the council were active on behalf of the Decree on Ecumenism and the Declaration on the Relation of the Church to Non-Christian Religions. The latter, after brief references to Hinduism and Buddhism, turned to relations with Islam and Judaism. American bishops, who had worked closely with Jewish representatives on an acceptable text, helped bring it to the floor and spoke for it. Cardinal Cushing announced that "there is no Christian rationale—neither theological nor historical—for any inequity, hatred or persecution of our Jewish brothers." Cardinal Meyer insisted that "we give explicit attention to the enormous impact of the wrongs done through the centuries to the Jews."[14]

The paramount American issue at the council, however, was religious liberty. American bishops spoke realistically from nearly two centuries' experience of church life in a religiously plural society. Their contentions were the same advanced by their predecessors in the spring of 1870; they had the advantages of John Courtney Murray's expertise and of broader international agreement with their arguments. They were also confident. When in November 1964 a parliamentary maneuver at the council's third session blocked all but certain approval of the Declaration on Religious Liberty, Cardinal Meyer took the lead in gathering within a half hour over eight hundred signatures to a protest petition which he and other cardinals then took to the pope. The Declaration was voted on September 21, 1965. Delegate-Observer Robert Cushman of Duke University felt that on that day "a very ancient order of things—at least in principle—passed away. In principle, the era of Constantine—sixteen hundred years of it—passed away."[15]

Broad media coverage and general interest in the council's proceedings led to sharply increased Catholic and American awareness of the inner workings of the Catholic Church. Protestant observers also were deeply involved in the proceedings. Even Paul Blanshard wrote a reasonably mellow book on his adventures in Rome during the sessions.[16] The monolithic image faded as old patterns of faith and order and life and work were challenged. Biblical metaphor replaced juridical analogy with the civil state as the primary way of imaging the church, which understood itself less as the medieval "perfect society" and more as a sinful but graced pilgrim people making its common way to God by living in and through the world, not by rejecting or fleeing it. Millennial trends were reversed. Sensitivity to local needs and abandonment of the presumption of Western superiority challenged the cultural centralization in vogue since the 11th-century Gregorian Reform. Its role in the growth of Western Christianity was recognized, but Europe was no longer the church, nor the church Europe. Neither was its American extension.

Collegiality, the notion of shared responsibility, tempered the papal spiritual monarchy which had reached its peak in the century after Vatican I. Catholic consciousness grew biblically and historically oriented as the influence of Greek metaphysics decreased. Its reign had begun with 3rd- and 4th-century church fathers and expanded to massive proportions in the high middle ages. Devotional styles now changed. Sentimental and popular paraliturgies disappeared—often without adequate replacement. The role of the mass, the central act of Catholic worship, changed. At the council, Cardinals Spellman and McIntyre defended retention of Latin as the language of the mass, with the cardinal of Los Angeles adding: "Furthermore, active participation is frequently a distraction."[17] The Constitution on the Sacred Liturgy adopted in 1963 said (n. 14) that, "in the restoration and promotion of the sacred liturgy, full and active participation by all the people is the aim to be considered before all else." Christian people, "'a chosen race, a royal priesthood, a holy nation, a redeemed people,' have a right and obligation by reason of their baptism" to participate actively. It is the "primary and indispensable source from which the faithful are to derive a true Christian spirit." Introduction of the vernacular into the mass began in 1964. The complete new rite was mandated in 1970.[18] Emphasis on the priest and bishops as servants in the church clashed with long-standing clerical attitudes. The council displayed new openness to other religious communities, particularly the Orthodox and the heirs of the 16th-century Reformation. It moved decisively to deploy its resources to promote peace and justice in the world. "Christians," the final paragraph (n. 93) of the Constitution on the Church in the Modern World declared, "can yearn for nothing more ardently than to serve the men of this age with ever growing generosity and success."

Catholics in the 1960s lived in most parts of the United States, weak only in Appalachia and the Southeast, and even there groups like the Glenmary missioners, founded in 1939 to serve home missions, were active. Traditional strongholds in the northeast and along the Great Lakes remained. There were large numbers of Spanish-speaking Catholics along the Mexican border and French-descended Creoles and Cajuns in Louisiana. The Cuban presence in south Florida was on the verge of enormous expansion. The McCarran-Walter Act was amended in 1965 to eliminate the national origins quota system and the result was large-scale immigration from outside northern Europe. By 1970, Filipinos led the non-Western Hemisphere immigrant parade, followed by Italians. Portuguese flocked to southeastern Massachusetts at a rate of more than four thousand a year and soon became the region's chief ethnic group.[19] Hispanics came in large numbers: American citizens from Puerto Rico, legal and illegal migrants from all over Latin America. In 1978 they would number between 20 and 30 percent of the total American Catholic population.[20] The stark poverty and political oppression endemic to their homeland brought Haitians, French-speaking black Catholics, from the island that had been Pierre Toussaint's birthplace. For Catholic American-born blacks also, the 1960s were a major period of growth: 127,389 converts were among the 220,000 newly baptized who increased their total in the church by 35 percent in the decade.[21]

By 1970 bishops familiar from council days were disappearing from the scene. Cardinal O'Hara had died in 1960. His successor in Philadelphia, John J. Krol, who served as under-secretary of the Council, became a cardinal in 1967 and was from 1972 to 1974 president of the National Conference of Catholic Bishops. Cardinal Spellman died in 1967 and was succeeded by Terence J. Cooke. Cardinal Cushing, remembered in Boston as "one of the most industrious, articulate, popular and colorful ecclesiastics in America during this century,"[22] had as successor in 1970 Humberto Medeiros. Cardinal Lawrence J. Shehan was archbishop of Baltimore from 1961 to 1974, while his neighbor, Cardinal Patrick A. O'Boyle, retired in 1973 after a quarter-century as Washington's archbishop. In the South Paul J. Hallinan's tenure as first archbishop of Atlanta was cut short by premature death in 1968. Philip M. Hannan has headed the archdiocese of New Orleans since 1965, when Cardinal John P. Cody went to Chicago. Cardinal John F. Dearden, Cardinal Mooney's successor in Detroit in 1958, was the first president of the National Conference of Catholic Bishops from 1966–1971. He retired in 1980. After Cardinal Ritter's death in 1967,

Cardinal John J. Carberry became archbishop of St. Louis where John L. May succeeded him in 1980. On the west coast, Cardinal McIntyre retired in 1970 after twenty-two years in Los Angeles and was succeeded by Archbishop Timothy Manning, who became a cardinal in 1973. The nation's first Hispanic archbishop was Robert Sánchez, named to Santa Fe in 1974.

Catholic lay people are found throughout business and government. By 1977, a third of the nation's governors were Catholics. John McCormack and Thomas P. O'Neill, Jr. of Massachusetts served as speakers of the House of Representatives and Senator Mike Mansfield of Montana succeeded Lyndon Johnson as Senate majority leader. Since 1960, over one hundred members of each Congress have been Catholics and two priests have served in the House, both in the 1970s, Robert J. Cornell, O. Praem., of Wisconsin, and Robert F. Drinan, S.J., of Massachusetts. After Drinan was asked to retire by religious superiors in 1980, there was an outpouring of praise from members of Congress for his devotion to "the oppressed, the indigent and the underprivileged" and for his effective advocacy of civil, constitutional, and human rights.[23] On the local scene, sisters and priests have served on city councils and in state legislatures. Monsignor Geno Baroni became an assistant secretary of housing and urban development in the Carter administration, while Notre Dame President Theodore M. Hesburgh, C.S.C., served on the National Civil Rights Commission and was named an ambassador to represent the United States at a United Nations conference on science and technology for development.

One index of the success of the church of the Gregorian reform, the Counter-Reformation, and Vatican I was the deepseated conviction implanted in all who came in contact with it, whether as members, observers, or opponents, of its immutability. American Catholics had now to cope with the staggering reality of dissent, change, and diversity at the highest levels of the church they had grown up believing was "the same all over the world," the one institution impervious to history. Dissent, change, and diversity quickly filtered down. Many American Catholics were also coping with their own unaccustomed prosperity and the new way of life, business, and leisure that came with it. Old moorings were cut. Catholics were more likely than others to move to suburbs. Parish and school structures had to be altered to fit new needs. A new generation experienced religious training and a cultural environment different from that which their parents and known. In a move freighted with symbolic import, "fish on Friday," universally recognized as a sign of Catholic identity, disappeared after the first Sunday of Advent 1966, with abrogation of obligatory abstinence from meat on that day each week. The Lenten discipline of fast and abstinence was modified almost to the vanishing point.[24] To this unstable if exciting mix were added the moral challenges of civil rights and Vietnam. Reactions ran the gamut. Some, uninterested, unwilling, or unable to cope, moved out of the Catholic Church to other Christian churches, Oriental religions, or the religious nothingarianism long ago familiar to Orestes Brownson. Belgian-born canon lawyer Gommar A. DePauw framed in 1965 a "Catholic Traditionalist Manifesto." He rejected the new liturgical rite of Pope Paul VI and kept to the formulary approved in 1570 by Pius V. French Archbishop Marcel Lefebvre's society of St. Pius X was one of several such groups to attract American followers alienated by the deeper change symbolized by liturgical updating.

The great majority of church leaders and lay people entered with varying degrees of enthusiasm and understanding into the new order of things. Others less sanguine busied themselves patrolling the battlements of defensive strongholds. Many turned to variants of enthusiastic religion or to religious-type encounter groups. Still others accepted the call to secular involvement: they walked from Selma to Montgomery behind Martin Luther King, Jr. and became the "Catholic Left" of the anti-Vietnam War movement.

Theological understandings elaborated in Vatican II's Dogmatic Constitution on the Church soon found their way into church life and structures. A great wave of structural change swept the Catholic Church in the United States. The NCWC gave way in 1966 to a two-tiered arrangement, the National Conference of Catholic Bishops (NCCB) and the United States Catholic Conference. Myriad "national conferences" and "bishops' committees" reported to them. On the international level, synods of bishops began meeting in Rome in 1967.

American priests, bishops and cardinals were appointed to the Vatican administrative staff, and a few Americans were named to the International Theological Commission. Americans headed several international men's and women's religious communities. In dioceses personnel boards discussed assignment of priests, taking into account criteria other than seniority. Retirement ages were set for bishops and pastors. In some places, non-territorial "floating" parishes were established and team ministry replaced the pastor-curate relationship. Sisters became parish assistants and a range of lay ministers came into being, some to assist in ministering the eucharist, others as readers or ministers of music. Married and single laymen were ordained deacons while continuing in secular occupations. The Canon Law Society of America, men and women whose profession is church law, made outstanding contributions: interdisciplinary seminars on renewal, study and application of due process, and elaboration of the "American procedural norms" for annulment proceedings, first approved by the Vatican in 1970, which have eased the lives of thousands. Diocesan conciliation and arbitration boards, priests' senates, and parish councils became common, but discussions in 1970 looking to a national pastoral council came to nothing.[25] Thirteen hundred delegates attended the Detroit Call to Action Congress in 1976 which was preceded by three years of planning and a series of regional meetings.[26]

Cooperation among religious communities of men and women has been a feature of the post-conciliar church. Superiors are linked in the Conference of Major Superiors of Men and the Leadership Conference of Women Religious, both founded in the 1950s. The Sister Formation Conference, begun in 1957, encouraged spiritual and professional growth of religious sisters. Other national organizations include the National Coalition of American Nuns (1969), the National Assembly of Women Religious (1970), and Consortium Perfectae Caritatis (1971), representing differing shades of opinion among sisters. The National Federation of Priests' Councils (1968) was founded to give associations of priests a representative voice in church affairs. There are organizations for contemplative nuns and for black, native American, and Hispanic clergy and members of religious communities. In 1975 four hundred men and women formed the Women's Ordination Conference to move the issue of ordination of women to priesthood. Other forms of consecrated life have developed. Twenty secular institutes, associations of lay men or women, or of diocesan priests, offer members a spirit and way of life without the external signs of community living proper to religious institutes. Since the late sixties there has also been a number of non-canonical communities, often created by former members of established institutes. They have no official church standing, some are ecumenical and some include both men and women.

Writing on the John Birch Society in 1962, Alan Westin saw signs that "the 1960s may see an even deeper division of American Catholics into warring ideological factions than has obtained at any time in the past." Political, economic, and religious positions were in contention. Sometimes, but not always, concerns coincided. President Kennedy was denounced for liberalism, for "selling out" the church and for being "soft on communism."[27] The social encyclicals of Popes John and Paul grated on the sensibilities of free enterprise enthusiasts of the more unrestrained sort. Loss of familiarity and stability in religious practice pained some; others were aesthetically appalled at gaucheries which passed for liturgical reform. Many missed the musical and artistic splendor, the sense of solemnity and awe, or the simple atmosphere of silence that had marked older worship forms. Achievement of a sense of continutiy with the historic Catholic tradition in the midst of change was made no easier by the reluctance which some—clergy and laity—felt for the effort or by those at the opposite pole who proclaimed with colossal insouciance that the past was in any case irrelevant and that the future would be essentially different.

Robert Welch once claimed that half the members of the John Birch Society were Catholics. *America* and other sources denied the claim, and the total number involved in any case was small, but the Society's extreme combination of economic conservatism and anti-communism did exercise an appeal.[28] Reporting to the bishops on behalf of NCWC's social action department in 1961, Archbishop William E. Cousins warned of the tendency to overrate the danger of domestic communism and spoke of the error of those who labeled as communists people whose views differed from their own.[29] "Commie" had replaced "APA" as a catchall term of abuse in some Catholic vocabularies. *Commonweal*'s editors read the bishops' 1961 statement, "Unchanging Duty in an Unchanging World," as a rebuke to "the means chosen by many Catholics to fight Communism," but that interpretation was by no means unanimous.[30]

Catholic organizations focusing on anti-communism included the Catholic Freedom Foundation and the St. Louis-based Cardinal Mindszenty Foundation. More explicitly concerned with religious aspects of change is Catholics United for the Faith (1968), a vigilant voice of conservatism in the areas of Catholic education and liturgy. The Catholic League for Religious and Civil Rights (1973) is a civil rights and anti-defamation organization. The Fellowship of Catholic Scholars (1978) is committed to upholding the teaching authority of Rome. The Latin Liturgy Association (1975), mindful of Vatican II's injunction (Constitution on the Sacred Liturgy, n. 36.1) that "the use of the Latin language, with due respect to particular law, is to be preserved in the Latin rites," encourages use of the Latin text of the new rite established by Pope Paul VI.

Isaac Hecker expected a great age of the Holy Spirit after the first Vatican council. The 1960s and 1970s saw unprecedented evidence of openness to the Spirit by Catholic Americans. The *Cursillo de Cristianidad* originated in Spain about 1949 and came to the United States by way of Hispanic Catholics in Texas. By 1961 it was spreading to "Anglo" Catholics in all parts of the country. An intensive and highly emotional weekend lived at close quarters, the *cursillo* brings together priests, religious, and lay people in an experience which lays heavy emphasis on the communitarian nature of Christianity. A second Spanish import, Marriage Encounter, intends to help married couples (and, more recently, engaged couples) search for, rediscover, or strengthen their love for one another. It was brought to the United States in 1967.

Some estimates of the number of charismatic Catholics in the United States hover around the one million mark.[31] Over three thousand prayer groups were counted in 1976. This movement began during the academic year 1966–67 among students and faculty members at Pittsburgh's Duquesne University, an institution founded by the religious community known as the Congregation of the Holy Spirit. From Duquesne, the charismatic or pentecostal movement spread to the University of Michigan, Michigan State University, and the University of Notre Dame campuses. It quickly became a national and then an international phenomenon with national and international congresses. A reassertion of the personal and the emotional in religion, the movement emphasizes baptism in the Spirit and charismatic gifts like speaking in tongues and prophecy. The Committee on Doctrine of the NCCB presented a report on November 14, 1969, entitled "The Pentecostal Movement in the Catholic Church in the U.S.A.," which stated:

> Theologically the movement has legitimate reasons for existence. It has a strong biblical basis. . . . The participants in the Catholic Pentecostal movement claim that they receive certain charismatic gifts. Admittedly, there have been abuses, but the cure is not a denial of their existence but their proper use. . . . Certainly, the recent Vatican Council presumes that the Spirit is active continuously in the Church.

Judging the validity of the movement by the effects on prayer meeting participants, the report continued:

> There are many indications that this participation leads to better understanding of the role the Christian plays in the Church. Many have experienced progress in their spiritual life. They are attracted to the reading of the scriptures and a deeper understanding of their faith. They seem to grow in their attachment to certain established devotional patterns such as devotion to the real presence and the rosary. . . . [32]

Like counterparts in mainline as well as in traditionally pentecostal Protestant churches, Catholic charismatics represent a degree of reaction against the seemingly excessive preoccupation with social activism that gripped many church people in the 1960s.

Participation in civil rights demonstrations primed some Catholics for direct action against unjust and oppressive structures in other areas of national life. By the mid-sixties, the dynamic in civil rights had shifted with the growth of black-power emphasis, and Catholics oriented to radical action cast about for a new theater. Growing American involvement in the Vietnam War fit the bill.[33] Catholic Workers Thomas C. Cornell and Christopher Kearns staged a public protest in New York City in the summer of 1963. The following year, Jesuit priest Daniel Berrigan and several companions at a Prague peace conference planned formation of the Catholic Peace Fellowship. In November, Thomas Merton invited to a retreat at his

Gethsemane, Kentucky, hermitage a group of Protestant and Catholic activists, nearly all of whom played a role in the future of the Catholic left. Merton had called on Christians to work for total abolition of war. He also shared Gandhi's belief that peace and justice could be assured by nonviolence and self-sacrifice.[34] Nonviolent resistance would be the characteristic approach of the Catholic left. They engaged in direct action, including symbolic property destruction, but avoided physical violence to persons.

On August 20, 1965, *Life* published a picture of Christopher Kearns publicly burning his draft card. By August 30, Congress had a law on the books making that a felony. Catholic Worker David J. Miller was the first to go to prison under it. Others followed. Then on November 9, another Worker, Roger LaPorte, using a form of protest employed by Buddhist monks in Vietnam, burned himself to death in the UN Plaza. The Jesuit provincial superior in New York instructed Daniel Berrigan's local superior to tell him not to involve himself in the aftermath of the LaPorte tragedy. When Berrigan seemed to be disregarding this directive and gave a talk comparing the young man's death to the death of Christ, his Jesuit superiors in New York and Rome believed he had ignored a direct order. In the tense situation, the editor of *Jesuit Missions,* the mission-support journal to which Berrigan was assigned, suggested that by way of a cooling-off period, he replace the editor himself on an already planned fact-finding trip to Latin America. This was taken as an attempt to exile Father Berrigan and within days nearly one thousand supporters signed a petition published in the *New York Times* demanding his recall. He was recalled. *Jesuit Missions* hosted a reception to celebrate his "triumphal return," and the mistaken information spread that Cardinal Spellman, a known advocate of American policy in Vietnam, had orchestrated the plot. In point of fact, he was not involved or consulted in the decisions made by Jesuit superiors.[35] But a legend had been born.

Subsequent activities of the Catholic left featured raids to disrupt files in Selective Service offices. A favorite tactic was to pour blood on the files. While awaiting sentence for doing that in a Baltimore office, Daniel Berrigan's brother Philip, a Josephite priest, organized a second raid, this time in suburban Catonsville, in which Daniel participated. Nine raiders doused files with homemade napalm and waited praying until they were arrested. Until the early 1970s, well over two hundred men and women were associated with the "action community," as they like to be called. Not all were Catholics. They included Jews and Moslems, as well as Protestants. Many were, or had been, religious sisters, brothers, or priests. The Catholic Left was a special object of J. Edgar Hoover's ire. Successful efforts were made to plant informers in their ranks, and several well-publicized trials were held. Ordered to prison after conviction in the Catonsville case, Daniel Berrigan led the FBI a merry and embarrassing chase for two months, punctuated by public appearances and the taping of a television documentary, "The Holy Outlaw." He was finally snared in August 1970 on Block Island at the mouth of Long Island Sound by an FBI posse posing as birdwatchers and with a Coast Guard vessel standing by.

A *Newsweek* poll in 1971 supports the view that the across-the-board impact of the anti-Vietnam actions was small. To adult American Catholics, pornography, abortion, and racial discrimination were more appropriate targets for a public stand by the church than was Vietnam. Of those polled 69 percent did not believe that Catholics who raided draft boards to protest the war were acting as responsible Christians. Six years after Daniel Berrigan's "exile" and four years after Philip Berrigan poured blood on the Baltimore records, 62 percent of Catholics surveyed had no idea who the brothers were.[36] This was not the case with many younger Catholics, including some who were counted among the nation's half million draft resisters. The Berrigans and those associated with them were seen as prophetic figures; their influence was considerable.[37]

The American Catholic community had not quite known their like before. Its members had long been suspect of being against the government. Goody Glover in 1688 and, thirty years later, Sébastien Râle had suffered because in different ways they were perceived as subversive of Puritan New England order. Robert Brooke and William Hunter were disturbers of the ecclesiastical and civil peace by law established in the royal colony of Maryland, and Governor Seymour bade them mend their ways. Colonel George Washington worried about the "unnatural and pernicious correspondence" of priests on the western frontier and in a later generation Lyman Beecher kept a sharp eye out for the papal invasion that never made it to the Mississippi Valley. The Mexican War had the San Patricio battalion, rebels in an unjust war and perhaps the nearest analogue. And there had been those fears back in 1893, when the APA was abroad in the land, of the St. Ignatius Day coup d'état that never was, not to mention tunnels from the Vatican to the White House abandoned in 1928. By the mid-1960s all those were historian's memories. Catholics manned the FBI, or seemed to do so, and the community was more blamed for excess of patriotism than for lack of it. At that point the Catholic Left introduced a new dimension to the dialogue.

The Catholic bishops had in 1966 reached a hesitant judgment that on balance American involvement in Vietnam was justified.[38] Two years later, in the wide-ranging pastoral letter "Human Life in Our Day," they were less sure. Defending the "fundamental right of political dissent," and advocating "rational debate" on public policy, the letter tried to

apply traditional "just war" criteria to the situation. The "inhuman dimension of suffering" and the physical losses being sustained in Vietnam
were weighed against prospective "disastrous" effects of "untimely withdrawal." The bishops did question the use of military force to solve
problems of "undernutrition, economic frustration, social stagnation and
political injustices."[39] In 1971 they issued a "Resolution on Southeast
Asia":

> At this point in history, it seems clear to us that whatever good we
> hope to achieve through continued involvement in this war is now out
> weighed by the destruction of human life and of moral values which it
> inflicts. It is our firm conviction, therefore, that the speedy end of this
> war is a moral imperative of the highest priority.[40]

In the 1968 letter the bishops had called for a change in the law to allow
for selective conscientious objection; by 1972 they were calling for amnesty for war resisters and deserters.[41]

While anti-war agitation continued, *America* wrote in August 1967 of
"the paroxysm of violence that is racking our cities."[42] With other Americans, Catholics suffered personal disillusionment and became impatient.
They suffered institutionally in cities and on university campuses. During
the five years of unrest that began in 1964 with Berkeley's Sproul Plaza as
backdrop, buildings were fired, president's offices occupied, and picket
lines thrown up on Catholic campuses as well as at Chicago and Columbia. A tiny minority of faculty and students struck St. John's University in
Queens, New York. The school became the first private university to sign
a labor contract with a faculty union.[43] The war, urban violence, and
academic unrest—and the psychological dislocation they occasioned—all
contributed to fray the ties that bound Americans to the past, whether
civil or ecclesiastical. Within Catholicism, as John Courtney Murray had
realized at the end of the Vatican Council, another fission was developing. Discussing the Declaration on Religious Liberty, Murray wrote that:

> The Council intended to make a clear distinction between religious free
> dom as a principle in the civil order and the Christian freedom that
> obtains even inside the Church. The two freedoms are distinct in kind
> and it would be perilous to confuse them. Nowhere does the declaration
> touch the issue of freedom within the Church.

"Undoubtedly, however," he added, "it will be a stimulus for the articulation of a full theology of Christian freedom in its relation to the doctrinal and disciplinary authority of the Church."[44] That articulation has not
taken place, and failure to understand the necessity for such a theology
has been a primary source of confusion and distress in the post-conciliar
church. Murray had rightly pointed to the need for theological under-

standing that reconciled two seeming opposites: the freedom of the Christian individual and the doctrinal and disciplinary authority claimed by the church. Problems arose whenever, from opposing points of view, either one was stressed without adequate attention to the other.

Pope Paul VI brought to New York City and the United Nations on October 4, 1965, the impassioned plea: "No more war; never again war." He offered mass in a packed Yankee Stadium and was gone that same night. By the time another pope, John Paul II, landed at Boston on October 1, 1979, to deliver fifty-three talks in a whirlwind seven days' visit to six cities and Irish Settlement, Iowa, Catholicism in the United States had experienced a decade and a half of tumultuous change.

In preparation for a meeting of the International Federation of Catholic Universities scheduled for Kinshasha, Zaire, in 1968, a group of educators met twice in 1967 to discuss the nature and role of the Catholic university. At the second meeting, held at the University of Notre Dame's retreat in Land O'Lakes, Wisconsin, from July 21 to 23, a statement was issued, signed by two bishops, twenty institutional representatives, and four foreign participants.[45] They agreed that, "to perform its teaching and research functions adequately, the Catholic university must have a true autonomy and academic freedom in the face of authority of whatever kind, lay or clerical, external to the academic community itself." The Land O'Lakes statement envisioned the Catholic university as "a community of learners or a community of scholars, in which Catholicism is *perceptibly present* and *effectively operative.*"

Philip Gleason has pointed out that at least from the mid-1920s "philosophy, rather than religion itself, was the critical element in integrating Catholic higher education." Catholic educators favored the approach of Father O'Hara of Notre Dame, who promoted "frequent reception of Holy Communion and a general intensification of piety and devotion." Few colleges offered a religion major—one survey found only three out of eighty-four—and serious theology courses for undergraduates began to be discussed only in 1939.[46] What was most radical about Land O'Lakes was its effort to find identity for a Catholic university "first of all and distinctively" in the presence of a group of scholars in all branches of theology. Their disciplines were termed essential to the integrity of such a university, their goal to achieve "the best possible intellectual understanding of religion and revelation and of man in all his varied relationships with God" by "exploring the depths of the Christian tradition and the total religious heritage of the world." The university was assigned the role of "critical reflective intelligence" for the church. Its research and its public service were to be oriented to "problems of greater human urgency or of greater public concern," with a special obligation to serve "the church and its component parts." The statement also contemplated a social dimension to university life in which students and faculty would explore together new forms of Christian living, witness, and service in an atmosphere of "meaningful liturgical and sacramental life" and "warm personal dialogue." Commitment to a more participatory style of university administration was advocated somewhat vaguely.

Idealistic visions quickly met the social reality of Catholic campus life in the late sixties. Restive faculties, many hastily recruited to handle booming enrollments and ignorant of or indifferent to the tradition being promoted, had other agenda. So did rebellious students, for whose multiple angers universities made fine surrogate targets. Catholic institutions also paid the price of decades of neglect of serious theological study. Theologians, biblical scholars, and historians capable of implementing the Land O'Lakes vision were in short supply and outnumbered by colleagues who did not understand or accept either the theological dimension of the plan or its advocacy of reflective, critical, and autonomous service to the church. Economics and the politics of state aid entered the picture with a vengeance. Catholic institutions, until the 1960s controlled by boards of trustees largely (in most cases, exclusively) made up of priests or members of sponsoring religious communities, moved in the sixties to boards with lay majorities.

Secularization was a further and quite different step. It was usually occasioned by the need to fulfill requirements for some form of state financial aid. One questionnaire in New Jersey asked for a count of "ikons" on campus and of books in the college library bearing an *imprimatur*. New York State hired a distinguished scholar, incidentally a Protestant minister, to determine whether Fordham's theology department was "indoctrinating" students (he found that they were not). All but four of the Empire State's Catholic colleges quietly altered listings in the *Official Catholic Directory* to indicate their secular status. The number of Catholic colleges and universities peaked in 1965 at three hundred nine. In 1980 there were two hundred thirty-nine.

Enrollment in Catholic elementary and secondary schools fell from 5.6 million in 1965 to less than 3.2 million in 1980. In 1965 there were 10,879 grade schools, against 8,149 in 1980. High schools in the same period dropped from 2,413 to 1,527. Despite the drop in schools and students, National Opinion Research Center surveys indicated that support among Catholics for parochial schools remained high.[47] In major urban centers a special feature is the inner-city school, financed by tuition payments and by diocesan or inter-parish programs in which more affluent segments of the community contribute to educational and social services in poorer areas. Catholic schools are prized by parents, many of them non-

Catholic. Explaining why she spent $1,100 of a $6,300 income on parochial school tuition, one mother, Diane Sánchez, told a *New York Times* reporter: "Education is the most important thing, and the kids learn more at Catholic schools."[48] Finances remain a serious problem, even though Catholic schools run at a per-pupil cost considerably lower than that of public schools ($462 against $2,607 in New York City in 1976–77), and some Title I funds to assist the educationally deprived have been available. In a series of decisions the Supreme Court has denied tax credits for parochial school parents, tuition reimbursement, and loan of wall maps and projectors, but allowed states to provide textbooks. The bishops repeated in 1967 their commitment to Catholic elementary and high schools as an "indispensable component of the Church's total commitment to education in the United States," and in 1970 declared that "the unfinished business on the agenda of Catholic schools includes the task of providing quality education for the poor and disadvantaged of our nation."[49]

The sixties cracked the melting-pot myth. Civil rights begat black pride and other Americans took a second look at their varied heritages. The age of ethnics arrived. Hispanics, already more than a quarter of the American population, increased when thousands fled Cuba in 1980. Vietnamese Catholics, "boat people" escaping communist victory in their country, settled across the United States. The longer-settled Italians and Poles exercised increasing influence in church circles. Eastern-rite Catholics, coldly received on arrival toward the end of the 19th century, counted eight dioceses of several rites and three archbishops. Other eastern-rite Catholics remained under the episcopal jurisdiction of local Latin-rite bishops, but carefully preserved their own identity.

The seventies saw changes in the Catholic black community. *Sepia* magazine headlined "CATHOLICS LOSING OUT AMONG BLACKS" and backed it up with statistics.[50] Between 1970 and 1975, 250 black seminarians withdrew from seminaries, 125 of 900 black sisters left their communities, and 25 of 190 black priests left the ordained ministry. Estimates were that 20 percent of black Catholics were no longer practicing, a figure not, however, out of line with more general statistics. The guard changed. In 1978 Dr. Thomas Wyatt Turner died.[51] A biology professor at Howard University and Hampton Institute, he was born in 1877 and in 1925 became a founder and first president of the Federated Colored Catholics of the United States, a vigorous advocacy group on black issues. In 1977 Marianist Brother Joseph Davis retired from the post of executive secretary of the National Office of Black Catholics, which he had held since its foundation in 1970. Associated with the NOBC are the National Black Catholic Clergy Caucus, the Black

Sisters' Conference, and the Black Catholic Lay Caucus. The first black bishop since Bishop Healy's death in 1900 was Auxiliary Bishop Harold R. Perry, S.V.D. (1966) in New Orleans. Bishop Joseph L. Howze of Biloxi became the first black to head a diocese in 1977.

Census estimates show slightly less than one-half the American Indian population—now preferring to be called Native Americans—living on reservations, with the rest largely congregated in urban areas. Catholic Native Americans have met in congress and formed a Federation of Catholic Indian Leaders. Interest is reviving in the stories of men like Black Elk, to the day of his death a practicing Catholic and catechist. Priests have engaged in dialogue with medicine men representing ancient tribal religions. Native American brothers, sisters, deacons, and priests work with missionaries on reservations in over forty dioceses. Most Native Americans live across the northern part of the country or in the Southwest. In recent years, the bishops have turned their attention to another part of the country and sponsored the Catholic Committee of Appalachia, which collaborates with others working in a thirteen-state eastern area. The bishops of the region issued in 1975 a statement entitled: "This Land Is Home to Me: A Pastoral Letter on Powerlessness in Appalachia."

The interfaith atmosphere in the United States as the 1980s begin is vastly superior to what it has been in the nation's past. Old fires are periodically rekindled on all sides, but cross-denominational cooperation is a reality far beyond the wildest imaginings of twenty years ago. Appointment by Presidents Nixon and Carter of personal representatives at the Vatican prompted only the most ritual of denunciations. Catholic priests belong to local ministerial associations, and sisters and priests have been staff members of the National Council of Churches. Reasonable arrangements are made for marriages of people belonging to different churches. Protestant ministers participate in Catholic services and Catholic priests in Protestant services. Inter-communion is not acknowledged and deep theological and cultural divides remain, but progress should not be gainsaid.

Besides close ecumenical cooperation on the parochial and local level, extensive relationships have developed in scholarly societies. Scholars of all faiths belong to the Society of Biblical Literature, of which Raymond E. Brown, S.S., has been President, and the Catholic Biblical Association. John Tracy Ellis, a Catholic, has been president of the Protestant-founded American Society of Church History and Methodist Albert Outler and Lutheran Martin E. Marty have headed the American Catholic Historical Association. Avery Dulles, S.J., has been president of the American Theological Society and Boston priest Philip King of the American Schools of Oriental Research. At four of the country's major theological centers—Chicago, Boston, Washington, and Berkeley—Catholic schools play significant roles in academic consortia which allow students to take courses in schools of differing Christian traditions. The Bishops' Committee for Interreligious and Ecumenical Affairs sponsors ongoing formal dialogues with the Orthodox and with a half-dozen Protestant traditions. A Secretariat for Catholic-Jewish relations has functioned since 1965.

Overseas missionary work among American Catholics has declined. The rapid pace of indigenization of the church in many parts of the globe is one reason. For internal reasons, countries like India severely discourage importation of clergy, but India has in fact begun to send its own Catholic missionaries to the Caribbean and Africa. To the extent that the great missionary expansion of the past century was a function of Western colonialism, it is largely dead. "Expatriate" brothers, sisters, priests, and lay volunteers remain, but as adjuncts of local churches. American missionaries work in one hundred twelve areas of the world outside the contiguous forty-eight states. Totals in 1977 were 2,882 priest-members of religious communities and 182 diocesan priests, 630 religious brothers and 42 seminarians, 2,781 sisters and 243 lay people. The Maryknoll Sisters were the largest single group of women. Among men's communities, the Jesuits and Maryknoll each had about 600 in the field. An important feature of American overseas work since World War II has been the work of Catholic Relief Services, already recognized by Merle Curti in 1963 as "the largest of the American volunteer overseas agencies."[52]

The segments of American labor on whose behalf the battles of the 1930s were fought have long since found their comfortable place in the American spectrum. Catholic efforts have more recently focused on the exploitation of Hispanics. In 1973 Bishop Sidney M. Metzger of El Paso wrote to every bishop in the United States asking support for the Farah boycott on behalf of Mexican-American workers.[53] Arizona-born César Chávez of the United Farm Workers had been perhaps the most explicitly religious labor leader in American history. Mary Hanna reported of him that "all of his thought, his work, spring from deeply Christian motivation."[54] Introduced to the corpus of Catholic social thought by San Francisco priests Donald McDonnell and Thomas McCullough, who had met him in the "Sal Si Puedes" barrio of San Jose in 1949, Chávez's range of action included strikes, picketing, and boycotts, but also pilgrimages behind the image of Our Lady of Guadalupe, fasting, and masses celebrated on flatbed trucks in the fields by priests wearing red *huelga* flags as vestments. Many of his opponents, the growers around Delano and in the San Joaquin valley were also Catholics, from families which had spent decades building up farms. Bishops like Aloysius J. Willinger, C.Ss.R., head of the diocese of Monterey-Fresno until 1967, were sympathetic to them. A major change occurred when Bishop Hugh A. Donohoe of Stockton appeared before a Senate investigating committee in 1966 to give the opinion of California's Catholic bishops that the farm problem was a moral problem, and that the farm workers had the right to form unions in their efforts to solve it, have access to labor organizers and to strike.[55]

The reductionist impulse which avoids confrontation with substantive issues and turns so many theological disputes among Catholics into tests of loyalty to the pope surfaced several times in the period after Vatican II in disputes at American universities and supplied criteria for judging the European—and later Latin American—theological luminaries whom Americans admired. It surfaced strongly in the controversy over the permissibility of married couples using "artificial" means of contraception.

The American bishops had discussed the topic of contraception for the first time in the pastoral letter of 1919. Their argument was that which had obtained in the Christian church since the 4th century. Referring to the story of Onan in Genesis 38:10, they rebuked those who with "fraudulent prudence would improve upon nature by defeating its obvious purpose."[56] Four years earlier, a public health nurse named Margaret Higgins Sanger had been indicted for sending information on birth control through the mails, and she was arrested in 1916 for running a birth control clinic in Brooklyn. On November 14, 1921, the *New York Times* carried the headline: "BIRTH CONTROL RAID MADE BY POLICE ON ARCHBISHOP'S ORDERS." Archbishop Hayes issued a statement in the aftermath of the police raid which climaxed the First American Birth Control Conference: "To take life after its inception is a horrible crime; but to prevent human life that the Creator is about to bring into being, is satanic."[57]

Not everyone appreciated the cardinal's rhetoric, or his priorities, but Catholic churchmen and theologians presented a solid front on the subject, as did most other churchmen until the 1930 Anglican Lambeth Conference moved to tolerate contraception under certain circumstances. Not until 1958 was the Anglican position altered to positive acceptance. A national sample in 1952 discovered that American Catholics were less committed to the sinfulness of "mechanical" birth control than they were to other points of church teaching, but 51 percent did think that it was sinful, while only 14 percent of Protestants and 10 percent of Jews thought so.[58] Chicago priest Andrew M. Greeley concluded in 1963:

> Most Catholics engage in family planning; most Catholics keep the Church's law (at least most of the time); upper class Catholics do better than lower class Catholics; Irish do better than Italians. . . . Catholic

education makes a difference. Rhythm is not as ineffective, at least relatively, as has been thought.[59]

Greeley's article appeared in the same year that Harvard gynecologist
John Rock published *The Time Has Come: A Catholic Doctor's Proposal
To End the Battle over Birth Control,* in which he defended use of the
contraceptive pill, in the development of which he had participated. Professor James Hitchcock of St. Louis University, a staunch defender of the
papal position on the subject, has documented subsequent stages in the
story.[60]

Vatican II made reference without elaboration to "unlawful contraceptive practices" in the Pastoral Constitution on the Church in the Modern
World (number 47 and number 51) noted that faithful Catholics were
"forbidden to use methods disapproved of by the teaching authority of
the Church in its interpretation of the divine law." Pope Paul had in
October 1964 reserved any final statement on the subject to himself.
Eighteen Americans were among the group of intellectuals, physicians,
and journalists who at the same time made a *démarche* at the council
questioning the continuing validity of the "particular conception and understanding of the natural law" on which the standard teaching on birth
control was based.[61] Writing on "Social Science and the Theology of
War," Gordon Zahn had asked a similar question when he noted that
no bishop had protested government boasts about weapons designed to
slaughter millions of noncombatants, but that the whole hierarchy condemned an advisory report to the President which "gave favorable attention to artificial birth control as a solution to overpopulation problems. . . . " Zahn felt the need for moral principles to "be continually
reinterpreted and re-applied to an ever-changing social reality."[62]

Early in the summer of 1966, the special commission created by Pope
John XXIII and expanded by Paul VI submitted three reports to the pope.
On April 19, 1967, the Kansas City-based *National Catholic Reporter* published the texts of the reports and it became clear that a majority of the
papal commission members favored a change in the official position. A
minority report, with American moral theologian John C. Ford, S.J., as a
principal author, upheld the ban on artificial contraception.

Just over a year later, on July 25, 1968, Pope Paul's encyclical letter *Humanae Vitae* reaffirmed the prohibition. The encyclical met a storm of protest in the United States, much of it centering in the Catholic University of
America. Within weeks, six hundred theologians had signed a statement
taking exception to "the ecclesiology implied and the methodology used"
by the pope and accused him of neglecting the witness of "the life of the
church in its totality," and the special witness of "many Catholic couples"

and of "the separated churches and ecclesial communities."[63] Cardinal O'Boyle had a difficult problem when fifty-one Washington priests publicly dissented from the encyclical's teaching. He announced that he could not permit them to teach what he himself was not allowed to teach. Two years later his position was upheld by the Vatican, but those of the priests who continued in the ministry were not held to public retraction of their dissent.[64] The November 1968 pastoral letter, *Human Life in Our Day*, supported the papal position. A federally financed national fertility study concluded in 1970 that "Catholics are becoming more and more like other parents in their use of the pill and other contraceptive devices,"[65] but theological discussion goes on. *Human Sexuality*, a cooperative study done under the aegis of the Catholic Theological Society of America, continued the dissenting tradition,[66] while in 1978 John C. Ford, with Germain Grisez, restated the positions on which *Humanae Vitae* was based.[67]

In 1980, just four years short of the bicentennial of John Carroll's appointment as first independent superior of the Catholic Church in the United States, the country's Catholic population stood by official count at 49,812,178 in a national population estimated at 221,719,000. The hierarchy numbered 10 cardinals, 37 archbishops, 306 bishops, and 85 abbots. Priests had increased since the last count a year before. There were 59,892, assisted by 4,093 deacons, nearly 800 of them ordained in the year just passed. The number of religious brothers and sisters continued to decline. The number of sisters had peaked in 1965, when there were 181,421, the mainstay of the church's extensive network of schools, hospitals, and charitable institutions. The figure stood at 126,517 in 1980.[68] Religious brothers, most of them also involved in schools and hospital work, were down from a high of 12,539 in 1965 to 8,563 fifteen years later. The number of seminarians stood at an all-time low. There had been 48,992 in 1964. In 1980 there were 13,226. A considerable proportion of those studying in Catholic seminaries in Chicago's southside ecumenical cluster, in Cambridge, and in Berkeley's Graduate Theological Union were women, ineligible for ordination.

The percentage of Catholics moving out of the church has increased since 1965. A rate of 7 percent was regular through the 1950s and early 1960s. By the early 1970s surveys calculated it at 14 percent, and Mary Hanna writes in 1979, "Surveys show that 16.1 percent of Americans who were raised as Catholics profess another or no religion when they reach adulthood."[69] A familiar index of Catholicity, attendance at mass, is confirmatory: Gallup found that 75 percent regular attendance in 1957 had slipped to 54 percent by 1975. The National Opinion Research Center's figures were not appreciably different: 71 percent attendance for 1966 and 50 percent in 1975, with an increase of those attending mass "practically never" from 6 percent to 12 percent in the same period.[70] Still, there were both statistical and impressionistic signs that not all was lost. A British professor, leaving for home after fourteen years on the west coast, wrote of his California parish: "Our parish community is, quite simply, the best community I have ever had the good fortune to live in during the whole of my life." He documented his praise with evidence of the parish's prayer and liturgical life, outreach to the sick, needy, and troubled, bible study groups, and ecumenical contacts.[71] Over eight million Catholics were in 1980 involved in religious education programs, under teachers who had scientific catechetical preparation. Summer school and year-round programs to prepare teachers and parish directors of religious education have become highly professional.

The Catholic Church entered the 1980s committed as a community to working out its salvation in and through this world. In new ways the world was less comfortable for the church. The news media, the therapist, the scientist were competitors. So was the widespread sense of freedom to be non-religious or utterly selective, of which Thomas Luckmann spoke in *The Invisible Religion*.[72] Moral problems not treated in old manuals are important. New values run through new generations. Tobacco is now a vice, but marijuana is less offensive than formerly. Ecology, environmentalism, energy-saving (but not by way of nuclear power), and equal rights for women are causes demanding recognition. Gay power is a fact. The understanding and valuation of human life and conditions under which it may legitimately be terminated—by abortion, euthanasia, legal execution, or hydrogen bomb—are questions which engage the Catholic community and divide it deeply, sometimes within itself, sometimes from others.

A degree of pessimism prevailed in the seventies. In 1957 Gallup pollsters had found that 79 percent of Catholics and 66 percent of Protestants thought the influence of religion in American life was increasing. In the interim, Catholic spirits fared less well than Protestant. By 1975, the percentages were 34 percent for Protestants and only 30 percent for Catholics.[73] The malaise must be balanced against enthusiasm in parishes and on campuses and the matter-of-fact religiousness that characterizes many more practicing Catholics. In their 1976 study, *Catholic Schools in a Declining Church,* NORC staffers Greeley, McCready, and McCourt placed high priority for the "decline of Catholic religiousness" on the impact of *Humanae Vitae,* which was followed by decline in acceptance of papal leadership and of the church's official ethic.[74] Douglas W. Johnson has concentrated in his analysis on the way in which changes in the church were "disruptive to the purposes and practices of some Roman Catholic adherents."[75] A process of demythologizing has been under way: of clergy and sisters, of the church itself as immutable even in manifestly mutable aspects, of the identification of the church with Western economic, social, and political interests. For many it was an exciting, challenging time in which to participate in change. Others were less active, but not disaffected.

The American Catholic community's roots lie in the soil of St. Clement's Island, Mount Desert, and St. Augustine and in the immigrant docks of New York and Boston, San Francisco and New Orleans. Others have ancestors who crossed the Rio Grande and the Canadian border. Nowadays new immigrants arrive by jet. A survey taken on the upper east side of Manhattan in the spring of 1976 summed up results of the past and hopes for the future.[76] Mass attendance was lower than in standard surveys: only about one-third came regularly. These Catholic New Yorkers were less disturbed by *Humanae Vitae* than NORC's results suggested. They did not reject reforms identified with Vatican II. Their major problems were far more significant. They had to do with central Catholic teachings: the existence of God, the divinity of Christ, the reality of heaven and hell. They were dissatisfied with the liturgy and particularly with poor preaching and they wanted clear explanations of church belief. Father Philip J. Murnion of the archdiocesan Office of Pastoral Research commented:

> The church, as a community of clear positions, strong leadership and important relationships has been lost somewhere along the way. People do not want "that old time religion." They are not asking for retrenchment to rigid rules and clerical dominance. They favor an outreaching church, lay participation, and a revival of a sense of community around faith and mutual caring. They want leadership.

A plainer statement of the end of the immigrant phase of American Catholic history could not be made. Whether one looks to the structuring and activities of the ecclesial community, to personal, paraliturgical or liturgical prayer life, or to the beliefs central to the core of it all, the fundamental challenges facing American Catholics in 1981 are challenges rooted in theology. The community will approach those challenges out of its own tradition, its own social memory, its own special understanding of reality. Michael Novak once tried to capture that special sense when he wrote that "Catholics *do* tend to differ [from others] in their sense of reality, in their version of realism, in their particular passion for justice, in their sense of the meaning of family and children, in facing death, in their approach to education, to suffering and to personal relations."[77] That special sense was characteristic of the original shareholders in Spanish and French America and on Maryland and Pennsylvania farms. It was evident in the tiny city parish of Philadelphia. It found different expressions, but preserved continuity, during the long and turbulent immigrant era from which the church is in many ways still emerging. How it will be verified in the new age is the story of the future.

Notes

INTRODUCTION

1. Henry Warner Bowden, "John Gilmary Shea; A Study of Method and Goals in Historiography," *Catholic Historical Review,* 54(1968):251.
2. Dogmatic Constitution on the Church, in Walter M. Abbott, S.J. and Joseph Gallagher (eds.), *The Documents of Vatican II* (New York 1966), pp. 24–37.
3. Sydney E. Ahlstrom, *A Religious History of the American People* (New Haven, 1972), pp. 1094–96.
4. John Gilmary Shea, *History of the Catholic Church in the United States* (4 vols.: Akron, 1886–92), 2:211.
5. For statistics of Catholic population, see Gerald Shaughnessy, S.M., *Has the Immigrant Kept the Faith?* (New York, 1925).
6. Rodney Stark and Charles Y. Glock, *American Piety: The Nature of Religious Commitment* (Berkeley, 1968), pp. 205–6.
7. *Ibid.,* p. 207.
8. Will Herberg, *Protestant-Catholic-Jew; An Essay in American Religious Sociology* (Garden City 1955).
9. Winthrop S. Hudson, "Reflections on the Meandering Career of Recent Protestant Theology," *The Christian Century,* September 6, 1972, pp. 868–71.
10. Ahlstrom, *Religious History,* pp. 1047–54.
11. See chapter 9, "Religion in American Society," in Elizabeth K. Nottingham, *Religion: A Sociological View* (New York 1971).
12. Henri de Lubac, S.J., *Catholicism: Christ and the Common Destiny of Man* (Universe Books ed.; London, 1962), p. xv.
13. William C. McCready and Andrew M. Greeley, "The End of American Catholicism?" *America,* October 28, 1972, p. 334.
14. John Whitney Evans, "American Youth and the Institutional Church; A Pastoral Reflection," *Proceedings of the Twentieth Annual Convention, The Catholic Theological Society of America* (Bronx, 1972), pp. 179–80.

CHAPTER I

1. On Florida see Michael V. Gannon, *The Cross in the Sand, the Early Catholic Church in Florida 1513–1870* (Gainesville, 1965), on which this section of the present chapter is largely based, Eugene Lyon, *The Enterprise of Florida: Pedro Menendez de Aviles and the Spanish Conquest of 1565–1568* (Gainesville, 1976); and John Tracy Ellis, *Catholics in Colonial America* (Baltimore, 1965), pp. 27–46.
2. Clifford M. Lewis, S.J., and Albert J. Loomie, S.J., *The Spanish Jesuit Mission to Virginia, 1570–1572* (Chapel Hill, 1953).
3. Gannon, *Cross in the Sand,* p. 54.
4. *Ibid.,* pp. 64–65; John Tracy Ellis (ed.), *Documents of American Catholic*

History (rev. ed.; Chicago, 1967), 1:18–23, has the complete text of the reports.

5. On Texas see Carlos E. Castañeda, *Our Catholic Heritage in Texas* (6 vols.; Austin, 1936–50); Ellis, *Colonial America,* pp. 75–106.
6. Wayne Moquin, with Charles Van Doren (eds.), *A Documentary History of the Mexican Americans* (New York, 1971), pp. 86–93.
7. Ellis, *Colonial America,* pp. 47–74.
8. Herbert E. Bolton, *Coronado on the Turquoise Trail: Knight of Pueblos and Plains* (Albuquerque, 1949).
9. Ellis, *Documents,* 1:9–10.
10. Moquin, *Mexican Americans,* pp. 26–30.
11. *Ibid.,* pp. 31–42; Ellis, *Documents,* 1:15–17.
12. Moquin, *Mexican Americans* pp. 43–58.
13. *Ibid.,* pp. 70–75.; Henry Warner Bowden, "Spanish Missions, Cultural Conflict and the Pueblo Revolt of 1680," *Church History,* 44(1975):217–28.
14. Howard Roberts Lamar, *The Far Southwest 1846–1912, A Territorial History* (New York, 1970), pp. 23–55; Moquin, *Mexican Americans* pp. 80–5; John L. Kissell, *Kiva, Cross and Crown: The Pecos Indians and New Mexico, 1540–1840* (Washington, 1979); *id., The Missions of New Mexico since 1776* (Albuquerque, 1979); Marta Weigle, *Brothers of Light, Brothers of Blood: The Pentitentes of the Southwest* (Albuquerque, 1976).
15. Herbert E. Bolton, *Rim of Christendom: A Biography of Eusebio Francisco Kino* (New York, 1936); Ellis, *Documents,* 1:24–27; John L. Kissell, *Friars, Soldiers and Reformers: Hispanic Arizona and the Sonora Mission, 1767–1856* (Tucson, 1976).
16. Ellis, *Colonial America,* pp. 107–22.
17. Moquin, *Mexican Americans,* pp. 14–18.
18. Clark Wissler, *Indians of the United States* (Garden City, 1966), pp. 202–5; Richard B. Morris (ed.), *Encyclopedia of American History* (New York, 1970), p. 8.
19. Maynard J. Geiger, O.F.M., *The Life and Times of Fray Junipero Serra, O.F.M., or the Man Who Never Turned Back, 1713–1784* (2 vols.; Washington, 1959).
20. Maynard Geiger, O.F.M., *Mission Santa Barbara 1782–1965* (Santa Barbara, 1965); Francis F. Guest, O.F.M., *Fermín Francisco de Lasuén (1736–1803, A Biography* Washington, 1973); Moquin, *Mexican Americans,* pp. 98–102; 110–15; Ellis, *Documents,* 1:34–47.
21. Leonard Pitt, *The Decline of the Californios: A Social History of the Spanish-Speaking Californians, 1846–1890* (Berkeley, 1971).
22. A vivid reconstruction is in Helen Hunt Jackson's 1884 novel, *Ramona.*
23. John B. McGloin, S.J., *California's First Archbishop: The Life of Joseph Sadoc Alemany, O.P., 1814–1888* (New York, 1966), p. 71.

CHAPTER II

1. Ellis, *Colonial America,* pp. 125–45. On the French American Empire, W. J. Eules, *France in America* (New York, 1973); Lucien Campeau, S.J., *La premiere mission d'Acadie 1602–1616* (Quebec, 1967); Antonio Dragon, S.J., *Le vrai visage de Sébastian Râle* (Montréal, 1975).

2. Reuben Gold Thwaites (ed.), *Jesuit Relations and Allied Documents* (73 vols.; Cleveland 1896–1901). See also Francois X. Charlevoix, S.J., *History and General Development of New France* (1744).
3. William V. Bangert, S.J., *A History of the Society of Jesus* (St. Louis, 1972), p. 265; Ellis, *Documents*, 1:49–51.
4. Francis X. Talbot, S.J., *Saint Among the Hurons: The Life of Jean de Brebeuf* (New York, 1949).
5. Ellis, *Colonial America*, pp. 146–67.
6. Francis X. Talbot, S.J., *Saint Among Savages: The Life of Isaac Jogues* (New York, 1935); Ellis, *Documents*, 1:52–60.
7. *Ibid.*, pp. 63–71.
8. Kenneth McNaught, *The Pelican History of Canada* (Baltimore, 1969), p. 39.
9. Bangert, *Society of Jesus*, p. 264.
10. Ellis, *Colonial America*, pp. 168–84.
11. Ellis, *Colonial America*, p. 180.
12. John Gilmary Shea (ed.), *Discovery and Exploration of the Mississippi Valley* (2nd ed.; Albany, 1903); Ellis, *Documents*, 1:60–63.
13. Joseph P. Donnelly, S.J., *Jacques Marquette: 1637–1675* (Chicago, 1968).
14. Ellis, *Colonial America*, pp. 185–231.
15. Ellis, *Documents*, 1:81–84.
16. Reuben Gold Thwaites, ed., *Louis Hennepin: A New Discovery of a Vast Country in America* (Chicago, 1903); Ellis, *Documents*, 1:72–81.
17. Lionel St. George Lindsay, ed., "Letters from the Archdiocesan Archives at Quebec, 1768–1788," *Records of the American Catholic Historical Society of Philadelphia*, 20(1909):414; Joseph P. Donnelly, S.J., *Pierre Gibault, Missionary, 1732–1802* (Chicago, 1971).
18. Martin I.J. Griffin, "Colonel John Francis Hamtramck, a Catholic Soldier of the Revolution, 1756–1803," *American Catholic Historical Researches*, 15 (1898):114–123.
19. Frank B. Woodford and Albert Hyma, *Gabriel Richard, Frontier Ambassador* (Detroit, 1958).

CHAPTER III

1. Ellis, *Colonial America*, 232–312; Charles E. O'Neill, S.J., *Church and State in French Colonial Louisiana: Policy and Politics to 1732* (New Haven, 1966).
2. Claude L. Vogel, O.F.M. Cap., *The Capuchins in French Louisiana, 1722–1766* (Washington, 1928); Jean Delanglez, S.J., *The French Jesuits in Lower Louisiana, 1700–1763* (*ibid.*, 1935); Ellis, *Documents*, 1:84–93.
3. John Gilmary Shea, *The History of the Catholic Church in the United Sates* (4 vols.; Akron, 1886–92), 2:579.
4. Richard E. Greenleaf, "The Inquisition in Spanish Louisiana, 1762–1800," *New Mexico Historical Review*, 50(1975):45–72.
5. Ellis, *Documents*, 1:184–8.
6. *Ibid.*, 1:185–88.

CHAPTER IV

1. *The Book of the General Lauues and Liberties concerning the Inhabitants of Massachusetts* (Cambridge, 1648), p. 26.

2. Colonial anti-Catholicism has been studied by Mary A. Ray, B.V.M., *American Opinion of Roman Catholicism in the Eighteenth Century* (New York, 1936). George Lincoln Burr, ed., *Narratives of the Witchcraft Cases, 1648–1706* (New York, 1914), pp. 103–17 (excerpt from Cotton Mather, *Memorable Providences*).

3. Raymond J. Lahey, "The Role of Religion in Lord Baltimore's Colonial Enterprise," *Maryland Historical Magazine,* 72(Winter, 1977):492–511.

4. Commager, *DAH,* pp. 21–22; Ellis, *DACH,* 1:95–98.

5. *Ibid.,* 1:98.

6. *Ibid.,* 1:104.

7. *The Archives of Maryland* (ed. William Hand Browne; 32 vols.; Baltimore, 1883–1912), 26:44–46. [Henceforth, *AM.*]

8. Robert Baird, *Religion in America* (abridged and introduced by Henry Warner Bowden; New York, 1970), p. 50.

9. *AM,* 1:82–84.

10. *AM,* 41:566–67. Although the assembly's acts speak of toleration for Christians, it extended in practice also to Jews, as the prominence in early colonial records of Jacob Lumbrozo attests.

11. Matthew Page Andrews, *The Founding of Maryland* (Baltimore, 1933), p. 144. For the Act of 1649, *AM,* 1:244–47; Commager, *DAH;* Ellis, *DACH,* 1.

12. Lawrence H. Gipson, *The British Empire before the American Revolution* (New York, 1958), 2:48–51, claims that "of all the British plantations in North America, Maryland had the severest anti-Catholic laws." See *AM* 24:91–98, 265–73; 26:340–41, 431–32; 30:228–29, 612–17; 33:287–89; 50:198.

13. Ellen Hart Smith, *Charles Carroll of Carrollton* (repr., New York, 1971), p. 87.

14. Thomas O'Brien Hanley, S.J. (ed.), *The John Carroll Papers* (3 vols.; Notre Dame, 1976), pp. 342–43. [Henceforth, *JCP.*]

15. Thomas Hughes, S.J., *History of the Society of Jesus in North America, Colonial and Federal* (4 vols.; New York, 1907–17), Documents, vol. 1, pt. 1:158–61.

16. *Ibid.,* 31.

17. Smith, *Charles Carroll,* p. 32.

18. Edward I. Devitt, S.J., "Letters of Father Joseph Mosley, 1757–1786," *Woodstock Letters,* 35(1906):44.

19. *Ibid.,* p. 50.

20. Edward I. Devitt, S.J., "History of the Maryland-New York Province, III; Newtown-Leonardtown," *Woodstock Letters,* 61(1932):15–16.

21. Edwin W. Beitzell, *The Jesuit Missions of St. Mary's County, Maryland* (Abell, Maryland, 1977), p. 26.

22. Thomas Hughes. S.J., "Educational Convoys to Europe in the Olden Time," *American Ecclesiastical Review,* 29(1903):24–39.

23. Joseph T. Durkin, S.J., "Catholic Training for Maryland Catholics," *Historical Records and Studies,* 32(1941), 70–82.

24. Hughes, *History,* Documents, vol. 1, pt. 1:136–37.

CHAPTER V

1. Hughes, Documents, vol. 1, pt. 1:103, 106.
2. Ibid., 112.
3. William W. Hening, ed., The Statutes at Large; Being a Collection of All the Laws of Virginia (Richmond, 1809), 1:268–69.
4. Hughes, Documents, vol. 1, pt. 1:123.
5. Ibid., 128–29.
6. Ibid., 130–31.
7. Ibid., 139–41.
8. Bruce E. Steiner, "The Catholic Brents of Colonial Virginia," The Virginia Magazine of History and Biography, 70(1962):387–409; Douglas Southall Freeman, George Washington, 1 (New York, 1948), Appendix I-1, "The Northern Neck Proprietary to 1745," pp. 447–513.
9. Carl Bridenbaugh, Cities in Revolt:Urban Life in America 1743–1776 (New York, 1955), p. 135.
10. American Catholic Historical Researches, 11(1894):58.
11. Hughes, Documents, vol. 1, pt. 1:220–21.
12. American Catholic Historical Researches, 22(1905):122.
13. Deborah Logan and Edward Armstrong, eds., Correspondence between William Penn and James Logan (Philadelphia, 1872), 2:354.
14. Dennis Clark, The Irish in Philadelphia: Ten Generations of Urban Experience (Philadelphia, 1973), p. 8.
15. John C. Fitzpatrick, ed., The Writings of George Washington (39 vols.; Washington, 1931–34), 1:498–99, 506. Hughes, Text, 2:546. Pennsylvania Archives (Philadelphia, 1853), 2:694.
16. J. Thomas Scharf and Thompson Westcott, History of Philadelphia 1609–1884 (Philadelphia, 1884), 2:1369–70.
17. American Catholic Historical Researches, 6(1889)182–85; Martin I. J. Griffin, "The Sir John James Fund," Records of the American Catholic Historical Society of Philadelphia, 9(1898):195–209.
18. Robert E. Quigley, "Catholic Beginnings in the Delaware Valley," in James F. Connelly, ed., The History of the Archdiocese of Philadelphia (Philadelphia, 1976), p. 20.
19. JCP, 1:65.
20. Bernhard Duhr, S.J., Geschichte der Jesuiten in den Ländern deutscher Zunge (4 vols.; Freiburg-Regensburg, 1907–28), 3:511; JCP, 1:406.
21. Edmund B. O'Callaghan, ed., Documents Relative to the Colonial History of the State of New York (15 vols.; Albany, 1853–87), 3:218.
22. John H. Kennedy, O.M.I., Thomas Dongan, Governor of New York, 1682–1688 (Washington, 1930).
23. Hugh Hastings, ed., Ecclesiastical Records, State of New York (7 vols.; Albany, 1901–16, 2:864.
24. Henry Foley, S.J., ed., Records of the English Province of the Society of Jesus (7 vols.; London, 1877–83), 7:343.

CHAPTER VI

1. With the suppression of their order, the priests came under the direct control of Bishop Richard Challoner, Vicar Apostolic of the London District,

who named their former Religious superior, John Lewis, his representative. One of the German priests in America died in 1775, and an Englishman in 1779. The rest remained through the war and after. Five American ex-Jesuits in Europe came home before the summer of 1776, another (the future Archbishop Leonard Neale) arrived in 1783, one day after Congress officially declared hostilities ended. Ten American ex-Jesuits and a secular priest remained abroad. One postwar American returnee became a Protestant Episcopal cergyman and one English priest in America abandoned the ministry when the Jesuit order was suppressed, but returned to it twenty years later.

2. Devitt, *Woodstock Letters*, 35:233–34.
3. *JCP*, 1:32.
4. Devitt, *loc. cit.*, 238.
5. *Boston Gazette*, April 11, 1768, quoted in Charles H. Metzger, S.J., *Catholics and the American Revolution: A Study in Religious Climate* (Chicago, 1962), p. 14.
6. John Webb Pratt, *Religion, Politics and Diversity: The Church-State Theme in New York History* (Ithaca, 1967), pp. 84–85.
7. John Adams, "On Canon and Feudal Law," in *Works* (ed. Charles Francis Adams; 10 vols.; Boston, 1850–56), 3:454.
8. "Deane Papers," *Collections of the New-York Historical Society* 2:475–77.
9. Worthington Chauncey Ford, ed., *Journals of the Continental Congress 1774–1789* (34 vols.; Washington, 1904), 1:34–35.
10. James H. Hutson, ed., *A Decent Respect for the Opinions of Mankind, Congressional State Papers 1774–1776* (Washington, 1975), p. 29.
11. *Ibid.*, p. 76.
12. *Ibid.*, p. 67.
13. Fitzpatrick, *Writings of Washington*, 3:492.
14. Peter S. Onuf, ed., *Maryland and the Empire, 1773: The Antilon-First Citizen Letters* (Baltimore, 1974), pp. 121–22.
15. *Ibid.*, p. 66.
16. *Ibid.*, pp. 225–26; Carroll to William Graves, August 15, 1774, in *Maryland Historical Magazine*, 32 (1928):223.
17. Edmund C. Burnett, ed., *Letters of Members of the Continental Congress* (5 vols.; Washington, 1921–31), 1:354.
18. George W. Corner, ed., *The Autobiography of Benjamin Rush* (Princeton, 1948), p. 151
19. Martin I. J. Griffin, *Catholics and the American Revolution* (3 vols.; Ridley Park Philadelphia, 1907–11), 1:352.
20. *JCP*, 1:59.
21. Dennis C. Kurjack, "St. Mary's and St. Joseph's Churches," in Luther P. Eisenhart, ed., *Historic Philadelphia* (Philadelphia, 1953), pp. 203–4.
22. *American Catholic Historical Researches*, 24(1907):329–38.
23. Griffin, *Catholics and the American Revolution, passim*.
24. *American Catholic Historical Researches*, 13(1896):171–72.
25. Corner, *Rush*, pp. 201–2.
26. *JCP*, 1:51; 56.
27. *Ibid.*, 1:343.
28. Joseph Zwinge, S.J., "Jesuit Farms in Maryland," *Woodstock Letters*, 42(1913).

29. *Ibid.*, 146–48.
30. Devitt, *Woodstock Letters*, 35:227–45; *JCP*, 1:338.
31. John M. Daley, S. J., "Pioneer Missionary: Ferdinand Farmer, S.J., 1720–1786," *Woodstock Letters*, 75(1946):105–15; 207–31; 311–21.
32. *JCP*, 1:66–67.
33. L. H. Butterfield, ed., *The Adams Papers* (Cambridge, 1961), 2nd ser., Adams Family Correspondence, 1(December, 1761-May, 1776):166–67; and 1st ser., Diary and Autobiography of John Adams, 2(Diary, 1771–1781):150; Ford, *Journal of the Continental Congress*, 2:439.
34. New York *Royal Gazette*, May 20, 1780.
35. *American Catholic Historical Researches*, 27(1910):218; *Collections of the Massachusetts Historical Society*, 5th ser., 2(Boston, 1882):61–62.
36. *JCP*, 1:278–79.
37. Ray W. Pettingill, ed., *Letters from America 1776–1779* (Boston/New York, 1924), p. 57; Samuel K. Wilson, "Bishop Briand and the American Revolution," *Catholic Historical Review*, 19(1933):133–47.
38. *American Catholic Historical Researches*, 23(1906):97–120.
39. *American Catholic Historical Researches*, 23(1906):203–39.
40. *Ibid.*:203; and 24(1907):7.
41. Burnett, *Letters of Members of the Continental Congress*, 1:354.
42. *JCP*, 1:46.
43. Peter Force, ed., *American Archives*, 4th ser., 3:1683.
44. Griffin, *Catholics and the American Revolution*, 1:105; Allan S. Everest, *Moses Hazen and the Canadian Refugees in the American Revolution* (Syracuse, 1976), pp. 40–41.
45. *American Catholic Historical Researches*, 16(1899):113; Mary Celeste Leger, *The Catholic Indians in Maine* (Washington, 1929), p. 144.
46. James Sullivan, "The History of the Penobscot Indians," *Collections of the Massachusetts Historical Society*, 1st ser., 9(1804):207.
47. Samuel G. Drake, *Book of the Indians* (Boston, 1861), p. 339.
48. Force, *American Archives*, 4:1:1349.
49. *Ibid.*, 4:3:1465–66.
50. *Ibid.*, 4:1:839, 184.
51. *American Catholic Historical Researches*, 25(1908):214.
52. A. Melançon, *Vie de L'Abbé Bourg* (Rimouski, 1921), p. 99.
53. John P. Donnelly, S.J., "Pierre Gibault," *New Catholic Encyclopedia*, 6: 464.
54. Richard K. MacMaster, S.J., "Parish in Arms: A Study of Father John MacKenna and the Mohawk Valley Loyalists, 1773–1778," *Historical Records and Studies*, 45(1957):107–25; Ewen J. MacDonald, "Father Roderick Macdonell at St. Regis and the Glen Garry Catholics," *Catholic Historical Review*, 19(1933):265–74.
55. *Collections of the Massachusetts Historical Society*, 5th ser., 3(1882):265.
56. *JCP*, 1:80–81.
57. *Ibid.*, 1:259.

CHAPTER VII

1. *JCP*, 1:66.
2. *Ibid.*, 1:71–77.

3. Edwin H. Burton, *The Life and Times of Bishop Challoner, 1691–1781* (2 vols.; New York, 1909), 2:127.
4. Hughes, Text, 2:591.
5. Burton, *Bishop Challoner*, p. 138.
6. *American Catholic Historical Researches*, 21(1904):118–20.
7. Carl Bridenbaugh, *Mitre and Sceptre* (New York, 1962), pp. 99–100.
8. Thorpe to Charles Plowden, Rome, March 3, 1784, Archives of the English Jesuit Province, London. [Henceforth AEP.]
9. *JCP*, 1:68.
10. Worthington C. Hunt *et al.*, eds., *Journals of the Continental Congress, 1774–1789* (33 vols.; Washington, 1904–36), 27:368.
11. AEP, Thorpe to Plowden, Rome, May 8, 1784.
12. Jules A. Baisnée, S.S., *France and the Establishment of the American Hierarchy: The Myth of French Interference, 1783–1784* (Baltimore, 1934), p. 79.
13. *JCP*, 1:146.
14. AEP, Thorpe to Plowden, Rome, July 27, 1785.
15. Shea, *History of the Catholic Church in the United States*, 2:243; Ellis, *Documents*, 1:143.
16. A. H. Smyth, ed., *The Writings of Benjamin Franklin* (10 vols.; New York, 1905–7), 10:349.
17. *JCP*, 1:162–63.
18. *Ibid.*, 1:155, 78.
19. *Ibid.*, 1:165.
20. AEP, Thorpe to Plowden, Rome, July 27, 1785.
21. *JCP*, 1:212.
22. *Ibid.*, 1:169–85.
23. *Ibid.*, 1:219.
24. *Ibid.*, 1:390.
25. *Ibid.*, 1:213.
26. *Ibid.*, 1:47.
27. Archives of the Congregation for Propagation of the Faith. Rome, Scritture riferite nei Congressi, I: America centrale dal Canada all'isthmo di Panama, 1673–1775, fols. 442rv, 443r, Charles M. Whelan, O.F.M. Cap., to Nuncio at Paris, New York, January 28, 1785.
28. See John Talbot Smith, *The Catholic Church in New York* (2 vols.; New York, 1908).
29. Bernard U. Campbell, "Memoirs of the Life and Times of Archbishop Carroll," *The U.S. Catholic Magazine*, 6(1846):103.
30. *JCP*, 1:202–3.
31. *Ibid.*, 1:196–97.
32. *Ibid.*, 1:208.
33. *Ibid.*, 1:203–6.
34. *Ibid.*, 1:204.
35. *Ibid.*, 1:272–73; 332; 356.
36. John Adams, *Works* (10 vols.; Boston, 1856), 9:355.
37. *Collections of the Massachusetts Historical Society*, 5th Series, 2:110.
38. John E. Sexton, "The First Foundation (1788–1789)," in Robert H. Lord, John E. Sexton, and Edward T. Harrington, *History of the Archdiocese of Boston* (3 vols.; New York, 1944), 2:375–411.
39. *JCP*, 1:354.

40. Poterie's pamphlet was *The Ressurection of Laurent Ricci; or A True and Exact History of the Jesuits* (Philadelphia, 1789).
41. *Collections of the Massachusetts Historical Society*, 5th Series, 2:123.
42. *JCP*, 1:197.
43. Charles Francis Adams, *Letters of Mrs. Adams* (Boston, 1848), p. 228.
44. Sexton, "First Foundation," pp. 364–65; 367.
45. *Ibid.*, p. 422.
46. *JCP*, 1:441.
47. Sexton, "First Foundation," pp. 448–49. See Mary Celeste Leger, R.S.M., *The Catholic Indian Missions in Maine (1611–1820)* (Washington, 1929).
48. Ford, *Journals of the Continental Congress*, 12:257.
49. *American Catholic Historical Researches*, 5(1888):28.
50. *JCP*, 2:129. See 2:131–32.
51. *Ibid.*, 2:256.
52. *Ibid.*, *2:112.*
53. Benjamin J. Webb, *The Centenary of Catholicity in Kentucky* (Louisville, 1884).
54. *JCP*, 1:326.
55. Victor F. O'Daniel, O.P., *The Dominican Province of St. Joseph* (New York, 1942), pp. 8–45.
56. *JCP*, 1:490.
57. Webb, *Catholicity in Kentucky*, p. 52.
58. Agnes G. McGann, S.C.N., "Sisters of Charity of Nazareth, Kentucky," *New Catholic Encyclopedia*, 3:476–77; Mary Matilda Barrett, S.L. "Sisters of Loretto," *ibid.*, 8:995.
59. *JCP* 1:348–49, 355, 361, etc. See "The First American Catholic Bible," *American Catholic Historical Researches*, 3(1887):64–68; Lawrence F. Flick, "Selections from the Correspondence of the Deceased Matthew Carey," *Records of the American Catholic Historical Society of Philadelphia*, 9(1898): 352–84; Joseph Jackson, "First Catholic Bible Printed in America," *ibid.*, 56 (1945):18–25.
60. Vincent J. Fecher, S.V.D., *A Study of the Movement for German National Parishes in Philadelphia and Baltimore, 1787–1802* (Rome, 1955).
61. *JCP*, 1:147.
62. *Ibid.*
63. *Ibid.*, 1:160.
64. *An Address to the Roman Catholics of the United States of America by a Catholic Clergyman* (Annapolis, 1784). Reprinted in *JCP*, 1:82–144.
65. *Ibid.*, 1:148–49.
66. *Ibid.*, 1:226–33.
67. *Ibid.*, 1:524.
68. *Ibid.*, 1:436–37. See James Hennesey, S.J., "An Eighteenth Century Bishop: John Carroll of Baltimore," *Archivum Historiae Pontificiae*, 16(1978):171–204; *id.*, "The Vision of John Carroll," *Thought*, 54(1979):322–33.
69. *JCP*, 1:516; Charles G. Herbermann, *The Sulpicians in the United States* (New York, 1916); Joseph W. Ruane, *The Beginnings of the Society of St. Sulpice in the United States, 1791–1829* (Washington, 1935).
70. *JCP*, 1:228–29.
71. *Ibid.*, 1:312.

72. *Ibid.*, 2:319.
73. *Ibid.*, 1:285.
74. *Ibid.*, 1:279–82.

CHAPTER VIII

1. Robert T. Handy, *A Christian America: Protestant Hopes and Historical Realities* (New York, 1971), pp. 27–64; Martin E. Marty, *Righteous Empire: The Protestant Experience in America* (New York, 1970).
2. *JCP*, 2:383. On Neale, see James Hennesey, S.J., "First American Foreign Missionary: Leonard Neale in Guyana," *Records of the American Catholic Historical Society of Philadelphia*, 83(1972):82–86.
3. M. Bernetta Brislen, O.S.F., "The Episcopacy of Leonard Neale, Second Archbishop of Baltimore," *Historical Records and Studies*, 34(1945):20–111.
4. Annabelle M. Melville, *Jean Lefebvre de Cheverus, 1768–1836* (Milwaukee, 1958).
5. See *Historical Records and Studies, passim;* and Benedict J. Fenwick, S.J., *Memoirs to Serve for the Future* (ed. Joseph M. McCarthy; New York, 1978), pp. 180–255.
6. J. Herman Schauinger, *Cathedrals in the Wilderness* (Milwaukee, 1952).
7. Martin I.J. Griffin, *History of the Rt. Rev. Michael Egan, First Bishop of Philadelphia* (Philadelphia, 1893).
8. Arthur J. Ennis, O.S.A., "The New Diocese of Philadelphia," in James F. Connelly, ed., *The History of the Archdiocese of Philadelphia* (Philadelphia, 1976), pp. 83–104.
9. Francis X. Curran, S.J., "The Jesuit Colony in New York, 1808–1817," *Historical Records and Studies*, 42(1954):51–97.
10. O'Daniel, *The Dominican Province of St. Joseph*, pp. 116–23.
11. *JCP*, 2:95.
12. *Ibid.*, 3:312.
13. APF, Lettere . . . dell'Anno 1821, Francesco Fontana to Ambrose Maréchal, Rome, July 21, 1821.
14. Francis E. Tourscher, O.S.A., *Old St. Augustine's* (Philadelphia, 1937).
15. Frederick J. Easterly, C.M., *The Life of the Rt. Rev. Joseph Rosati, First Bishop of St. Louis, 1789–1843* (Washington, 1942).
16. Charles W. Currier, C.Ss.R., *Carmel in America* (Baltimore, 1890).
17. Annabelle M. Melville, *Elizabeth Bayley Seton, 1774–1821* (New York, 1951).
18. Anna C. Minogue, *Loretto, Annals of the Century* (New York, 1912); Anna B. McGill, *The Sisters of Charity of Nazareth, Kentucky* (New York, 1917).
19. Louise Callan, R.S.C.J., *The Society of the Sacred Heart in North America* (New York, 1937); *id.*, *Philippine Duchesne, Frontier Missionary of the Sacred Heart, 1769–1852* (Westminster, 1957).
20. Anna C. Minogue, *Pages from a Hundred Years of Dominican History: the Story of the Congregation of Saint Catherine of Siena* (New York, 1922).
21. Grace M. Sherwood. *The Oblates' One Hundred and One Years* (New York, 1931); Joseph B. Code, "Negro Sisterhoods in the United States," *America*, January 8, 1938, pp. 318–19.
22. Ellis, *Documents*, 1:170–172.

23. *American Catholic Historical Researches,* 9(1892):124–127; 18(1901): 168–70; *JCP,* 1:293; 2:264; 527.

24. Hughes, Documents, Vol. 1, pt. 1:238, 241.

25. APF, Scritture riferite nei Congressi, 5, fols. 243rv and 244rv, John Connolly to Propaganda, February 26, 1818.

26. Ennis, "The New Diocese of Philadelphia," p. 97; Francis E. Tourscher, O.S.A., *The Hogan Schism and Trustee Troubles in St. Mary's Church, Philadelphia, 1820–1829* (Philadelphia, 1930), pp. 43–46.

27. Hugh J. Nolan, "Francis Patrick Kenrick, First Coadjutor-Bishop," in Connelly, pp. 195–96.

28. Peter Guilday, *The Life and Times of John England, First Bishop of Charleston, 1786–1842* (2 vols.; New York, 1927), 1:225.

29. Richard Shaw, *Dagger John: The Unquiet Life and Times of Archbishop John Hughes of New York* (New York, 1977), p. 227.

30. Vincent J. Fecher, S.V.D., *A Study of the Movement for German National Parishes in Philadelphia and Baltimore, 1787–1802* (Rome, 1955).

31. O'Daniel, *The Dominican Province of St. Joseph,* pp. 131–38.

32. Tourscher, *Hogan Schism;* Ennis, pp. 92–93.

33. Tourscher, *Hogan Schism,* p. 78, Ennis, p. 95.

34. Peter Guilday, *The Catholic Church in Virginia, 1815–1822* (New York, 1924); *id., John England,* 1:164–282.

Chapter IX

1. J. Herman Schauinger, *William Gaston, Carolinian* (Milwaukee, 1949).

2. Carl B. Swisher, *Roger B. Taney* (New York, 1935); Vincent C. Hopkins, S.J., *Dred Scott's Case* (New York, 1951).

3. Alexis de Tocqueville, *Democracy in America* (ed. Phillips Bradley; 2 vols.; New York, 1945), 1:311–12; 2:28, 30.

4. Annabelle M. Melville, *Elizabeth Bayley Seton, 1774–1821* (New York, 1951); Joseph I. Dirvin, C.M., *Mrs. Seton* (New York, 1962).

5. Hudson Mitchell, S.J., "Virgil Horace Barber," *Woodstock Letters,* 79 (1950): 297–334.

6. Edwin V. Sullivan, "James Roosevelt Bayley," in *The Bishops of Newark 1853–1978* (South Orange, 1978), pp. 1–22; Alfred C. Rush, C.Ss.R., and Thomas J. Donaghy, F.S.C., "The Saintly John Neumann and His Coadjutor Archbishop Wood," in Connelly, ed., *History of the Archdiocese of Philadelphia,* pp. 237–70.

7. Walter Elliott, C.S.P., *The Life of Father Hecker* (New York, 1891); Joseph McSorley, C.S.P., *Father Hecker and His Friends* (St. Louis, 1952; Vincent F. Holden, C.S.P., *The Yankee Paul: Isaac Thomas Hecker* (Milwaukee, 1958).

8. Juliana Wadhams, *The Case of Cornelia Connelly* (New York, 1957).

9. Thomas R. Ryan, C.Pp.S., *Orestes A. Brownson* (Huntington, 1976); Arthur M. Schlesinger, Jr., *Orestes A. Brownson: A Pilgrim's Progress* (Boston, 1939).

10. Joseph and Helen McCadden, *Father Varela: Torch Bearer from Cuba* (New York, 1969). On pre–Civil War Catholic New York, see Jay P. Dolan, *The Immigrant Church: New York's Irish and German Catholics, 1815–1865* (Baltimore, 1975).

11. Anon., *Memoir of Pierre Toussaint, Born a Slave in St. Domingo* (Boston, 1854).
12. Oliver Carlson, *The Man Who Made News: James Gordon Bennett* (New York, 1942). Shaw, *Dagger John,* gives a running account of the Hughes-Bennett skirmishes.
13. Elsa Loacher Jones, "Francis Martin Drexel's Years in America," *Records of the American Catholic Historical Society of Philadelphia,* 85(1974):129–40; Consuela M. Duffy, S.B.S., *Katharine Drexel: A Biography* (Philadelphia, 1966).
14. William M. Halsey, *The Survival of American Innocence: Catholicism in an Era of Disillusionment, 1920–1940* (Notre Dame, 1980), p. 100.
15. John M. Daley, S.J., *Georgetown University: Origin and Early Years* (Washington, 1957).
16. Mary M. Meline and Edward F. X. McSweeny, *The Story of the Mountain: Mount Saint Mary's College and Seminary* (2 vols.; Emmitsburg, 1911).
17. Robert I. Gannon, S.J., *Up to the Present: The Story of Fordham* (Garden City, 1967).
18. Thomas J. Schlereth, *The University of Notre Dame: A Portrait of Its History and Campus* (Notre Dame/London, 1976).
19. Gower and Leliaert, pp. 104–6.
20. Gabriel Gravier, *Relation du voyage des dames religieuses ursulines de Rouen á Nouvelle Orlèans* (Paris, 1872); Henry C. Semple, S.J., ed., *The Ursulines in New Orleans and Our Lady of Prompt Succor* (New York, 1925).
21. Lawrence Kehoe, ed., *Complete Works of the Most Rev. John Hughes, D.D., Archbishop of New York* (2 vols.; New York, 1865), 2:708. The quotation is from a pastoral letter of February 10, 1847.
22. William Kailer Dunn, *What Happened to Religious Education? The Decline of Religious Teaching in the Public Elementary Schools, 1776–1861* (Baltimore, 1958).
23. Vincent P. Lannie, *Public Money and Parochial Education: Bishop Hughes, Governor Seward and the New York School Controversy* (Cleveland, 1968); Diane Ravitch, *The Great School Wars: New York City, 1805–1973* (New York, 1974), pp. 3–84; John Webb Pratt, *Religion, Politics, and Diversity: The Church-State Theme in New York History* (Ithaca, 1967), pp. 161–90; Raymond A. Mohl, "Education as Social Control in New York City, 1784–1825," *New York History,* 51(1970):231.
24. Harold A. Buetow, *Of Singular Benefit: The Story of Catholic Education in the United States* (New York, 1970).
25. G. E. Baker, ed., *Works of William H. Seward* (2 vols.; New York, 1853–54), 2:215.
26. Hugh J. Nolan, ed., *Pastoral Letters of the American Hierarchy, 1792–1970* (Huntington, L. I., 1971), pp. 6, 7.
27. Buetow, *Of Singular Benefit,* p. 146.
28. *Concilium Plenarium totius Americae septentrionalis foederatae . . . Anno 1852* (Baltimore, 1853), p. 47.
29. John H. Lamott, *History of the Archdiocese of Cincinnati* (New York, 1921), pp. 214–15.
30. Paul Horgan, *Lamy of Santa Fe: His Life and Times* (New York, 1975), p. 40.

31. John H. Lamott, *History of the Archdiocese of Cincinnati, 1821–1921* (New York, 1921); Robert F. Trisco, *The Holy See and the Nascent Church in the Middle Western United States, 1826–1850* (Rome, 1962), pp. 212–14.

32. Charles Lemarié, *Monseigneur Bruté de Rémur, premier évêque de Vincennes aux États-Unis (1834–1839)* (Paris, 1974); id., *Les Missionaires bretons de l'Indiana au XIXe siècle* (Angers, 1973); John J. Hogan, *On the Mission in Missouri 1857–1868* (Kansas City, 1892; reprinted, Westminster, 1972); Timothy Walch, "Catholic Institutions and Urban Development: The View from Nineteenth-Century Chicago and Milwaukee," *Catholic Historical Review*, 64(1978):16–32; John Rothensteiner, *History of the Archdiocese of St. Louis* (2 vols.; St. Louis, 1928); William B. Faherty, S.J., *Dream by the River: Two Centuries of St. Louis Catholicism, 1766–1967* (St. Louis, 1973); Frederick J. Easterley, C.M., *The Life of the Rt. Rev. Joseph Rosati, First Bishop of St. Louis, 1789–1843* (Washington, 1942); Samuel J. Miller, "Peter Richard Kenrick, Bishop and Archbishop of St. Louis, 1806–1896," *Records of the American Catholic Historical Society of Philadelphia*, 84(1973):3-163; Peter L. Johnson, *Centennial Essays for the Milwaukee Archdiocese, 1843–1943* (Milwaukee, 1943); Roger Baudier, *The Catholic Church in Louisiana* (New Orleans, 1939).

33. Trisco, *The Holy See and the Nascent Church*, p. 232.

34. Theodore Roemer, O.F.M. Cap., *Ten Decades of Alms* (St. Louis, 1942).

35. Colman Barry, O.S.B., *The Catholic Church and German Americans* (Milwaukee, 1953), p. 17.

36. Daniel Callahan, *The Mind of the Catholic Layman* (New York, 1963), p. 48.

37. Vincent F. Holden, C.S.P., "Father Hecker's Vision Vindicated," *Historical Records and Studies*, 50(1964):49.

38. Mary Ramona Mattingly, *The Catholic Church on the Kentucky Frontier 1785–1812* (Washington, 1936), pp. 139–40.

39. Francis E. Tourscher, O.S.A., *The Kenrick-Frenaye Correspondence* (Philadelphia, 1920), p. 156.

40. Shaw, *Dagger John*, pp. 304–5; 328–29.

41. Peter Guilday, *A History of the Councils of Baltimore, 1791–1884* (New York, 1932); id., *The National Pastorals of the American Hierarchy, 1792–1919* (Washington, 1923); Eugenio Corecco, *La Formazione della Chiesa Cattolica negli Stati Uniti d'America attraverso l'attività sinodale* (Brescia, 1970); James Hennesey, S.J., "Councils of Baltimore," *The New Catholic Encyclopedia* (15 vols.; New York, 1967), 2:38–43.

42. *Diurnal of the Right Rev. John England, D.D., First Bishop of Charleston, S.C., from 1820 to 1823* (Philadelphia, 1895), pp. 66–67.

43. For the text of England's Constitution, see Ignatius A. Reynolds, ed., *The Works of the Right Rev. John England, First Bishop of Charleston* (5 vols.; Baltimore, 1849), 5:91–108.

CHAPTER X

1. Harland Hogue, *Christian Seed in Western Soil* (Berkeley, 1965), p. 11.

2. William G. McLoughlin, *Revivals, Awakenings and Reform* (Chicago/London, 1978), pp. 98–140.

3. Federalist Paper 2 (October 31, 1787), in Jacob E. Cooke, ed., *The Federalist Papers* (Middletown, 1961), p. 9.
4. Sexton, 1:772.
5. *Ibid.,* p. 806.
6. *Ibid.,* p. 774.
7. Robert Baird, *Religion in America* (ed., Henry Warner Bowden; New York, 1970), pp. 261–62.
8. Carleton Beals, *Brass-Knuckle Crusade: The Great Know-Nothing Conspiracy, 1820–1860* (New York, 1960), p. 99. See Ray Allen Billington, *The Protestant Crusade 1800–1860* (Chicago, 1938).
9. Beals, *Brass-Knuckle Crusade,* p. 36, from Beecher's August 10, 1834, sermon, repeated in several Boston churches that Sunday, on the eve of the burning of the Charlestown convent.
10. Horace Bushnell, *Barbarism, the First Danger* (New York, 1847). The line quoted is the capitalized final line of the sermon.
11. Archivio Segreto Vaticano, Fondo Segretariato di Stato, Consolari Pontifici, 1854, file 292.
12. Billington, *The Protestant Crusade,* p. 422.
13. Dagmar R. Lebreton, *Chahta-Ima: The Life of Adrien-Emmanual Rouquette* (Baton Rouge, 1947).
14. Gower and Leliaert, *Brownson-Hecker Correspondence,* p. 126.
15. Billington, *The Protestant Crusade,* pp. 46–47; Shaw, *Dagger John,* p. 67.
16. Shaw, *Dagger John,* pp. 64–70, Billington, *The Protestant Crusade,* p. 55.
17. Billington, *The Protestant Crusade,* pp. 62–63; Shaw, *Dagger John* pp. 94–100.
18. James H. Smylie, "Phases in Protestant-Roman Catholic Relations in the United States: Monologue, Debate and Dialogue," *Religion in Life,* 34 (1965):258–69.
19. Billington, *The Protestant Crusade,* pp. 122–25.
20. *Ibid.,* pp. 90–92; 99–108.
21. *Ibid.,* pp. 68–76; James J. Kenneally, "The Burning of the Ursuline Convent; A Different View," *Records of the American Catholic Historical Society of Philadelphia,* 90(1979):15–21.
22. Billington, *The Protestant Crusade,* pp. 220–34; Michael Feldberg, *The Philadelphia Riots of 1844: A Study of Ethnic Conflict* (Westport, 1975).
23. *American Catholic Historical Researches,* 8(1891):89–90; repr., *Records of the American Catholic Historical Society of Philadelphia,* 80(1969):108–10.
24. *Ibid.*
25. Reply of George W. Biddle, Philadelphia, June 18, 1844, to "Address of the Catholic Lay Citizens," *ibid.,* p. 146.
26. Shaw, *Dagger John,* p. 197.
27. Billington, *The Protestant Crusade,* pp. 200–211.
28. James F. Connelly, *The Visit of Archbishop Gaetano Bedini to the United States, June, 1853—February, 1854* (Rome, 1960).
29. Leo F. Stock, *United States Ministers to the Papal States: Instructions and Despatches, 1848–1868* (Washington, 1933).
30. Miller, *"Peter Richard Kenrick,"* p. 57.
31. *Woodstock Letters,* 16 (1887):324–25.
32. Thomas W. Spalding, *Martin John Spalding: American Churchman* (Washington, 1973), pp. 70–71.

33. *Ibid.,* p. 72, from a "card" in the Louisville *Journal,* August 8, 1855.
34. *Ibid.*
35. Roy P. Basler, ed., *The Collected Works of Abraham Lincoln* (9 vols.; New Brunswick, 1953–55), 2:323.
36. Gower and Leliaert, *Brownson-Hecker Correspondence,* p. 182.

CHAPTER XI

1. Mathias M. Hoffman, *The Church Founders of the Northwest* (Milwaukee, 1937).
2. Mary Nona McGreal, O.P., "Samuel Mazzuchelli, Participant in Frontier Democracy," *Records of the American Catholic Historical Society of Philadelphia* 87(1976):99–116; Mary Gilbert Kelly, O.P., *Catholic Immigrant Colonization Projects in the United States, 1815–1860* (New York, 1937); Henry J. Browne, "Archbishop Hughes and Western Colonization," *Catholic Historical Review,* 36(1950):269–73.
3. Mathias M. Hoffman, *Arms and the Monk! The Trappist Saga in Mid-America* (Dubuque, 1952).
4. M. Jane Coogan, B.V.M., *The Price of Our Heritage: History of the Sisters of Charity of the Blessed Virgin Mary* (2 vols.; Dubuque, 1975).
5. Peter L. Johnson, *Crosier on the Frontier: A Life of John Martin Henni* (Madison, 1959).
6. Peter Beckman, O.S.B., *The Catholic Church on the Kansas Frontier, 1850–1877* (Washington, 1943). On Miége, See Gilbert J. Garraghan, S.J., *The Jesuits of the Middle United States* (3 vols.; New York, 1938), *passim.*
7. Thomas T. McAvoy, C.S.C., *The Catholic Church in Indiana, 1789–1834* (New York, 1940), p. 19.
8. Garraghan, *Jesuits,* 2:177.
9. Joseph Gregorich, *The Apostle of the Chippewas: The Life Story of the Most Rev. Frederick Baraga, the First Bishop of Marquette* (Chicago, 1932).
10. Garraghan, *Jesuits,* 2:183, n.18.
11. *Ibid.,* p. 197.
12. For Hoecken's diary, see Thomas A. Kinsella, *A Centenary of Catholicity in Kansas, 1822–1922* (Kansas City, 1921).
13. Garraghan, *Jesuits,* p. 186.
14. *Ibid.,* p. 205.
15. *Ibid.,* pp. 229ff.; 442ff.; 493ff.
16. Howard L. Harrod, *Mission among the Blackfeet* (Oklahoma City, 1971).
17. Garraghan, *Jesuits,* pp. 236ff.
18. Hiram M. Chittenden and Albert T. Richardson, *Life, Letters and Travels of Father Pierre-Jean DeSmet, S.J., 1801–1873* (4 vols.; New York, 1905).
19. Nicolas Point, S.J., *Wilderness Kingdom: Indian Life in the Rocky Mountains, 1840–1847* (tr. Joseph P. Donnelly, S.J.; New York, 1967).
20. Frederick V. Holman, *John McLoughlin, the Father of Oregon* (Cleveland, 1907).
21. Clarence B. Bagley, ed., *Early Catholic Missions in Old Oregon* (2 vols.; Seattle, 1932); Letitia M. Lyons, *Francis Norbert Blanchet and the Founding of the Oregon Missions, 1838–1848* (Washington, 1940).
22. Garraghan, *Jesuits,* p. 267.
23. *Ibid.*

24. *Ibid.*, pp. 276ff.
25. For the general picture, see Robert I. Burns, S.J., *Jesuits and the Indian Wars of the Northwest* (New Haven, 1966).
26. Garraghan, *Jesuits*, pp. 370–72.
27. James P. Shannon, *Catholic Colonization on the Western Frontier* (New Haven, 1957).
28. Beckman, *Kansas Frontier,;* Henry W. Casper, S.J., *History of the Catholic Church in Nebraska* (3 vols.; Milwaukee, 1960–1966).
29. Mary Ursula Thomas, "The Catholic Church and the Oklahoma Frontier, 1824–1907," unpub. Ph.D. diss., St. Louis University, 1938.
30. William J. Howlett, *Life of the Right Reverend Joseph P. Machebeuf* (Pueblo, 1908).
31. Robert J. Dwyer, *The Gentile Comes to Utah* (Washington, 1941); Thomas F. O'Dea, *The Mormons* (Chicago, 1957), p. 107.
32. Jean Baptiste Salpointe, *Soldiers of the Cross: Notes on the Ecclesiatical History of New Mexico, Arizona and Colorado* (Banning, 1898); Francis J. Weber, "Arizona Catholicism in 1878: A Report by John Baptist Salpointe," *The Journal of Arizona History*, 9(1968):119–39.
33. Carlos E. Castañeda, *Our Catholic Heritage in Texas* (6 vols.; Austin, 1936–50), vol. 6.
34. Ellis, *Documents*, 1:253–58, a letter from Odin to the Vincentian superior-general.
35. Horgan, *Lamy*, pp. 233–36.
36. James F. Meline, *Two Thousand Miles on Horseback: Santa Fe and Back* (New York, 1867), pp. 189–90.
37. Howard Roberts Lamar, *The Far Southwest 1846–1912: A Territorial History* (New York, 1970), p. 29.
38. Horgan, *Lamy*, p. 196.
39. Wayne Moquin and Charles Van Doren, ed., *A Documentary History of the Mexican Americans* (New York, 1971), pp. 151–52.
40. For a sympathetic view of Martinez, see Lamar, *Far Southwest*, pp. 39–41 and *passim.*
41. Horgan, *Lamy*, p. 440.
42. "PADRES Organizing for 'Chicano Power,' " *National Catholic Reporter*, April 2, 1971, p. 18.
43. Garraghan, *Jesuits*, 2:401.
44. Ellis, *Documents*, 1:305–6.
45. John Bernard McGloin, S.J., *California's First Archbishop: The Life of Joseph Sadoc Alemany, O.P., 1814–1888* (New York, 1966), pp. 124–26.
46. *Ibid.*, pp. 100–101.
47. Ellis, *Documents*, 1:306.
48. Louis B. Wright, *Culture on the Moving Frontier* (New York, 1961), p. 141.
49. Gerald J. McKevitt, S.J., *The University of Santa Clara: A History* (Stanford, 1979); John B. McGloin, S.J., *Jesuits by the Golden Gate: The Society of Jesus in San Francisco, 1849–1969* (San Francisco, 1972).
50. McGloin, *Jesuits by the Goldon Gates*, pp. 80–82.
51. Leonard Pitt, *The Decline of the Californios: A Social History of the Spanish-Speaking Californians, 1846–1890* (Berkeley, 1971), p. 146.
52. Francis J. Weber, *California's Reluctant Prelate: The Life and Times of Right Reverend Thaddeus Amat. C.M. (1811–1878)* (Los Angeles, 1964).

53. Moquin and Van Doren, *Mexican Americans,* pp. 111–12.
54. Pitt, *Decline of the Californios,* pp. 48–68.
55. Josiah Royce, *California from the Conquest of 1846 to the Second Vigilance Committee in San Francisco: A Study of American Character* (ed. Robert G. Cleland; New York, 1948), p. 287.
56. Pitt, *Decline of the Californios,* pp. 136–37.
57. Andrew F. Rolle, *California: A History* (New York, 1963), pp. 124–25.

CHAPTER XII

1. *JCP,* 3:313.
2. "Brother Mobberley's Diary," *Woodstock Letters,* 32(1903):13–14.
3. Robert K. Judge, S.J., "Foundation and First Administration of the Maryland Province, V: The Slave Question," *Woodstock Letters,* 88(1959):392–401.
4. Nathaniel E. Green, *The Silent Believers* (Louisville, 1972), p. 23.
5. APF, Lettere, 346, fols. 70v, 71r; 350, fol. 10r; 354, fols. 289r, 446v, 447r; 355, fol. 417r; Scritture, 20, fols. 238r, 239v, 290r, 291v, 333rv, 334v, 892rv, 893rv, 1562rv, 1563rv; Congressi, America Centrale, 16, fols. 644rv, 645r, 1197r, 1198r; 17, fols. 173r, 375r; 18, fols. 339rv, 340r, 453rv, 456r, 1188rv; 19, fols. 872r, 873rv.
6. Joseph B. Code, "Negro Sisterhoods in the United States," *America,* January 8, 1938, pp. 318–19; Minogue, *Loretto Annals,* pp. 95–97.
7. Billington, *Protestant Crusade,* p. 425. For a survey of Catholic reaction, see Madeleine Hooke Rice, *American Catholic Opinion on the Slavery Controversy* (New York, 1944).
8. John England, *Letters to the Honorable John Forsyth on the Subject of Domestic Slavery* (Baltimore, 1844).
9. Joseph D. Brockhage, *Francis Patrick Kenrick's Opinion on Slavery* (Washington, 1955), p. 242;
10. Shaw, *Dagger John,* pp. 334–35.
11. George P. Rawick, gen. ed., *The American Slave: A Composite Autobiography* (Westport, 1972), 16:190036.
12. *American Catholic Historical Researches,* 8(1891):71.
13. *Proceedings of the Massachusetts Historical Society, 1871–1873,* pp. 445–47.
14. Green, *Silent Believers,* pp. 34–35, from *The Catholic Advocate,* September 14, 1839; January 26, 1836.
15. Mary Alphonsine Frawley, S.S.J., *Patrick Donahoe* (Washington, 1946).
16. Edward Allen, O.S.B., "The Slavery Question in Catholic Newspapers," *Historical Records and Studies,* 26(1936):99–167.
17. Shaw, *Dagger John,* p. 360.
18. *Ibid.,* p. 335.
19. Theodore Maynard, *Orestes Brownson: Yankee, Radical, Catholic* (New York, 1943), pp. 321–22. Vincent A. Lapomarda, S.J., "Orestes Augustus Brownson: A Nineteenth-Century View of the Blacks in American Society," *Mid-America,* 53(1971):160–69.
20. Ellis, *Documents,* 1:379–83.
21. Pitt, *Decline of the Californios,* p. 183.
22. Spalding, *Martin John Spalding,* pp. 130–31.

23. Shaw, *Dagger John,* p. 343. On McMaster, see Mary Augustine Kwitchin, O.S.F., *James Alphonsus McMaster: A Study in American Thought* (Washington, 1949).
24. Shaw, *Dagger John,* p. 355.
25. *Ibid.,* p. 337.
26. *Ibid.,* p. 342.
27. *Ibid.,* p. 344.
28. *Ibid.,* p. 360.
29. Ellis, *Documents,* 1:348–56, (Lynch); Lawrence Kehoe, ed., Complete Works of the Most Rev. John Hughes, D.D., Archbishop of New York (2 vols.; New York, 1866), 2:513–20 (Hughes).
30. Rena M. Andrews, "Archbishop Hughes and the Civil War," Ph.D. diss., University of Chicago, 1935.
31. Shaw, *Dagger John,* p. 356.
32. James McCague, *The Second Rebellion: The Story of the New York City Draft Riots of 1863* (New York, 1968); Thomas F. Meehan, "Archbishop Hughes and the Draft Riots," *Historical Records and Studies,* 1(1899):171–90. Shaw, *Dagger John,* pp. 361–69.
33. Spalding, *Martin John Spalding,* pp. 162–63.
34. Oscar Hugh Lipscomb, "The Administration of John Quinlan, Second Bishop of Mobile, 1859–1883," *Records of the American Catholic Historical Society of Philadelphia,* 78(1967):37.
35. *Ibid.,* pp. 34–35.
36. Michael V. Gannon, *Rebel Bishop; The Life and Era of Augustin Verot* (Milwaukee, 1964), pp. 31–32.
37. Lipscomb, "Quinlan," p. 38.
38. Leo Francis Stock, "Catholic Participation in the Diplomacy of the Southern Confederacy," *Catholic Historical Review,* 16(1930):1–18.
39. Ignatius L. Ryan, C.P. "Confederate Agents in Ireland," *Historical Records and Studies,* 26(1936): 40–91; "Father John Bannon, S.J.," ibid., 92–98. Bannon became a Jesuit in Ireland in 1865.
40. Lipscomb, "Quinlan," p. 60. In James J. Pillar, O.M.I., *The Catholic Church in Mississippi 1837–1865* (New Orleans, 1964), pp. 151–347, deal with the war years.
41. McGloin, *Alemany,* p. 183.
42. Pitt, *Decline of the Californios,* pp. 230–33.
43. Horgan, *Lamy,* pp. 288–94.
44. Samuel J. Miller, "Peter Richard Kenrick, Bishop and Archbishop of St. Louis, 1806–1896," *Records of the American Catholic Historical Society of Philadelphia,* 84(1973):64–70.
45. Spalding, *Martin John Spalding,* pp. 138–39; Lipscomb, "Quinlan," p. 37.
46. Paul E. Ryan, *History of the Diocese of Covington, Kentucky* (Covington, 1954), p. 172.
47. Spalding, *Martin John Spalding,* pp. 128ff.
48. O'Daniel, *Dominican Province of St. Joseph,* pp. 202–6.
49. James Gibbons, "My Memories," *Dublin Review,* 110(1917):165.
50. James H. Bailey, *A History of the Diocese of Richmond: The Formative Years* (Richmond, 1956), p. 145.
51. Lipscomb, "Quinlan," p. 42.
52. Lamar, *The Far Southwest,* p. 115.

53. Roger Baudier, *The Catholic Church in Louisiana* (New Orleans, 1939).
54. Joseph T. Durkin, S.J., *Stephen R. Mallory, Confederate Navy Chief* (Chapel Hill, 1954).
55. Gannon, *Verot,* pp. 94–107.
56. Lipscomb, "Quinlan," pp. 50–54; Ellis, *Documents,* 1:368–70; Ewens, *Role of the Nun,* pp. 221–40.
57. Stock, "Catholic Participation," pp. 1–18.
58. Shaw, *Dagger John,* pp. 355–56.
59. Noel Blakiston, ed., *The Roman Question: Extracts from the Despatches of Odo Russell from Rome, 1858–1870* (London, 1962), p. 288.
60. Loretta C. Feiertag, *American Public Opinion on Diplomatic Relations between the United States and the Papal States, 1847–1867* (Washington, 1933), pp. 112–14.
61. David [Thomas W.] Spalding, C.F.X., "Martin John Spalding's 'Dissertation on the American Civil War,' " *Catholic Historical Review,* 52(1966): 66–85; Spalding, *Martin John Spalding,* pp. 140–44.

CHAPTER XIII

1. Spalding, *Martin John Spalding,* pp. 180, 191; 149–50.
2. Gannon, *Verot,* pp. 109–14; Spalding, *Martin John Spalding,* pp. 164–65.
3. *Ibid.,* p. 166.
4. Guy W. Moore, *The Case of Mrs. Surratt: Her Controversial Trial and Execution for Conspiracy in the Lincoln Assassination* (Norman, 1954); William O. Madden, S.J., "American Catholic Support for the Papal Army, 1866–1868," H.E.D. dissertation, Pontifical Gregorian University, Rome, 1968, pp. 44–52.
5. Spalding, *Martin, John Spalding,* pp. 194–237.
6. James Hennesey, S.J., "The Baltimore Council of 1866: An American Syllabus," *Records of the American Catholic Historical Society of Philadelphia,* 76(1965):165–72.
7. *Ibid.,* p. 171. See *id.,* "Papacy and Episcopacy in Nineteenth Century American Catholic Thought, " *ibid.,* 77(1966):175–89.
8. Nolan, *Pastoral Letters,* p. 136.
9. *Ibid.,* p. 154.
10. Miller, "Peter Richard Kenrick," pp. 76–81; Spalding, *Martin John Spalding,* pp. 219–33.
11. Edward Misch, "The American Bishops and the Negro from the Civil War to the Third Plenary Council of Baltimore (1865–1884)," H.E.D. dissertation, Pontifical Gregorian University, Rome, 1968; Spalding, *Martin John Spalding,* pp. 221–22.
12. Gannon, *Rebel Bishop,* pp. 115–44.
13. E. Merton Coulter, *The South During Reconstruction, 1865–1877* (Baton Rouge, 1947), p. 338.
14. Gannon, *Rebel Bishop,* p. 117.
15. Albert J. Raboteau, *Slave Religion: The "Invisible Institution" in the Antebellum South* (Oxford/New York, 1978), pp. 87–89; 271–75.
16. Albert S. Foley, S.J., *God's Men of Color: The Colored Catholic Priests of the United States, 1854–1954* (New York, 1954).

17. Albert S. Foley, S.J., *Bishop Healy: Beloved Outcaste* (New York, 1954); Thomas J. O'Donnell, S.J., "For Bread and Wine," *Woodstock Letters,* 80 (1951):99–142.
18. John T. Gillard, S.S.J., *The Catholic Church and the American Negro* (Baltimore, 1929); *id., Colored Catholics in the United States* (Baltimore, 1941).
19. William D'Arcy, *The Fenian Movement in the United States, 1858–1886* (Washington, 1947); Spalding, *Martin John Spalding,* pp. 245–50.
20. James Hennesey, S.J., "Prelude to Vatican I: American Bishops and the Definition of the Immaculate Conception," *Theological Studies,* 25(1964): 409–19.
21. Hennesey, "Baltimore Council," pp. 161–65.
22. Madden, "Papal Army," pp. 34–44.
23. Robert F. Trisco, "Bishops and Their Priests in the United States," in John Tracy Ellis, ed., *The Catholic Priest in the United States: Historical Investigations* (Collegeville, 1971), pp. 111–292. Spalding, *Martin John Spalding,* pp. 276–79.
24. Frederick J. Zwierlein, *The Life and Letters of Bishop McQuaid* (3 vols., Rochester, 1925–1927), 2:11–41.
25. Spalding, *Martin John Spalding,* pp. 328–31. Henry B. Leonard, "Ethnic Conflict and Episcopal Power: The Diocese of Cleveland, 1847–1870," *Catholic Historical Review,* 62(1976):388–407.
26. *Ibid.,* pp. 265–79; Gilbert J. Garraghan, S.J., *The Catholic Church in Chicago, 1673–1871* (Chicago, 1921), pp. 137–218.
27. Spalding, *Martin John Spalding,* pp. 268–75; 279–81; Robert Emmett Curran, S.J., "Prelude to 'Americanism': The New York Accademia and Clerical Radicalism in the Late Nineteenth Century," *Church History,* 47(1978):48–65.
28. Kwitchen, *James Alphonsus McMaster,* pp. 184–95; Trisco, "Bishops and Their Priests," pp. 150–94; Nelson J. Callahan, *A Case for Due Process in the Church: Father Eugene O'Callaghan, American Pioneer of Dissent* (Staten Island, 1971).
29. James Hennesey, S.J., *The First Council of the Vatican: The American Experience* (New York, 1963); *id.,* "Nunc Venio de America: The American Church and Vatican I," *Annuarium Historiae Conciliorum* 1(1969):348–73; James H. Smylie, "American Protestants Interpret Vatican I," *Church History,* (1969): 459–74.
30. James Hennesey, S.J., "James A. Corcoran's Mission to Rome, 1868–1869," *Catholic Historical Review,* 48(1962):157–81.
31. *Id., First Council of the Vatican,* p. 84.

CHAPTER XIV

1. John Hope Franklin, *From Slavery to Freedom, A History of Negro Americans* (3rd ed., New York, 1969), pp. 328–43.
2. Charles N. Glaab and A. Theodore Brown, *A History of Urban America,* (New York, 1967), pp. 107–66.
3. Frederick Merk, *Manifest Destiny and Mission in American History, a Reinterpretation* (New York, 1966), pp. 231–66. Josiah Strong, *Our Country, Its Possible Future and Present Crisis* (New York, 1885), listed among dangers to the American Protestant way of life: immigrants, Roman Catholicism,

rum, tobacco, socialism, misuse of wealth, and urban evils. John Fiske, *American Political Ideas* (New York, 1885), advanced the thesis of Anglo-Saxon racial superiority and John William Burgess, *Political Science and Comparative Constitutional Law* (Boston, 1890), extended the thesis to all Teutonic peoples.

4. Winthrop Hudson, *American Protestantism* (Chicago, 1961), pp. 124–27. *Id., Religion in America, an Historical Account of the Development of American Religious Life* (New York, 1965), pp. 207–304; Martin Marty, *Righteous Empire, the Protestant Experience in America* (New York, 1970), pp. 173–76; Richard Hofstadter, *Social Darwinism in American Thought* (rev. ed., Boston, 1955); Winthrop Hudson, *The Great Tradition of the American Churches* (New York, 1963), pp. 157–94.

5. Hudson, *Religion in America,* p. 247. See Thomas T. McAvoy, C.S.C., "The Growth of the American Catholic Minority in the Later Nineteenth Century," *Review of Politics,* 15(1953):275–302.

6. Maldwyn A. Jones, *American Immigration* (Chicago, 1960); Oscar Handlin, *The Uprooted: the Epic Story of the Great Migration That Made the American People* (New York, 1951); *id., Immigration as a Factor in American History* (Englewood Cliffs, 1959); Marcus Hansen, *The Immigrant in American History* (Cambridge, 1940).

7. Gerald Shaughnessy, S.M., *Has the Immigrant Kept the Faith?* (New York, 1925), p. 190.

8. Nathan Glazer and Daniel P. Moynihan, *Beyond the Melting Pot* (Cambridge, 1963), p. 219.

9. Rudolph Vecoli, "Prelates and Peasants: Italian Immigrants and the Catholic Church," *Journal of Social History;* 3(1969):268; Silvano M. Tomasi and Edward C. Stibili, eds., *Italian-Americans and Religion: An Annotated Bibliography* (Staten Island, 1978); Silvano Tomasi and M. Engels, ed., *The Italian Experience in the United States* (Staten Island, 1970); Keith P. Dyrud, *et al., The Other Catholics* (New York, 1978), an anthology on Catholics from eastern and southern Europe; James W. Sanders, *The Education of an Urban Minority: Catholics in Chicago, 1833–1965* (New York, 1977), pp. 56–71; Humbert S. Nelli, *The Italians in Chicago, 1880–1930* (New York, 1970), 181–200; Ellis, *Life of Gibbons,* 1:341, Henry J. Browne, "The Italian Problem in the Catholic Church of the United States, 1880–1900," *Historical Records and Studies,* 35(1946):46–72.

10. Howard R. Lamar, *The Far Southwest 1846–1912, A Territorial History* (New York, 1970); Leonard Pitt, *The Decline of the Californios, A Social History of the Spanish-Speaking Californians, 1846–1890* (Berkeley, 1966); Wayne Moquin *et al., A Documentary History of the Mexican Americans* (New York, 1971). Mason Wade, "The French Catholic Parish and 'Survivance' in 19th Century New England," *Catholic Historical Review,* 36(1950):163–89.

11. Stephen Thernstrom, "Irish Life in a Yankee City," in Philip Gleason, ed., *Catholicism in America* (New York, 1960), p. 61.

12. "Relazione sullo stato presente della chiesa cattolica negli stati uniti dell' America," APF, Scritture riferite nei Congressi, America Centrale, 36 (1882): fol. 195–97.

13. Gower and Leliaert, *Brownson-Hecker Correspondence,* p. 292; Sanders, *Education of an Urban Minority,* p. 102.

14. Paul R. Messbarger, *Fiction with a Parochial Purpose: Social Uses of American Catholic Literature, 1884–1900* (Boston, 1971).
15. American Catholic Historical Society Collections (Philadelphia), Heuser Papers, Elliott to Herman Heuser, New York, June 6, 1909. Opposition to abandonment of Latin liturgy was one point on which Ireland and his great adversary, Archbishop Corrigan, agreed. Corrigan "simply foamed at the bare mention of vernacularity" *(ibid.)*.
16. Jay P. Dolan, *Catholic Revivalism* (Notre Dame/London, 1978).
17. Donna Merwick, *Boston Priests, 1848–1910: A Study of Social and Intellectual Change* (Cambridge, 1973), p. 74.
18. Merwick deals with this era, seeing it as one of devolution from an earlier integration of Catholicism in Boston. See also Robert H. Lord *et al., History of the Archdiocese of Boston*, 3:3–437.
19. Francis G. McManamin, S.J., *The American Years of John Boyle O'Reilly, 1870–1890* (Washington, 1959); Mary Alphonsine Frawley, S.S.J., *Patrick Donahoe* (Washington, 1946).
20. John T. Smith, *The Catholic Church in New York* (2 vols.; New York, 1908), 2:414–29; Robert Emmett Curran, S.J., *Michael Augustine Corrigan and the Shaping of Conservative Catholicism in America, 1878–1902* (New York, 1978).
21. Glazer and Moynihan, *Beyond the Melting Pot*, pp. 219–20. A sociological analysis follows, to p. 287. See also William Shannon, *The American Irish* (New York, 1963), pp. 68–85; Sanders, *Education of an Urban Minority*, pp. 124–25.
22. James P. Rodechko, *Patrick Ford and His Search for America: A Case Study of Irish-American Journalism 1870–1913* (New York, 1976).
23. Peter Guilday, "John Gilmary Shea, Father of American Catholic History, 1824–1892," *Historical Records and Studies*, 17(1926):7–171; Henry W. Bowden, "John Gilmary Shea, A Study of Methods and Goals of Historiography," *Catholic Historical Review*, 54(1968):235–60.
24. Frederick J. Zwierlein, *The Life and Letters of Bishop McQuaid* (3 vols.; Rochester, 1925–1927); *id., Letters of Archbishop Corrigan to Bishop McQuaid and Allied Documents* (Rochester, 1946); Robert F. McNamara, *The Diocese of Rochester 1868–1968* (Rochester, 1968), pp. 110–251.
25. Alfred C. Rush, C.Ss.R., and Thomas J. Donaghy, F.S.C., "The Saintly John Neumann and His Coadjutor, Archbishop Wood," in Connelly, ed., *History of the Archdiocese of Philadelphia*, pp. 237–70; Wayne Broehl, *The Molly Maguires* (New York, 1964); Mary Consuela, I.H.M., "The Church of Philadelphia (1884–1918)," in Connelly, pp. 271–321.
26. John Tracy Ellis, *The Life of James Cardinal Gibbons, Archbishop of Baltimore, 1834–1921* (2 vols.; Milwaukee, 1952).
27. Patrick H. Ahern, *The Life of John J. Keane, Educator and Archbishop, 1839–1918* (Milwaukee, 1954).
28. Miller, "Peter Richard Kenrick," pp. 129–39.
29. M. Edmund Hussey, "The 1878 Financial Failure of Archbishop Purcell," *Cincinnati Historical Society Bulletin*, 36 (1978):6–41.
30. Colman Barry, O.S.B., *The Catholic Church and German Americans* (Milwaukee, 1953); Peter Johnson, *Crosier on the Frontier, A Life of John Martin Henni* (Madison, 1959); M. Ludwig, *Right Hand Glove Uplifted, A*

Biography of Archbishop Michael Heiss (New York, 1968); James Moynihan, *The Life of Archbishop John Ireland* (New York, 1953).

31. John Tracy Ellis, *John Lancaster Spalding, First Bishop of Peoria, American Educator* (Milwaukee, 1961); David Sweeney, O.F.M. *The Life of John Lancaster Spalding, First Bishop of Peoria, 1840–1916,* (New York, 1965). See J. L. Spalding, *The Religious Mission of the Irish Race and Catholic Colonization* (New York, 1880); *id., Means and Ends of Education* (Chicago, 1895).

32. Philip Gleason, *The Conservative Reformers, German-American Catholics and the Social Order* Notre Dame, 1968), is a study of the Central-Verein.

33. M. Sevina Pahorezki, *The Social and Political Activities of William James Onahan* (Washington, 1942).

34. Francis Weber, ed., "The Church in Utah, 1882, a Contemporary Account," *Records of the American Catholic Historical Society of Philadelphia,* 81(1970):199–208.

35. Jean Baptiste Salpointe, *Soldiers of the Cross: Notes on the Ecclesiastical History of New Mexico, Arizona, and Colorado* (Banning, 1898).

36. Blandina Segale, S.C., *At the End of the Santa Fe Trail* (Milwaukee, 1948).

37. McGloin, *California's First Archbishop;* James Gaffey, *Citizen of No Mean City: Archbishop Patrick Riordan of San Francisco (1841–1914)* (Washington, 1976). See pp. 213–43 for the Pious Fund case.

38. Wilfred P. Schoenberg, S.J., *A Chronicle of Catholic History of the Pacific Northwest, 1743–1960* (Spokane, 1962).

39. Mary G. Balcom, *The Catholic Church in Alaska* (Chicago, 1969).

40. Maggie Bunson, *Faith in Paradise: A Century and a Half of the Roman Catholic Church in Hawaii* (Boston, 1977); John Farrow, *Damien the Leper* (Garden City, 1954); Gavan Daws, *Holy Man: Father Damien of Molokai* (New York, 1973); John Beevers, *A Man for Now: The Life of Damien de Veuster, Friend of Lepers* (Garden City, 1973).

41. Matthew McDevitt, F.S.C., *Joseph McKenna, Associate Justice of the United States* (Washington, 1946); Marie Carolyn Klinkhamer, O.P., *Edward Douglass White, Chief Justice of the United States* (Washington, 1943).

42. "Cum Magnopere," *Acta Sanctae Sedis,* 12(1879–80):88–92; Trisco, "Bishops and Their Priests," pp. 111–292; Ellis, *Life of Cardinal Gibbons,* 1:203–63; James Hennesey, S.J., "Councils of Baltimore," *New Catholic Encyclopedia,* 2:42–43; Guilday, *History of the Councils of Baltimore,* pp. 221–49.

43. John Higham, *Strangers in the Land, Patterns of American Nativism,* 1860–1925 (rev. ed.; New York, 1965), pp. 35–96; *id.,* "Another Look at Nativism," *Catholic Historical Review,* 44(1958):147–58.

44. Donald Kinzer, *An Episode in Anti-Catholicism, the American Protective Association* (Seattle, 1964).

CHAPTER XV

1. Aaron Abell, *American Catholicism and Social Action: A Search for Social Justice, 1865–1950* (Garden City, 1960).

2. Joan Bland, S.N.D., *Hibernian Crusade, The Story of the Catholic Total Abstinence Union of America,* (Washington, 1951).

3. Abell, *American Catholicism and Social Action,* pp. 128–29.

4. Mary Evangela Henthorne, B.V.M., *The Irish Catholic Colonization Association of the United States* (Champaign, 1932); James Shannon, *Catholic Colonization on the Western Frontier* (New Haven, 1957).
5. Eric F. Goldman, *Charles J. Bonaparte, Patrician Reformer, His Earlier Career* (Baltimore, 1943).
6. Abell, *American Catholicism and Social Action,* pp. 120; 87–88.
7. Lyman Beecher, *Plea for the West* (Cincinnati, 1835), p. 12; Sanders, *Education of an Urban Minority,* pp. 18–25.
8. Marie Carolyn Klinkhamer, O.P., "The Blaine Amendment of 1875, Private Motives for Public Action," *Catholic Historical Review* 42(1956):15–49.
9. John W. Pratt, *Religion, Politics, and Diversity, the Church-State Theme in New York History* (Ithaca, 1967), pp. 247–56.
10. Justice Felix Frankfurter, Concurring Opinion in People of the State of Illinois vs. Board of Education, 1948, in Joseph Blau, ed., *Cornerstones of Religious Freedom in America* (New York, 1964), p. 262.
11. Charles W. Eliot, "Recent Changes in Secondary Education," *The Atlantic Monthly,* 84(1899):443.
12. Daniel F. Reilly, O.P., *The School Controversy, 1891–1893* (Washington, 1943); Buetow, *Of Singular Benefit,* pp. 170–75; Ellis, *Life of Cardinal Gibbons,* 1:653–707. Zwierlein, *Life and Letters of Bishop McQuaid,* 3:160–81.
13. Thomas Bouquillon, *Education: To Whom Does it Belong?* (Baltimore, 1892); René Holaind, S.J., *The Parent First: An Answer to Dr. Bouquillon's Query* (New York, 1891). By another Jesuit, James Conway, S.J., *The State Last, A Study of Dr. Bouquillon's Pamphlet* (New York, 1892).
14. Reilly, *The School Controversy,* pp. 250–66; 160–62; Zwierlein, *Life and Letters of Bishop McQuaid,* 3:171–74.
15. *Ibid.,* 3:182–86. Denis O'Connell, progressive agent in Rome, helped draw up the points.
16. Reilly, *School Controversy,* pp. 180–83.
17. Buetow, *Of Singular Benefit,* pp. 179–80.
18. *Ibid.,* pp. 180–84.
19. John Tracy Ellis, "A Tradition of Autonomy," in Neil P. McCluskey, *The Catholic University: A Modern Appraisal* (Notre Dame, 1970), p. 220; Mary David Cameron, S.S.N.D., *The College of Notre Dame of Maryland, 1895–1945* (New York, 1947).
20. John E. Copus, S.J., "Count Creighton's Princely Gift," *Woodstock Letters* 35(1906):373–76.
21. John Tracy Ellis, *The Formative Years of the Catholic University of America* (Washington, 1946); *id., Life of Cardinal Gibbons,* 1:389–438. Both M.G. Caldwell and her sister Elizabeth, also a benefactress of the University, left the Catholic church. Elizabeth, Baroness von Zedtwitz, published *The Double Doctrine of The Church of Rome* (New York, 1906).
22. Fergus Macdonald, C.P., *The Catholic Church and the Secret Societies* (New York, 1946); William D'Arcy, *The Fenian Movement in the United States, 1858–1886* (Washington, 1947).
23. Terence V. Powderly, *Thirty Years of Labor, 1859–1889* (Columbus, 1890); *id., The Path I Trod, the Autobiography of Terence V. Powderly* (New York, 1940); Henry J. Browne, *The Catholic Church and the Knights of Labor* (Washington, 1949); Ellis, *Life of Cardinal Gibbons,* 1:486–546. Powderly left the Catholic Church to become a freemason in 1901.

24. Henry Pelling, *American Labor* (Chicago, 1960), p. 118; Shannon, *American Irish*, p. 140.
25. Philip Taft, *The A. F. of L. in the Time of Gompers* (New York, 1957), p. 335.
26. Curran, *Michael Augustine Corrigan;* Zwierlein, *Life and Letters of McQuaid*, 3:1–83; Ellis, *Life of Gibbons*, 1:547–94; Stephen Bell, *Rebel, Priest and Prophet* (New York, 1937); Sylvester Malone, *Dr. Edward McGlynn* (New York, 1918).
27. Walter Rauschenbusch, *Christianizing the Social Order* (New York, 1912), pp. 91–92.
28. *The Standard* (New York), April 2, May 7, July 16, 1887. Excerpts from McGlynn's lecture, "The Cross of a New Crusade," are in Aaron Abell, ed., *American Catholic Thought on Social Questions* (Indianapolis, 1968), pp. 162–76.
29. M. Adele Gorman, O.S.F., "Evolution of Catholic Lay Leadership, 1820–1920," *Historical Records and Studies*, 50(1964):130–65; *id.*, "Lay Activity and the Catholic Congresses of 1889 and 1893," *Records of the American Catholic Historical Society*, 74(1963):3–22.
30. Gorman, "Evolution," p. 141.
31. Ellis, *Life of Gibbons*, 2:14.
32. *Progress of the Catholic Church in America and the Great Columbian Catholic Congress of 1893* (4th ed., Chicago, 1897), 2:83.
33. *Ibid.*, pp. 91–93.
34. *Ibid.*, pp. 121–25.
35. *Ibid.*, p. 202.
36. *Ibid.*, pp. 39–40.
37. David [Thomas W.] Spalding, C.F.X., "The Negro Catholic Congresses, 1889–1894," *Catholic Historical Review*, 55(1969):337–57; *Three Catholic Afro-American Congresses* (Cincinnati, 1893; repr., New York, 1978).
38. Peter J. Rahill, *The Catholic Indian Missions and Grant's Peace Policy* (Washington, 1953); Francis P. Prucha, S.J., *American Indian Policy in Crisis: Christian Reformers and the Indian* (Norman, 1976), pp. 53–56.
39. John T. Gillard, S.S.J., *The Catholic Church and the American Negro* (Baltimore, 1929); *id.*, *Colored Catholics in the United States* (Baltimore, 1941); William Osborne, *The Segregated Covenant: Race Relations and American Catholics* (New York, 1967), pp. 19–42.
40. Dimitri Grigorieff, "The Orthodox Church in America from the Alaska Mission to Autocephaly," *St. Vladimir's Theological Quarterly*, 14 (1970):202–3; Gerald P. Fogarty, S.J., "The American Hierarchy and Oriental Rite Catholics, 1890–1907," *Records of the American Catholic Historical Society of Philadelphia*, 85(1974):17–28; Bohdan P. Procko, "Soter Ortynsky: First Ruthenian Bishop in the United States, 1907–1916," *Catholic Historical Review*, 58(1973):513–33.
41. Barry, *Catholic Church and German Americans*, pp. 3–43.
42. Buffalo *Volksfreund*, February 17, 1890. See George Zurcher, *Foreign Ideas in the Catholic Church in America* (East Aurora, 1896), p. 29.
43. Anton Walburg, *The Question of Nationality in Its Relation to the Catholic Church in the United States* (Cincinnati, 1889). See Barry, *Catholic Church and German Americans*, pp. 82–85.
44. *Ibid.*, pp. 45–50.

45. *Ibid.*, pp. 50–62.
46. March 15, 1890, cited in Ellis, *John Lancaster Spalding,* pp. 55–56.
47. Barry, *Catholic Church and German Americans,* is largely a study, favorable to its subject, of Cahensly.
48. The Abbelen memorial is in Barry, pp. 289–96, together with a reply submitted by Ireland and Keane, December 6, 1886, pp. 296–312. Corrigan wrote the archbishops' response.
49. *Ibid.*, pp. 131–82; 313–16.
50. Albert Houtin, *L'Américanisme* (Paris, 1904); Thomas T. McAvoy, C.S.C., *The Great Crisis in American Catholic History, 1895–1900* (Chicago, 1957); Margaret Mary Reher, "The Church and the Kingdom, a Catholic Contribution," unpublished diss., Fordham University, 1972; *id.,* "Pope Leo XIII and 'Americanism,' " *Theological Studies,* 34(1973):679–89; Ellis, *Life of Cardinal Gibbons,* 2:1–80.
51. See Isaac Hecker, *Questions of the Soul* (New York, 1855); *Aspirations of Nature* (New York, 1857); *The Church and the Age* (New York, 1887); Reher, "Church and Kingdom," pp. 79–81.
52. Gower and Leliaert, *Brownson-Hecker Correspondence,* p. 291.
53. "American Catholicity," *American Catholic Quarterly Review,* 16(1891): 396–408.
54. Gerald P. Fogarty, S.J., *The Vatican and the Americanist Crisis: Denis J. O'Connell, American Agent in Rome, 1885–1903* (Rome, 1974).
55. Ellis, *Life of Cardinal Gibbons,* 2:11.
56. James Hennesey, S.J., "Leo XIII's Thomistic Revival: A Political and Philosophical Event," *The Journal of Religion,* 58 (Supplement, 1978):S 185–97.
57. Christoph Weber, *Kirchliche Politik zwischen Rom, Berlin und Trier 1876–1888* (Mainz, 1970), p. 100, n. 18.
58. Fogarty, *Vatican and the Americanist Crisis,* p. 260.
59. Ireland's speeches were published, *L'Église et le siècle, conférences et discours* (Paris, 1894).
60. Fogarty, *Vatican and the Americanist Crisis,* pp. 219–50; Ellis, *Life of Gibbons,* 1:595–652; Sweeney, *Life of Spalding,* pp. 209–19; Zwierlein, *Life and Letters of McQuaid,* 3:150–59.
61. Francesco Satolli, *Loyalty to Church and State* (Baltimore, 1895), p. 150.
62. Zwierlein, *Life and Letters of McQuaid,* pp. 203–28.
62. Ellis, *Documents of American Catholic History,* 2:499–511; *id., Life of Gibbons,* 2:30.
64. James F. Cleary, "Catholic Participation in the World's Parliament of Religions," *Catholic Historical Review,* 55(1970):605.
65. Ellis, *Life of Gibbons,* 2:41.
66. Fogarty, *Vatican and the Americanist Crisis,* pp. 263–67 (analysis); 319–26 (text). Text also in Felix Klein, *Americanism, a Phantom Heresy,* (Atchinson, 1951), pp. 71–75.
67. Ralph Weber, *Notre Dame's John Zahm* (Notre Dame, 1961), pp. 103, 106–23.
68. Walter Elliott, C.S.P., *The Life of Father Hecker* (New York, 1891); *Le Père Hecker Fondateur des "Paulistes" Américains, 1819–1888,* par le Père W. Elliott, de la même Compagnie. Traduit et adapté de l'anglais avec autorization de l'auteur. Introduction par Mgr. Ireland. Preface par l'Abbé Félix Klein (Paris, 1897).

69. Ellis, *Life of Gibbons,* 2:50–51.
70. William Clebsch, *American Religious Thought: A History* (Chicago, 1973), p. 114.
71. Halsey, *Survival of American Innocence,* pp. 4, 128.
72. Reher, "The Church and the Kingdom of God," pp. 175–234.

CHAPTER XVI

1. William R. Thayer, *The Life and Letters of John Hay* (2 vols.; Boston, 1915), 2:337.
2. Joseph T. Durkin, S.J., *General Sherman's Son* (New York, 1959), p. 170.
3. V. E. McDevitt, *The First California's Chaplain* (Berkeley, 1956).
4. George Barton, "A Story of Self-Sacrifice; Being a Record of the Labors of the Catholic Sisterhoods in the Spanish-American War," *Records of the American Catholic Historical Society of Philadelphia,* 37 (1926):104–92; Ellis, *Life of Cardinal Gibbons,* 2:81–140; Aidan H. Germain, O.S.B., *Catholic Military and Naval Chaplains, 1776–1917* (Washington, 1929), pp. 136–55.
5. Fogarty, *Vatican and the Americanist Crisis,* p. 280.
6. Sweeney, *Life of Spalding,* pp. 249–57; Daniel B. Schirmer, *Republic or Empire: American Resistance to the Philippine War* (Cambridge, 1972).
7. Charles S. Olcott, *The Life of William McKinley* (2 vols.; Boston, 1916), 2:110–11.
8. Henry F. May, "The Rebellion of the Intellectuals, 1912–1917," *American Quarterly,* 8(1956):114–26.
9. *Acta Sanctae Sedis,* 41(1908):432.
10. Francis C. Kelley, *The Bishop Jots It Down* (New York, 1939); *id., The Story of Extension* (Chicago, 1922); James P. Gaffey, *Francis Clement Kelley and the American Catholic Dream* (2 vols.; Bensenville, 1980), 1:73–202.
11. Abell, *American Catholicism and Social Action,* pp. 118–19.
12. Titus Cranny, S.A., *Father Paul, Apostle of Unity* (2nd ed.; Peekskill, 1965); Charles Angell, S.A., and Charles LaFontaine, S.A., *Prophet of Reunion: The Life of Paul of Graymoor* (New York, 1975); Charles LaFontaine, S.A., "Repairer of the Breach—Mother Lurana White, Co-Founder of the Society of the Atonement," *Catholic Historical Review,* 62 (1976):434–54.
13. Edwin O'Connor's novel *The Last Hurrah* (Boston, 1956) catches the spirit of political Boston. See also James M. Curley, *I'd Do It Again: A Record of All My Uproarious Years* (Englewood Cliffs, 1957); Shannon, *American Irish,* p. 185.
14. Henry Morton Robinson, *The Cardinal* (New York, 1950), is a novel about ecclesiastical Boston. See William Cardinal O'Connell, *Recollections of Seventy Years* (Boston, 1944); Merwick, *Boston Priests,* pp. 142–96. Merwick notes (p. 142) that O'Connell was the model for the fictional bishop Shyrne in William L. Sullivan's novel, *The Priest, A Tale of Modernism in New England* (Boston, 1911).
15. Jones, *American Immigration,* p. 237.
16. Glaab and Brown, *History of Urban America,* p. 139; Sanders, *Education of an Urban Minority,* pp. 50–51; Abell, *American Catholicism and Social action, p. 160.*

17. William Galush, "The Polish National Catholic Church: A Survey of Its Origins, Development and Missions," *Records of the American Catholic Historical Society of Philadelphia,* 83(1972):131–49; Theodore Andrews, *The Polish National Catholic Church in America and Poland* (London, 1953); John P. Gallagher, *A Century of History: the Diocese of Scranton, 1868–1968* (Scranton, 1968); Warren C. Platt, "The Polish National Catholic Church: An Inquiry into Its Origins," *Church History,* 46(1977):74–89.

18. Sanders, *Education of an Urban Minority,* pp. 62–64; Barry, *Catholic Church and German Americans,* pp. 253–54; Victor Greene, "For God and Country, the Origins of Slavic Catholic Self-Consciousness in America," *Church History,* 35(1966):446–60; Anthony J. Kuzniewski, S.J., *Faith and Fatherland: The Polish Church War in Wisconsin, 1896–1918* (Notre Dame/London, 1980).

19. Sanders, *Education of an Urban Minority,* pp. 130–31.

20. Buetow, *Of Singular Benefit,* pp. 213–14; Henry J. Browne, "The American Parish School in the Last Half Century," *NCEA Bulletin,* 50(1953):323–34; Raymond G. Fuller, *Child Labor and the Constitution* (New York, 1923), p. 2.

21. Buetow, *Of Singular Benefit,* pp. 187–93; 183–84.

22. Sweeney, *Life of Spalding,* pp. 316–23.

23. Francis G. McManamin, S.J., "Peter Muldoon, First Bishop of Rockford, 1862–1927," *Catholic Historical Review,* 48(1962):365–78.

24. Bernard C. Cronin, *Father Yorke and the Labor Movement in San Francisco, 1900–1910* (Washington, 1944); Joseph S. Brusher, S.J., *Consecrated Thuderbolt: Father Yorke of San Francisco* (Hawthorne, 1973).

25. Humphrey J. Desmond, *Chats within the Fold: A Series of Little Sermons from a Lay Standpoint* (Baltimore, 1901), pp. 16–22; Abell, *American Catholicism and Social Action,* pp. 154–55.

26. James Addison White, *The Founding of Cliff Haven* (New York, 1950).

27. *Ibid.,* p. 89.

28. Abell, *American Catholicism and Social Action,* p. 169.

29. Betten, *Catholic Activism and the Industrial Worker,* p. 5.

30. M. Adele Gorman, O.S.F., "Evolution of Catholic Lay Leadership, 1820–1920," *Historical Records and Studies,* 50(1964):149–65.

31. Philip Gleason, *The Conservative Reformers: German-American Catholics and the Social Order* (Notre Dame, 1968).

32. Mary Harrita Fox, B.V.M., *Peter E. Dietz, Labor Priest* (Notre Dame, 1953). Philip Taft, *The A. F. of L. in the Time of Samuel Gompers* (New York, 1957), pp. 335–38, dismisses the Militia as "largely a paper organization."

33. John A. Ryan, *Social Doctrine in Action, A Personal History* (New York, 1941); Francis L. Broderick, *Right Reverend New Dealer John A. Ryan* (New York, 1963); Patrick W. Gearty, *The Economic Thought of Monsignor John A. Ryan* (Washington, 1953).

34. Abell, *American Catholicism and Social Action,* p. 152.

35. Robert Doherty, "Thomas J. Hagerty, The Church and Socialism," *Labor History,* 3(1962):39–56; Melvin Dubofsky, *We Shall Be All, A History of the Industrial Workers of the World* (Chicago, 1969), pp. 79–86, 91–93.

36. Dale Fetherling, *Mother Jones the Miners' Angel: A Portrait* (Carbondale/Edwardsville, 1974), pp. 203–4.

37. *Ibid.*, p. 121.
38. *Ibid.*, pp 107–8.
39. *Ibid.*, pp. 205–9.
40. Benjamin Gitlow, *The Whole of Their Lives* (New York, 1948), p. 37.
41. Elizabeth Gurley Flynn, *The Rebel Girl: An Autobiography* (rev. ed.; New York, 1973), pp. 41–44.
42. Sally M. Miller, *The Radical Immigrants* (Boston, 1974).
43. Neil Betten, *Catholic Activism and the Industrial Worker* (Gainsville, 1976).
44. Henry F. Pringle, *The Life and Times of William Howard Taft* (2 vols.; New York, 1939), 2:834.
45. Colman J. Barry, O.S.B., *The Catholic University of America, 1903–1909, the Rectorship of Denis J. O'Connell* (Washington, 1950).
46. *Ibid.*, pp. 177–83.
47. John Ireland, "Three and a Half Years of Pius X," *North American Review,* 184(1907):35–45; *id.*, "The Dogmatic Authority of the Papacy," *ibid.*, 187 (1908):486–87.
48. Ahern, *Life of Keane*, pp. 357–66.
49. John Tracy Ellis, "The Formation of the American Priest: An Historical Perspective," and Michael V. Gannon," Before and after Modernism: The Intellectual Isolation of the American Priest," in Ellis, ed., *Catholic Priest in the United States*, pp. 60–74; 330–50.
50. John Ratté, *Three Modernists* (New York, 1967), pp. 259–336; William L. Sullivan, *Under Orders, the Autobiography of William L. Sullivan* (New York, 1944); Michael B. McGarry, C.S.P., "Modernism in the United States: William Laurence Sullivan, 1872–1935," *Records of the American Catholic Historical Society of Philadelphia,* 90(1979):33–52.
51. McNamara, *Diocese of Rochester,* pp. 242–45, 259.
52. See John R. Slattery, "The Workings of Modernism," *The American Journal of Theology,* 13(1909):555–74.
53. Joseph T. Lienhard, S.J., "The New York Review and Modernism in America," *Records of the American Catholic Historical Society of Philadelphia,* 82(1971):67–82; Michael J. DeVito, *The New York Review 1905–1908* (New York, 1977).
54. Frank J. Reuter, *Catholic Influence on American Colonial Policies, 1898–1904* (Austin, 1967); John T. Farrell, "Archbishop Ireland and Manifest Destiny," *Catholic Historical Review,* 33(1947):269–301; Dorothy Dohen, *Nationalism and American Catholicism* (New York, 1967); Frederick J. Zwierlein, *Theodore Roosevelt and Catholics, 1882–1919* (St. Louis, 1956).
55. Fogarty, *Americanist Agent to the Vatican,* pp. 279–81; McAvoy, *Great Crisis,* pp. 206–10.
56. Richard K. MacMaster, "Bishop Barron and the West African Missions, 1841–1845," *Historical Records and Studies,* 50(1964):83–129.
57. Colman J. Barry, O.S.B., *Upon These Rocks: Catholics in the Bahamas* (Collegeville, 1973); Francis J. Osborne, S.J., *History of the Catholic Church in Jamaica* (Aylesbury, 1977), pp. 125–85; John Francis Bannon, S.J., *The Missouri Province S.J.: A Mini-History* (St. Louis, 1977), pp. 17–19.
58. Albert J. Nevins, M.M., *The Meaning of Maryknoll* (New York, 1954).
59. Pedro de Achutegui, S.J., and Miguel Bernad, S.J., *Religious Revolution in the Philippines: the Life and Church of Gregorio Aglipay* (2 vols.; Manila, 1960–66); Ellis, *Life of Cardinal Gibbons,* 2:81–140.

60. Edward F. Goss S.J., "The Taft Commission to the Vatican, 1902," *Records of the American Catholic Historical Society of Philadelphia,* 46(1935):183–201; John T. Farrell, "Background of the 1902 Taft Mission to Rome," *Catholic Historical Review,* 36(1950):1–22.
61. Ellis, *Life of Cardinal Gibbons,* 2:132–38.
62. Edward J. Berbusse, S.J., *The United States in Puerto Rico* (Chapel Hill, 1966).

CHAPTER XVII

1. Halsey, *The Survival of American Innocence,* p. 51, supplied both examples.
2. John Higham, *Strangers in the Land: Patterns of American Nativism 1860–1925* (New York, 1965), p. 180.
3. *Congressional Record,* 62nd Cong., 1st sess., February 15, 1913, vol. IL, p. 3216, repr. in Thomas E. Brown, *Bible Belt Catholicism: A History of the Roman Catholic Church in Oklahoma, 1905–1945* (New York, 1977), pp. 228–30. Sections in the bogus oath are said to date back to the 1678 Popish Plot in England.
4. Higham, *Strangers in the Land,* p. 181.
5. Ellis, *Life of Gibbons,* 2:205–21; Arthur S. Link, *Wilson: The Struggle for Neutrality 1914–1915* (Princeton, 1960), pp. 640–44; Gaffey, *Francis Clement Kelley,* 2:3–57.
6. Dean R. Esslinger, "American Catholicism and Irish attitudes toward Neutrality, 1914–1917: A Study of Catholic Minorities," *Catholic Historical Review,* 53(1967):194–216, studies all the minority groups. See also Edward Cuddy, "Pro-Germanism and American Catholicism, 1914–1917," *ibid.,* 53(1968):427–54, excerpted in Philip Gleason, ed., *Catholicism in America* (New York/Evanston/London, 1970), pp. 92–100. For the Wilson remark, Stephen Bonsal, *Unfinished Business* (London, 1944), p. 138. Link, *The Struggle for Neutrality,* p. 24; *id., Wilson: Campaigns for Progressivism and Peace 1916–1917* (Princeton, 1965), pp. 130–34.
7. John B. Sheerin, C.S.P., *Never Look Back: The Career and Concerns of John J. Burke* (New York/Paramus, 1975), p. 29.
8. Philip Gleason, *The Conservative Reformers: German-American Catholics and the Social Order* (Notre Dame/London, 1968), pp. 160, 171.
9. Ellis, *Life of Gibbons,* 2:237.
10. *Ibid.,* p. 239.
11. Thomas T. McAvoy, C.S.C., *A History of the Catholic Church in the United States* (Notre Dame/London, 1969), p. 364.
12. Ellis, *Life of Gibbons,* 2:246–47.
13. Patricia McNeal, "Catholic Conscientious Objection during World War II," *Catholic Historical Review,* 61(1975):232, n. 32.
14. Ray H. Abrams, *Preachers Present Arms* (Philadelphia, 1933), p. 197.
15. Ellis, *Life of Gibbons,* 2:270.
16. Maurice F. Egan and John B. Kennedy, *The Knights of Columbus in Peace and War* (2 vols.; New Haven, 1920).
17. Michael Williams, *American Catholics in the War* (New York, 1921); Ellis, *Life of Gibbons,* 2:293–95; Sheerin, *Never Look Back,* pp. 36–43; Elizabeth

McKeown, "War and Welfare: A Study of American Catholic Leadership," unpub. Ph.D. diss., University of Chicago, 1972.

18. Williams, *American Catholics*, pp. 97–153; Ellis, *Life of Gibbons*, 2:295–97; Sheerin, *Never Look Back*, pp. 44–48.
19. *Ibid.*, p. 90.
20. Ellis, *Life of Gibbons*, 2:243–46; Jules Jusserand in *American Historical Review*, 37(1932):818; Ellis, *ibid.*, 2:257; 276.
21. James Gibbons, "The War Policy of the Pope," *America*, February 23, 1918, pp. 487–88.
22. Ellis, *Life of Gibbons*, 2:286.
23. Gaffey, *Francis Clement Kelley*, 1:233–56.
24. Sheerin, *Never Look Back*, p. 45.
25. McKeown, "War and Welfare," pp. 179–94.
26. Ellis, *Documents*, 2:589–607; Broderick, *Right Reverend New Dealer*, pp. 104–8. For Ryan's own account: John Ryan, *Social Reconstruction* (New York, 1920).
27. For a documented précis, Ellis, *Documents*, 2:607–13. See Sheerin, *Never Look Back*, pp. 56–84.
28. Joan Bland, S.N.D., *Hibernian Crusade: The Story of the Catholic Total Abstinence Union of America* (Washington, 1951), p. 267.
29. Ellis, *Life of Gibbons*, 2:535–39.
30. Fetherling, *Mother Jones*, pp. 165–66; 174.
31. Broderick, *Right Reverend New Dealer*, pp. 90; 165–70.
32. Brown, *Bible-Belt Catholicism*, pp. 65–87.
33. James J. Kenneally, "Catholicism and Woman Suffrage in Massachusetts," *Catholic Historical Review*, 53(1967):43–57, repr. in Philip Gleason, ed., *Catholicism in America* (New York/Evanston/London, 1970), pp. 81–91; D. Owen Carrigan, "Martha Moore Avery: Crusader for Social Justice," *Catholic Historical Review*, 54(1968):31–32.
34. Ellis, *Life of Gibbons*, 2:579; 539.
35. Fetherling, *Mother Jones*, p. 163.
36. Kenneally, "Catholicism and Woman Suffrage," in Gleason, *Catholicism in America*, pp. 86–90.
37. Ellis, *Life of Gibbons*, 2:542.
38. Broderick, *Right Reverend New Dealer*, pp. 98–99.
39. *Ibid.*, pp. 155–59; Vincent A. McQuade, *The American Catholic Attitude on Child Labor Since 1891* (Washington, 1938), pp. 79–100.

CHAPTER XVIII

1. Reinhold Niebuhr, "Religion's Limitations," *The World Tomorrow*, 3(1920):77, quoted by Eldon G. Ernst, *Moment of Truth for Protestant America: Interchurch Campaigns Following World War One* (Missoula, 1972), p. 157.
2. *Ibid.*, pp. 170–71.
3. Robert T. Handy, *A History of the Churches in the United States and Canada* (New York, 1977), p. 381.
4. Charles G. Marshall, "An Open Letter to the Honorable Alfred E. Smith," *Atlantic Monthly*, 139(1927):540. See *id.*, *The Roman Catholic Church in the Modern State* (New York, 1928).

5. Handy, *History of the Churches,* p. 399.
6. *Catholic World,* 116(1922):137.
7. Halsey, *The Survival of American Innocence,* p. 103; Robert C. Holiday, ed., *Joyce Kilmer* (2 vols.; New York, 1918), 2:204, 109–10.
8. Raymond H. Schmandt, "Catholic Intellectual Life in the Archdiocese of Philadelphia: An Essay," in Connelly, *History of the Archdiocese of Philadelphia,* p. 623. The tribute is from an honorary degree citation written by Shakespearean scholar Horace Howard Furness, Sr.
9. Halsey, *The Survival of American Innocence,* pp. 124–37; William V. Shannon, *The American Irish* (New York/London, 1963); Dennis Flynn, "James T. Farrell and His Catholics." *America,* September 15, 1979, pp. 111–13.
10. Thomas F. Curley, "Catholic Novels and American Culture," *Commentary* 36(1963):38.
11. Henry D. Piper, *F. Scott Fitzgerald: A Critical Portrait* (Carbondale, 1965), p. 48.
12. Andrew Turnbull, ed., *The Letters of F. Scott Fitzgerald* (New York, 1963), p. 325.
13. Shannon, *American Irish,* pp. 261–81.
14. Halsey, *Survival of American Innocence,* p. 124; George N. Shuster, *The Church and Current Literature* (New York, 1930), pp. 27–33; *id., On the Side of Truth: An Evaluation with Readings* (ed. Vincent P. Lannie; Notre Dame/London, 1974).
15. Marty, *Righteous Empire,* p. 211.
16. Moquin and Van Doren, eds., *Documentary History of the Mexican Americans,* p. 253.
17. Nolan, "Native Son," in Connelly, ed., *History of the Archdiocese of Philadelphia,* p. 380.
18. McAvoy, *History of the Catholic Church,* pp. 395–96.
19. Sanders, *Education of an Urban Minority,* pp. 100–101.
20. Henry J. Browne, "The American Parish School in the Last Half Century," *National Catholic Education Association Bulletin,* 50(1953):326.
21. Paul A. FitzGerald, S.J., is writing *The History of the Jesuit Educational Association,* which treats the emergence of national Jesuit educational cooperation in the 1920s.
22. Thomas T. McAvoy, C.S.C., "Notre Dame 1919–1922: The Burns Revolution," *Review of Politics,* 25(1963):431–50.
23. Sanders, *Education of an Urban Minority,* p. 174.
24. *Ibid.,* pp. 175–76.
25. *The Fiery Cross,* January 2, 1925, repr. in Michael Williams, *The Shadow of the Pope* (New York/London, 1932), p. 315.
26. Abell, *American Catholicism and Social Action,* p. 216.
27. Nolan, "Native Son," in Connelly, *History of the Archdiocese of Philadelphia,* p. 366.
28. For the wealthy Irish, see Stephen Birmingham, *Real Lace: America's Irish Rich* (New York, 1973).
29. Sheerin, *Never Look Back,* pp. 99–100.
30. Nolan, "Native Son," in Connelly, ed., *History of the Archdiocese of Philadelphia,* p. 340.
31. *Ibid.,* p. 357.
32. *Ibid.,* p. 368.

33. *Ibid.*, p. 354.
34. *Ibid.*, p. 379.
35. Sanders, *Education of an Urban Minority*, p. 128.
36. *Ibid.*, pp. 129–30.
37. McAvoy, *History of the Catholic Church*, p. 389.
38. Newman C. Eberhardt, C. M., "John Joseph Cantwell," *New Catholic Encyclopedia*, 3:73–74; Francis J. Weber, *John Joseph Cantwell: His Excellency of Los Angeles* (Los Angeles, 1971).
39. Robert McNamara, "Archbishop Hanna, Rochesterian," *Rochester History*, 25(1963):1–24.
40. John A. Ryan, *The Church and Socialism and Other Essays* (Washington, 1919), p. 159.
41. Nolan, *Pastoral Letters*, pp. 212–61.
42. Abell, *American Catholicism and Social Action*, p. 203.
43. John A. Ryan, "Criticism of the Social Action Department," *NCWC Bulletin*, (1929), p. 17.
44. Nolan, "Native Son," in Connelly, ed., *History of the Archdiocese of Philadelphia*, p. 346.
45. David J. O'Brien, "The American Priest and Social Action," in Ellis, ed., *Catholic Priest in the United States*, pp. 438–39.
46. Broderick, *Right Reverend New Dealer*, p. 126.
47. J. G. Shaw, *Edwin Vincent O'Hara, American Prelate* (New York, 1957); Raymond P. Witte, S.M., *Twenty-Five Years of Crusading: A History of the National Catholic Rural Life Conference* (Des Moines, 1948).
48. Abell, *American Catholicism and Social Action*, p. 228.
49. Halsey, *Survival of American Innocence*, p. 66.
50. Higham, *Strangers in the Land*, p. 291.
51. Rodger Van Allen *The Commonweal and American Catholicism* (Philadelphia, 1974), pp. 15–16.
52. *Ibid.*, p. 16; "The Roman Church and Taxation," *Christian Century*, January 22, 1925, pp. 114–15.
53. Michael Williams, *The Shadow of the Pope* (New York/London, 1932), pp. 145–298; Allan J. Lichtman, *Prejudice and the Old Politics: The Presidential Election of 1928* (Chapel Hill, 1979), p. 321.
54. Abell, *American Catholicism and Social Action*, p. 227; John A. Ryan, "A Question of Tactics for Catholic Citizens," *Catholic Charities Review*, 8(1924):314–17; Patrick H. Callahan, "Tactics for Catholic Citizens," *Fortnightly Review*, 31(1924):481–83.
55. Broderick, *Right Reverend New Dealer*, pp. 114–15, 140–43.
56. M. Paul Holsinger, "The Oregon School Bill Controversy, 1922–1925," *Pacific Historical Review*, 37(1968):327–42; Lloyd P. Jorgensen, "The Oregon School Law of 1922: Passage and Sequel," *Catholic Historical Review*, 54(1968):455–66.
57. Ellis, *Life of Gibbons*, 2:543–45; Sheerin, *Never Look Back*, pp. 97–100; Browne, "Parochial Schools," pp. 331–32; Sanders, *Education of an Urban Minority*, p. 129; Nolan, "Native Son," in Connelly, ed., *History of the Archdiocese of Philadelphia*, pp. 363–64.
58. John Whitney Evans, *The Newman Movement: Roman Catholics in American Higher Education, 1883–1971* (Notre Dame/London, 1980).
59. *Woodstock Letters*, 36(1907):392–93; 37(1908):123.

60. Herbert C. Noonan, S.J., "The Need of Jesuit Universities," *Woodstock Letters,* 54(1924):238–48; Thomas T. McAvoy, C.S.C., *Father O'Hara of Notre Dame, the Cardinal-Archbishop of Philadelphia* (Notre Dame/London, 1967), pp. 139–40.
61. David C. Bailey, *¡Viva Cristo Rey! The Cristero Rebellion and the Church-State Conflict in Mexico* (Austin/London, 1974); Sheerin, *Never Look Back,* pp. 108–90; Louis J. Gallagher, S.J., *Edmund A. Walsh, S.J.* (New York, 1962).
62. Broderick, *Right Reverend New Dealer,* pp. 118–20; 170–78.
63. Charles G. Marshall, "An Open Letter to the Honorable Alfred E. Smith," *Atlantic Monthly* 139(1927):540–49.
64. Reinhold Niebuhr, "Catholics and the State," *The New Republic,* October 17, 1960, p. 15; Alfred E. Smith, "Catholic and Patriot: Governor Smith Replies," *Atlantic Monthly,* 139(1927):721–28.
65. "What Shall the Catholic Do?" *Commonweal,* January 2, 1929, p. 251.
66. *Catholic World,* 128(1928):357.

Chapter XIX

1. Philip Gleason, "In Search of Unity: American Catholic Thought 1920–1960," *Catholic Historical Review,* 65(1979):185–205.
2. Carl P. Hensler, review of *Christian Life and Worship, Homiletic and Pastoral Review,* 34(1934):665.
3. Fulton J. Sheen, "Educating for a Catholic Renaissance," *National Catholic Educational Association Bulletin,* 26(1929):45–54. See Gleason, "In Search of Unity," pp. 196–97.
4. *National Catholic Educational Association Bulletin,* 32(1935):70–71; Gleason, p. 198.
5. Halsey, *Survival of Innocence,* p. 150.
6. John O. Riedl, "Everyman's Philosophy," *Proceedings of the American Catholic Philosophical Association,* 11(1935):186–87; Halsey, pp. 148–49.
7. George Bull, S.J., "The Function of the Catholic Graduate School," *Thought,* 13(1938):368–78.
8. Halsey, *Survival of Innocence,* pp. 94–95.
9. *Ibid.,* pp. 78–83.
10. McAvoy, *Father O'Hara,* pp. 90–123.
11. Halsey, *Survival of Innocence,* p. 93.
12. J. Leo Klein, S.J., "The Role of Gerald Ellard (1894–1963) in the Development of the Contemporary American Catholic Liturgical Movement," unpub. Ph.D. diss. (Fordham University, 1971), pp. 111–38.
13. William J. Leonard, S.J., "The Liturgical Movement in the United States," in William Barauna and Jovian Lang, eds., *The Liturgy of Vatican II* (2 vols.; Chicago, 1966), 2:293–312.
14. Gleason, "In Search of Unity," pp. 199–201.
15. John P. Delaney, S.J., "Catholic Maryland Gives Thanks," *Woodstock Letters,* 63(1934):427–36.
16. Daniel A. Lord, S.J., *Played by Ear* (Chicago, 1956); Mary Florence [Bereniece] Wolff, S.L., *The Sodality Movement in the United States, 1926–1936* (St. Louis, 1939).

17. Patrick O'Farrell, ed., *Documents in Australian Catholic History* (2 vols.; London/Dublin/Melbourne, 1968), 2:392.
18. Francis P. Lally, *The Catholic Church in A Changing America* (Boston, 1962), p. 48.
19. John Tracy Ellis, *American Catholicism* (2nd rev. ed., Chicago, 1969), p. 145.
20. John A. Ryan, "Are We on the Right Road?" *Commonweal,* October 12, 1934, pp. 547–49.
21. David J. O'Brien, *American Catholics and Social Reform: The New Deal Years* (New York, 1968), pp. 240–41, n. 31.
22. George Q. Flynn, *American Catholics and the Roosevelt Presidency 1932– 1936* (Lexington, 1968), pp. 36–41.
23. *Ibid.,* p. 17.
24. *The Christian Century,* August 23, 1933, p. 1070.
25. William E. Leuchtenburg, *Franklin Roosevelt and the New Deal* (New York, 1963), pp. 184–85.
26. Thomas E. Blantz, C.S.C., "Francis J. Haas: Priest and Government Servant," *Catholic Historical Review,* 57(1972):571–92.
27. Neil Betten, *Catholic Activism and the Industrial Worker* (Gainesville, 1976), pp. 108–23; O'Brien, *American Catholics and Social Reform;* pp. 97–119.
28. See John Brophy, *A Miner's Life* (ed. John O. P. Hall; Madison, 1946); Betten, *Catholic Activism,* pp. 114–15; Abell, *American Catholicism and Social Action,* pp. 257–58.
29. O'Brien, *American Catholics and Social Reform,* p. 103.
30. *Ibid.,* p. 110.
31. *Ibid.,* pp. 143–49.
32. *Catholic Worker,* 5(July 1937):5.
33. Abell, *American Catholicism and Social Action,* pp. 267–69.
34. Nolan, ed., *Pastoral Letters of the American Hierarchy,* pp. 287–353.
35. Sanders, *Education of an Urban Minority,* p. 189.
36. Roger L. Treat, *Bishop Sheil and the CYO* (New York, 1951).
37. O'Brien, *American Catholics and Social Reform,* pp. 108–9.
38. *Ibid.,* pp. 113; 255, n. 40; Betten, *Catholic Activism,* p. 116.
39. Edward S. Shapiro, "Catholic Agrarian Thought and the New Deal," *Catholic Historical Review,* 65(1979):583–99; *id.,* "The Catholic Rural Life Movement and the New Deal Farm Program," *American Benedictine Review,* 28(1977):307–32.
40. John LaFarge, S.J. *The Manner Is Ordinary* (Garden City, 1957), pp. 290– 302; *id., Interracial Justice: A Study of the Catholic Doctrine of Race Relations* (New York, 1937); *id., No Postponement* (New York, 1950); *id., The Catholic Viewpoint on Race Relations* (Garden City, 1956).
41. Lord, *Played by Ear,* pp. 269–313; Nolan, "Native Son," in Connelly, *History of the Archdiocese of Philadelphia,* pp. 384–85.
42. O'Brien, *American Catholics and Social Reform,* pp. 184–85.
43. *Ibid.,* pp. 185–89.
44. *Ibid.,* p. 189.
45. *Ibid.,* pp. 189–92; Paul B. Marx, *Virgil Michel and the Liturgical Movement* (Collegeville, 1967).
46. *Ibid.,* p. 208; O'Brien, *American Catholics and Social Reform,* p. 191.

47. *Ibid.*, pp. 191–211; Betten, *Catholic Activism and the Industrial Worker*, pp. 48–72; William D. Miller, *A Harsh and Dreadful Love: Dorothy Day and the Catholic Worker Movement* (New York, 1973); Arthur Sheehan, *Peter Maurin: Gay Believer* (Garden City, 1959); Dorothy Day, *From Union Square to Rome* (Silver Springs, 1938); *id.*, *The Long Loneliness* (New York, 1963); *id.*, *Loaves and Fishes* (Garden City, 1952); Mary C. Segers, "Equality and Christian Anarchism: The Political and Social Ideas of the Catholic Worker Movement," *Review of Politics*, 40 (1978):196–230.

48. Thomas C. Cornell and James H. Forest, eds., *A Penny A Copy: Readings from the Catholic Worker* (New York/London, 1968), p. 15.

49. Day, *Long Loneliness*, pp. 148–49.

50. O'Brien, *American Catholics and Social Reform*, p. 209.

51. Miller, *Harsh and Dreadful Love*, p. 133.

52. Richard Deverall, "The Way It Was," *Social Order*, 11(1961–1962):195–200, 259–64, 302–8, 351–55, 403–8, 451–56; 12(1962):35–41, 59–64, 125–30, 178–83, 287–90. Mel Piehl, "The Liberal Wing of the Catholic Worker Movement," unpub. paper, Notre Dame-Jesuit House Seminar, Chicago, 1976.

53. O'Brien, *American Catholics and Social Reform*, pp. 114–19; Betten, *Catholic Activism and the Industrial Worker*, pp. 124–25; Day, *The Long Loneliness*, pp. 215–16.

54. Piehl, "Liberal Wing"; John A. Cogley, *A Canterbury Tale: Experiences and Reflections, 1916–1976* (New York, 1976).

55. O'Brien, *American Catholics and Social Reform*, pp. 56–64; Flynn, *American Catholics and the Roosevelt Presidency*, pp. 197–99.

56. O'Brien, *American Catholics and Social Reform;* pp. 111–12.

57. *America*, October 22, 1938, p. 60.

58. Flynn, *American Catholics and the Roosevelt Presidency*, pp. 122–49.

59. *Ibid.*, pp. 150–94.

60. Nolan, *Pastoral Letters*, p. 320.

61. George Q. Flynn, *Roosevelt and Romanism: Catholics and American Diplomacy, 1937–1945* (Westport/London, 1976), pp. 29–62.

62. Hugh Thomas, *The Spanish Civil War* (New York/Evanston/London, 1961), p. 173.

63. Van Allen, *Commonweal and American Catholicism*, p. 64.

64. *Ibid.*, pp. 70–74.

65. Thomas, *Spanish Civil War*, p. 450.

66. Flynn, *Roosevelt and Romanism*, p. 36; Nolan, *Pastoral Letters*, pp. 323–24.

67. Flynn, *Roosevelt and Romanism*, pp. 39–40; J. David Valaik, "American Catholic Dissenters and the Spanish Civil War," *Catholic Historical Review* 53(1968):537–55; Thomas P. Anderson, "The Spanish Rehearsal," *Continuum*, 2(1964):193–202.

68. Charles J. Tull, *Father Coughlin and the New Deal* (Syracuse, 1965); Betten, *Catholic Activism and the Industrial Workers*, pp. 90–107; O'Brien, *American Catholics and Social Reform*, pp. 150–81. James Shenton began a revisionist trend on Coughlin, suggesting that he was confused and inconsistent, rather than fascist. See his "The Coughlin Movement and the New Deal," *Political Science Quarterly*, 73(1958):352–73; and "Fascism and Father Coughlin," *Wisconsin Magazine of History*, 44(1960):6–11.

69. Van Allen, *Commonweal and American Catholicism,* pp. 54–55.
70. O'Brien, *American Catholics and Social Reform,* p. 173.
71. James M. Curley, *I'd Do It Again* (Englewood Cliffs, 1957), p. 296.
72. Seymour Lipset, "Three Decades of the Radical Right Coughlinites, Mc-Carthyites and Birchers" in Daniel Bell, ed., *The Radical Right* (Garden City, 1964), p. 382; Seymour Lipset and Earl Raab, *The Politics of Unreason: Right-Wing Extremism in America 1790–1970* (New York, 1970) pp. 172–75.
73. Forrest Davis, "Father Coughlin," *Atlantic,* 156(1935):659–58.
74. Francis Biddle, *In Brief Authority* (Garden City, 1962), pp. 238; 246–47.
75. O'Brien, *American Catholicism and Social Reform,* pp. 161–81; Deverall, "The Way It Was," *Social Order* 11(1961):198–99.
76. Flynn, *Roosevelt and Romanism,* p. 7.
77. O'Brien, *American Catholics and Social Reform,* p. 82; Patricia McNeal, "Origins of the Catholic Peace Movement," *Review of Politics,* 35(1973): 346–74.
78. O'Brien, *American Catholics and Social Reform,* p. 172.
79. Flynn, *Roosevelt and Romanism,* p. 65.
80. *Ibid., pp. 163–73.*
81. *Ibid.,* p. 69.
82. *Ibid.,* p. 72.
83. Robert I. Gannon, S.J., *The Cardinal Spellman Story* (Garden City, 1962).
84. Flynn, *Roosevelt and Romanism,* p. 78.
85. Nolan, *Pastoral Letters,* pp. 372–77.
86. *Ibid.,* p. 379.
87. *Ibid.,* pp. 380–84.
88. *Ibid.,* pp. 385–89; see Moquin and Van Doren, eds., *Documentary History of Mexican Americans,* pp. 303–20.
89. Nolan, *Pastoral Letters,* pp. 390–93.
90. *Ibid.,* pp. 394–97.
91. There is no overall study of the role of Catholics and their church in World War II.
92. Patricia McNeal, "Catholic Conscientious Objection during World War II," *Catholic Historical Review,* 51(1965):222–42; Gordon C. Zahn, *Another Part of the War: the Camp Simon Story* (Amherst, 1979).
93. Gannon, *Cardinal Spellman,* p. 164. See Robert A. Graham, S.J., *Vatican Diplomacy: A Study of Church and State on the International Plane* (Princeton, 1959), pp. 326–48; Flynn, *Roosevelt and Romanism,* pp. 98–126; Anson Phelps Stokes, *Church and State in the United States* (3 vols.; New York, 1950), 2:103–10.
94. Harold H. Tittman, Jr., "Vatican Mission," *Social Order,* 10(1960):113–17.
95. Myron C. Taylor, ed., *Wartime Correspondence between President Roosevelt and Pope Pius XII* (New York, 1947).
96. Graham, *Vatican Diplomacy,* pp. 344–45. See Igino Cardinale, *Le Saint-Siège et la diplomatie* (Paris, 1962).
97. Gannon, *Cardinal Spellman,* pp. 176–97.
98. Edward E. Swanstrom, "War Relief Services, NCWC," in Benjamin L. Masse, S.J., ed., *The Catholic Mind through Fifty Years, 1903–1953* (New York, 1952), pp. 594–96.

Chapter XX

1. Flynn, *Roosevelt and Romanism*, p. 194.
2. Francis J. Spellman, "American at War," *Catholic Mind*, 41(1943):1–5.
3. McAvoy, *Father O'Hara*, p. 207.
4. Will Herberg, *Protestant, Catholic, Jew* (Garden City, 1955).
5. Flynn, *Roosevelt and Romanism*, pp. 192, 193.
6. Nolan, *Pastoral Letters*, pp. 380–84.
7. Dennis J. Dunn, *The Catholic Church and the Soviet Government, 1939–1949* (Boulder, 1977), pp. 98–105.
8. Nolan, *Pastoral Letters*, pp. 394–97.
9. Thomas E. Murray, "Morality and Security: The Forgotten Equation," in William J. Nagle, ed., *Morality and Modern Warfare: The State of the Question* (Baltimore, 1960), pp. 58–68.
10. John C. Ford, S.J., "The Morality of Obliteration Bombing," *Theological Studies*, 5(1944):261–309.
11. *Id.*, "The Hydrogen Bombing of Cities," in Nagle, ed., *Morality and Modern Warfare*, pp. 98–103.
12. Hadley Cantrill, *Public Opinion 1935–1946* (Princeton, 1951), p. 23; Flynn, *Roosevelt and Romanism*, pp. 209–11.
13. Cornell and Forest, *A Penny A Copy*, p. 67.
14. Van Allen, *The Commonweal and American Catholicism*, pp. 92–93; *Catholic World*, 161(1945):449–52.
15. Cantrill, *Public Opinion*, p. 1069.
16. *Ibid.*
17. Gannon, *Cardinal Spellman*, pp. 242–44.
18. John M. Blum, *From the Morgenthau Diaries* (3 vols.; Boston, 1959–1967). 3:380–81.
19. *Ibid.*, 3:395, 397.
20. *Ibid.*, 3:353.
21. Liston Pope, "Religion and Class Structure," *Annals of the American Academy of Political and Social Science*, 256(1948):85–86. See Hadley Cantrill, "Educational and Economic Compositions of Religious Groups," *American Journal of Sociology*, 47(1943):574–79.
22. Robert M. Hutchins. "The Integrating Principle of Catholic Higher Education," *College Newsletter, Midwest Regional Unit, NCEA* (1937), p. 1, cited in John Tracy Ellis, "American Catholics and the Intellectual Life." *Thought*, 30(1955):374–75.
23. Handy, *Churches in the United States*, pp. 400–401.
24. *Ibid.*
25. Cited by Ellis, "American Catholics and the Intellectual Life," p. 368; from *The Pilot* (Boston), October 17, 1947.
26. John D. Donovan, "The American Catholic Hierarchy: A Social Profile," *American Catholic Sociological Review*, 19(1958):98–112.
27. Archives of the Archdiocese of St. Louis, Ritter to Sister Matthew Marie, March 28, 1947; Donald J. Kemper, "Catholic Integration in St. Louis, 1935–1947," *Missouri Historical Review*, 73(1978):1–22.
28. Daniel B. Carroll, "The O'Hara Years," in Connelly, ed., *History of the Archdiocese of Philadelphia*, pp. 434–35.
29. Nolan, "Native Son," *ibid.*, pp. 411–12.

30. Statistics gathered by Joseph M. Becker, S.J., "Changes in U. S. Jesuit Membership, 1958–1975: A Symposium," *Studies in the Spirituality of Jesuits,* 9(1977):81.
31. McAvoy, *History of the Catholic Church,* p. 454.
32. Bernard Lazerwitz, "Some Factors Associated with Variations in Church Attendance," *Social Forces,* 39(1960):303.
33. Andrew M. Greeley, "Some Information on the Present Situation of American Catholics," *Social Order,* 13(1963):19.
34. *Ibid.,* pp. 20–21.
35. *America,* September 14, 1957, p. 410.
36. William B. Clebsch, *American Religious Thought* (Chicago, 1973).
37. For a study unfavorable to the role played by Catholics in various events of the period, see David Caute, *The Great Red Fear: The Anti-Communist Purge under Truman and Eisenhower* (New York, 1978).
38. Gannon, *Cardinal Spellman,* pp. 336–37.
39. L'inesauribile mistero," *Acta Apostolicae Sedis,* 49(1957):17–19; *The Pope Speaks,* 3 (1956):342; See Paul Higginson, "The Vatican and Communism from 'Divini Redemptoris' to Pope Paul VI," *New Blackfriars,* 61(1980): 158–70, 234–44.
40. Donald F. Crosby, S.J., *God, Church, and Flag: Senator Joseph R. McCarthy and the Catholic Church, 1950–1957* (Chapel Hill, 1978), p. 11; Gannon, *Cardinal Spellman,* p. 338.
41. Crosby, *God, Church, and Flag,* p. 10: Gannon, *Cardinal Spellman,* p. 339.
42. Crosby, *God, Church, and Flag,* p. 12.
43. Betten, *American Catholicism and the Industrial Worker,* pp. 139–45.
44. Joseph H. Fichter, S.J., review of *God, Church, and Flag* in *America,* October 7, 1978, p. 229.
45. Van Allen *Commonweal and American Catholicism,* p. 116.
46. Crosby, *God, Church, and Flag,* pp. 58–63. See Louis Budenz, *This Is My Story* (New York, 1947); id., *The Bolshevik Invasion of the West: An Account of the Great Political War for a Soviet America* (Linden, 1966); Owen Lattimore, *Ordeal by Slander* (Boston, 1950).
47. *New York Times,* November 22, 1951; *Christian Century,* November 28, 1951.
48. Nolan, *Pastoral Letters,* p. 457.
49. See Crosby, *God, Church, and Flag,* pp. 83–86. Vincent P. De Santis, "American Catholics and McCarthyism," *Catholic Historical Review,* 51(1965):8, does not think the reference is to McCarthy.
50. Crosby, *God, Church, and Flag,* pp. 26–42.
51. *Congressional Record,* 81st Cong., 2nd Sess., February 20, 1950, p. 1954. See Robert Griffith, *The Politics of Fear: Joseph R. McCarthy and the Senate* (Lexington, 1970), pp. 48–51.
52. Crosby, *God, Church, and Flag,* pp. 165–67.
53. *Ibid.,* pp. 71–75; 88–117.
54. Seymour Martin Lipset, "Three Decades of the Radical Right: Coughlinites, McCarthyites, and Birchers," in Daniel Bell, ed., *The Radical Right* Garden City, 1964), p. 395, quoting Nelson W. Polsby, "Towards an Explanation of McCarthyism," *Political Studies,* 8(1960):250–71.
55. Lipset, "Three Decades," p. 407.
56. Crosby, *God, Cross, and Flag,* p. 196.

57. *Ibid.*, pp. 231–34.
58. *Ibid.*, pp. 134, 158–60.
59. Ibid., pp. 104, 188, 113, 174, 175.
60. Van Allen, *Commonweal and American Catholicism*, pp. 107–16.
61. Miller, *Harsh and Dreadful Love*, pp. 229–32.
62. Crosby, *God, Church, and Flag*, pp. 178–84.
63. *Ibid.*, pp. 167–69.
64. Donald E. Pelotte, S.S.S., *John Courtney Murray: Theologian in Conflict* (New York/Ramsey/Toronto, 1976), pp. 17–18.
65. F. William O'Brien, S.J., "General Clark's Nomination as Ambassador to the Vatican: American Reaction," *Catholic Historical Review*, 44(1958/1959):421–39.
66. Lawrence P. Creedon and W. D. Falcon, *United for Separation* (Milwaukee, 1959).
67. Marty, *Righteous Empire*, p. 246.
68. Handy, *History of the Churches*, p. 404; Crosby, *God, Church, and Flag*, p. 135.
69. *Ibid.*, p. 136.
70. *Ibid.*, p. 137.
71. *Ibid.*, p. 126; *Christian Century*, May 6, 1953, p. 531.
72. Alson J. Smith, "The Catholic-Protestant Feud," *American Mercury*, 65(1947):536–42.
73. William E. McManus, "Federal Aid to Education," in Masse, ed., *Catholic Mind through Fifty Years*, p. 189.
74. Richard E. Morgan, "The Establishment Clause and Sectarian Schools: A Final Installment?" in Philip B. Kurland, ed., *Church and State: The Supreme Court and the First Amendment* (Chicago, 1975), p. 233.
75. McAvoy, *Father O'Hara*, p. 401.
76. McManus, "Federal Aid," 189–200.
77. Paul Blanshard, *God and Man in Washington* (Boston, 1960), pp. 143–44.
78. Gannon, *Cardinal Spellman*, pp. 308–14.
79. *Ibid.*, pp. 314–21; Anson Phelps Stokes, *Church and State in the United States* (3 vols.; 1950), 2:755.
80. Morgan, in Kurland, ed., *Church and State*, pp. 232–72; Buetow, *Of Singular Benefit*, pp. 267–80. Texts of many relevant opinions are in Blau, *Cornerstones of Religious Freedom*, pp. 252–92.
81. Text of the Holy Office Letter, *American Ecclesiastical Review*, 127(1952): 307–11 (Latin), 311–15 (English); Robert Connor, *Walled In: The True Story of a Cult* (New York, 1979).
82. Van Allen, *Commonweal and Catholicism*, pp. 17–21; George N. Shuster, "Have We Any Scholars?" *America*, August 15, 1925.
83. Denis W. Brogan, *U.S.A. An Outline of the Country, Its People and Institutions* (London, 1941), p. 65.
84. John Tracy Ellis, "American Catholics and the Intellectual Life," *Thought*, 30(1955):351–88.
85. Thomas F. O'Dea, *American Catholic Dilemma: An Inquiry into Intellectual Life* (New York, 1958): Walter J. Ong, S.J., *Frontiers in American Catholicism* (New York, 1957): Gustave Weigel, S.J., "*American Catholic Intellectualism*—A Theologian's Reflections," *Review of Politics*, 19(1957): 275–307.

86. McAvoy, *Father O'Hara*, p. 405.
87. John Courtney Murray, S.J., "The Problem of Religious Freedom," *Theological Studies*, 25(1964):503–75; also, *The Problem of Religious Freedom* (Westminster, 1965), pp. 17–19.
88. Pelotte, *John Courtney Murray*, pp. 11–12.
89. John Tracy Ellis, *Perspectives in American Catholicism* (Baltimore/Dublin, 1963), pp. 7–8.
90. Blanshard, *American Freedom*, pp. 49–50 and *passim*.
91. Pelotte, *John Courtney Murray, passim;* Thomas T. Love, *John Courtney Murray: Contemporary Church-State Theory* (Garden City, 1965); Elwyn A. Smith, *Religious Liberty in the United States* (Philadelphia, 1972), pp. 226–44; John Courtney Murray, S.J., *We Hold These Truths: Catholic Reflections on The American Proposition* (New York, 1960).
92. William B. Faherty, S.J., *Dream by the River: Two Centuries of St. Louis Catholicism, 1766–1967* (St. Louis, 1971), p. 180.
93. George H. Dunne, S.J., "The Sin of Segregation," *Commonweal*, September 21, 1945, pp. 542–45.
94. Pelotte, *John Courtney Murray*, p. 11.
95. McAvoy, *Father O'Hara*, p. 192.
96. Alice Renard, "A Negro Looks at the Church," *Commonweal*, p. 211.
97. Jesse O. McKee, "A Geographical Analysis of the Origin, Diffusion, and Spatial Diffusion of the Black American in the United States," *The Southern Quarterly*, 12(1974):203–16.
98. Clarence E. Williams, C.PP.S., "The Growth of Black Catholicism in Chicago: An Oral History," unpub. paper, Garrett Evangelical Seminary, 1976.
99. George Shuster, S.S.J., and Robert M. Kearns, S.S.J., *Statistical Profile of Black Catholics* (Washington, 1976): Green, *Silent Believers*, p. 17.
100. Gannon, *Cardinal Spellman*, pp. 269–70; William A. Osborne, *The Segregated Covenant: Race Relations and American Catholics* (New York, 1967), pp. 126–53.
101. *Ibid.*, pp. 112–18; 97–112.
102. *Ibid.*, 46–47.
103. *Ibid.*, pp. 69–89.
104. Nolan, *Pastoral Letters*, pp. 506–10.

Chapter XXI

1. Patrick W. Collins, "Gustave Weigel: Ecclesiologist and Ecumenist," unpub. Ph.D. diss., Fordham University, 1972, pp. 348–49; Gustave Weigel, S.J., "The Role of the Laity," *Act*, 14(1961):3, 5.
2. Theodore H. White, *The Making of the President 1960* (New York, 1962), pp. 260–62; 391–93; Lawrence Fuchs, *John F. Kennedy and American Catholicism* (New York, 1967).
3. Van Allen, *Commonweal and American Catholicism*, p. 133.
4. Theodore C. Sorensen, *Kennedy* (New York, 1965), pp. 188–89.
5. *Ibid.*, pp. 143–44.
6. *Ibid.*, p. 194.
7. *Ibid.*, p. 217.

8. Anne Fremantle, ed., *The Papal Encyclicals in Their Historical Context* (New York, 1963), p. 318.
9. Higginson, "Vatican and Communism," pp. 164–71; 234–44.
10. Vincent A. Yzermans, ed., *American Participation in the Second Vatican Council* (New York, 1967).
11. *Papal Teachings: The Church* (Boston, 1962), p. 196; Brian Fothergill, *Nicholas Wiseman* (London, 1963), p. 170.
12. Yzermans, ed., *American Participation,* pp. 449–51.
13. Van Allen, *Commonweal and American Catholicism,* pp. 141–47.
14. Yzermans, ed., *American Participation,* pp. 577; 586–94.
15. *Ibid.,* pp. 617–64.
16. Paul Blanshard, *Paul Blanshard on Vatican II* (Boston, 1967).
17. Yzermans, ed., *American Participation,* p. 154.
18. Nolan, *Pastoral Letters,* pp. 587–99.
19. Bill Kovach, "Eased Laws Alter U.S. Ethnic Profile," *New York Times,* June 14, 1971.
20. Mary T. Hanna, *Catholics and American Politics* (Cambridge/London, 1979), p. 247.
21. Green, *The Silent Believers,* p. 17.
22. Francis J. Lally, "Richard James Cushing," *New Catholic Encyclopedia* (Washington, 1974), 16:113.
23. *Congressional Record,* 96th Cong., 2nd Sess., June 11, 1980, H 4808–H 4823.
24. Nolan, *Pastoral Letters,* pp. 608–12.
25. *A National Pastoral Council Pro and Con* (Washington, 1971).
26. Documentation on the Call to Action Conference including the resolutions, is in *A.D. 1977,* published by the Quixote Center, Washington, D.C.
27. Alan F. Westin, "The John Birch Society: 'Radical Right' and 'Extreme Left' in the Political Context of Post World War II," in Bell, ed., *Radical Right,* p. 260.
28. *Ibid.,* p. 250; and Lipset, "Three Decades of the Radical Right," *ibid.,* p. 431; Edward T. Gargan, "Radical Catholics of the Right," *Social Order,* 11 (1961):409–19.
29. Nolan, *Pastoral Letters,* p. 451.
30. "The Bishops' Meeting," *Commonweal,* December 1, 1961.
31. Kevin and Dorothy Ranaghan, *Catholic Pentecostals* (New York, 1969); Joseph H. Fichter, S.J., *The Catholic Cult of the Paraclete* (New York, 1975); Edward D. O'Connor, C.S.C., *The Pentecostal Movement in the Catholic Church* (rev. ed., Notre Dame, 1974).
32. *Ibid.,* pp. 291–93.
33. Charles A. Meconis, *With Clumsy Grace: The American Catholic Left 1961–1975* (New York, 1979).
34. Thomas Merton, "The Root of War," *Catholic Worker,* 28(1961):1, 7; Gordon Zahn, ed., *Thomas Merton on Peace* (New York, 1971), p. 182.
35. This statement of the facts in the case is based on the personal recollections of the author, who was at the time executive assistant to the Jesuit provincial superior in New York, in whose office the relevant decisions were made and directives issued.
36. *Newsweek,* October 4, 1971, quoted by Meconis, *With Clumsy Grace,* p. 170.

37. Lawrence M. Baskir and William A. Strauss, *Chance and Circumstance: The Draft, the War and the Vietnam Generation* (New York, 1978), p. 67.
38. Nolan, *Pastoral Letters,* pp. 604–7.
39. *Ibid.,* pp. 701–2.
40. Hanna, *Catholics and American Politics,* p. 44.
41. Nolan, *Pastoral Letters,* pp. 702–4; Hanna, *Catholics and American Politics,* p. 44.
42. *America,* August 12, 1967, cover.
43. George A. Kelly, *The Battle for the American Church* (Garden City, 1979), pp. 65–69.
44. John Courtney Murray, S.J., in Walter M. Abbott, S.J., and Joseph Gallagher, eds., *The Documents of Vatican II* (New York, 1966), pp. 694–95.
45. "The Catholic University of Today," *America,* August 12, 1967, pp. 154–56.
46. Gleason, "In Search of Unity," pp. 194, 195, 196, 199.
47. Andrew M. Greeley *et al., Catholic Schools in a Declining Church* (New York, 1976); Greeley, *The American Catholic: A Social Portrait* (New York, 1977), pp. 167–69.
48. Edward B. Fiske, "Catholic Schools Attain Stability in Urban Cores," *New York Times,* October 9, 1977.
49. *Ibid.;* Nolan, *Pastoral Letters,* pp. 621–24.
50. *Sepia,* 24(1975):10.
51. Marilyn Wenzke Nickels, "Journey of a Black Catholic," *America,* July 10, 1976, pp. 6–8.
52. Merle Curti, *American Philanthropy Abroad: A History* (New Brunswick, 1963), p. 523.
53. Hanna, *Catholics and American Politics,* p 40.
54. *Ibid.,* pp. 38–39.
55. Ronald B. Taylor, *Chavez and the Farm Workers* (Boston, 1975).
56. Nolan, *Pastoral Letters,* pp. 241–42.
57. Peter Fryer, *The Birth Controllers* (New York, 1966), p. 214.
58. Andrew M. Greeley, "Some Information on the Present Situation of American Catholics," *Social Order,* 13(1963):20.
59. *Id.,* "Family Planning Among American Catholics," *Chicago Studies,* 2(1963):57.
60. James Hitchcock, "The American Press and Birth Control: Preparing the Ground for Dissent," *Homiletic and Pastoral Review,* 80(1980):10–26.
61. Yzermans, *American Participation,* p. 193.
62. Gordon C. Zahn, "Social Science and the Theology of War," in Nagle, *Morality and Modern War,* pp. 108–9.
63. *New York Times,* July 30, 1968.
64. Kelly, *Battle,* pp. 166–72.
65. John Tracy Ellis, "The U.S.A.," in Roger Aubert *et al., The Church in a Secularised Society* (New York/London, 1978), p. 272.
66. Anthony Kosnik, ed., *Human Sexuality: New Directions in Catholic Thought* (New York, 1977).
67. John C. Ford, S.J., and Germain Grisez, "Contraception and the Authority of the Ordinary Magisterium," *Theological Studies,* 39(1978):258–312.
68. Margaret Mary Modde, O.S.F., "Departures from Religious Institutes," *New Catholic Encyclopedia,* 17:570–71.

69. Greeley, *American Catholic*, p. 143; Hanna, *Catholics and American Politics*, p. 105.
70. Jackson W. Carroll *et al.*, *Religion in America 1950 to the Present* (New York, 1979), pp. 19–20.
71. Donald Nicholl, "To Be an American," *The Tablet* (London), May 24, 1980, pp. 495–98.
72. Thomas Luckmann, *The Invisible Religion* (New York, 1969).
73. Carroll *et al.*, *Religion in America*, p. 33.
74. Greeley *et al.*, *Catholic Schools*, p. 129.
75. Carroll *et al.*, *Religion in America*, p. 96.
76. "Catholics Reflect Shifts in Belief," *New York Times*, February 10, 1977.
77. Michael Novak, "The Communal Catholic," *Commonweal*, January 17, 1975, p. 342.

Index